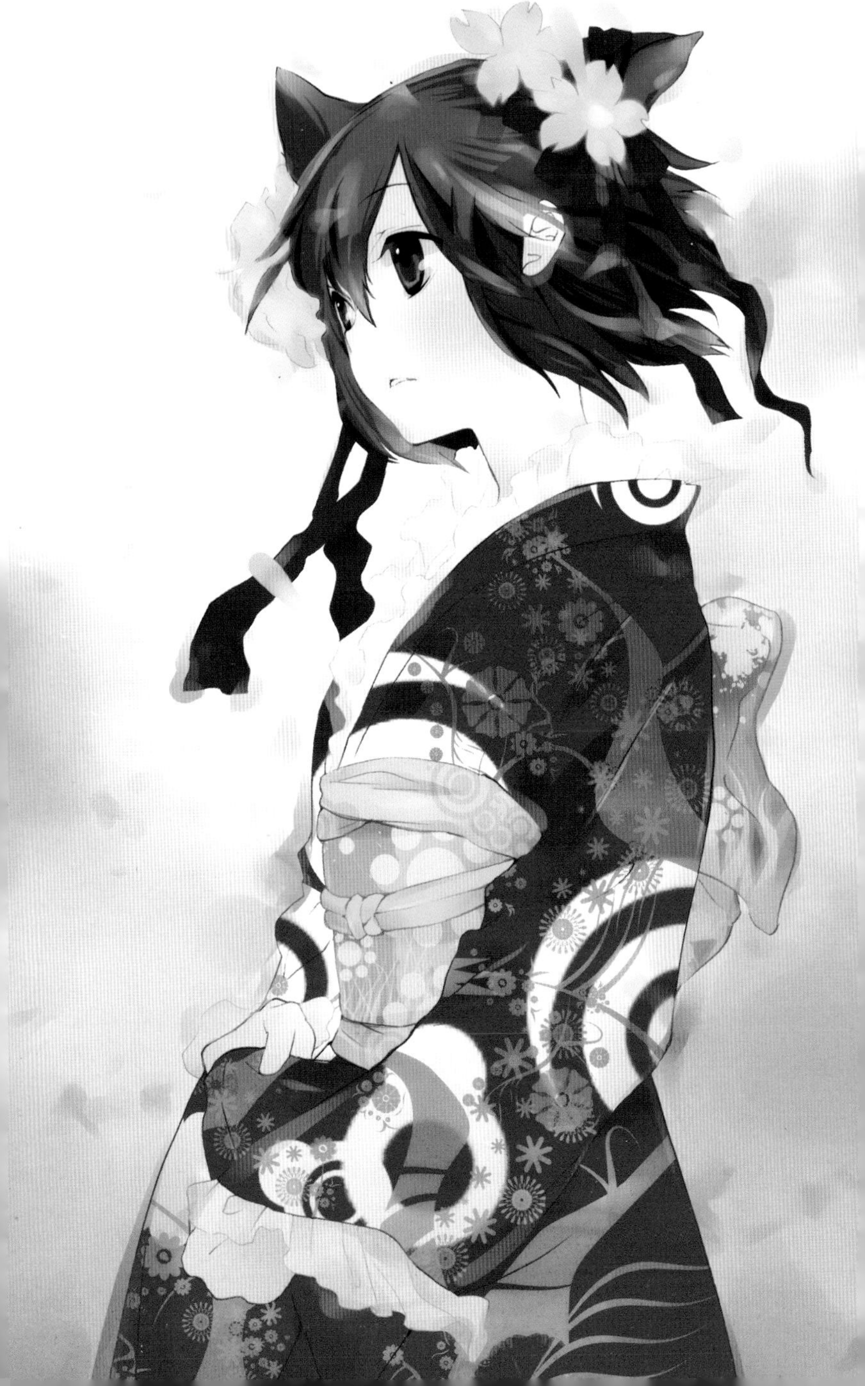

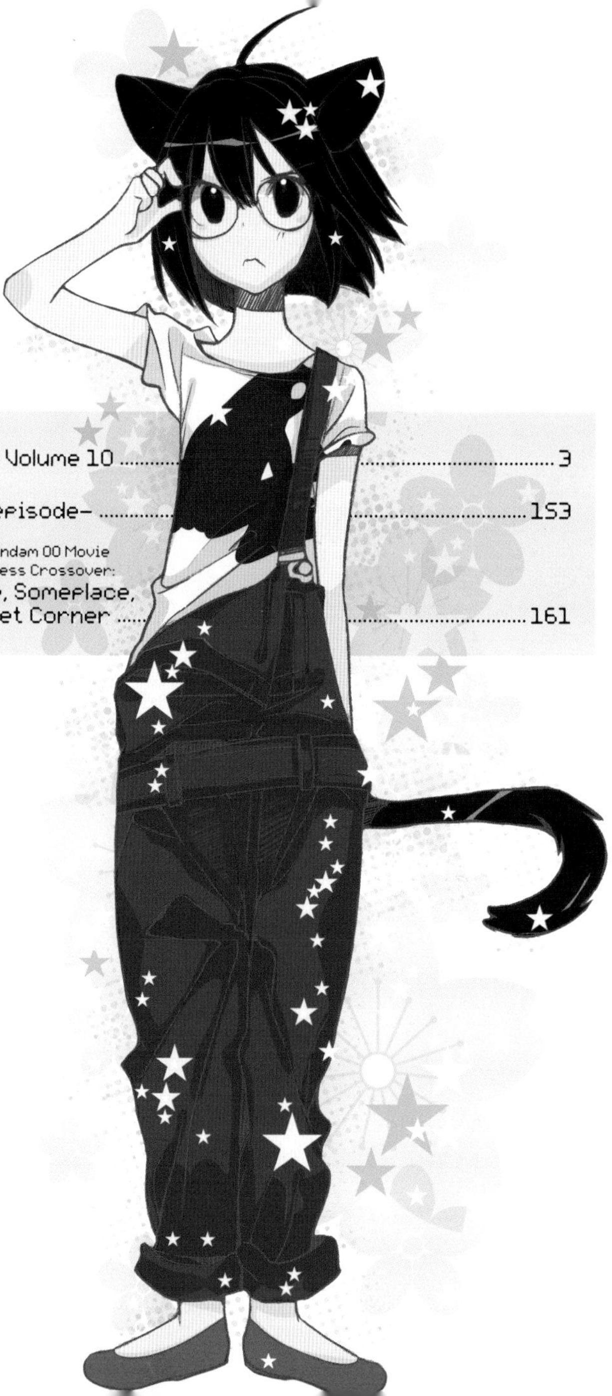

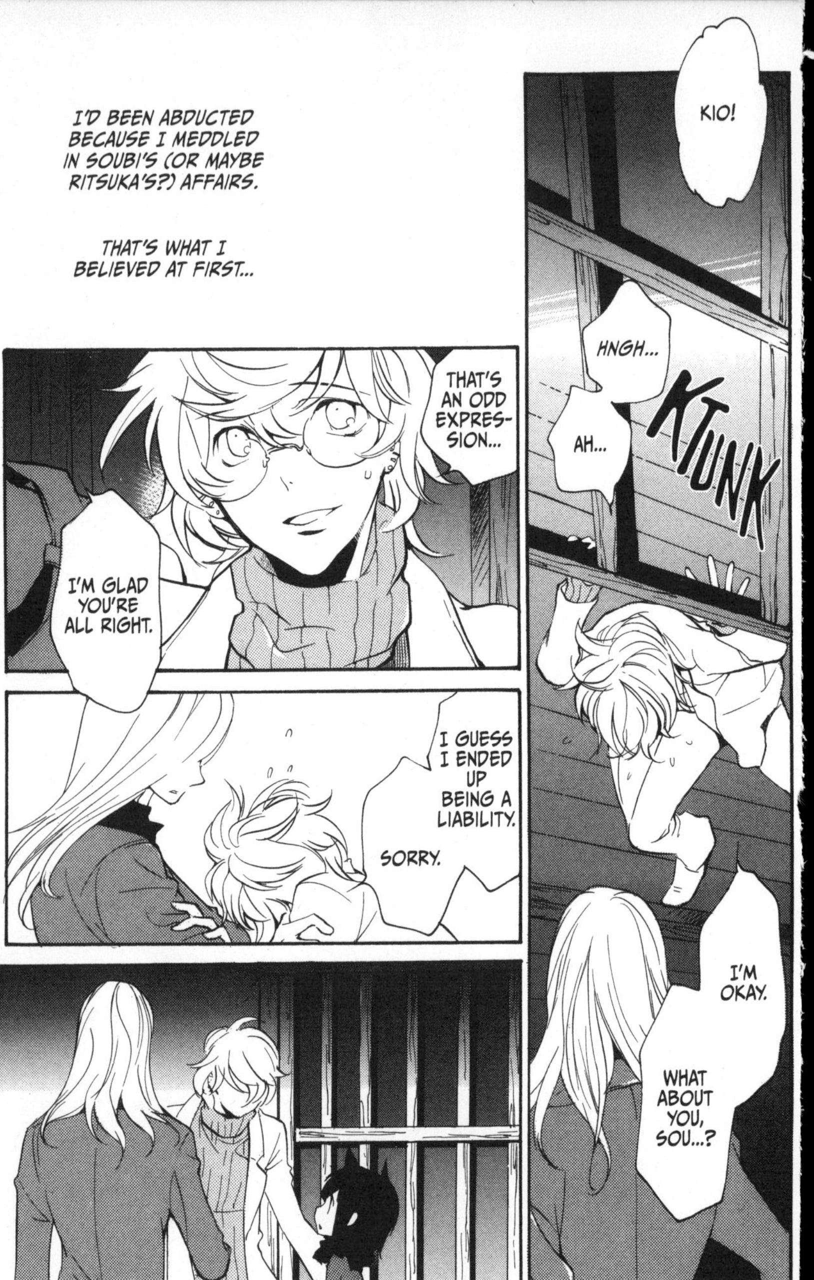
KIO!
HNGH...
AH...
KTUNK
I'M OKAY.
WHAT ABOUT YOU, SOU...?
I'D BEEN ABDUCTED BECAUSE I MEDDLED IN SOUBI'S (OR MAYBE RITSUKA'S?) AFFAIRS.
THAT'S WHAT I BELIEVED AT FIRST...
THAT'S AN ODD EXPRES-SION...
I'M GLAD YOU'RE ALL RIGHT.
I GUESS I ENDED UP BEING A LIABILITY.
SORRY.

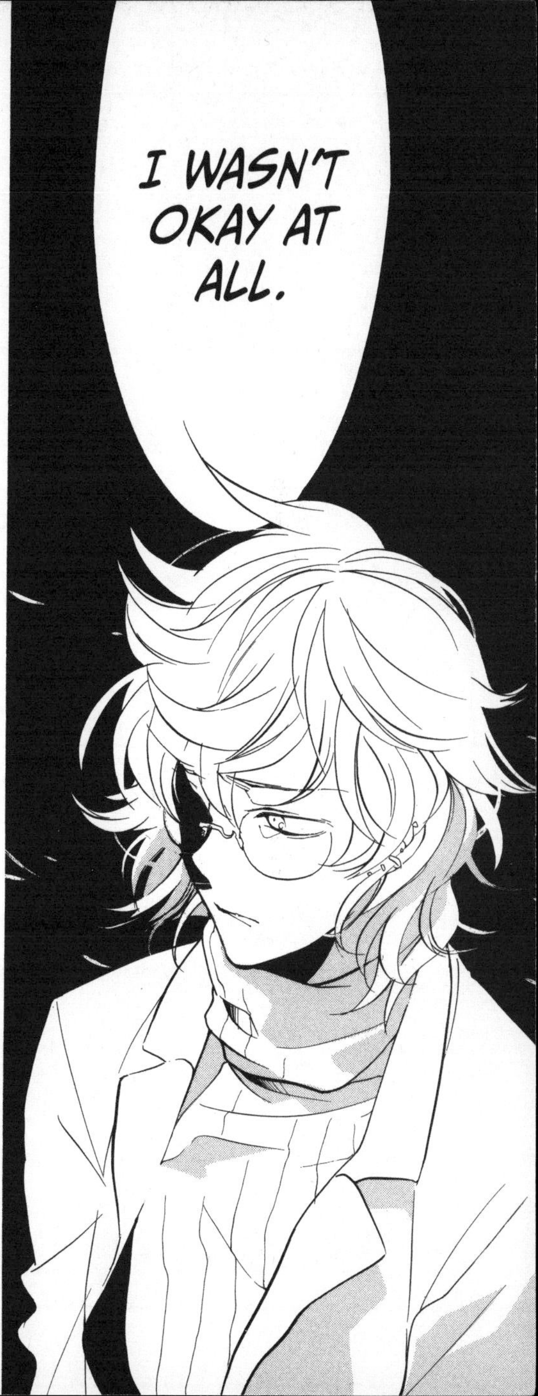
I WASN'T OKAY AT ALL.

LOVELESS

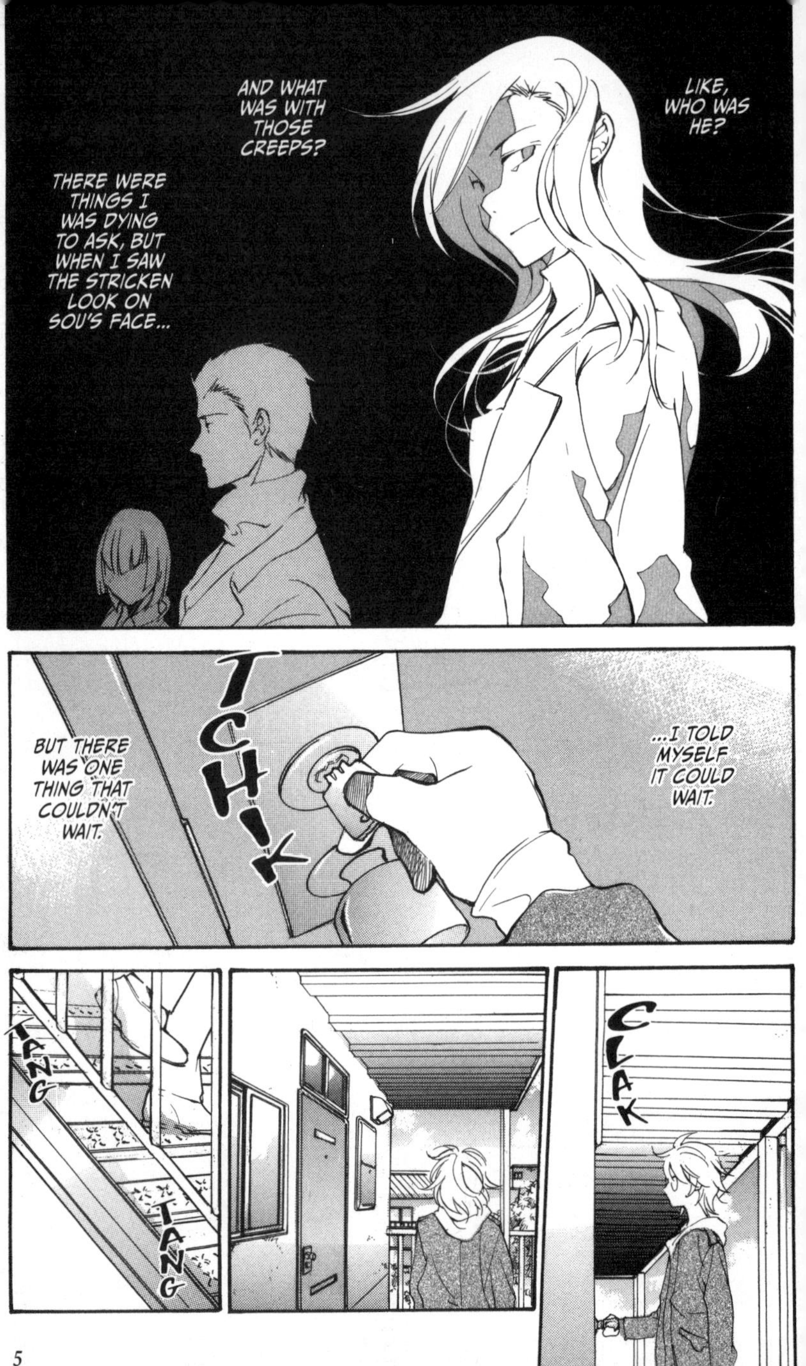
LIKE, WHO WAS HE?
AND WHAT WAS WITH THOSE CREEPS?
THERE WERE THINGS I WAS DYING TO ASK, BUT WHEN I SAW THE STRICKEN LOOK ON SOU'S FACE...
...I TOLD MYSELF IT COULD WAIT.
TCHIK
BUT THERE WAS ONE THING THAT COULDN'T WAIT.
CLAK
TANG TANG TANG

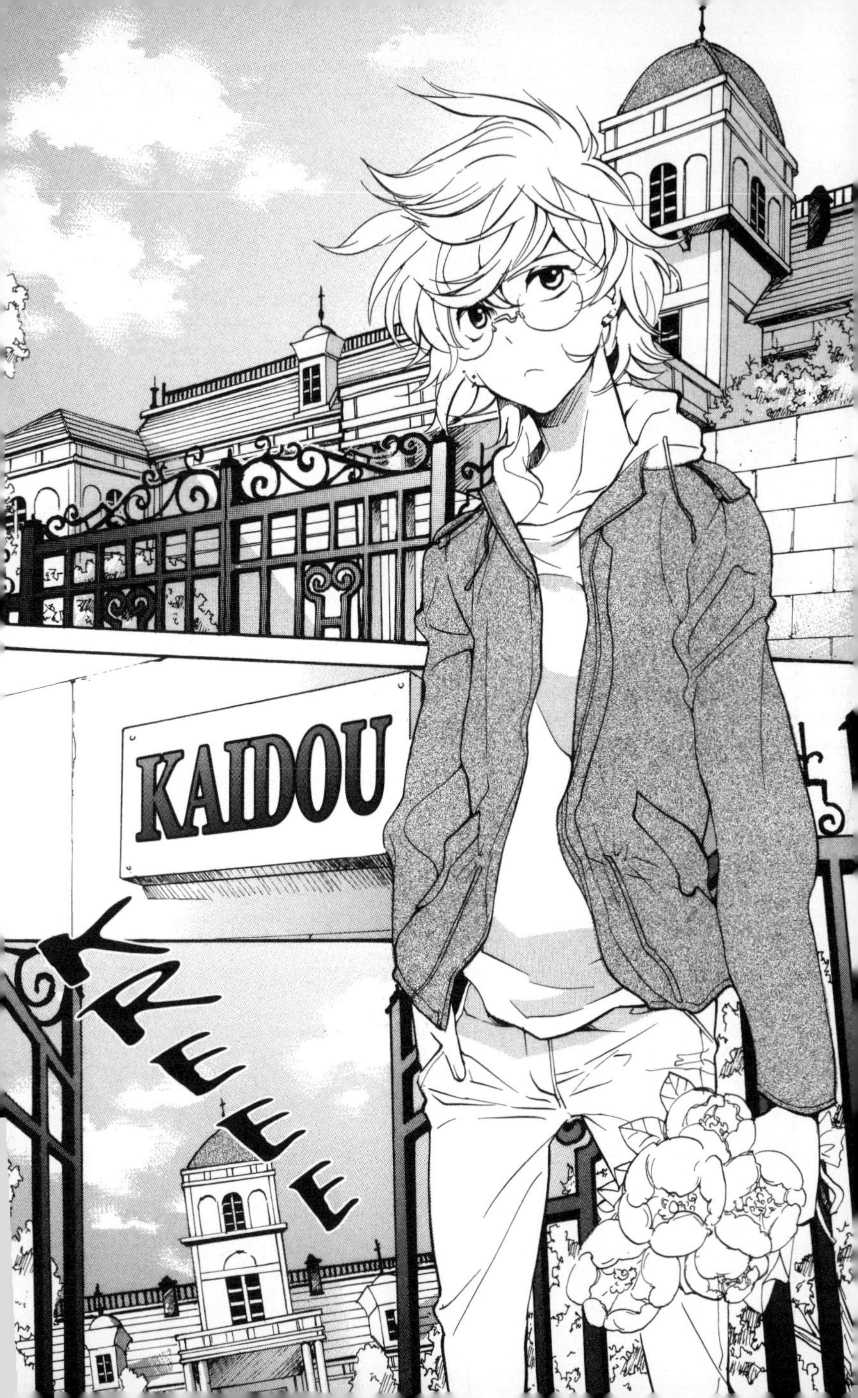
KAIDOU
KREEEE

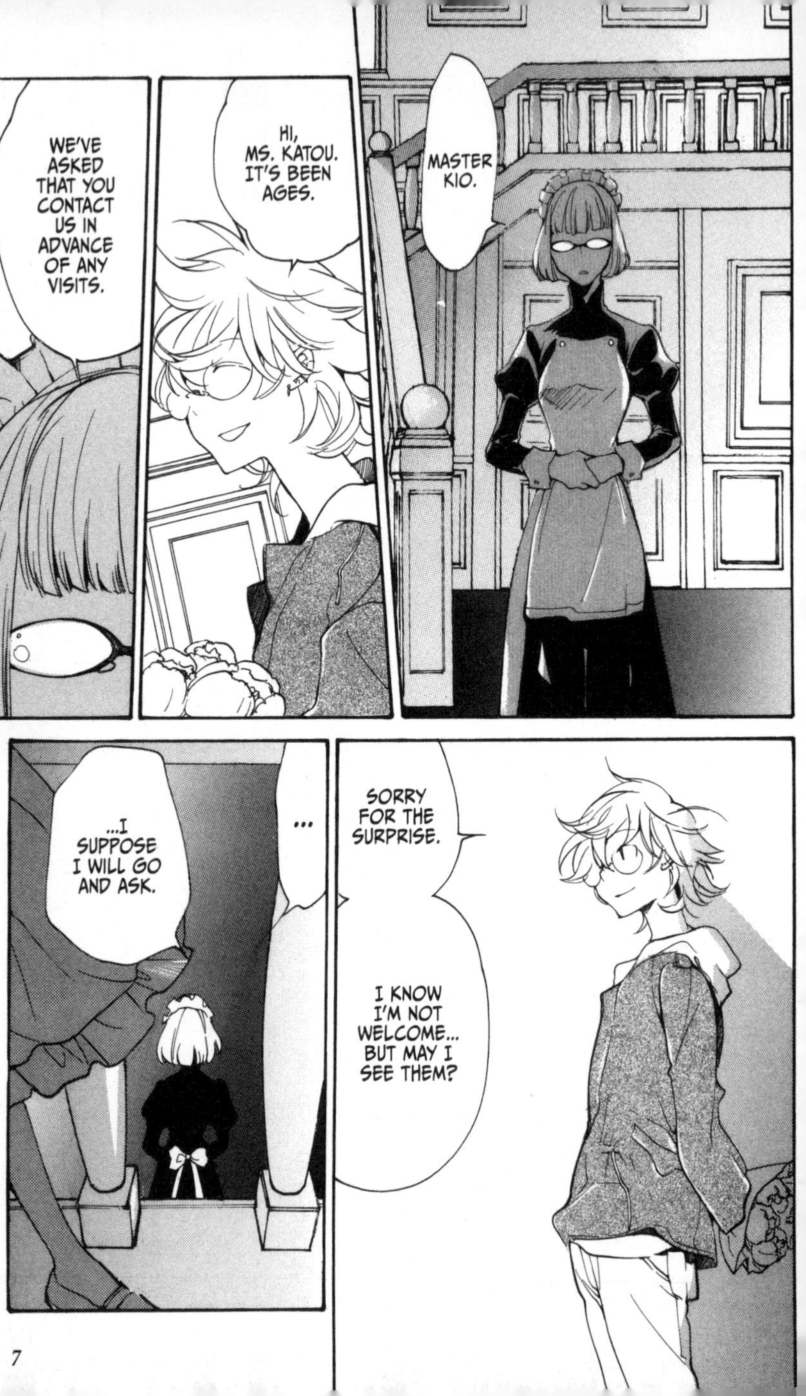
MASTER KIO.
HI, MS. KATOU. IT'S BEEN AGES.
WE'VE ASKED THAT YOU CONTACT US IN ADVANCE OF ANY VISITS.
SORRY FOR THE SURPRISE.
I KNOW I'M NOT WELCOME... BUT MAY I SEE THEM?
...
...I SUPPOSE I WILL GO AND ASK.

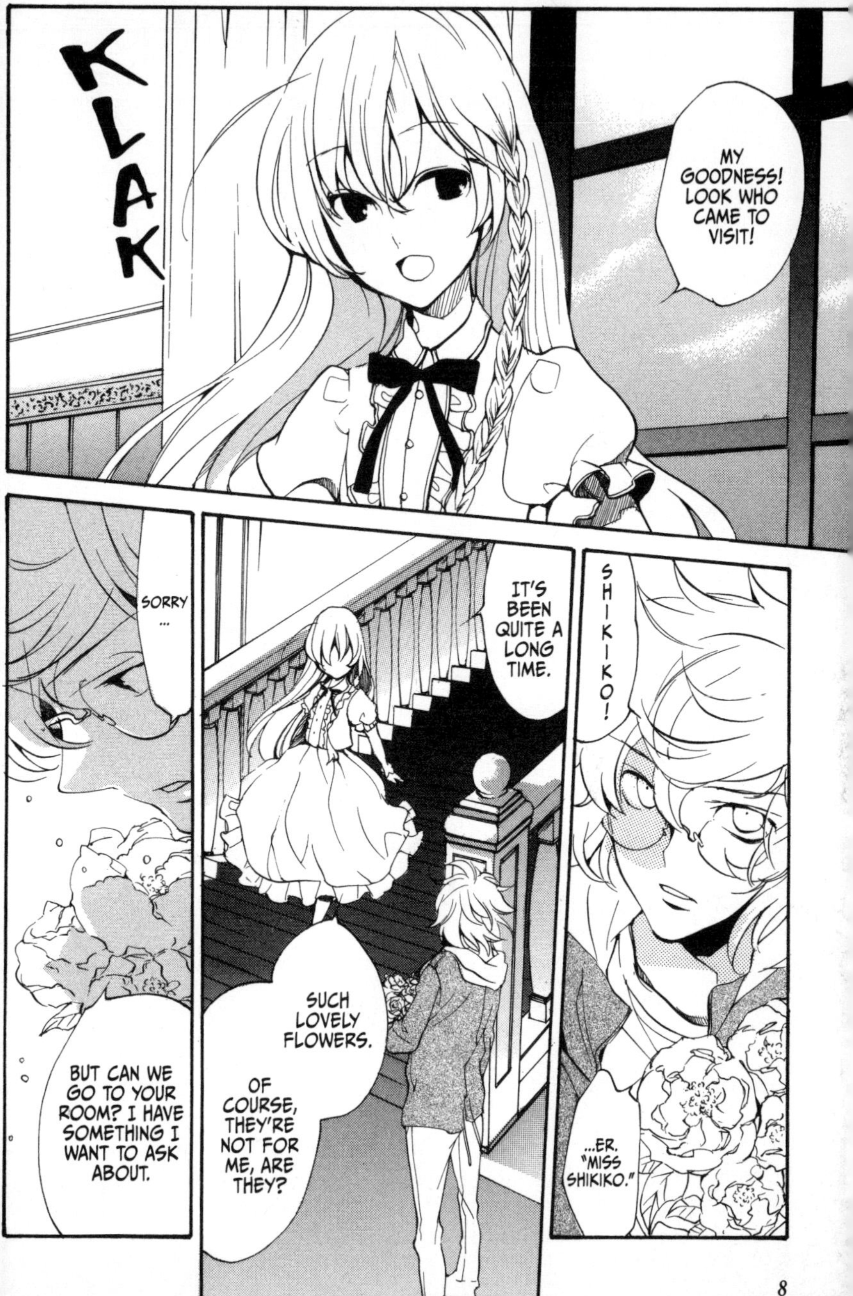
MY GOODNESS! LOOK WHO CAME TO VISIT!
KLAK
SHIKIKO!
...ER. "MISS SHIKIKO."
IT'S BEEN QUITE A LONG TIME.
SUCH LOVELY FLOWERS.
OF COURSE, THEY'RE NOT FOR ME, ARE THEY?
SORRY...
BUT CAN WE GO TO YOUR ROOM? I HAVE SOMETHING I WANT TO ASK ABOUT.

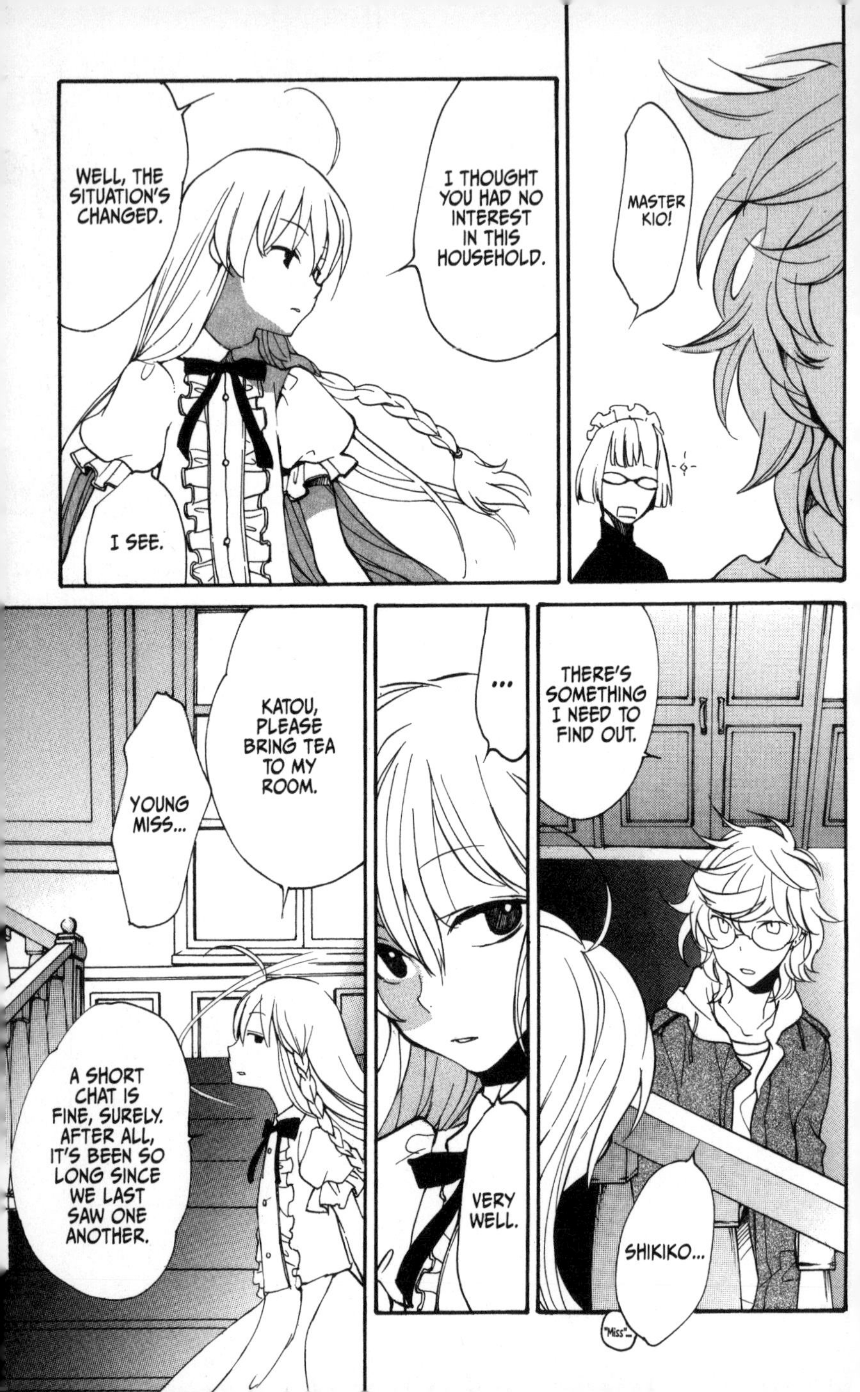
MASTER KIO!
I THOUGHT YOU HAD NO INTEREST IN THIS HOUSEHOLD.
WELL, THE SITUATION'S CHANGED.
I SEE.
THERE'S SOMETHING I NEED TO FIND OUT.
SHIKIKO...
"Miss"...
...
VERY WELL.
KATOU, PLEASE BRING TEA TO MY ROOM.
YOUNG MISS...
A SHORT CHAT IS FINE, SURELY. AFTER ALL, IT'S BEEN SO LONG SINCE WE LAST SAW ONE ANOTHER.

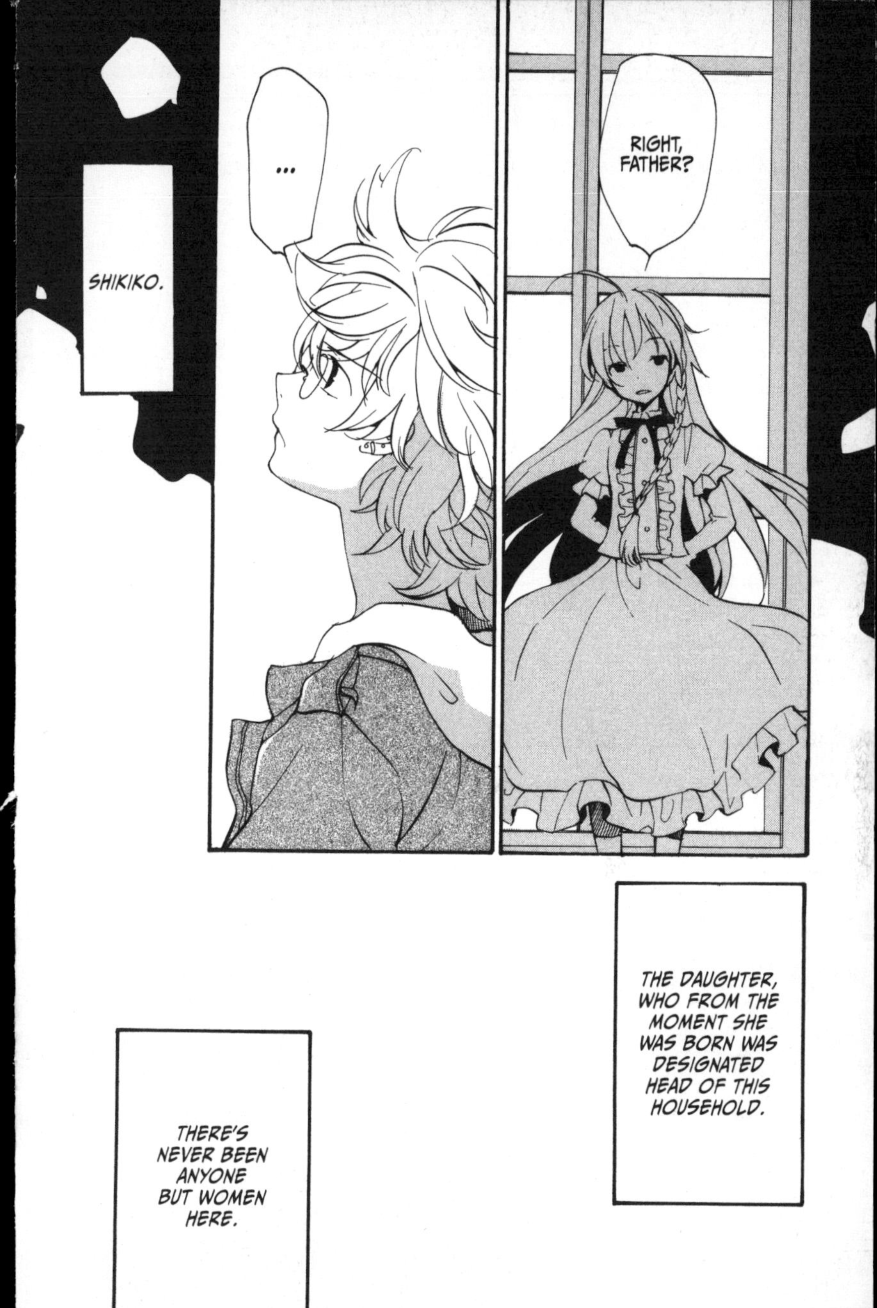
RIGHT, FATHER?
...
SHIKIKO.
THE DAUGHTER, WHO FROM THE MOMENT SHE WAS BORN WAS DESIGNATED HEAD OF THIS HOUSEHOLD.
THERE'S NEVER BEEN ANYONE BUT WOMEN HERE.

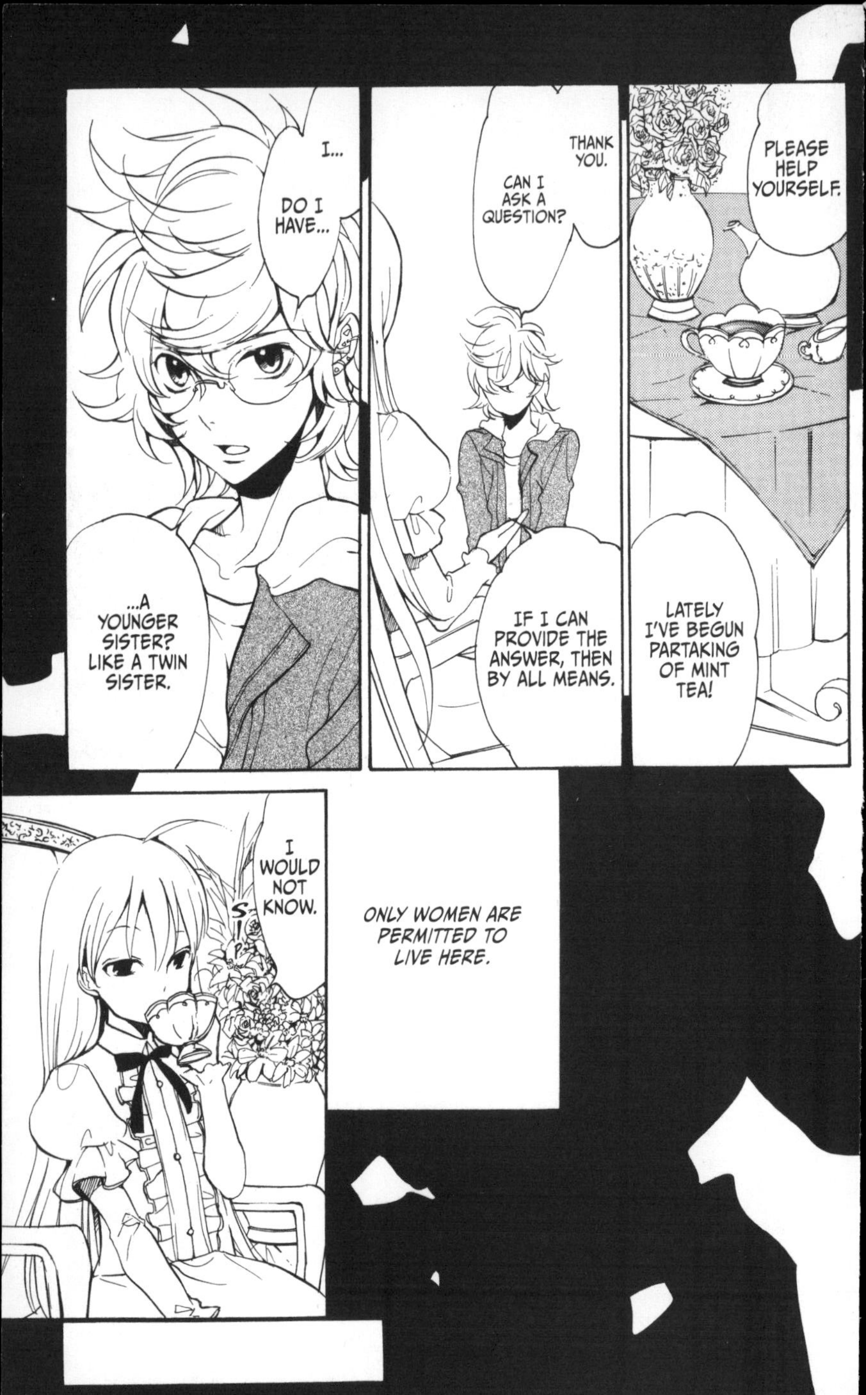
PLEASE HELP YOURSELF.
LATELY I'VE BEGUN PARTAKING OF MINT TEA!
THANK YOU.
CAN I ASK A QUESTION?
IF I CAN PROVIDE THE ANSWER, THEN BY ALL MEANS.
I...
DO I HAVE...
...A YOUNGER SISTER? LIKE A TWIN SISTER.
ONLY WOMEN ARE PERMITTED TO LIVE HERE.
I WOULD NOT KNOW.
SIP

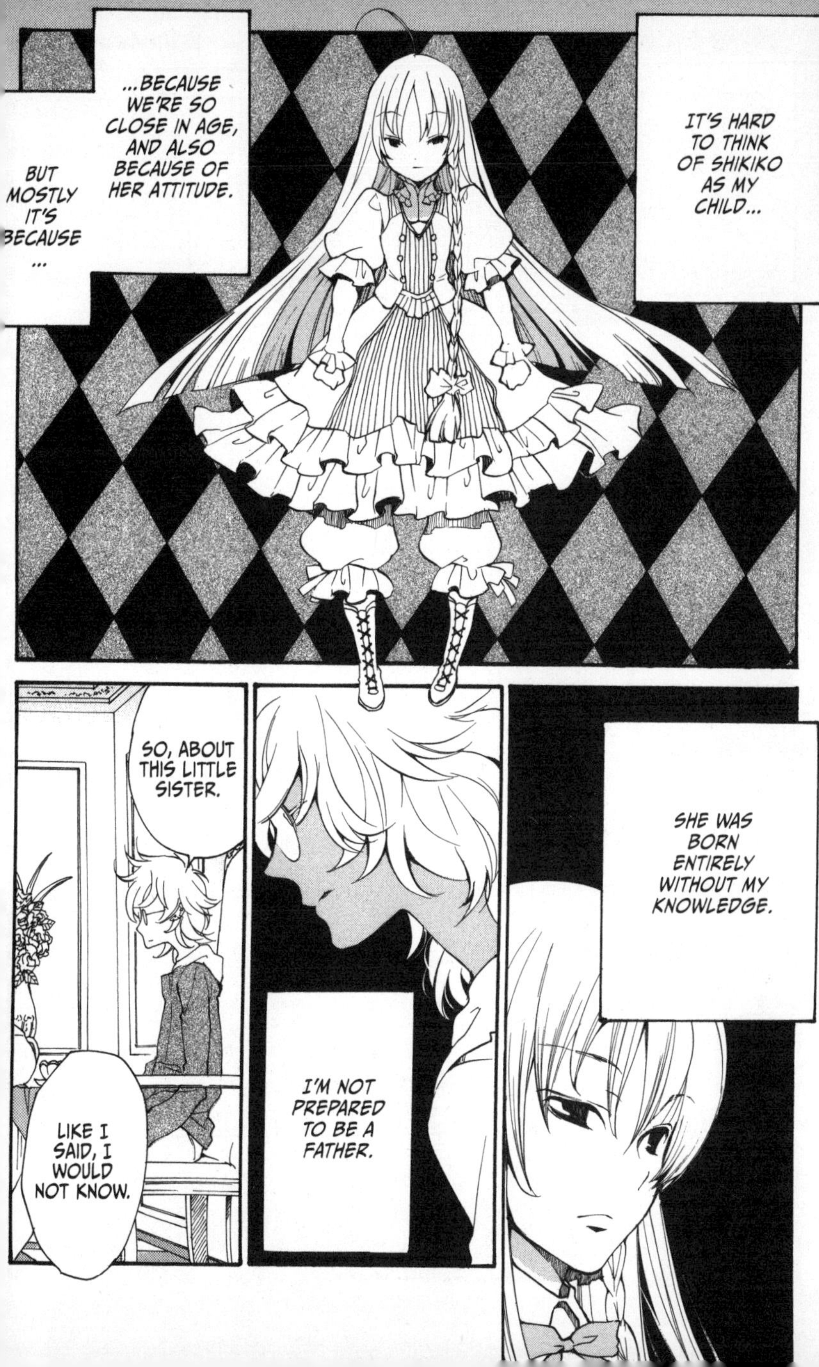
IT'S HARD TO THINK OF SHIKIKO AS MY CHILD...
...BECAUSE WE'RE SO CLOSE IN AGE, AND ALSO BECAUSE OF HER ATTITUDE.
BUT MOSTLY IT'S BECAUSE ...
SHE WAS BORN ENTIRELY WITHOUT MY KNOWLEDGE.
I'M NOT PREPARED TO BE A FATHER.
SO, ABOUT THIS LITTLE SISTER.
LIKE I SAID, I WOULD NOT KNOW.

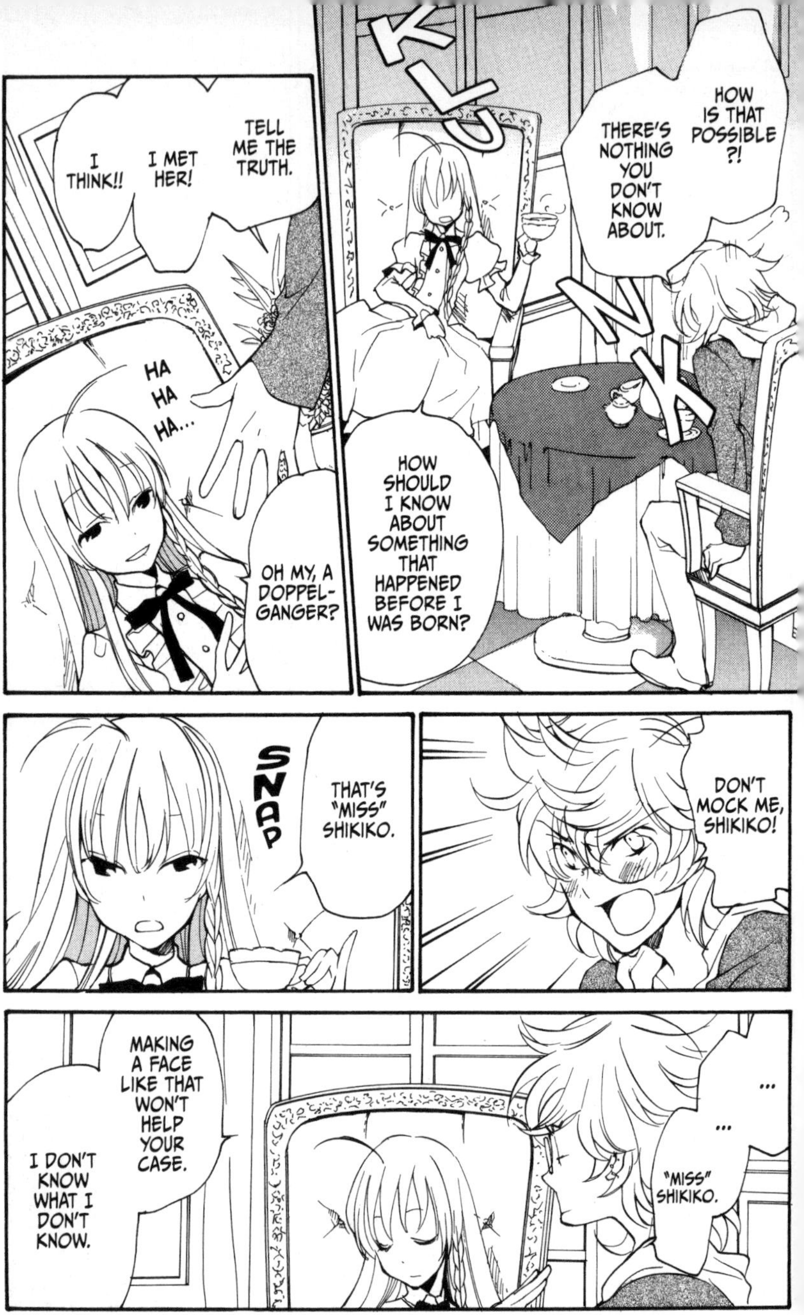
HOW IS THAT POSSIBLE?!
THERE'S NOTHING YOU DON'T KNOW ABOUT.
KLUNK
HOW SHOULD I KNOW ABOUT SOMETHING THAT HAPPENED BEFORE I WAS BORN?
TELL ME THE TRUTH.
I MET HER!
I THINK!!
HA HA HA...
OH MY, A DOPPEL-GANGER?
DON'T MOCK ME, SHIKIKO!
SNAP
THAT'S "MISS" SHIKIKO.
...
...
"MISS" SHIKIKO.
MAKING A FACE LIKE THAT WON'T HELP YOUR CASE.
I DON'T KNOW WHAT I DON'T KNOW.

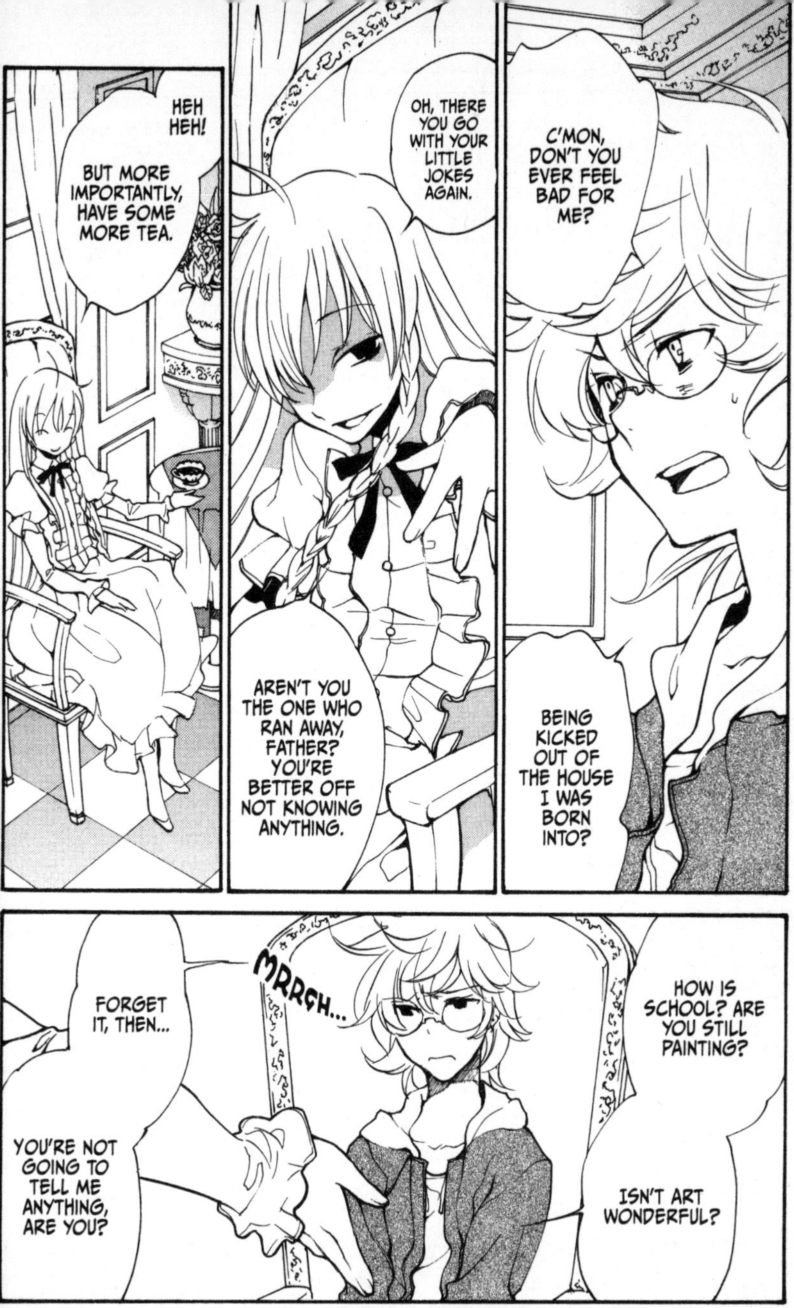
C'MON, DON'T YOU EVER FEEL BAD FOR ME?
BEING KICKED OUT OF THE HOUSE I WAS BORN INTO?
OH, THERE YOU GO WITH YOUR LITTLE JOKES AGAIN.
AREN'T YOU THE ONE WHO RAN AWAY, FATHER? YOU'RE BETTER OFF NOT KNOWING ANYTHING.
HEH HEH!
BUT MORE IMPORTANTLY, HAVE SOME MORE TEA.
HOW IS SCHOOL? ARE YOU STILL PAINTING?
ISN'T ART WONDERFUL?
MRRGH...
FORGET IT, THEN...
YOU'RE NOT GOING TO TELL ME ANYTHING, ARE YOU?

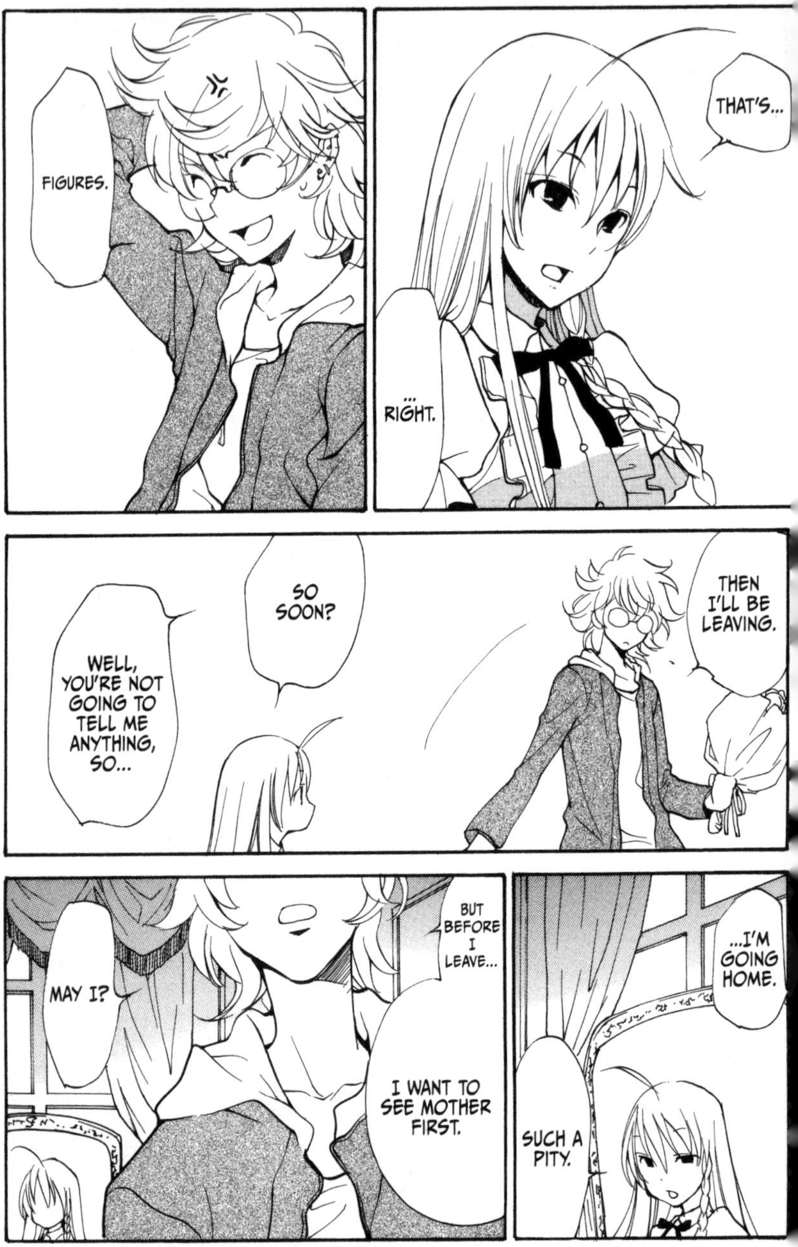
THAT'S...
... RIGHT.
FIGURES.
THEN I'LL BE LEAVING.
SO SOON?
WELL, YOU'RE NOT GOING TO TELL ME ANYTHING, SO...
...I'M GOING HOME.
SUCH A PITY.
BUT BEFORE I LEAVE...
I WANT TO SEE MOTHER FIRST.
MAY I?

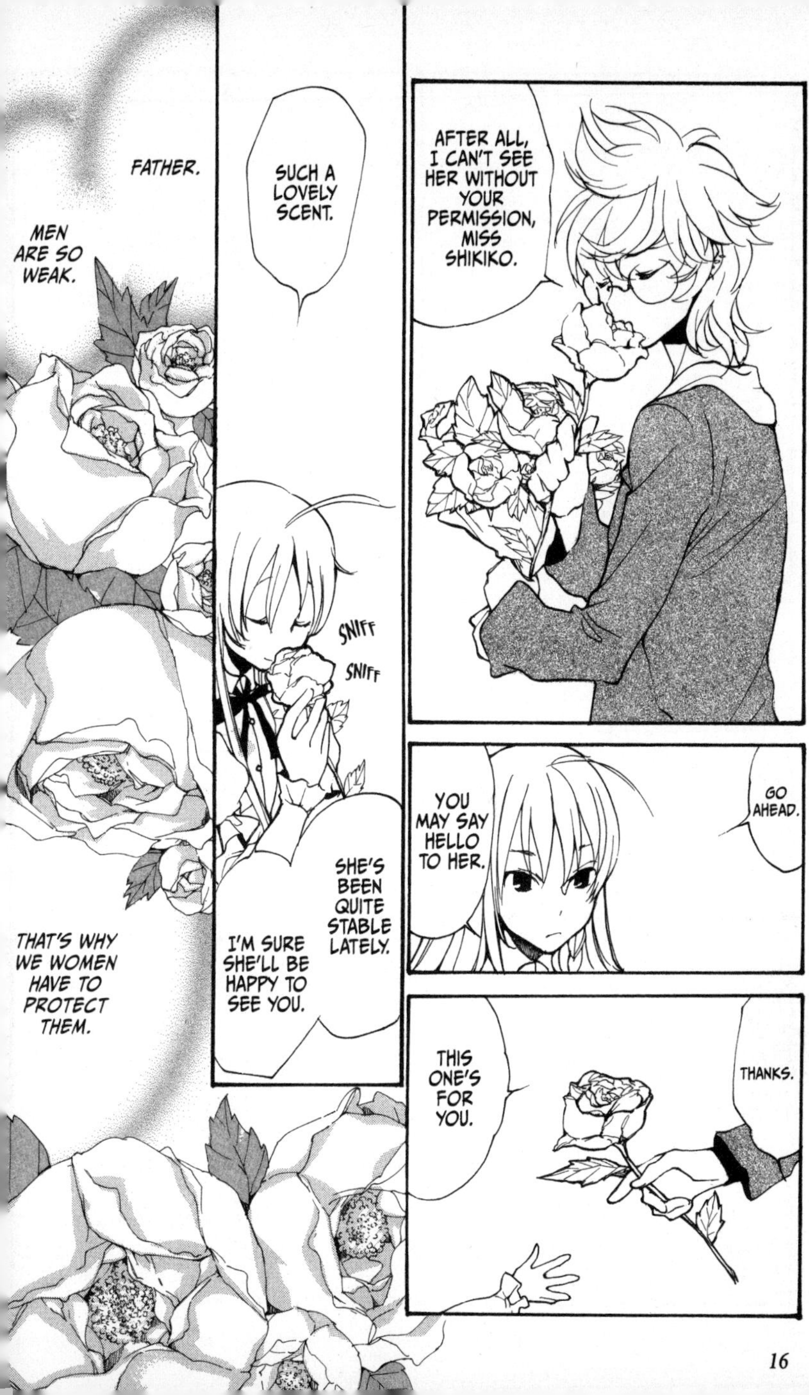
AFTER ALL, I CAN'T SEE HER WITHOUT YOUR PERMISSION, MISS SHIKIKO.
GO AHEAD.
YOU MAY SAY HELLO TO HER.
THANKS.
THIS ONE'S FOR YOU.
SUCH A LOVELY SCENT.
SNIFF
SNIFF
SHE'S BEEN QUITE STABLE LATELY.
I'M SURE SHE'LL BE HAPPY TO SEE YOU.
FATHER.
MEN ARE SO WEAK.
THAT'S WHY WE WOMEN HAVE TO PROTECT THEM.

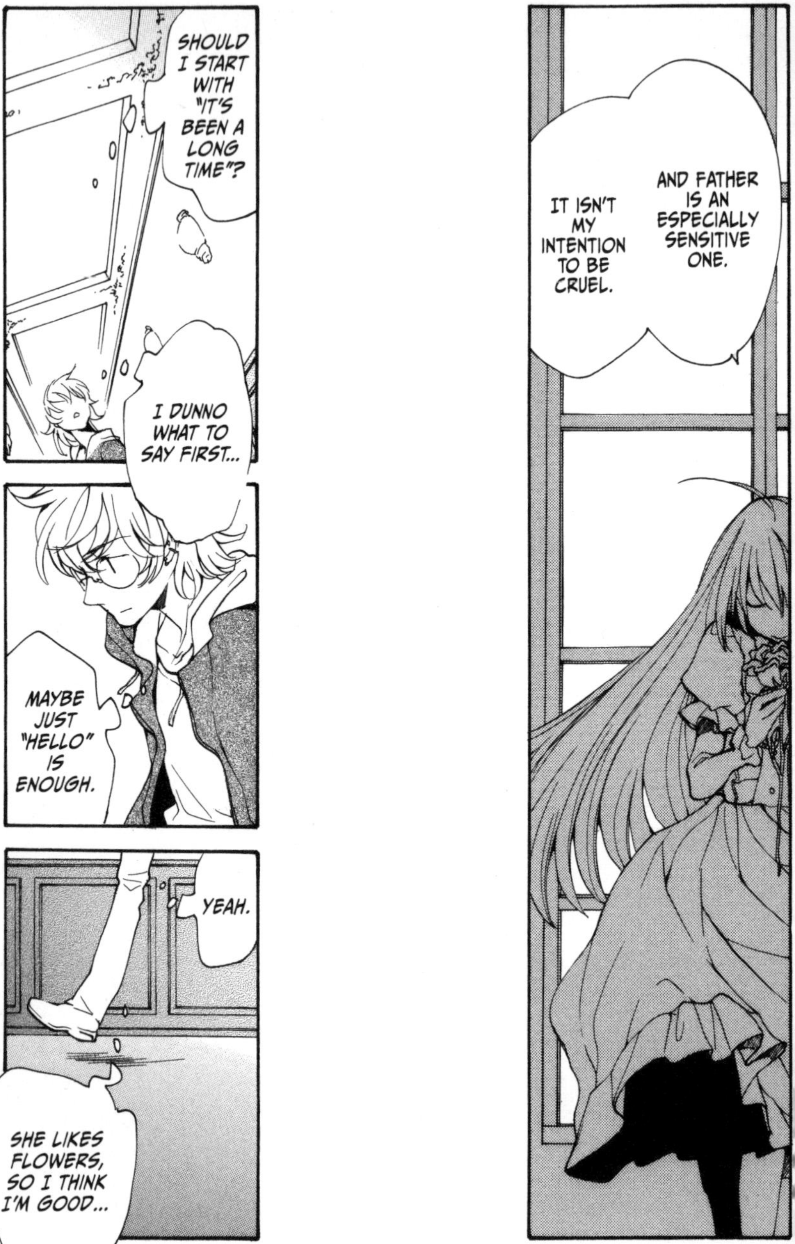
AND FATHER IS AN ESPECIALLY SENSITIVE ONE.
IT ISN'T MY INTENTION TO BE CRUEL.
SHOULD I START WITH "IT'S BEEN A LONG TIME"?
I DUNNO WHAT TO SAY FIRST...
MAYBE JUST "HELLO" IS ENOUGH.
YEAH.
SHE LIKES FLOWERS, SO I THINK I'M GOOD...

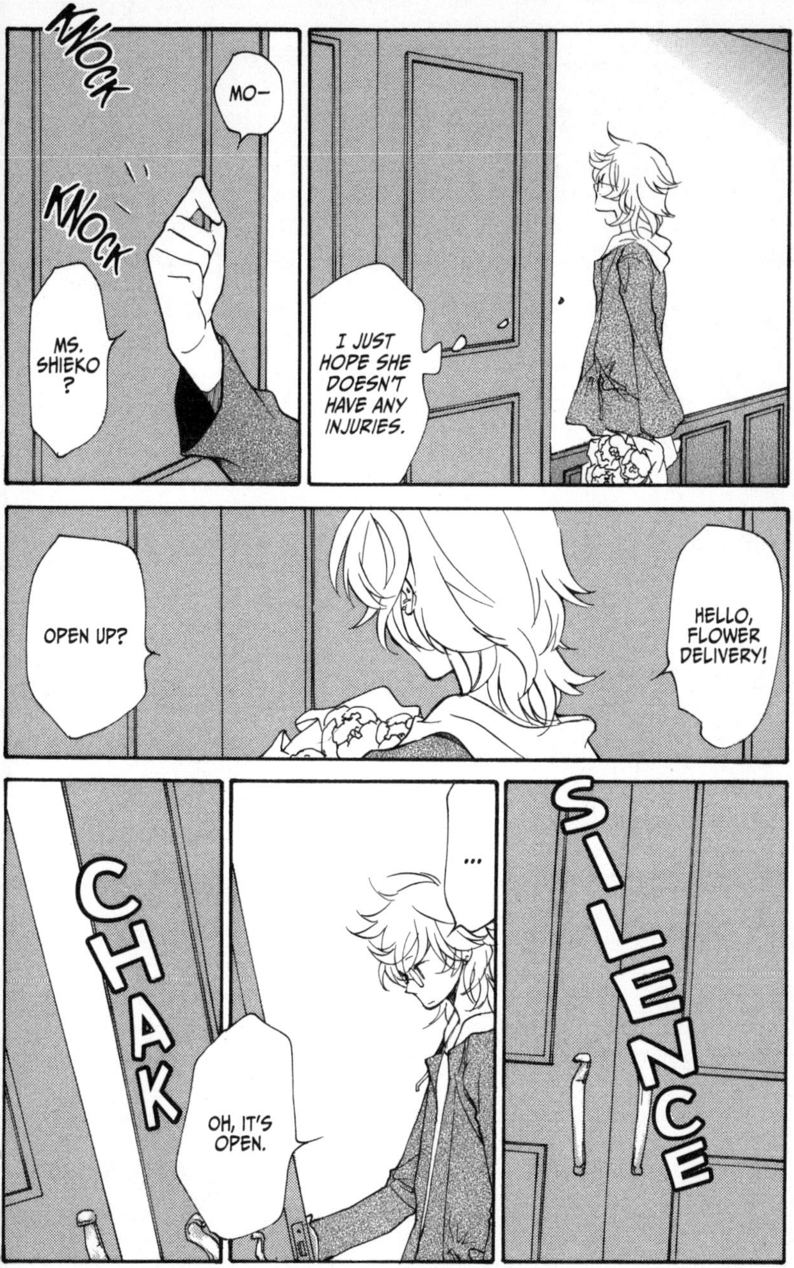
I JUST HOPE SHE DOESN'T HAVE ANY INJURIES.
MO–
KNOCK
KNOCK
MS. SHIEKO?
HELLO, FLOWER DELIVERY!
OPEN UP?
SILENCE
...
OH, IT'S OPEN.
CHAK

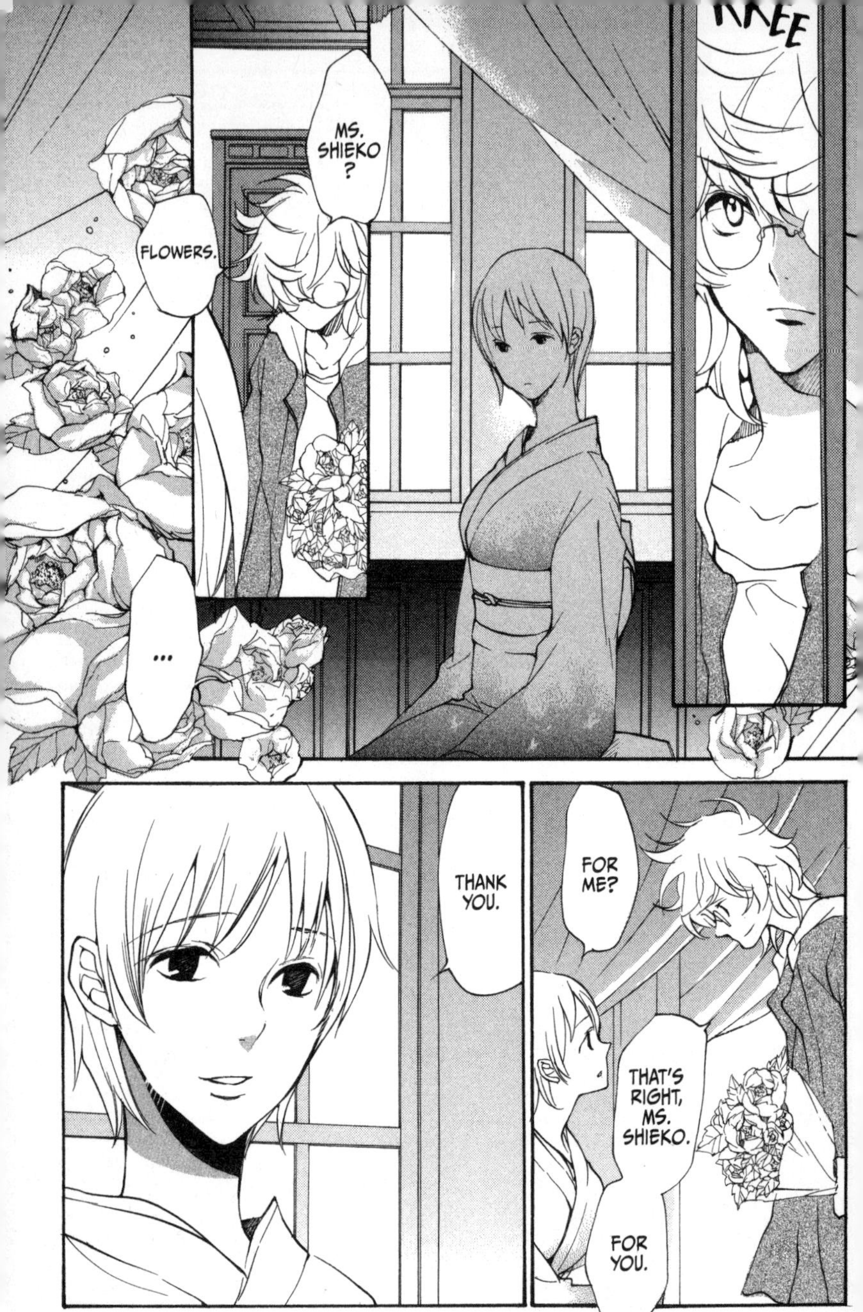
MS. SHIEKO?
FLOWERS.
...
FOR ME?
THAT'S RIGHT, MS. SHIEKO.
FOR YOU.
THANK YOU.

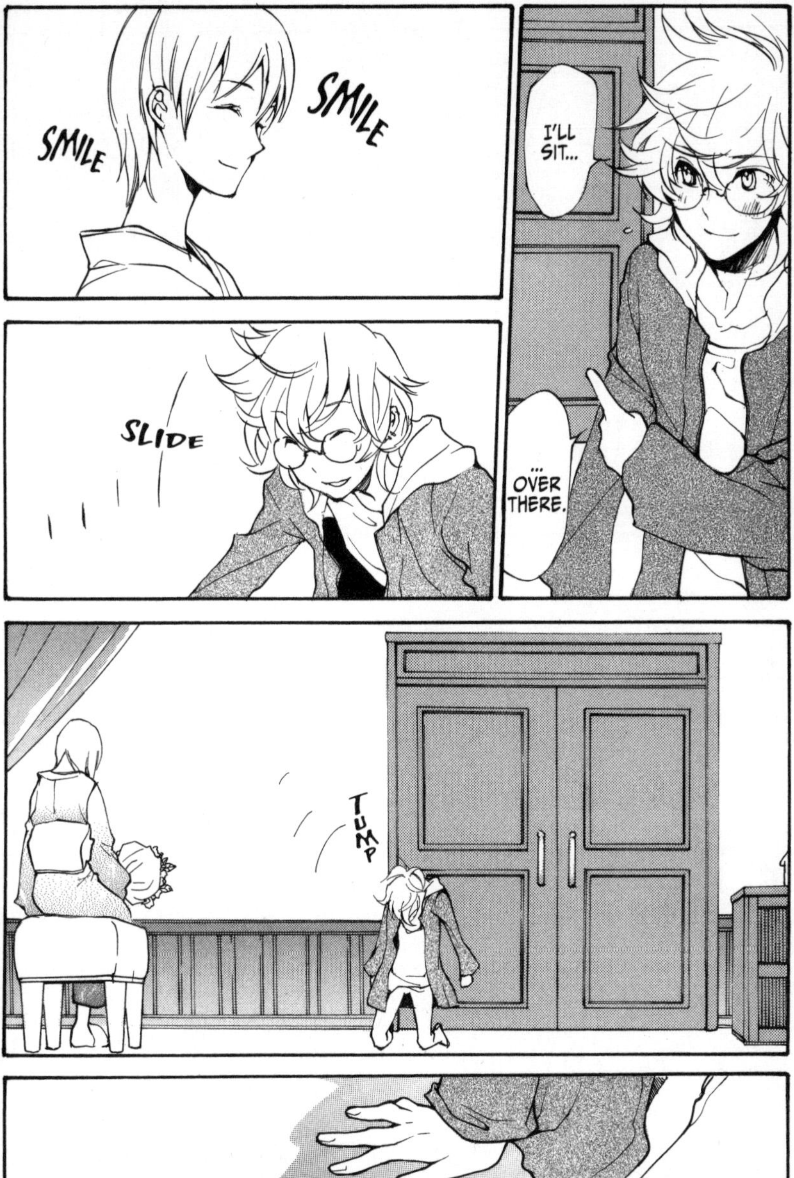
I'LL SIT...
...OVER THERE.
SMILE
SMILE
SLIDE
TUMP

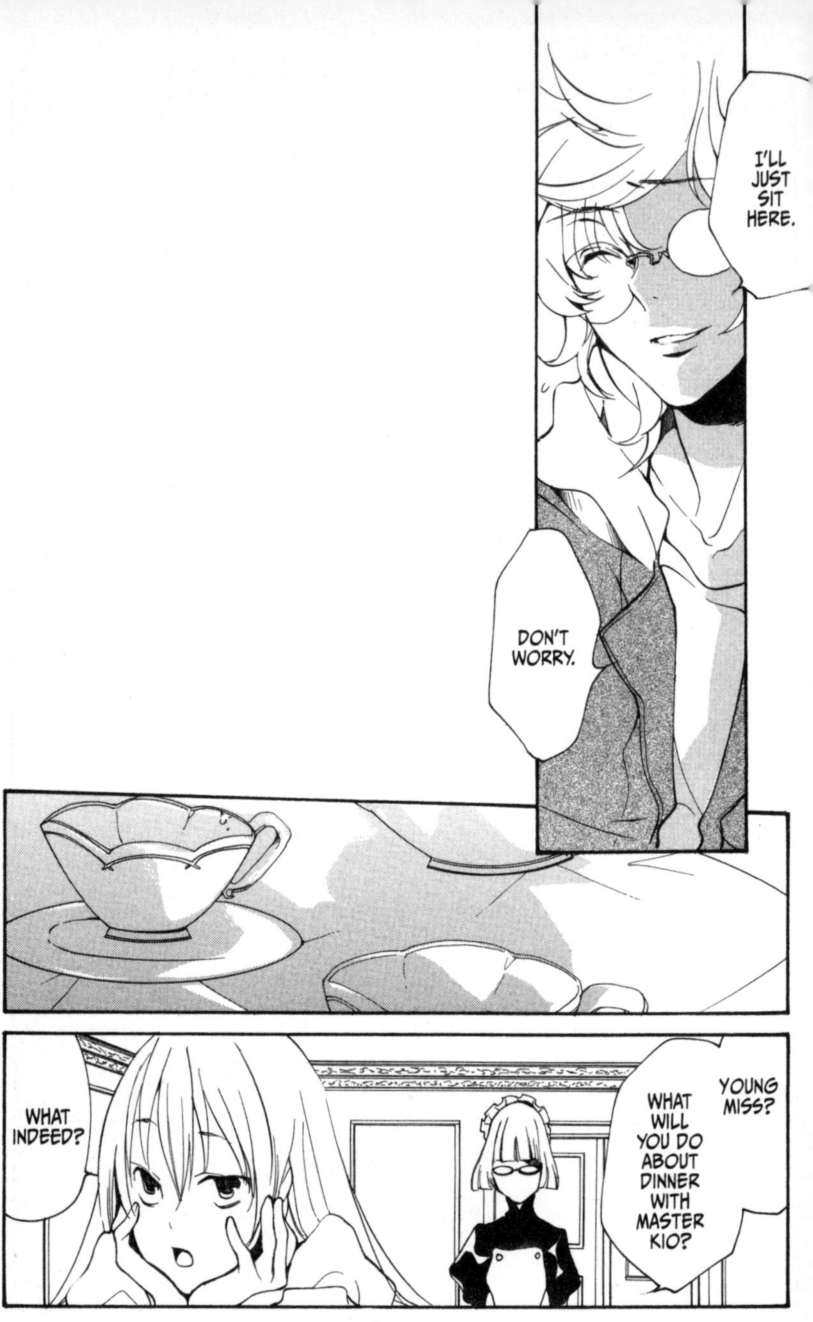
I'LL JUST SIT HERE.
DON'T WORRY.
YOUNG MISS?
WHAT WILL YOU DO ABOUT DINNER WITH MASTER KIO?
WHAT INDEED?

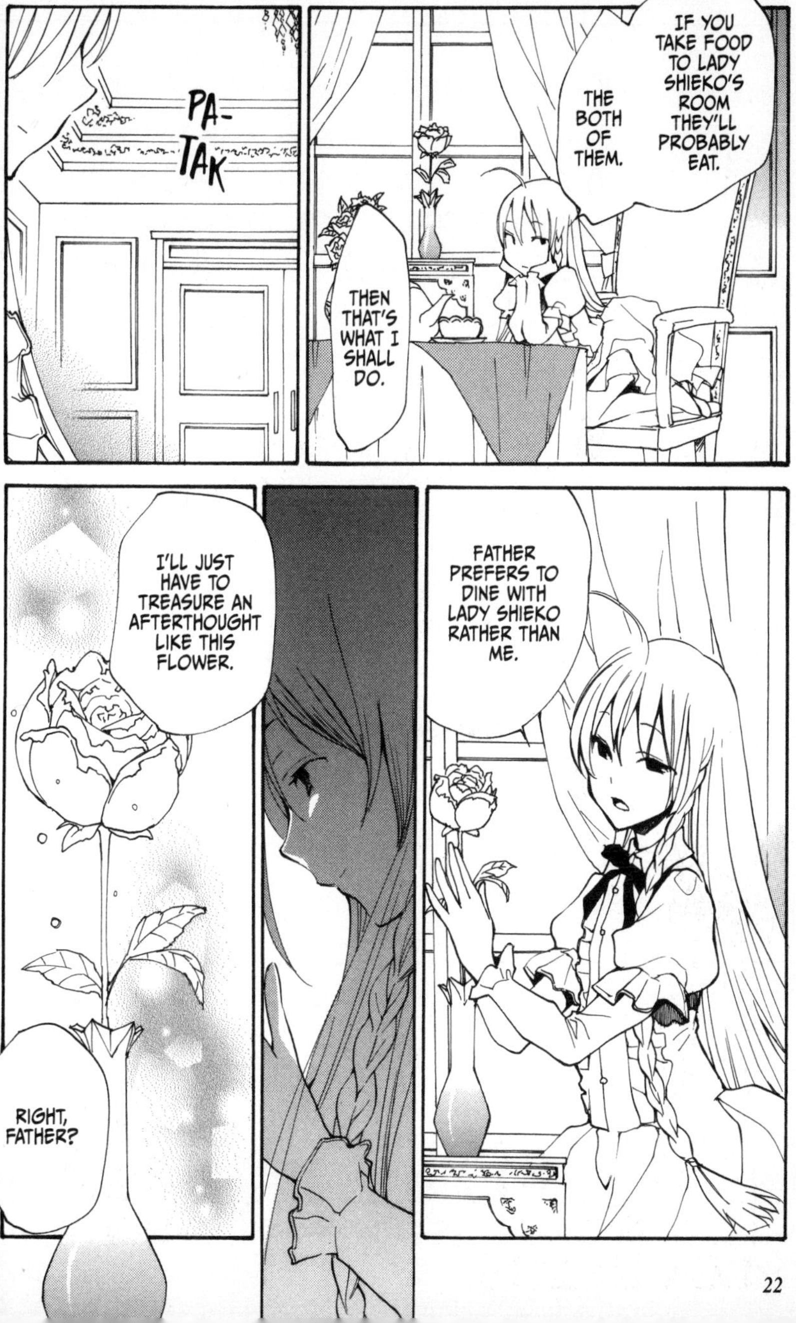
IF YOU TAKE FOOD TO LADY SHIEKO'S ROOM THEY'LL PROBABLY EAT.
THE BOTH OF THEM.
THEN THAT'S WHAT I SHALL DO.
PA-TAK
FATHER PREFERS TO DINE WITH LADY SHIEKO RATHER THAN ME.
I'LL JUST HAVE TO TREASURE AN AFTERTHOUGHT LIKE THIS FLOWER.
RIGHT, FATHER?

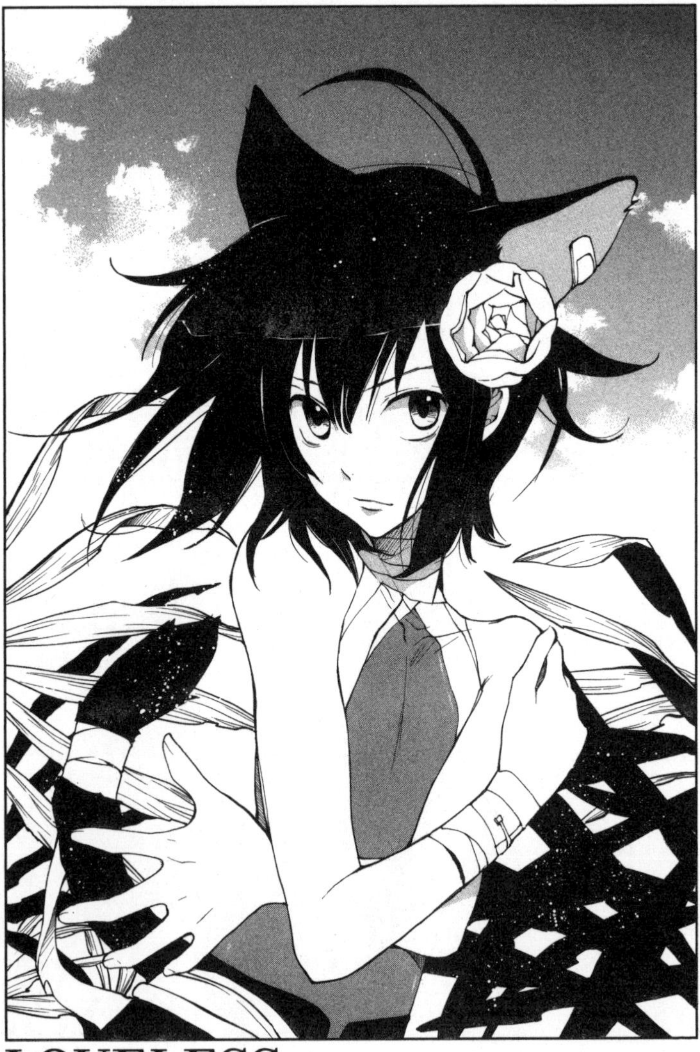

LOVELESS

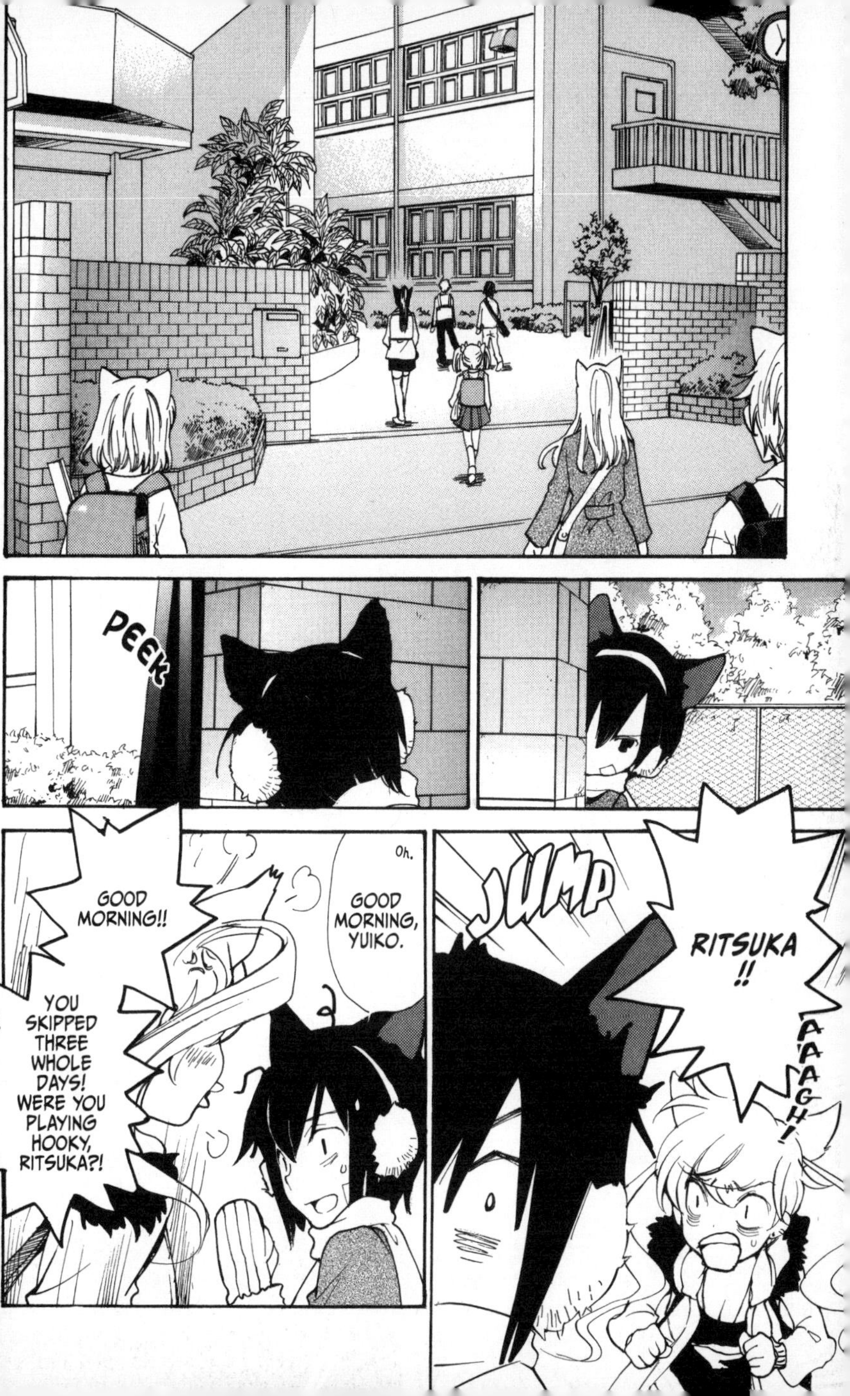
PEEK
RITSUKA !!
AAAGH!
JUMP
Oh.
GOOD MORNING, YUIKO.
GOOD MORNING!!
YOU SKIPPED THREE WHOLE DAYS! WERE YOU PLAYING HOOKY, RITSUKA?!

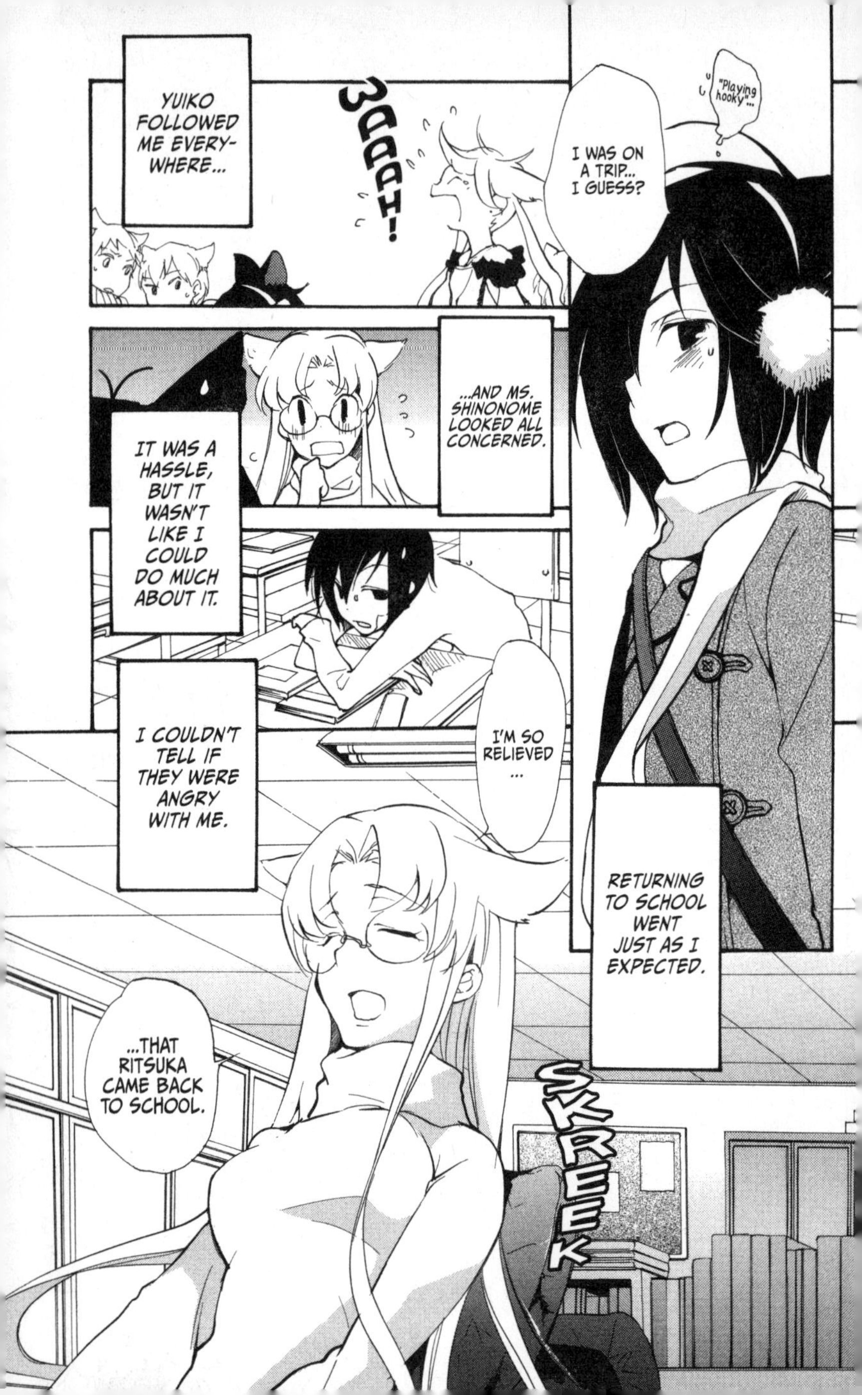
"Playing hooky"...
I WAS ON A TRIP... I GUESS?
RETURNING TO SCHOOL WENT JUST AS I EXPECTED.
YUIKO FOLLOWED ME EVERY-WHERE...
BAAAAH!
...AND MS. SHINONOME LOOKED ALL CONCERNED.
IT WAS A HASSLE, BUT IT WASN'T LIKE I COULD DO MUCH ABOUT IT.
I COULDN'T TELL IF THEY WERE ANGRY WITH ME.
I'M SO RELIEVED ...
...THAT RITSUKA CAME BACK TO SCHOOL.
SKREEK

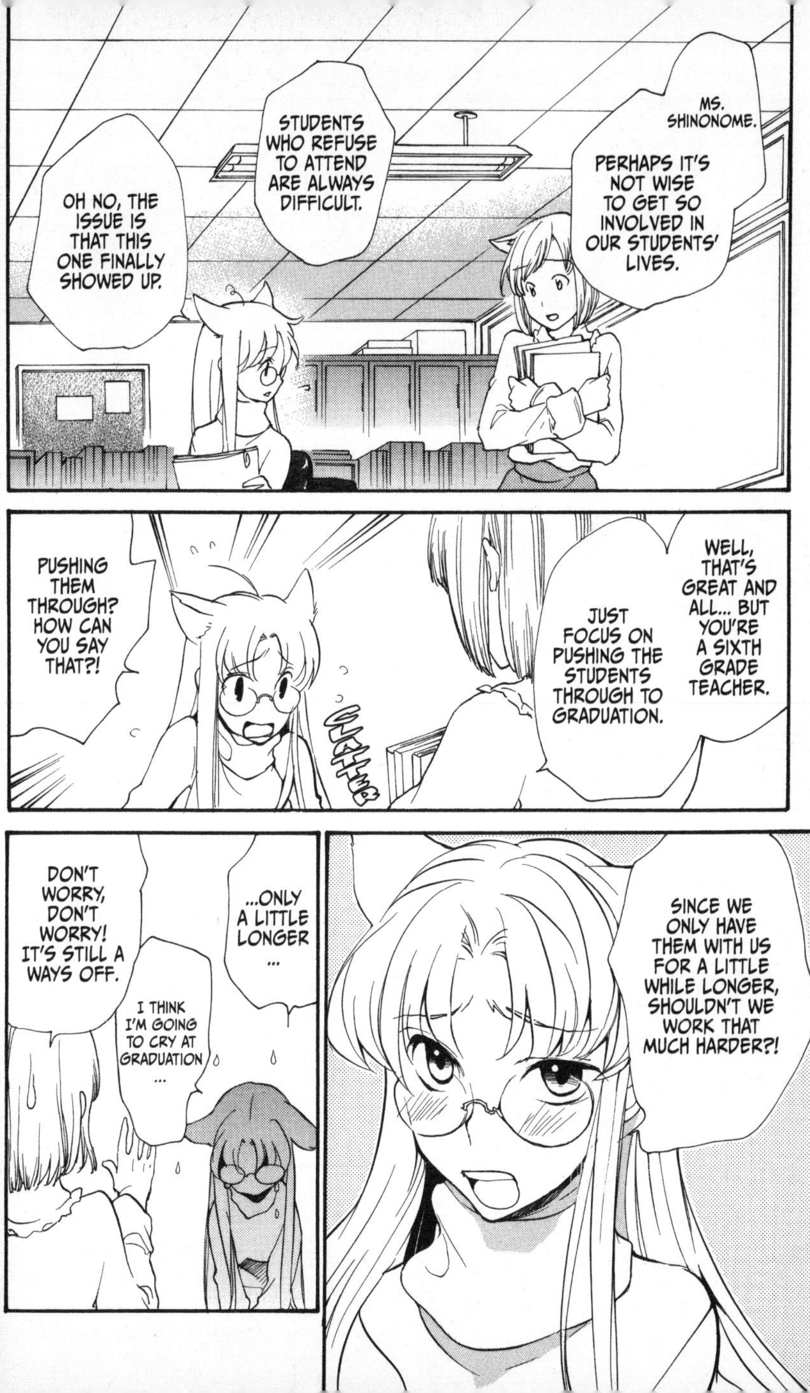
MS. SHINONOME.
PERHAPS IT'S NOT WISE TO GET SO INVOLVED IN OUR STUDENTS' LIVES.
STUDENTS WHO REFUSE TO ATTEND ARE ALWAYS DIFFICULT.
OH NO, THE ISSUE IS THAT THIS ONE FINALLY SHOWED UP.
WELL, THAT'S GREAT AND ALL... BUT YOU'RE A SIXTH GRADE TEACHER.
JUST FOCUS ON PUSHING THE STUDENTS THROUGH TO GRADUATION.
PUSHING THEM THROUGH? HOW CAN YOU SAY THAT?!
SINCE WE ONLY HAVE THEM WITH US FOR A LITTLE WHILE LONGER, SHOULDN'T WE WORK THAT MUCH HARDER?!
...ONLY A LITTLE LONGER ...
DON'T WORRY, DON'T WORRY! IT'S STILL A WAYS OFF.
I THINK I'M GOING TO CRY AT GRADUATION ...

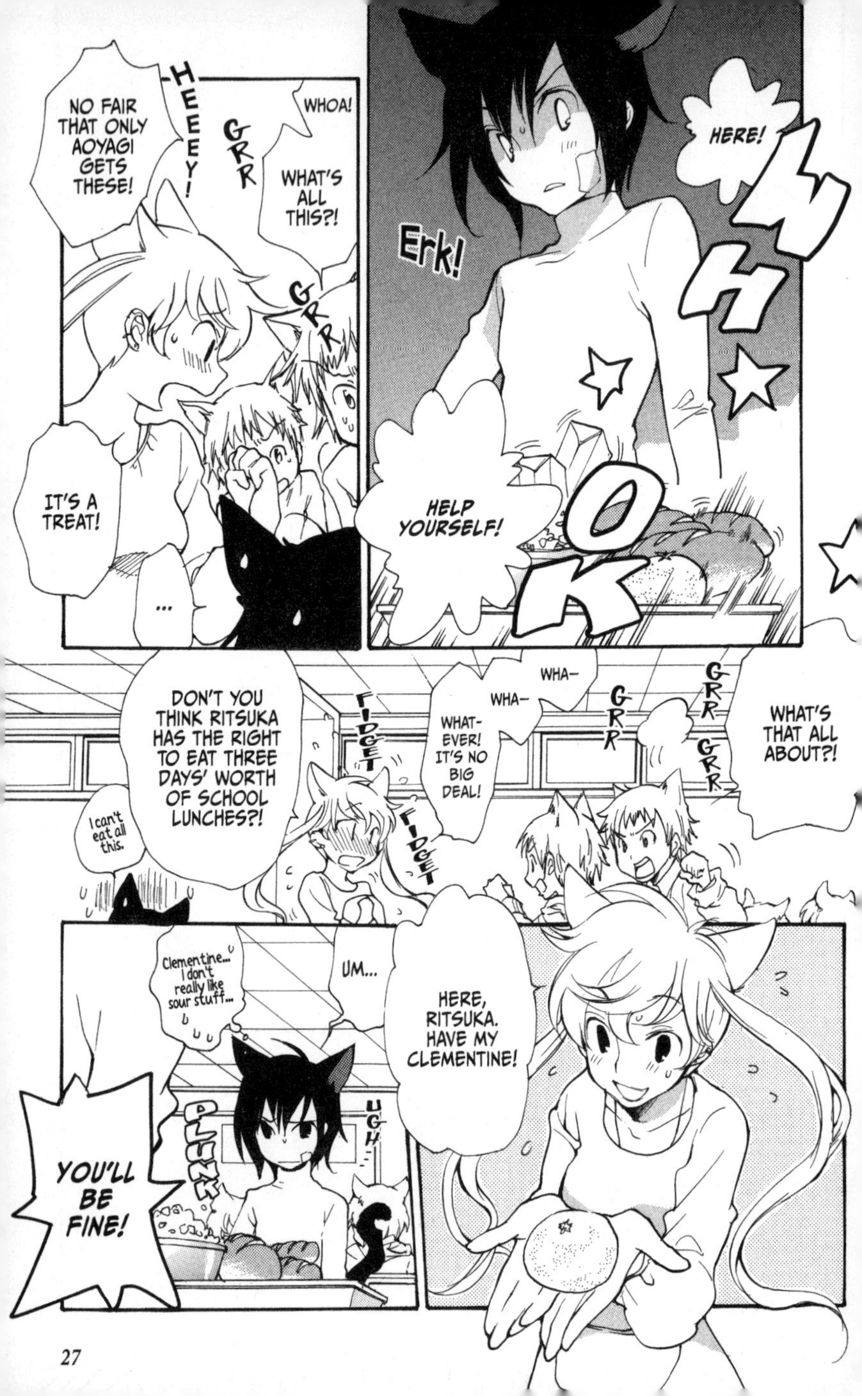
HERE!
Erk!
HELP YOURSELF!
HEEEEY!
NO FAIR THAT ONLY AOYAGI GETS THESE!
WHOA!
GRR
WHAT'S ALL THIS?!
GRR
IT'S A TREAT!
...
WHAT'S THAT ALL ABOUT?!
GRR GRR
GRR
WHA-
WHA-
WHATEVER! IT'S NO BIG DEAL!
FIDGET
FIDGET
DON'T YOU THINK RITSUKA HAS THE RIGHT TO EAT THREE DAYS' WORTH OF SCHOOL LUNCHES?!
I can't eat all this.
HERE, RITSUKA. HAVE MY CLEMENTINE!
UM...
Clementine... I don't really like sour stuff...
UGH
PLUNK
YOU'LL BE FINE!

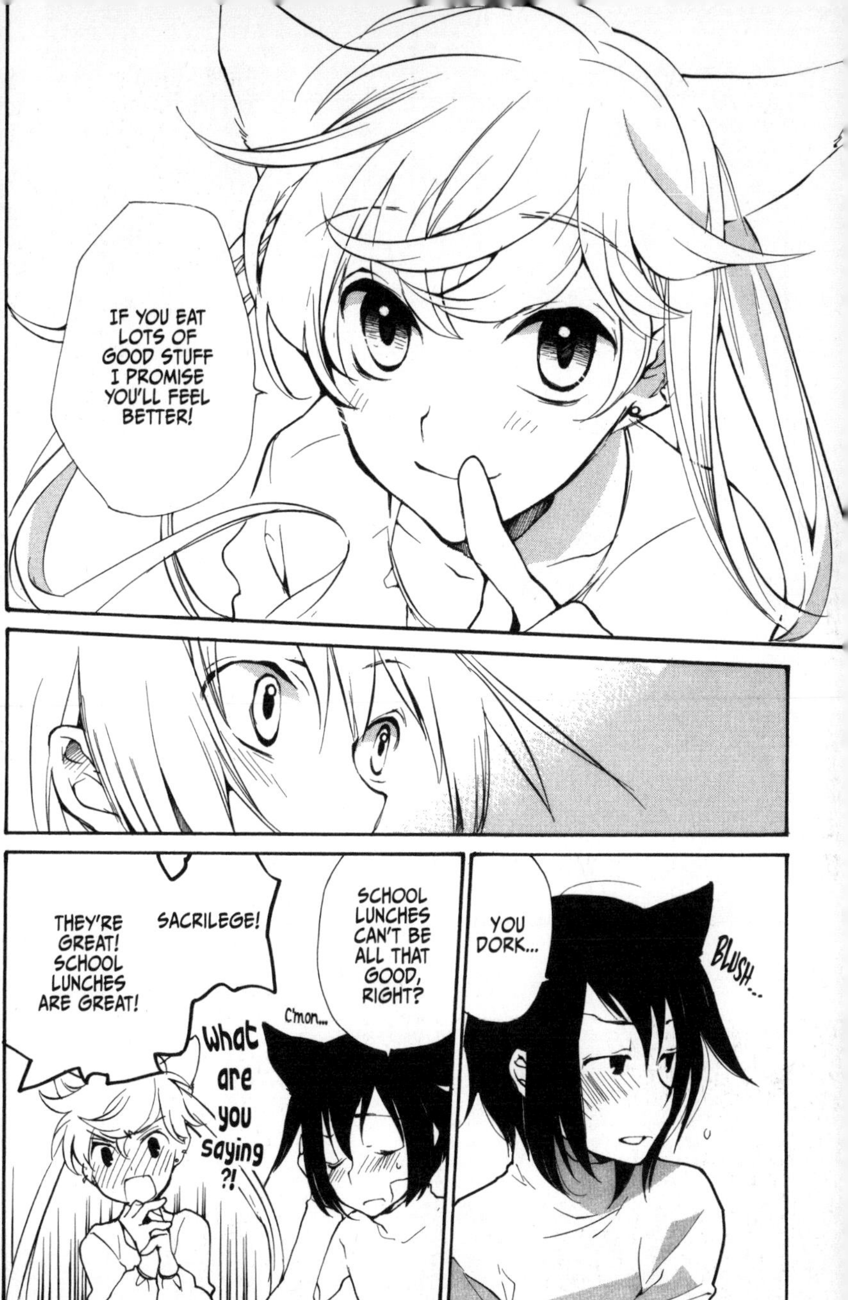
IF YOU EAT LOTS OF GOOD STUFF I PROMISE YOU'LL FEEL BETTER!
YOU DORK...
BLUSH...
SCHOOL LUNCHES CAN'T BE ALL THAT GOOD, RIGHT?
C'mon...
SACRILEGE!
THEY'RE GREAT! SCHOOL LUNCHES ARE GREAT!
What are you saying?!

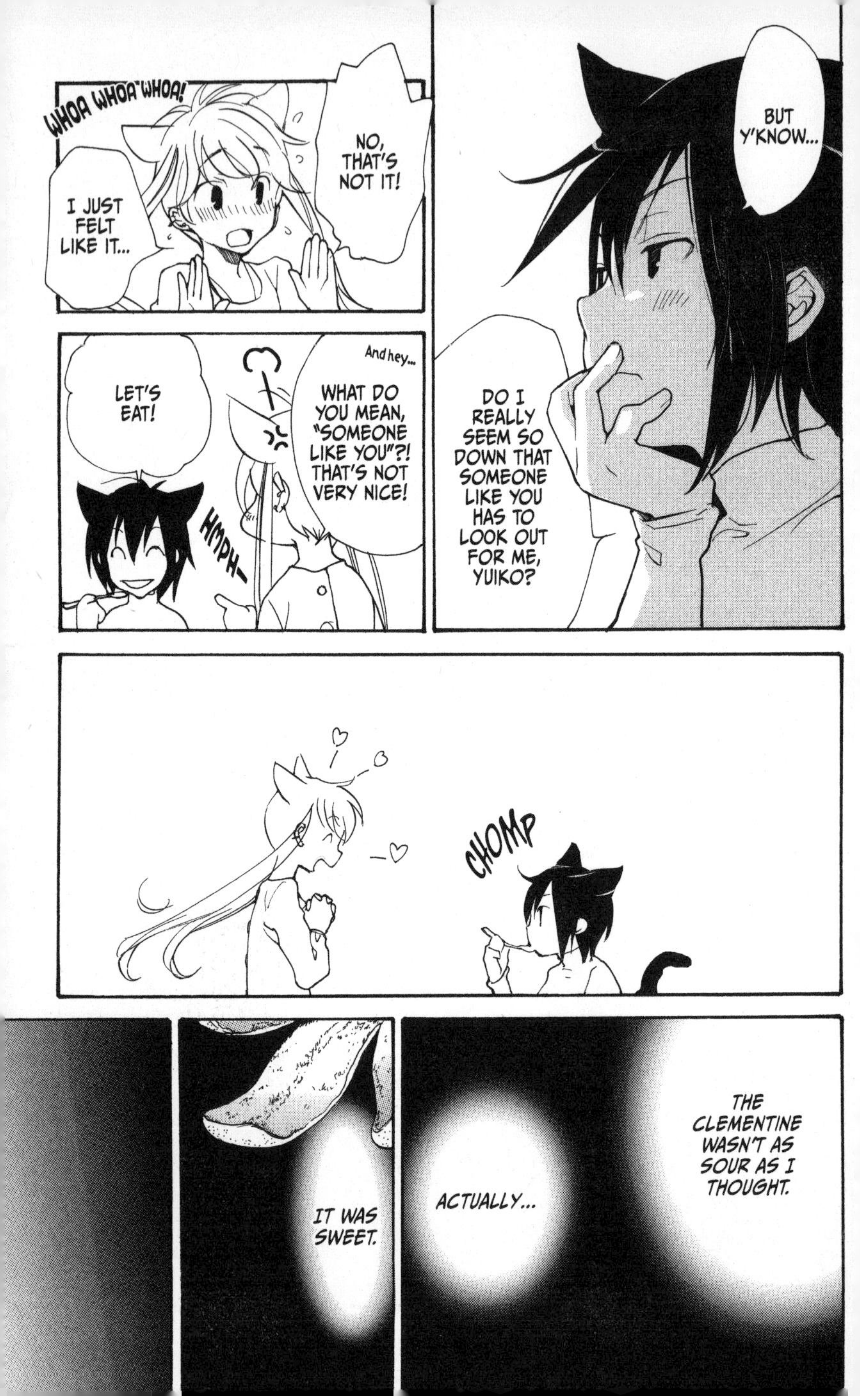
BUT Y'KNOW...
DO I REALLY SEEM SO DOWN THAT SOMEONE LIKE YOU HAS TO LOOK OUT FOR ME, YUIKO?
NO, THAT'S NOT IT!
WHOA WHOA WHOA!
I JUST FELT LIKE IT...
And hey...
WHAT DO YOU MEAN, "SOMEONE LIKE YOU"?! THAT'S NOT VERY NICE!
HMPH-
LET'S EAT!
CHOMP
THE CLEMENTINE WASN'T AS SOUR AS I THOUGHT.
ACTUALLY...
IT WAS SWEET.

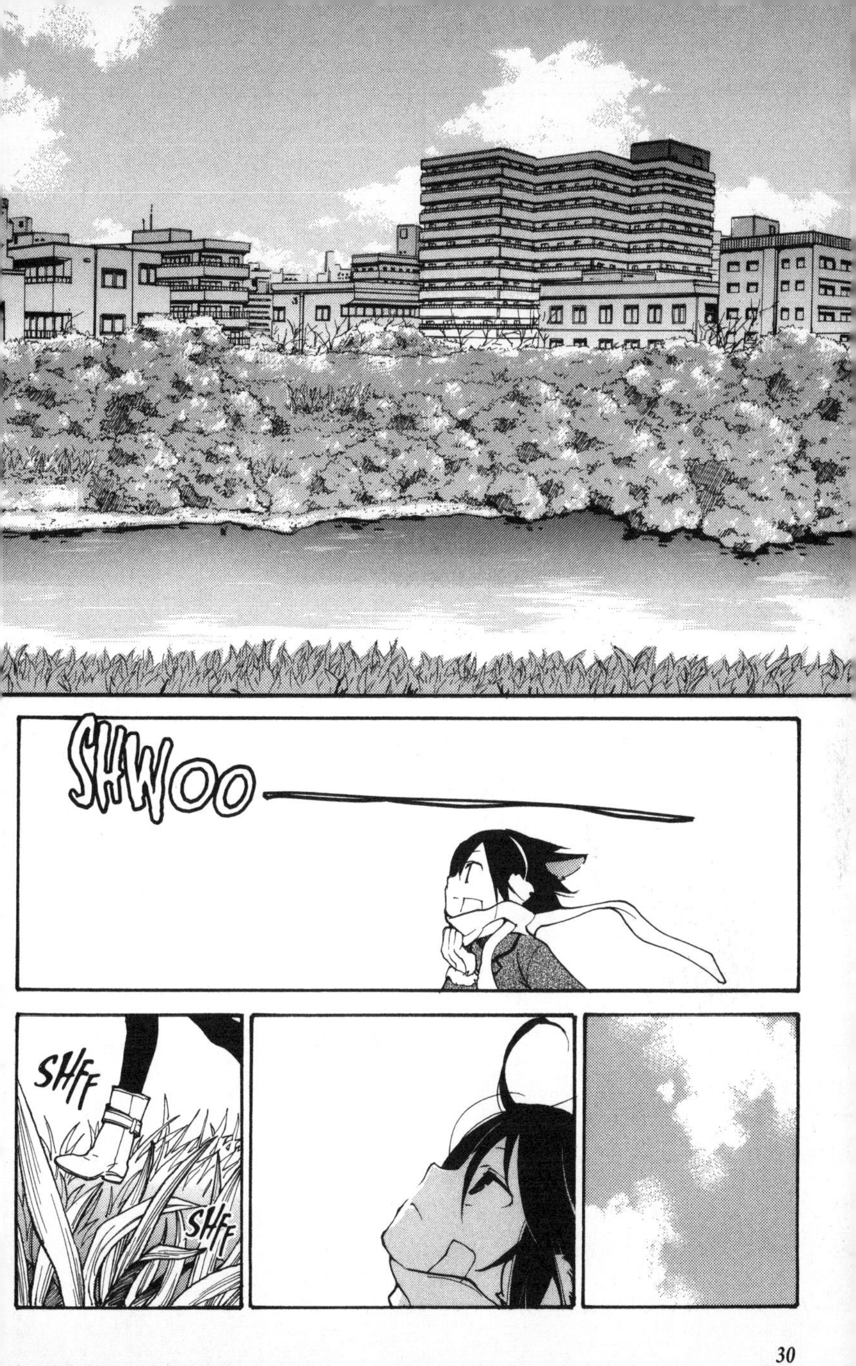
SHWOO
SHFF
SHFF

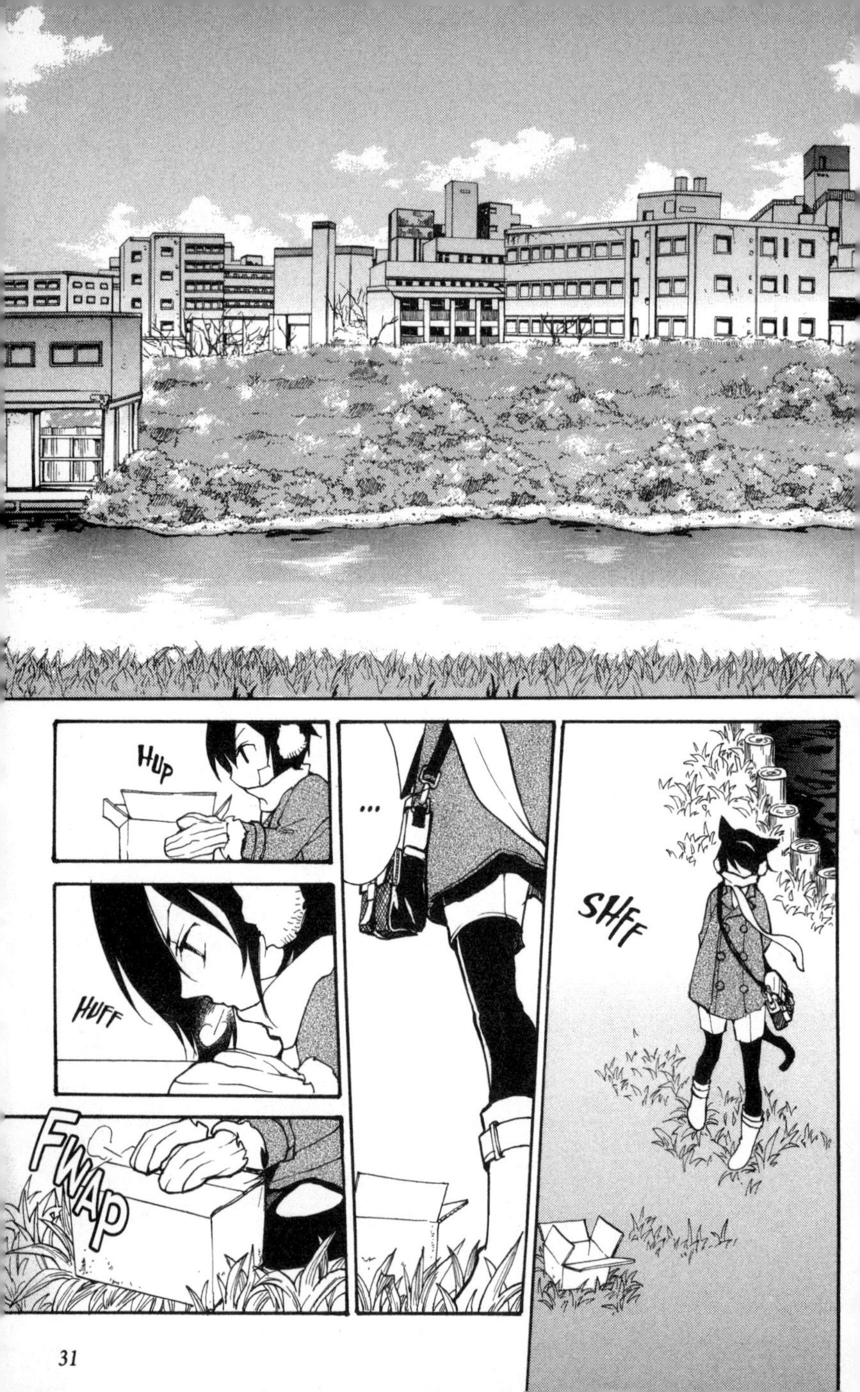
SHFF
...
HUP
HUFF
FWAP

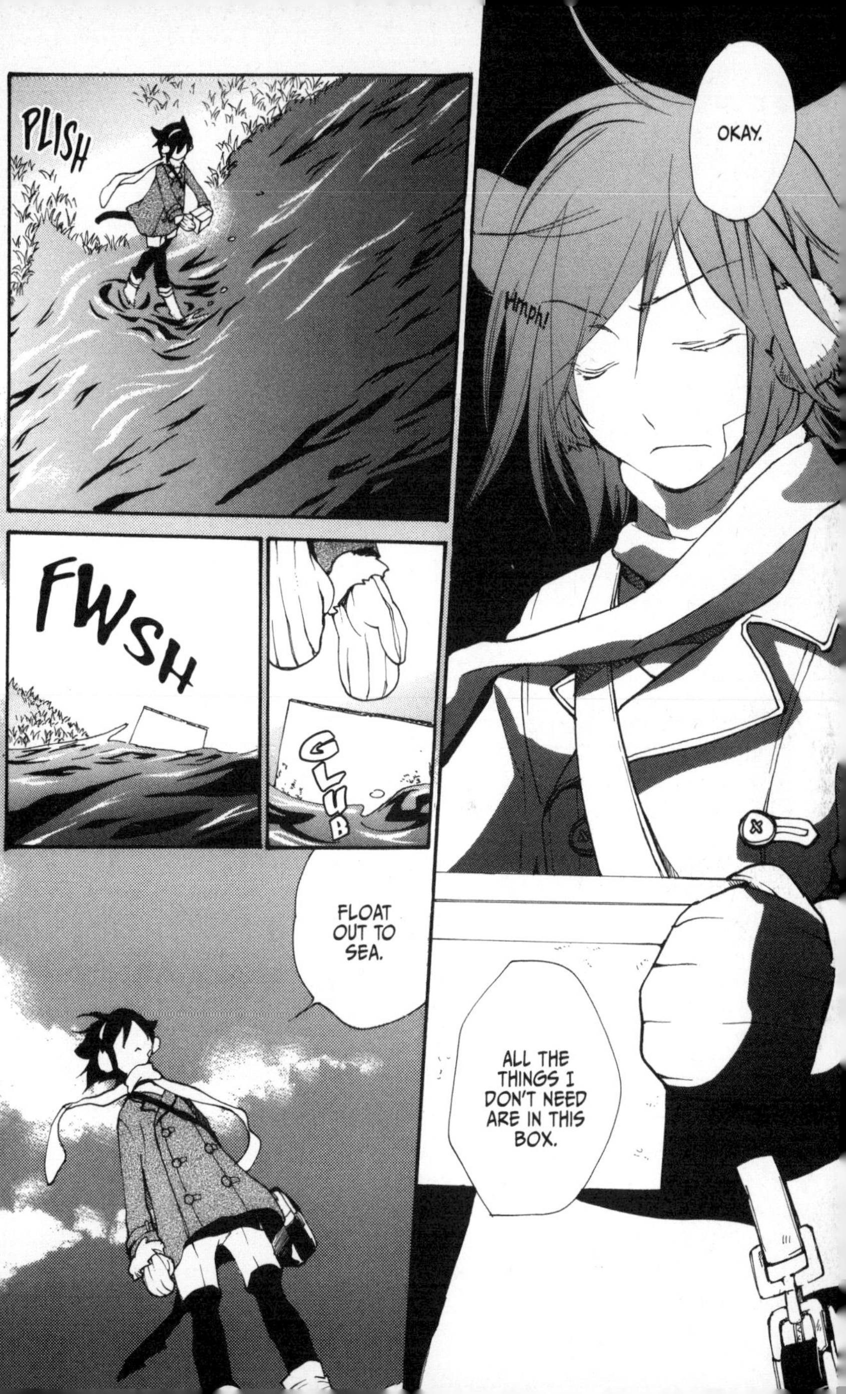
OKAY.
Hmph!
ALL THE THINGS I DON'T NEED ARE IN THIS BOX.
PLISH
GLUB
FWSH
FLOAT OUT TO SEA.

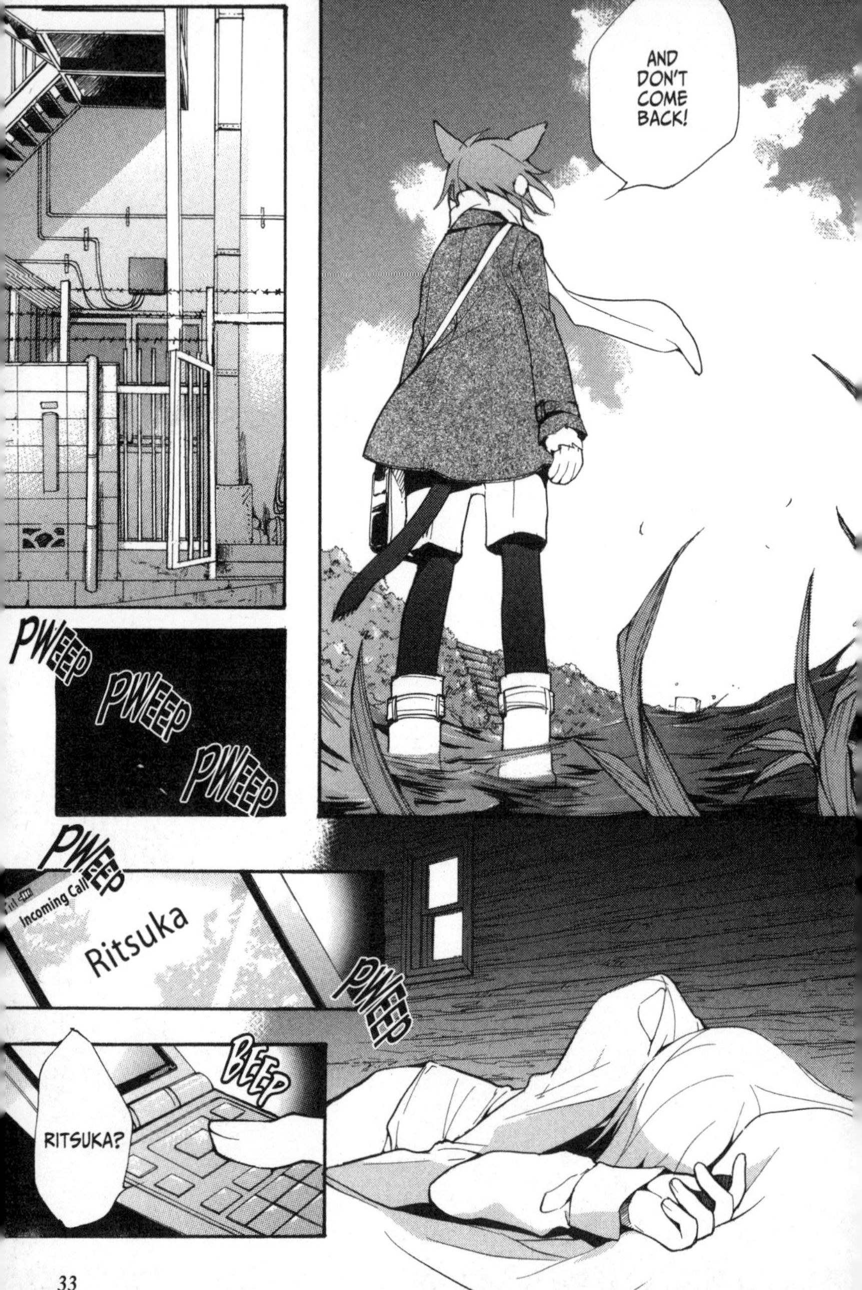
AND DON'T COME BACK!
PWEEP
PWEEP
PWEEP
PWEEP
PWEEP
Incoming Call
Ritsuka
BEEP
RITSUKA?

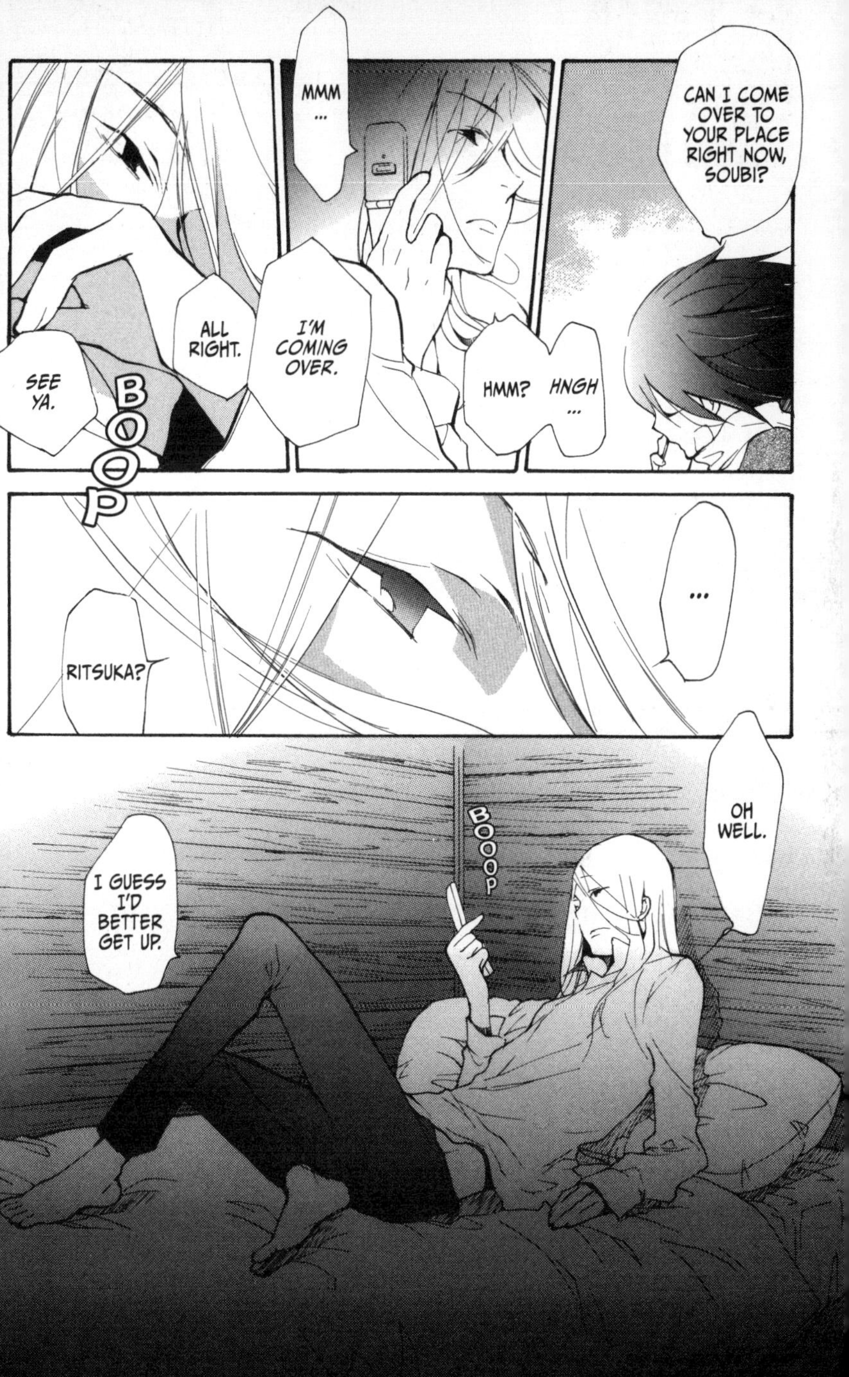
CAN I COME OVER TO YOUR PLACE RIGHT NOW, SOUBI?
HNGH ...
HMM?
MMM ...
I'M COMING OVER.
ALL RIGHT.
SEE YA.
BOOOP
...
RITSUKA?
OH WELL.
BOOOP
I GUESS I'D BETTER GET UP.

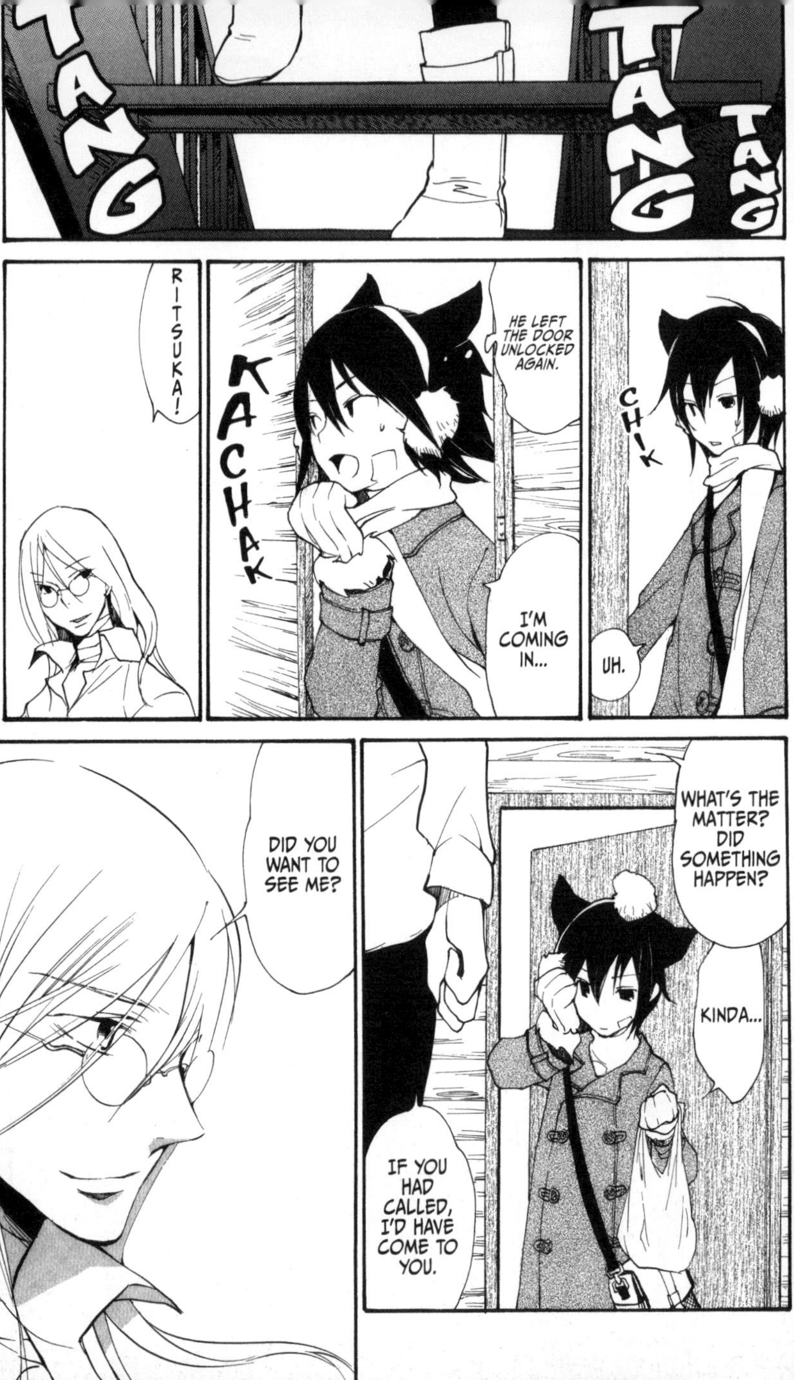
TANG
TANG
TANG
CHIK
UH.
HE LEFT THE DOOR UNLOCKED AGAIN.
KACHAK
I'M COMING IN...
RITSUKA!
WHAT'S THE MATTER? DID SOMETHING HAPPEN?
KINDA...
IF YOU HAD CALLED, I'D HAVE COME TO YOU.
DID YOU WANT TO SEE ME?

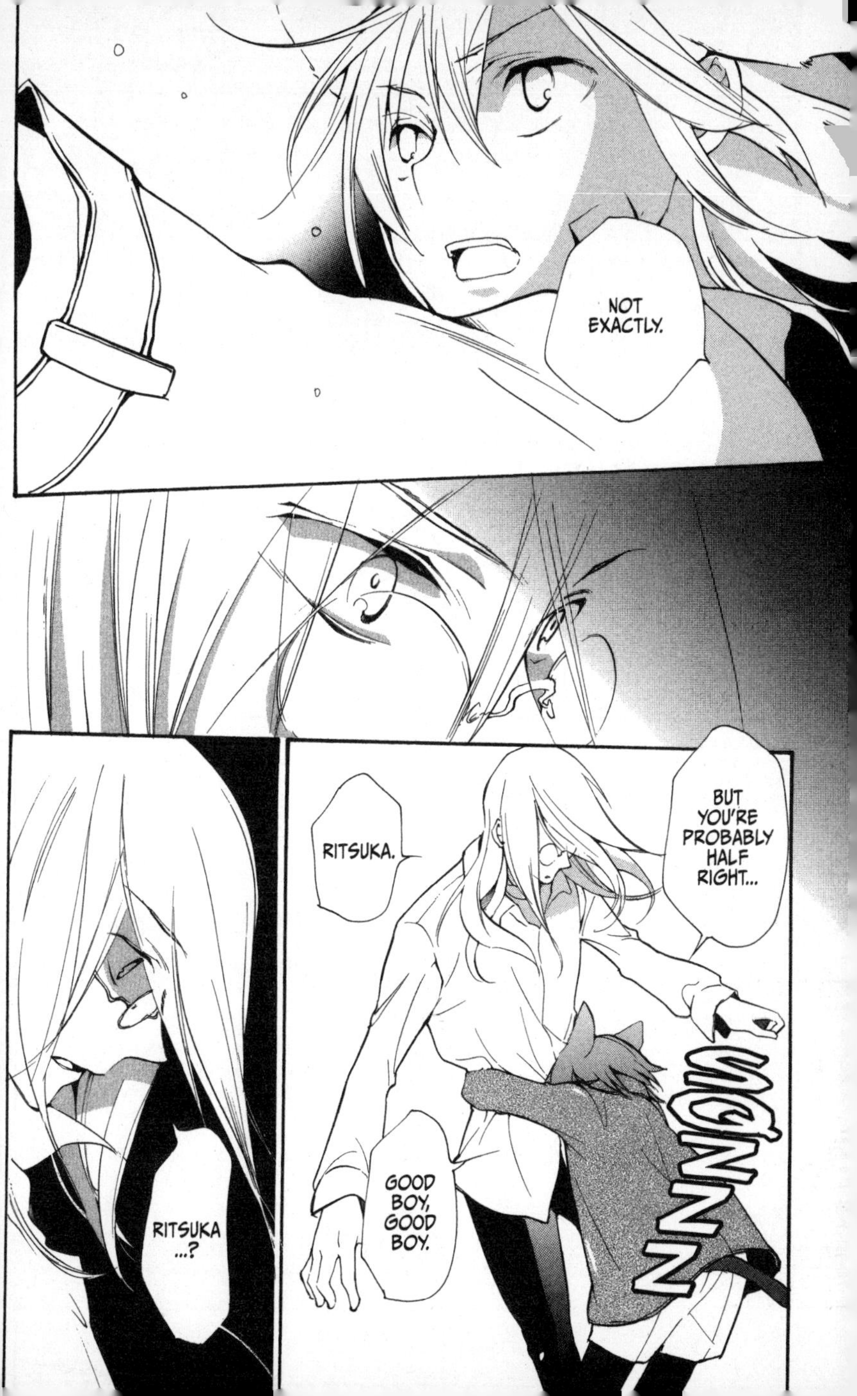
NOT EXACTLY.
BUT YOU'RE PROBABLY HALF RIGHT...
RITSUKA.
GOOD BOY, GOOD BOY.
RITSUKA ...?

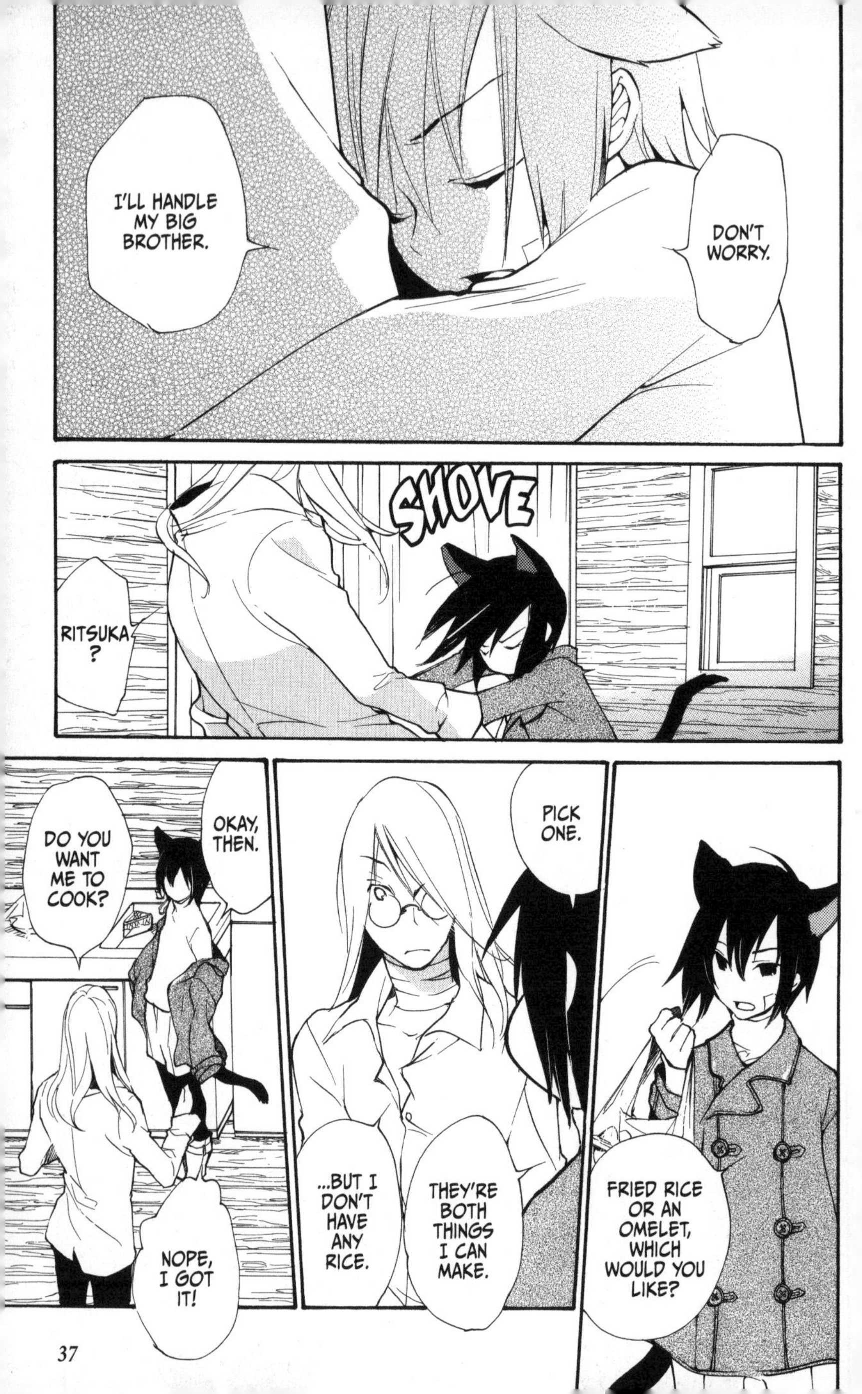
DON'T WORRY.
I'LL HANDLE MY BIG BROTHER.
SHOVE
RITSUKA?
FRIED RICE OR AN OMELET, WHICH WOULD YOU LIKE?
PICK ONE.
THEY'RE BOTH THINGS I CAN MAKE.
...BUT I DON'T HAVE ANY RICE.
OKAY, THEN.
DO YOU WANT ME TO COOK?
NOPE, I GOT IT!

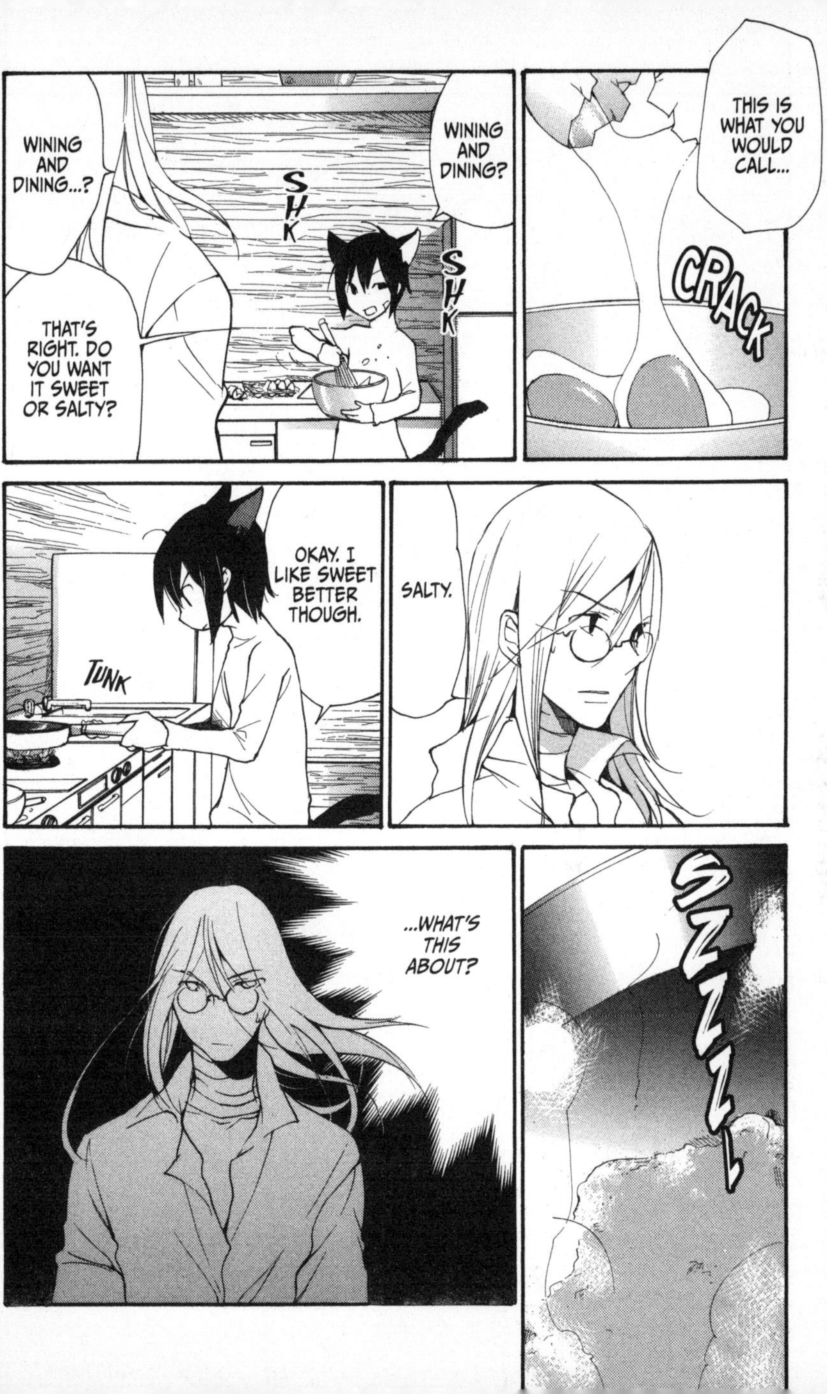
THIS IS WHAT YOU WOULD CALL...
CRACK
WINING AND DINING?
SHK
SHK
WINING AND DINING...?
THAT'S RIGHT. DO YOU WANT IT SWEET OR SALTY?
SALTY.
OKAY. I LIKE SWEET BETTER THOUGH.
TUNK
SZZZZ
...WHAT'S THIS ABOUT?

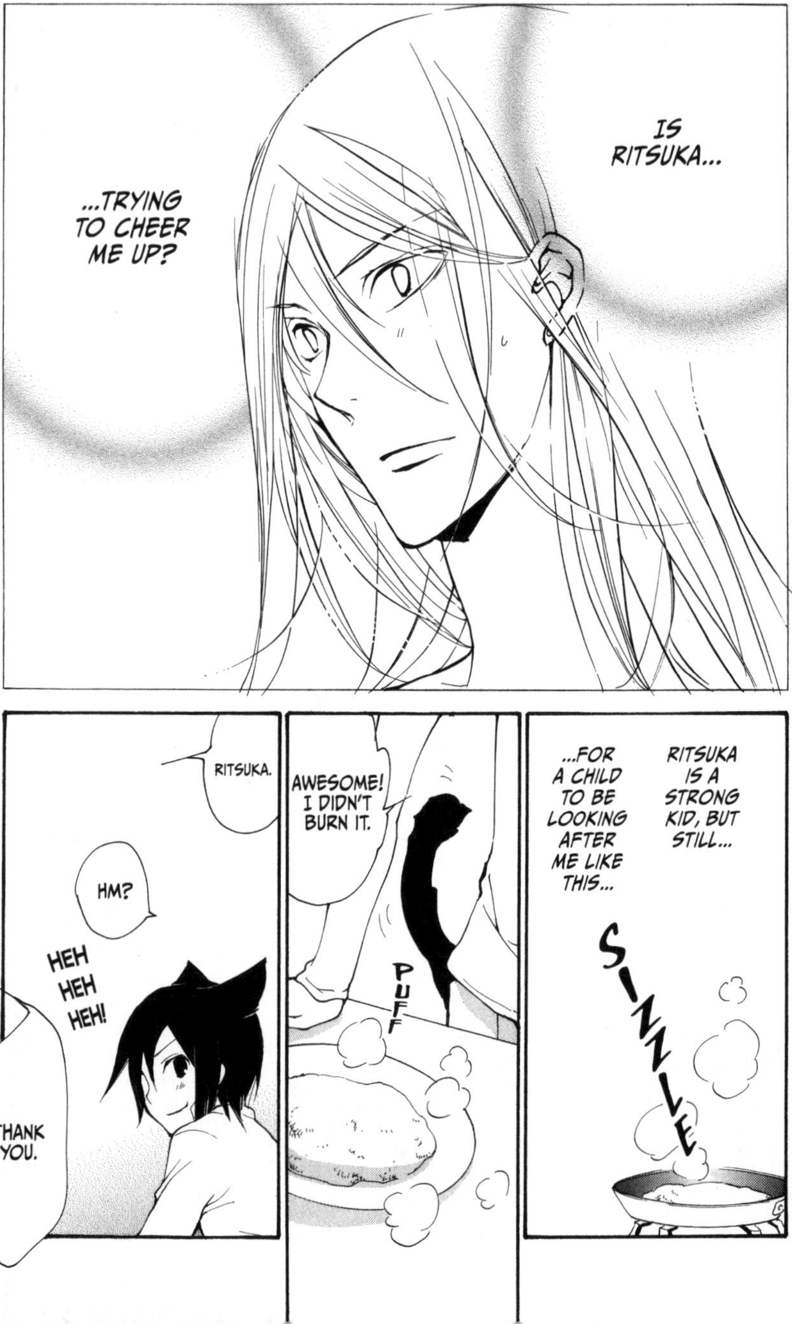
IS RITSUKA...
...TRYING TO CHEER ME UP?
RITSUKA IS A STRONG KID, BUT STILL...
...FOR A CHILD TO BE LOOKING AFTER ME LIKE THIS...
SIZZLE
AWESOME! I DIDN'T BURN IT.
PUFF
RITSUKA.
HM?
HEH HEH HEH!
THANK YOU.

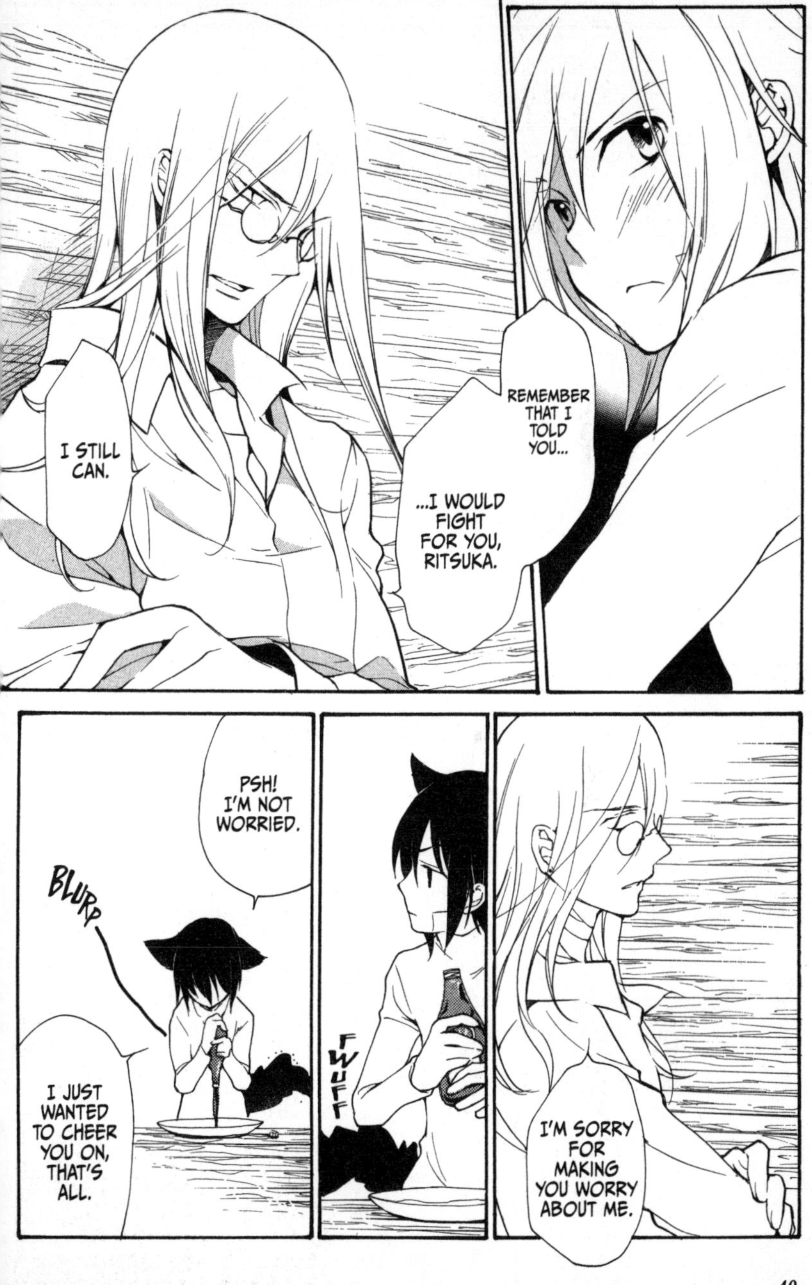
REMEMBER THAT I TOLD YOU...
...I WOULD FIGHT FOR YOU, RITSUKA.
I STILL CAN.
I'M SORRY FOR MAKING YOU WORRY ABOUT ME.
FWUFF
PSH! I'M NOT WORRIED.
BLURP
I JUST WANTED TO CHEER YOU ON, THAT'S ALL.

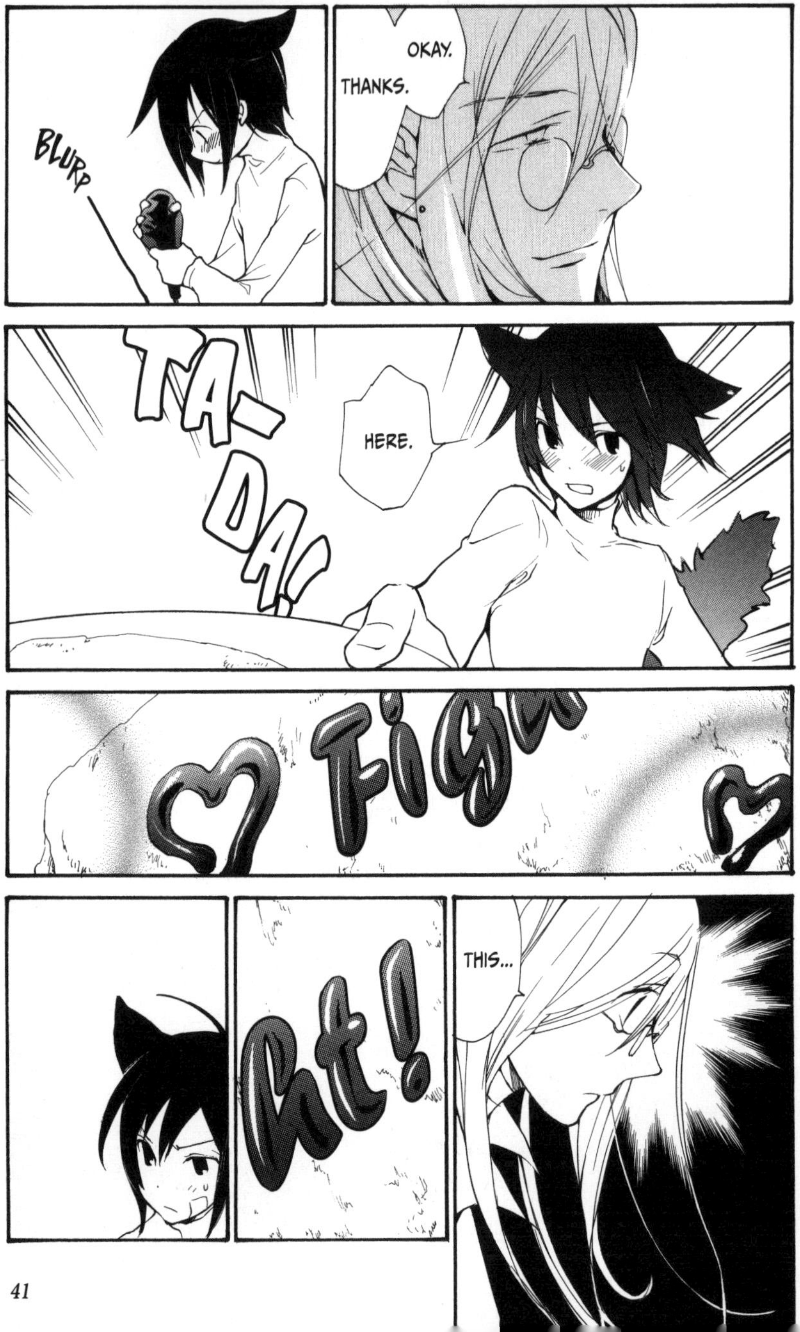
OKAY.
THANKS.
BLURP
HERE.
TA-DA!
♡ Figh
ht!
THIS...

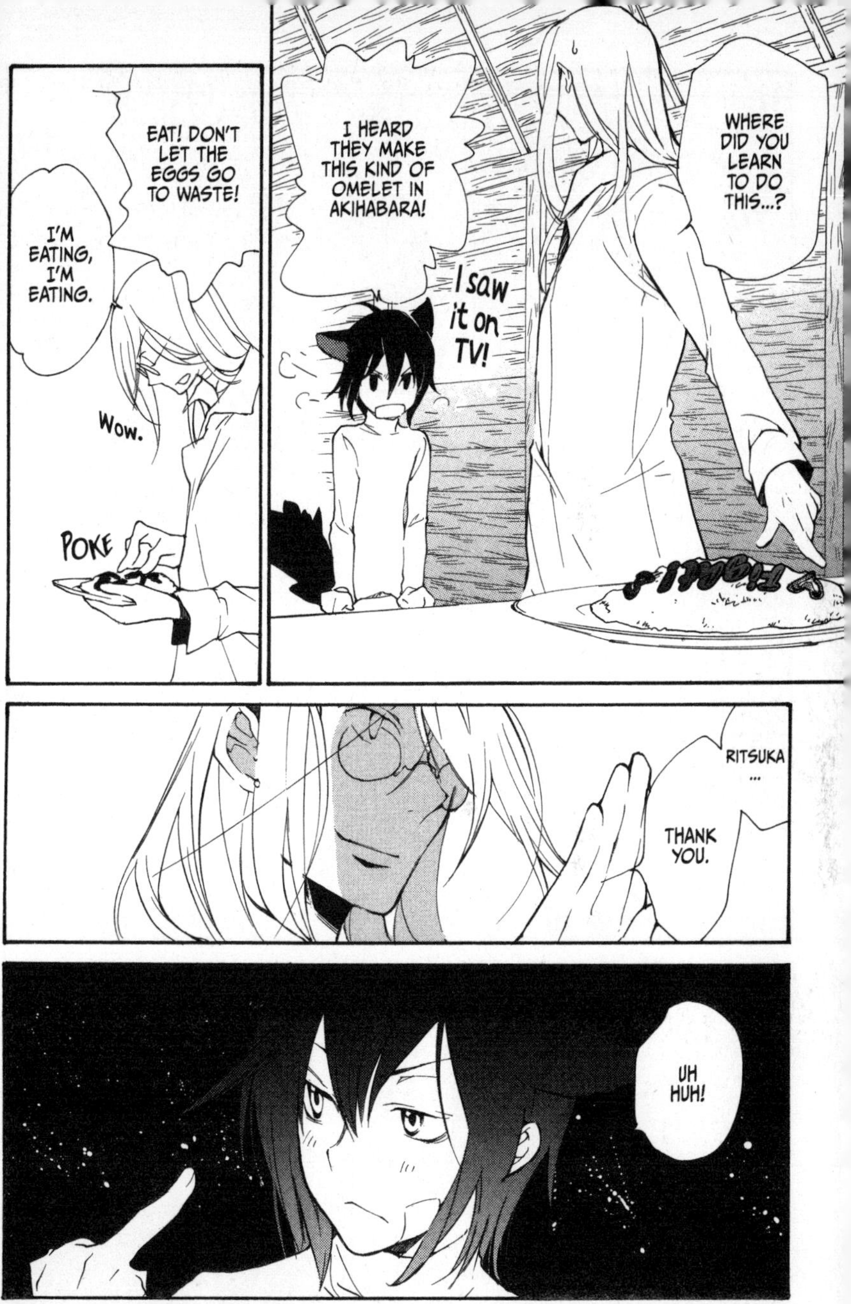
WHERE DID YOU LEARN TO DO THIS...?
I HEARD THEY MAKE THIS KIND OF OMELET IN AKIHABARA!
I saw it on TV!
EAT! DON'T LET THE EGGS GO TO WASTE!
I'M EATING, I'M EATING.
Wow.
POKE
RITSUKA ...
THANK YOU.
UH HUH!

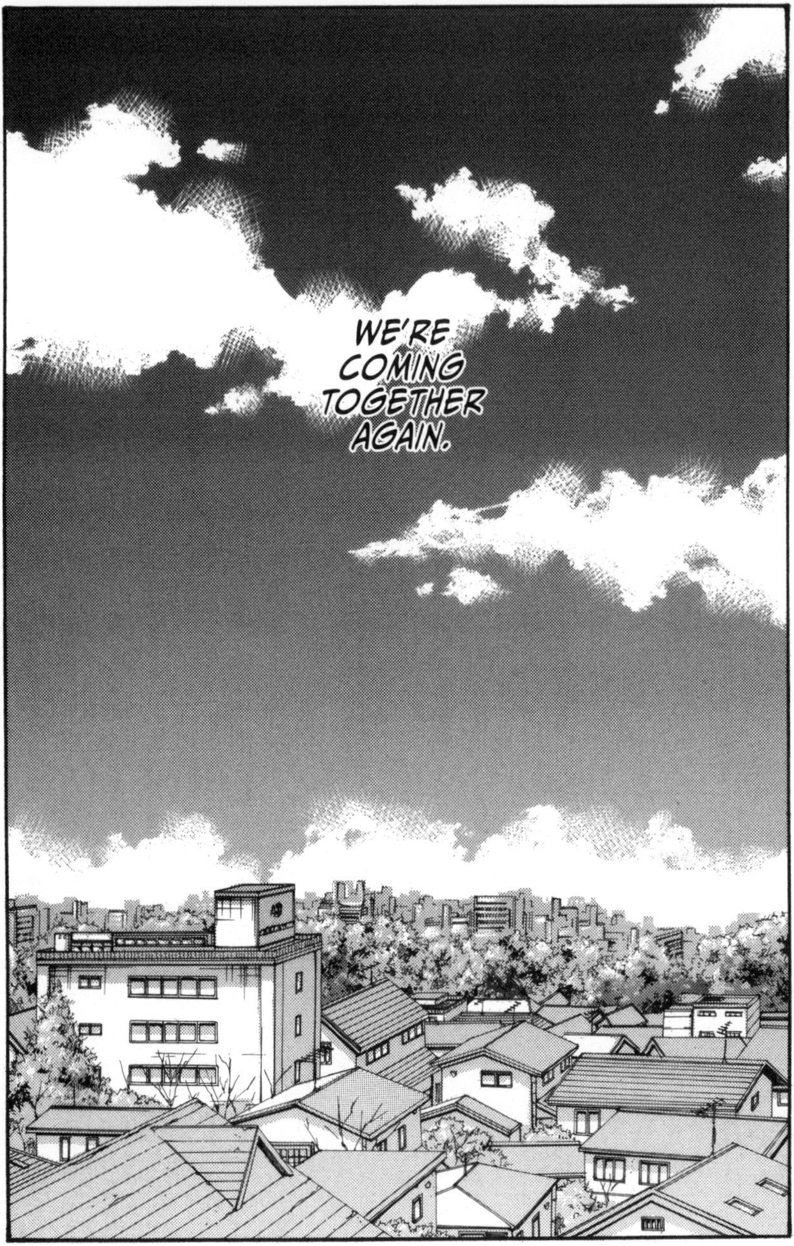
WE'RE COMING TOGETHER AGAIN.

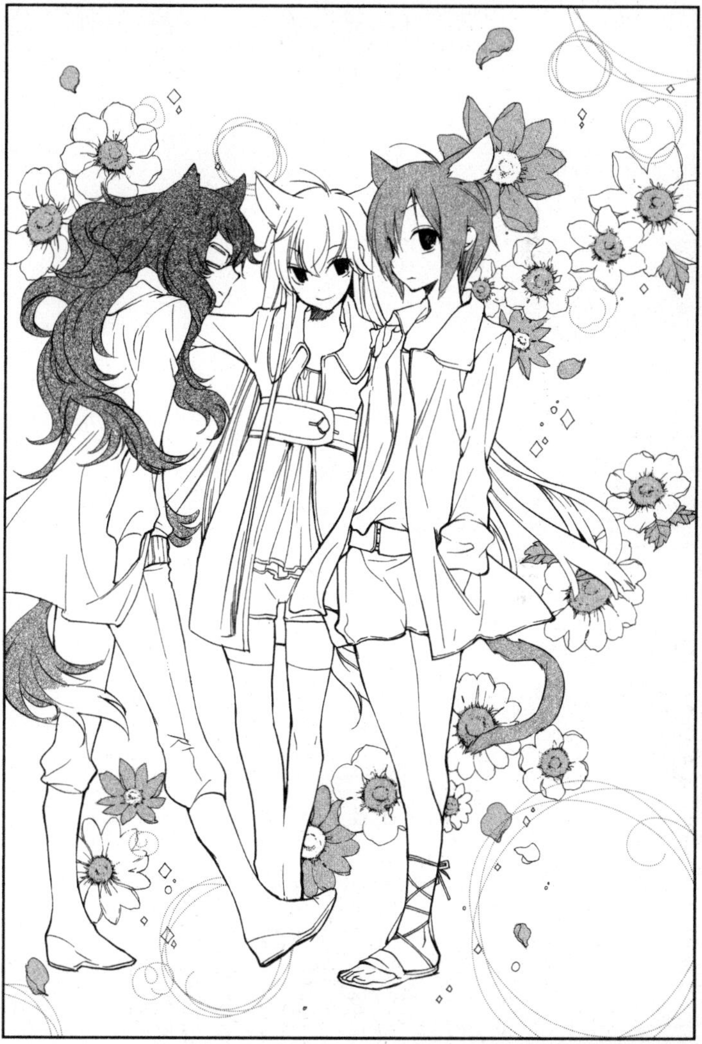

LOVELESS

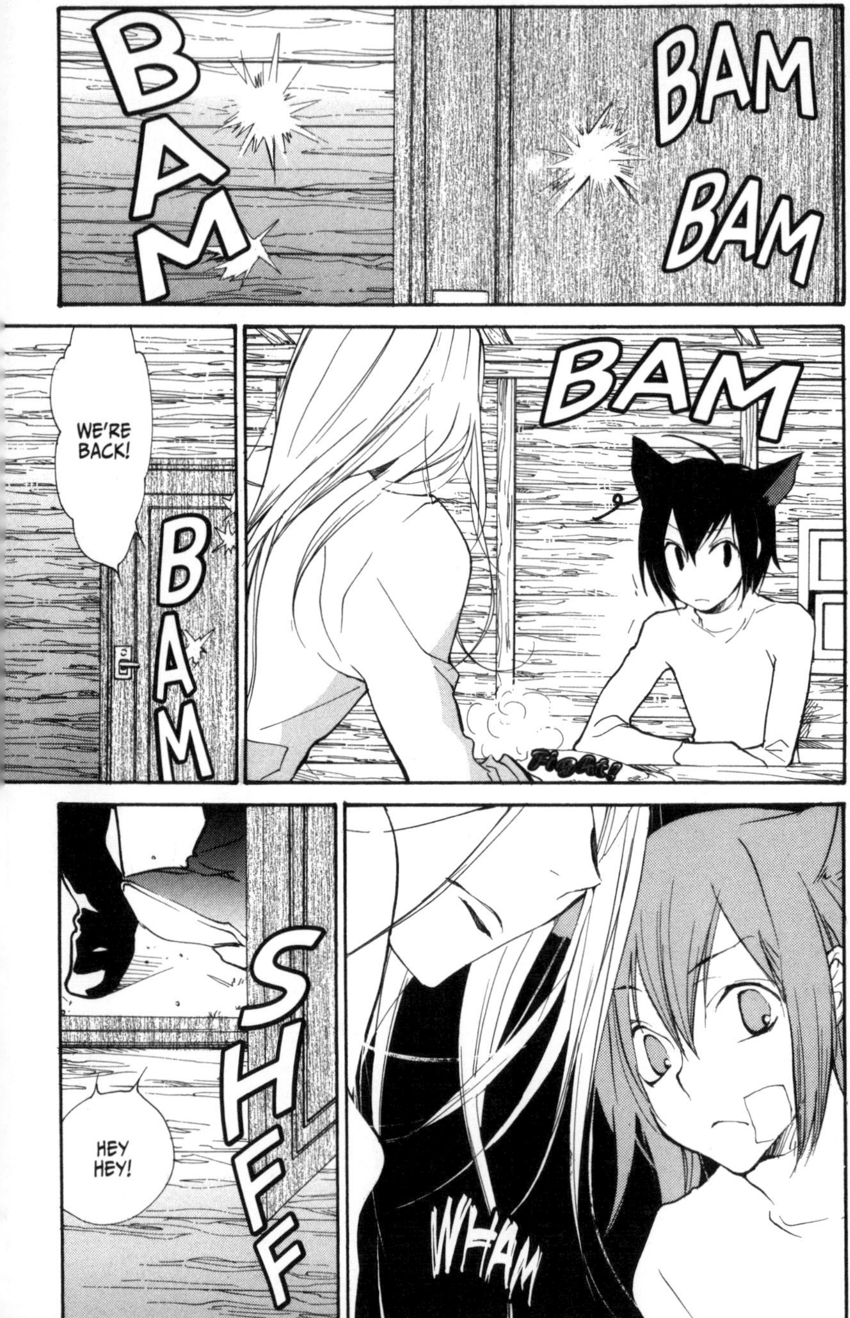
BAM
BAM
BAM
BAM
BAM
FIGHT!
WE'RE BACK!
BAM
WHAM
SHFF
HEY HEY!

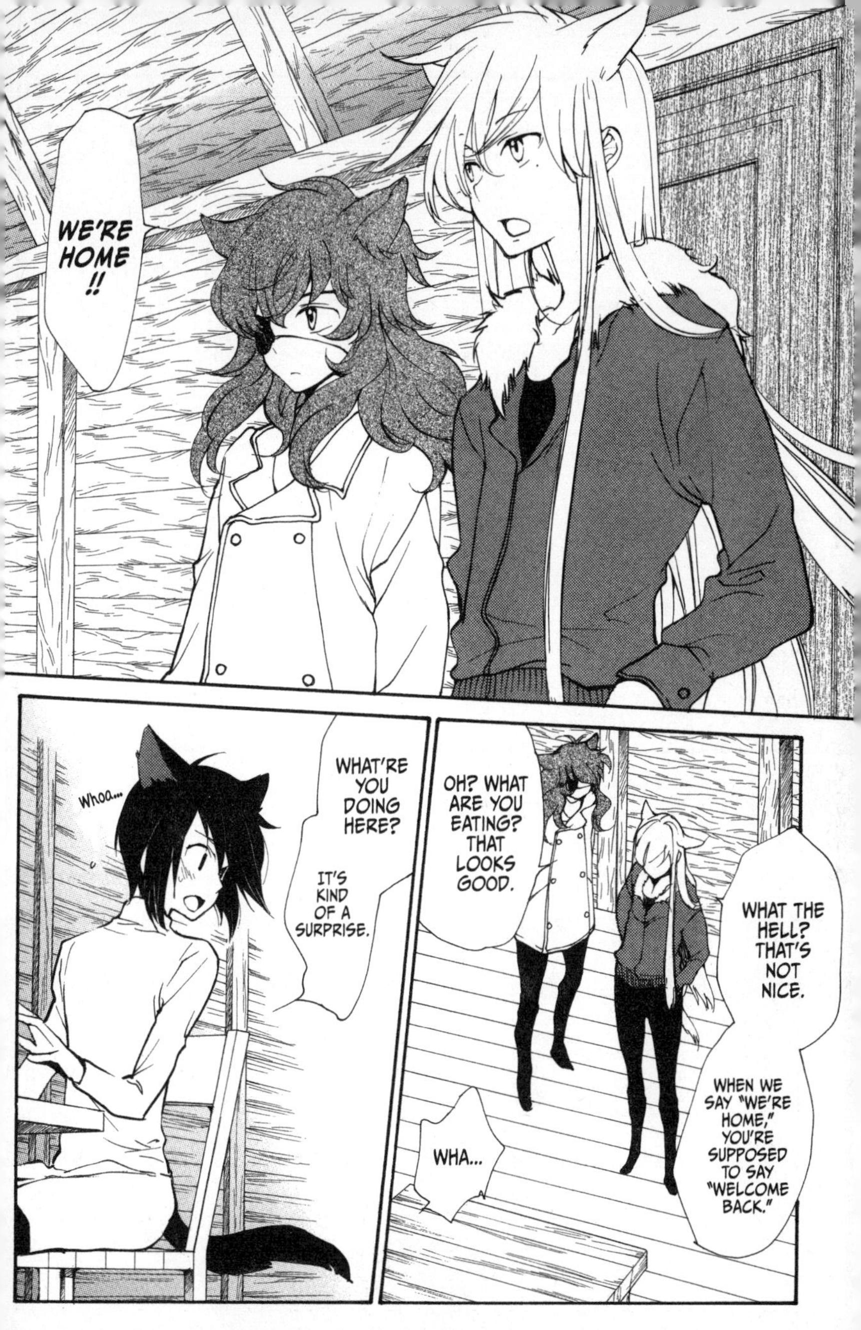
WE'RE HOME !!
OH? WHAT ARE YOU EATING? THAT LOOKS GOOD.
WHAT THE HELL? THAT'S NOT NICE.
WHEN WE SAY "WE'RE HOME," YOU'RE SUPPOSED TO SAY "WELCOME BACK."
WHA...
WHAT'RE YOU DOING HERE?
IT'S KIND OF A SURPRISE.
Whoa...

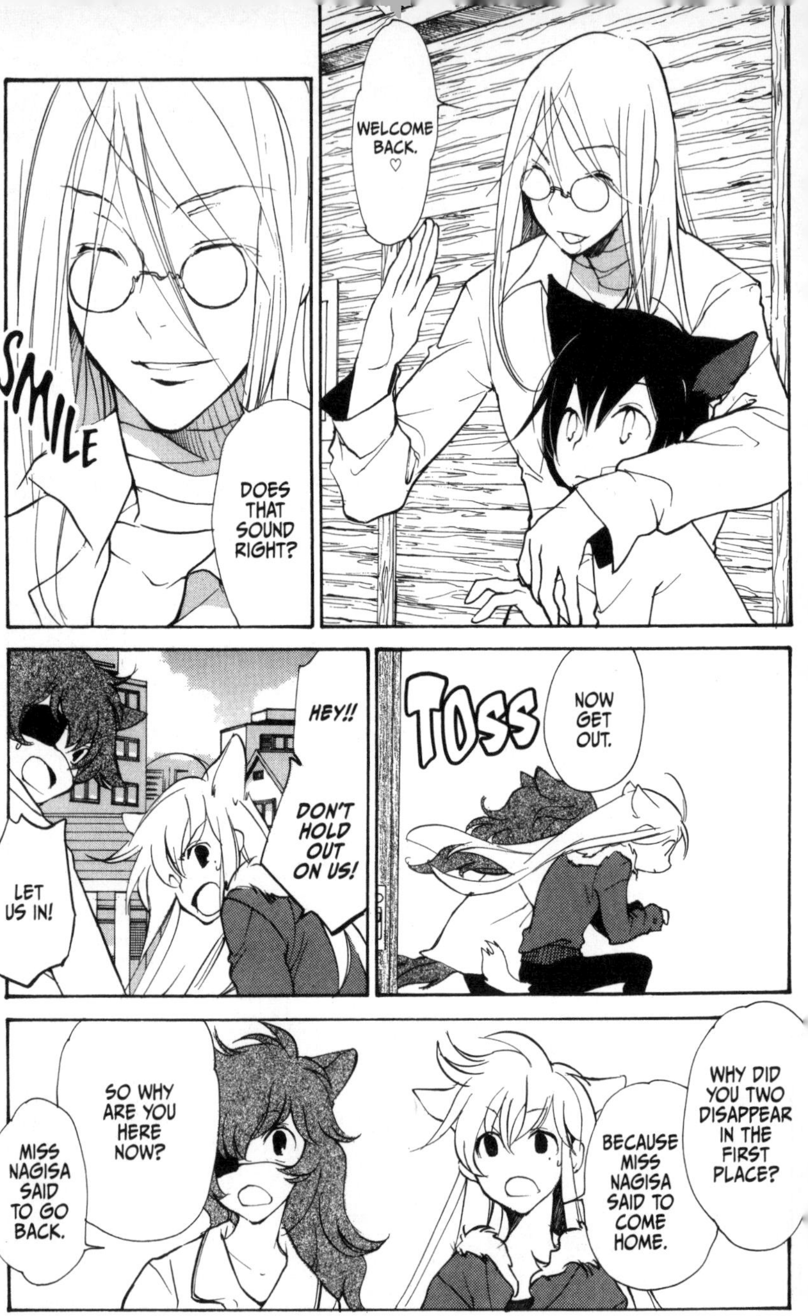
WELCOME BACK. ♡
SMILE
DOES THAT SOUND RIGHT?
TOSS
NOW GET OUT.
HEY!!
DON'T HOLD OUT ON US!
LET US IN!
WHY DID YOU TWO DISAPPEAR IN THE FIRST PLACE?
BECAUSE MISS NAGISA SAID TO COME HOME.
SO WHY ARE YOU HERE NOW?
MISS NAGISA SAID TO GO BACK.

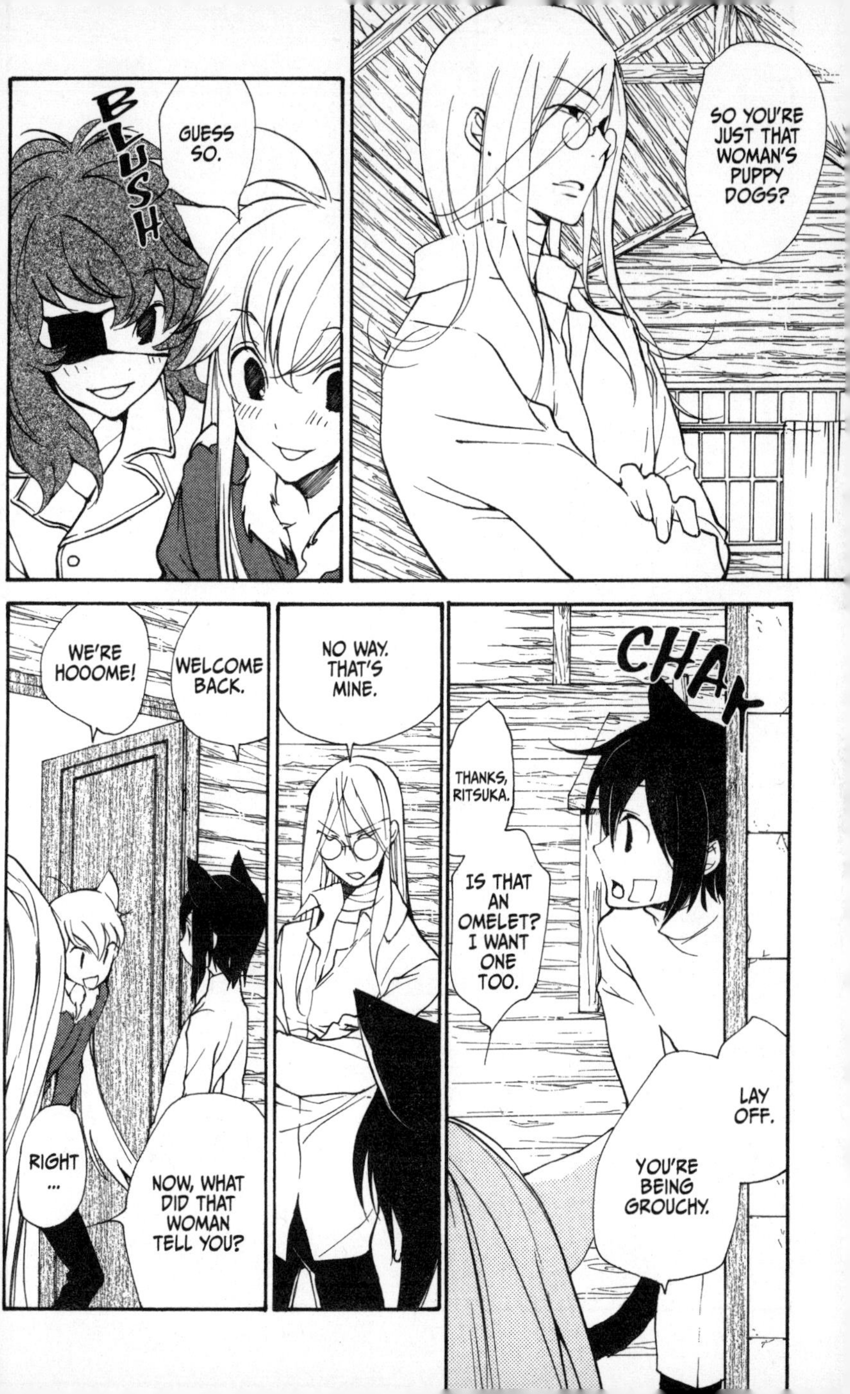
SO YOU'RE JUST THAT WOMAN'S PUPPY DOGS?
BLUSH
GUESS SO.
CHAK
THANKS, RITSUKA.
IS THAT AN OMELET? I WANT ONE TOO.
LAY OFF.
YOU'RE BEING GROUCHY.
NO WAY. THAT'S MINE.
WELCOME BACK.
WE'RE HOOOME!
RIGHT ...
NOW, WHAT DID THAT WOMAN TELL YOU?

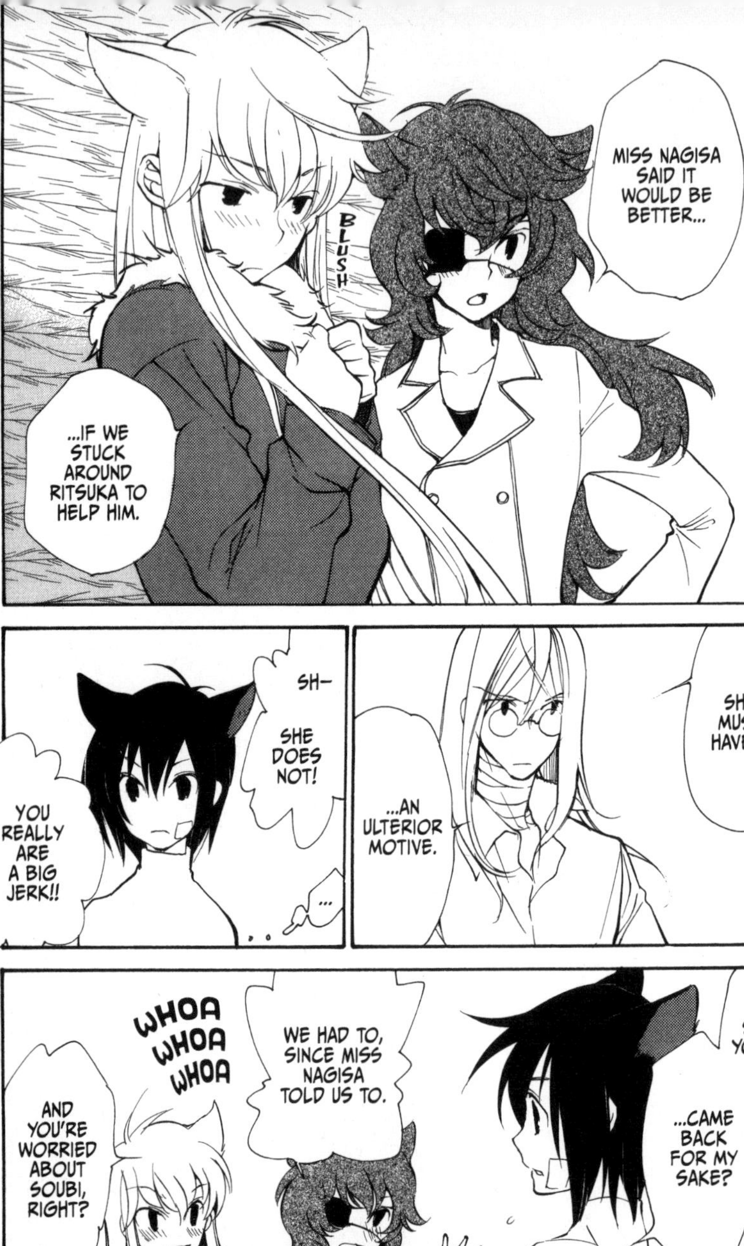
MISS NAGISA SAID IT WOULD BE BETTER...
BLUSH
...IF WE STUCK AROUND RITSUKA TO HELP HIM.
SHE MUST HAVE...
...AN ULTERIOR MOTIVE.
SH—
SHE DOES NOT!
...
YOU REALLY ARE A BIG JERK!!
SO YOU...
...CAME BACK FOR MY SAKE?
WE HAD TO, SINCE MISS NAGISA TOLD US TO.
WHOA WHOA WHOA
AND YOU'RE WORRIED ABOUT SOUBI, RIGHT?

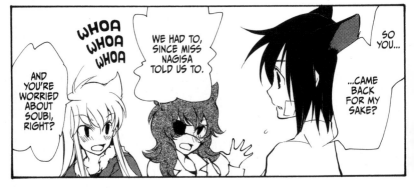

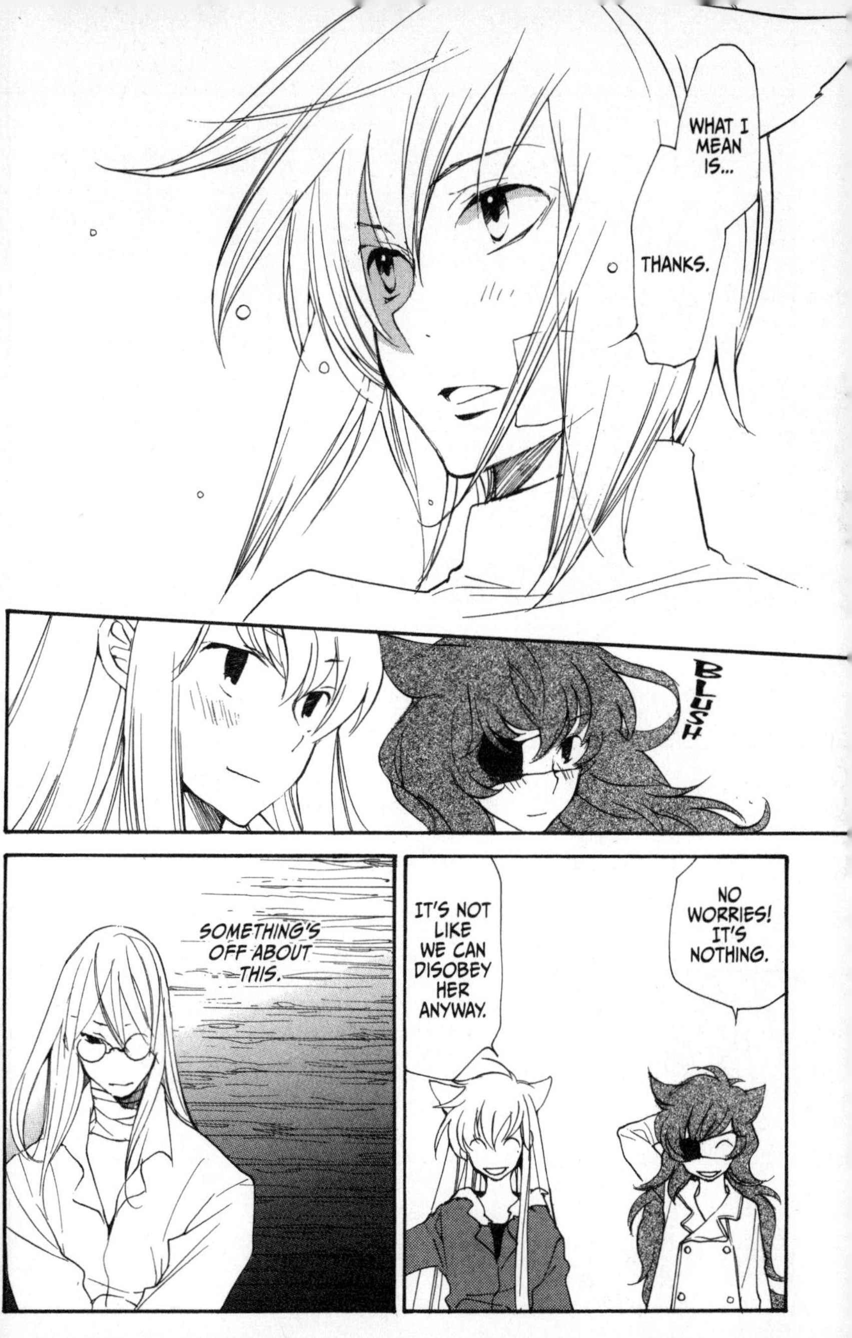
WHAT I MEAN IS...
THANKS.
BLUSH
NO WORRIES! IT'S NOTHING.
IT'S NOT LIKE WE CAN DISOBEY HER ANYWAY.
SOMETHING'S OFF ABOUT THIS.

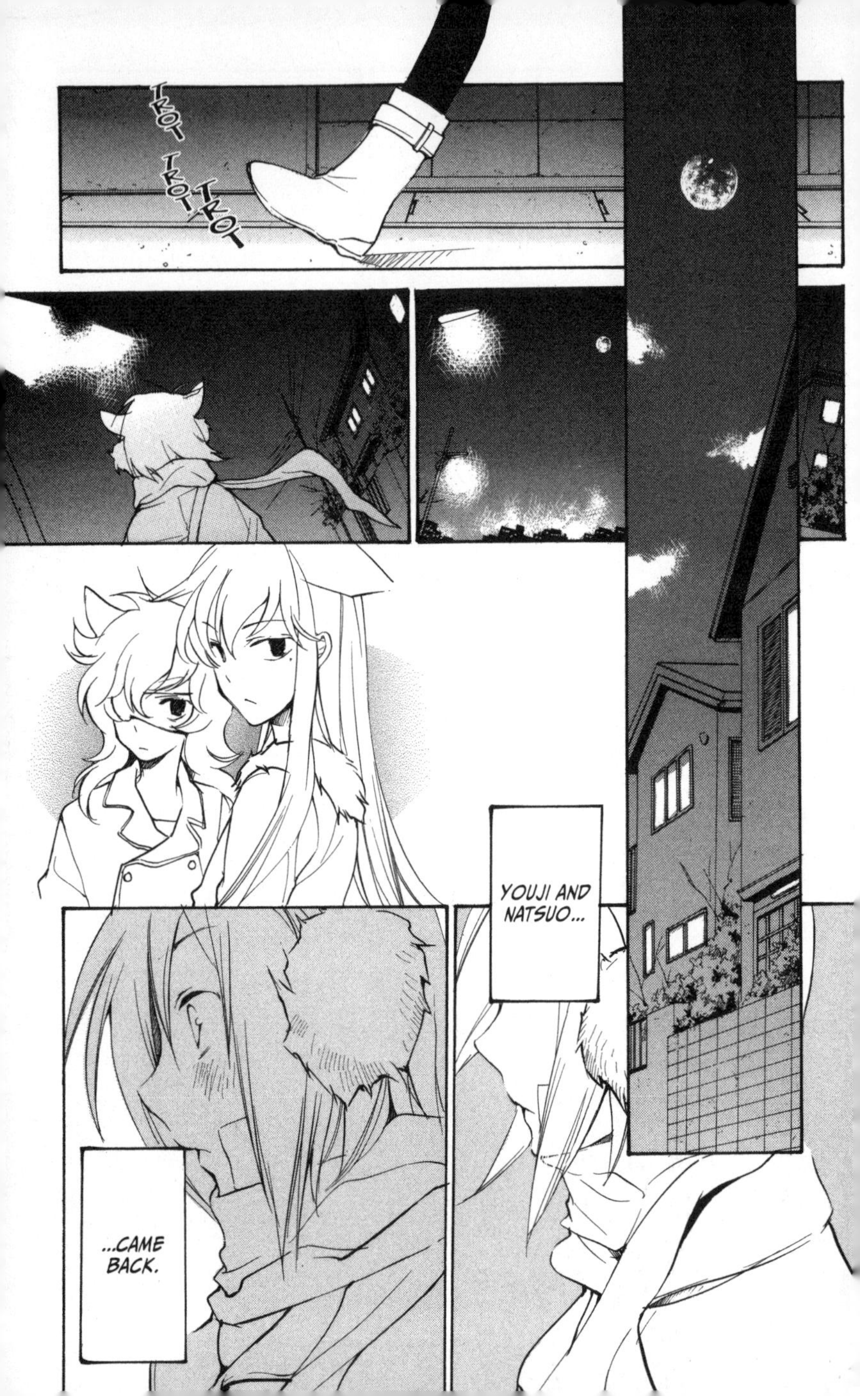
TROT TROT TROT
YOUJI AND NATSUO...
...CAME BACK.

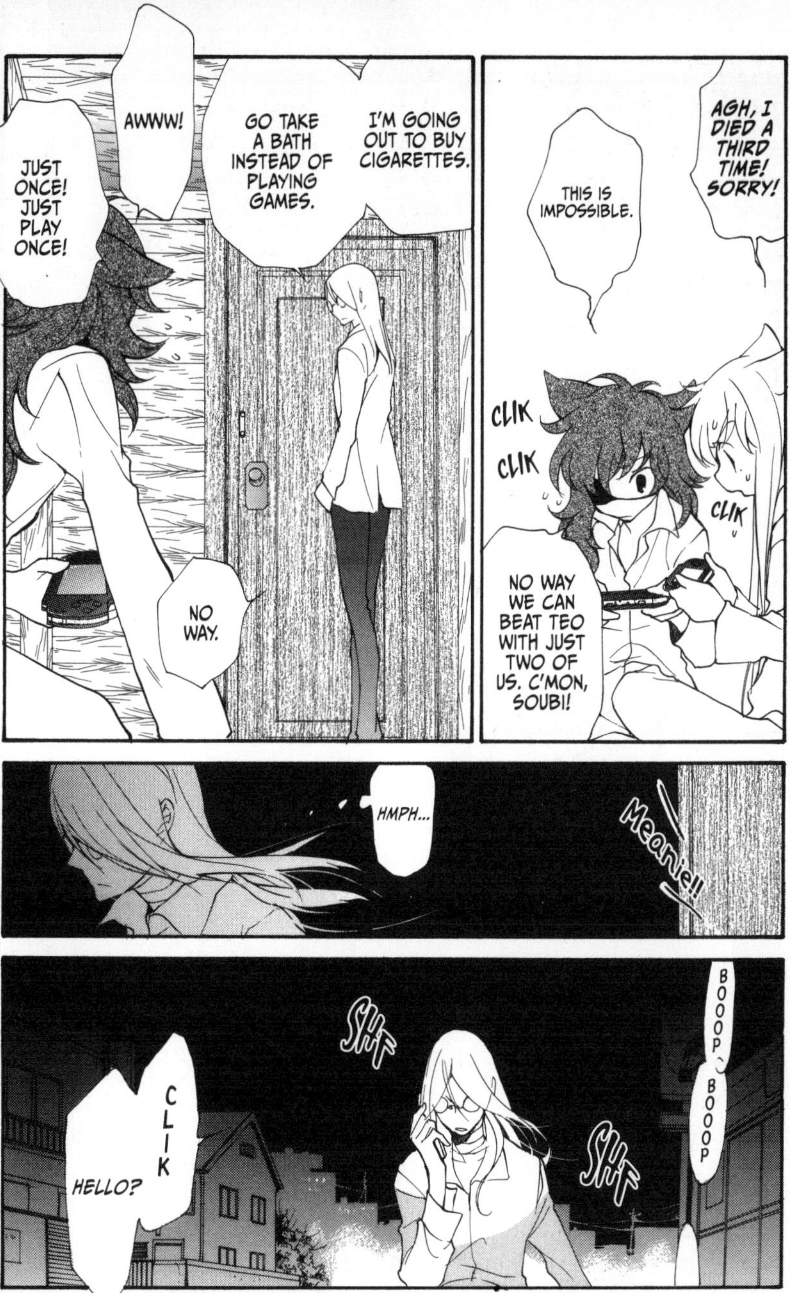

AGH, I DIED A THIRD TIME! SORRY!
THIS IS IMPOSSIBLE.
CLIK
CLIK
CLIK
NO WAY WE CAN BEAT TEO WITH JUST TWO OF US. C'MON, SOUBI!
I'M GOING OUT TO BUY CIGARETTES.
GO TAKE A BATH INSTEAD OF PLAYING GAMES.
AWWW!
JUST ONCE! JUST PLAY ONCE!
NO WAY.
Meanie!!
HMPH...
BOOOP BOOOP
SHF
SHF
CLIK
HELLO?

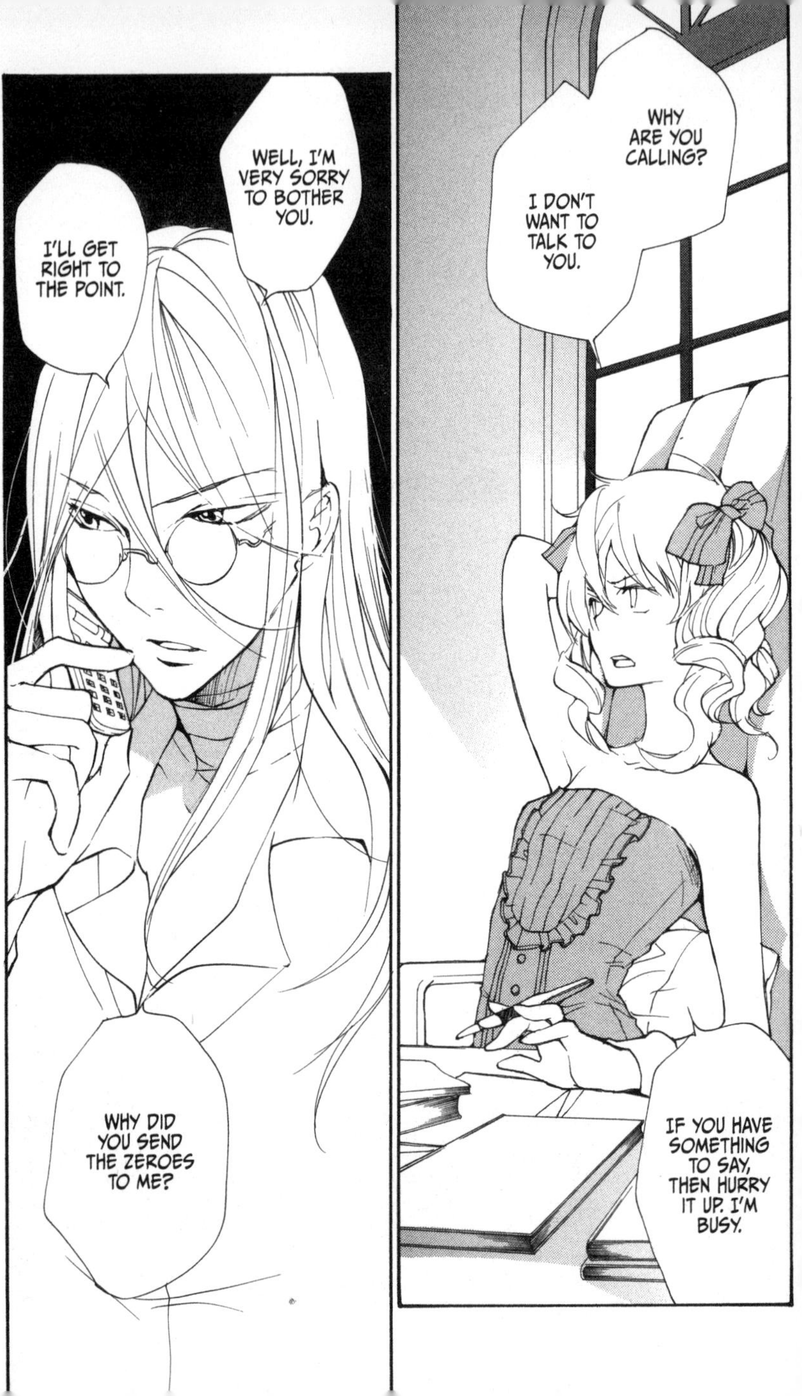
WHY ARE YOU CALLING?
I DON'T WANT TO TALK TO YOU.
IF YOU HAVE SOMETHING TO SAY, THEN HURRY IT UP. I'M BUSY.
WELL, I'M VERY SORRY TO BOTHER YOU.
I'LL GET RIGHT TO THE POINT.
WHY DID YOU SEND THE ZEROES TO ME?

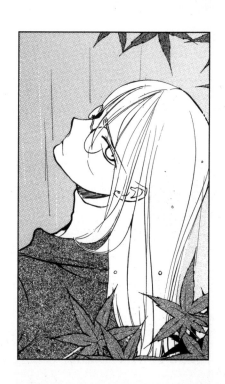

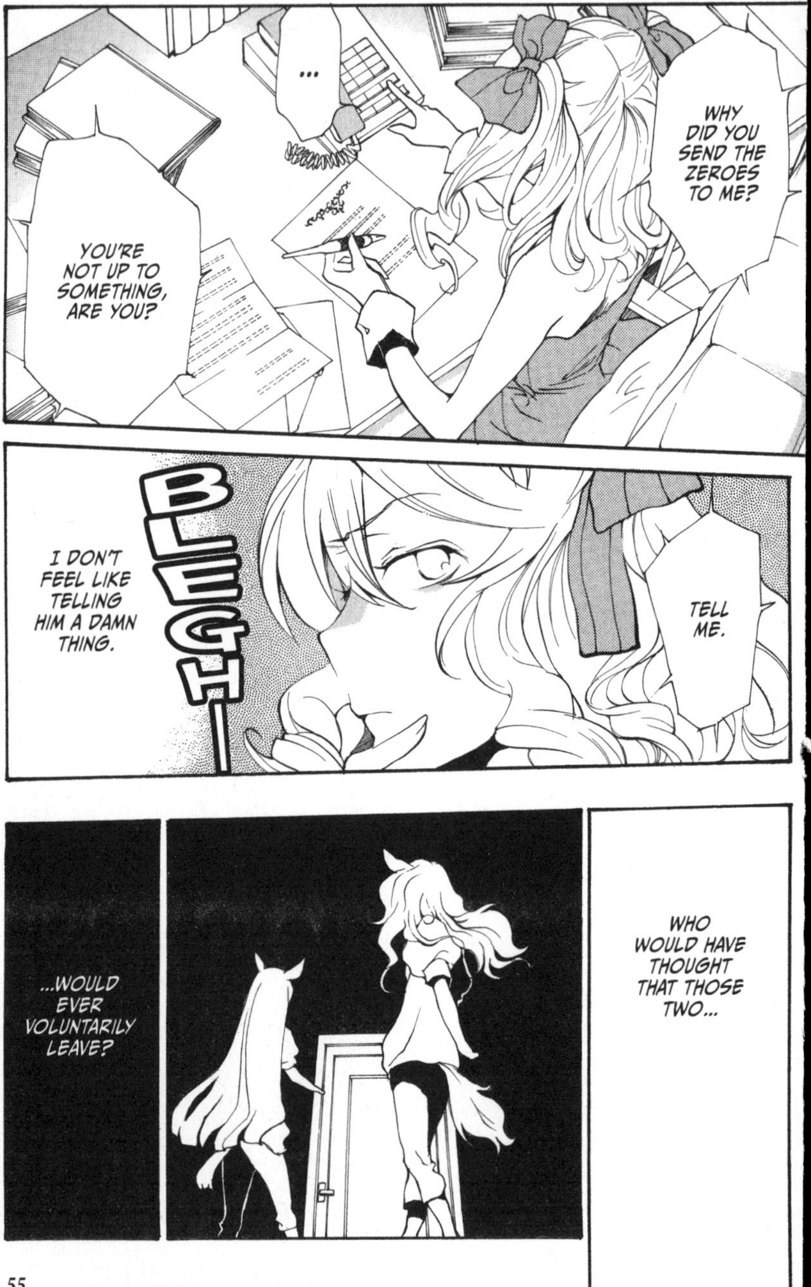
WHY DID YOU SEND THE ZEROES TO ME?
...
YOU'RE NOT UP TO SOMETHING, ARE YOU?
TELL ME.
BLEGH!
I DON'T FEEL LIKE TELLING HIM A DAMN THING.
WHO WOULD HAVE THOUGHT THAT THOSE TWO...
...WOULD EVER VOLUNTARILY LEAVE?

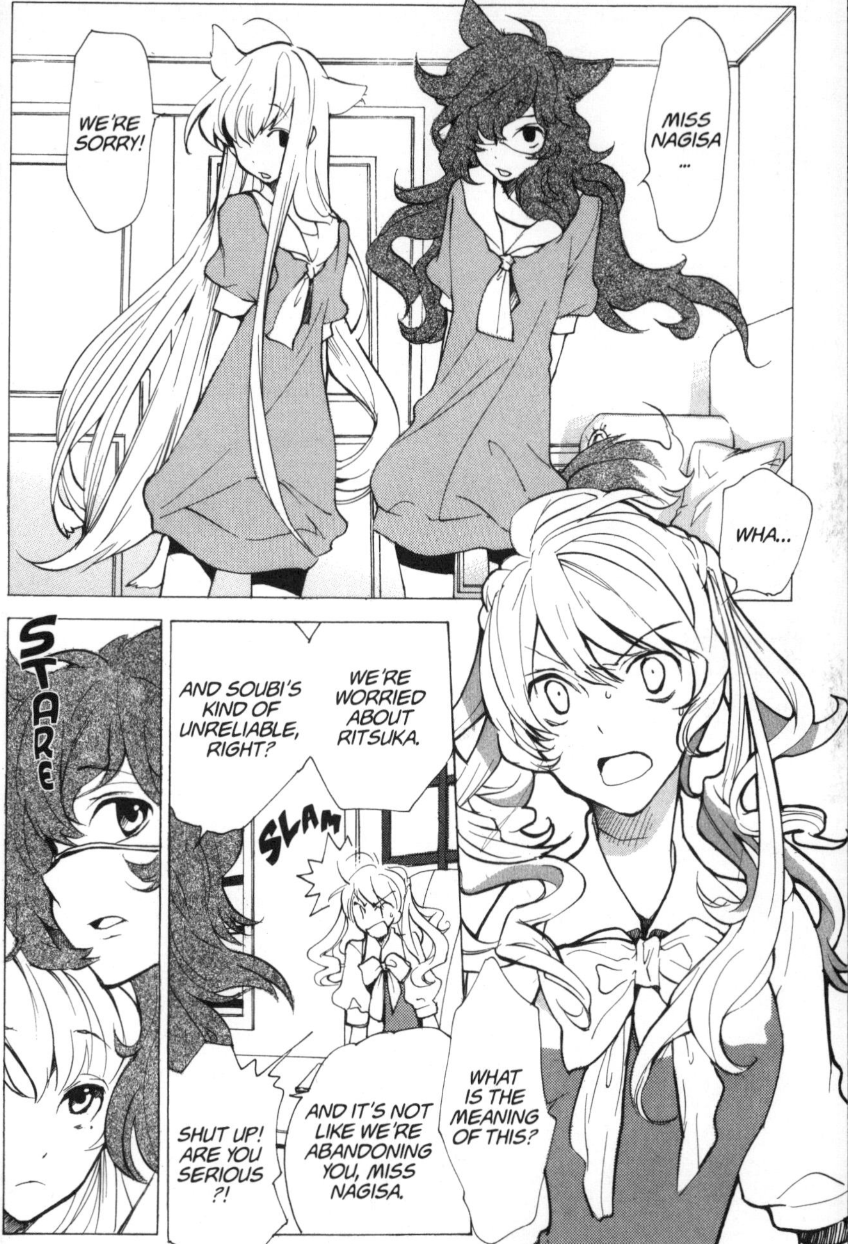
MISS NAGISA ...
WE'RE SORRY!
WHA...
WHAT IS THE MEANING OF THIS?
WE'RE WORRIED ABOUT RITSUKA.
AND SOUBI'S KIND OF UNRELIABLE, RIGHT?
SLAM
AND IT'S NOT LIKE WE'RE ABANDONING YOU, MISS NAGISA.
SHUT UP! ARE YOU SERIOUS ?!
STARE

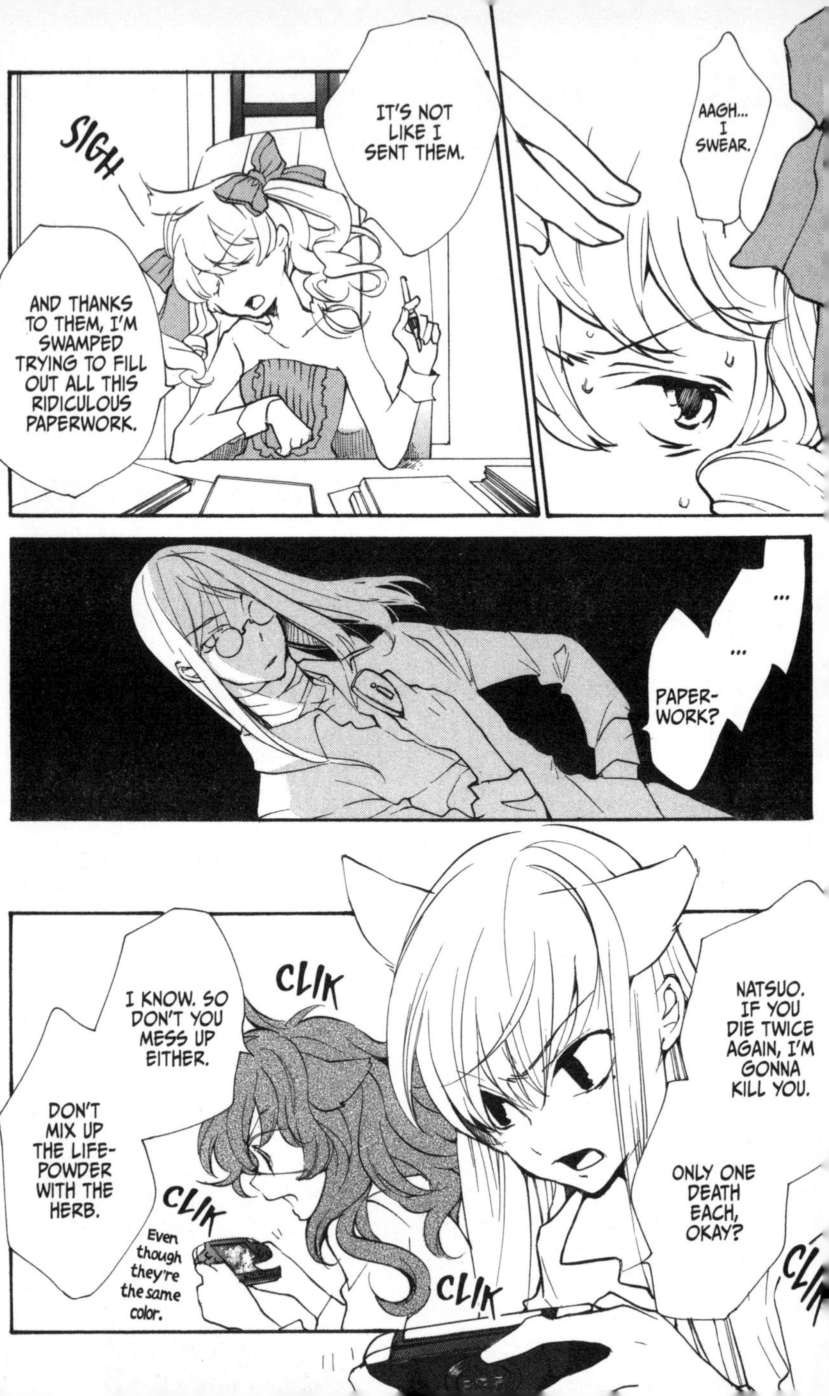
AAGH... I SWEAR.
IT'S NOT LIKE I SENT THEM.
SIGH
AND THANKS TO THEM, I'M SWAMPED TRYING TO FILL OUT ALL THIS RIDICULOUS PAPERWORK.
...
...
PAPER-WORK?
NATSUO. IF YOU DIE TWICE AGAIN, I'M GONNA KILL YOU.
ONLY ONE DEATH EACH, OKAY?
CLIK
I KNOW. SO DON'T YOU MESS UP EITHER.
DON'T MIX UP THE LIFE-POWDER WITH THE HERB.
CLIK
Even though they're the same color.
CLIK

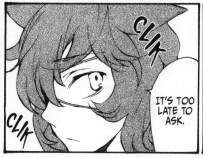

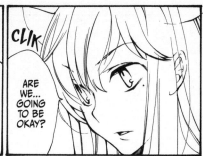

CLIK
ARE WE... GOING TO BE OKAY?
CLIK
IT'S TOO LATE TO ASK.
CLIK
WHAT IF WE GET BULLIED?
SHOULD WE JUST BULLY THEM BACK?
OR SHOULD WE KILL THEM?
I DUNNO... BOTH SOUND PRETTY GOOD.
ACK! I'M GETTING TROUNCED!
KICK!! KICK!!

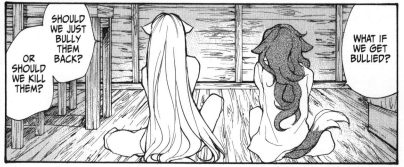

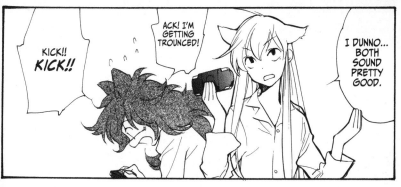

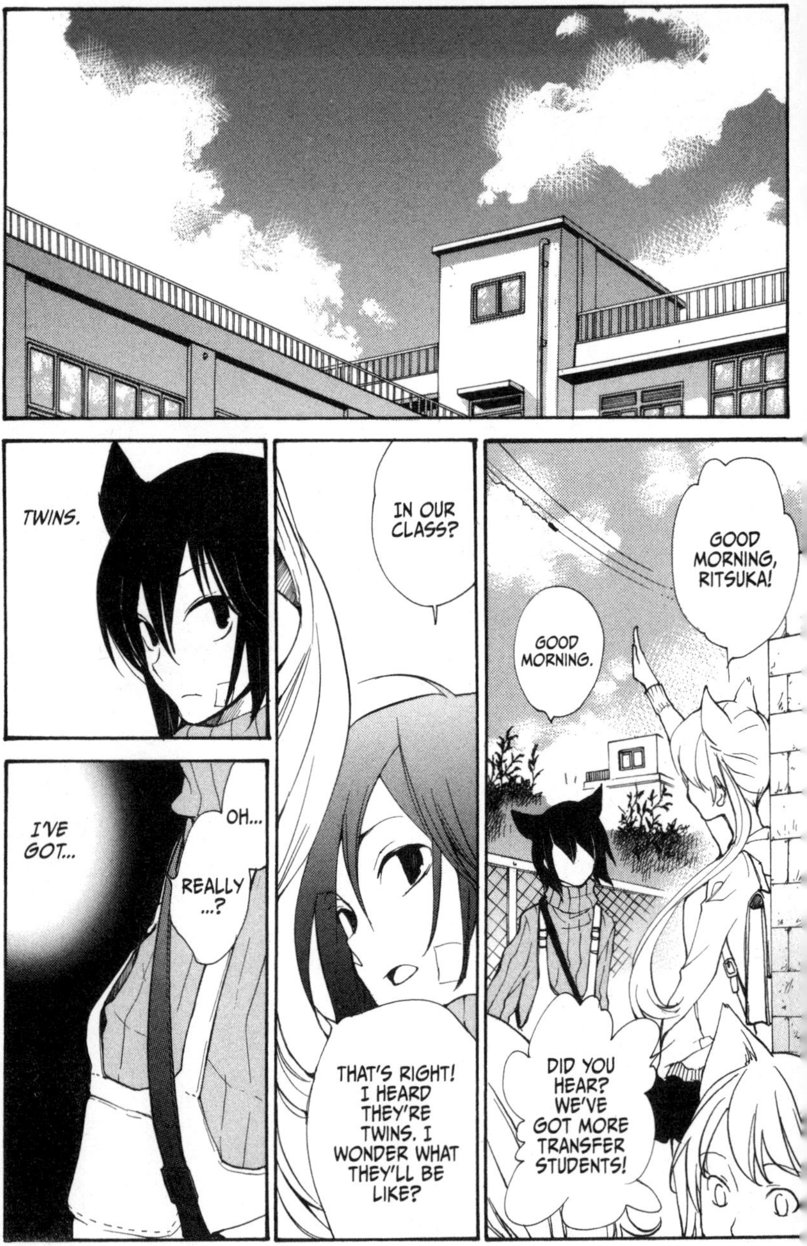
GOOD MORNING, RITSUKA!
GOOD MORNING.
DID YOU HEAR? WE'VE GOT MORE TRANSFER STUDENTS!
IN OUR CLASS?
THAT'S RIGHT! I HEARD THEY'RE TWINS. I WONDER WHAT THEY'LL BE LIKE?
TWINS.
OH...
REALLY ...?
I'VE GOT...

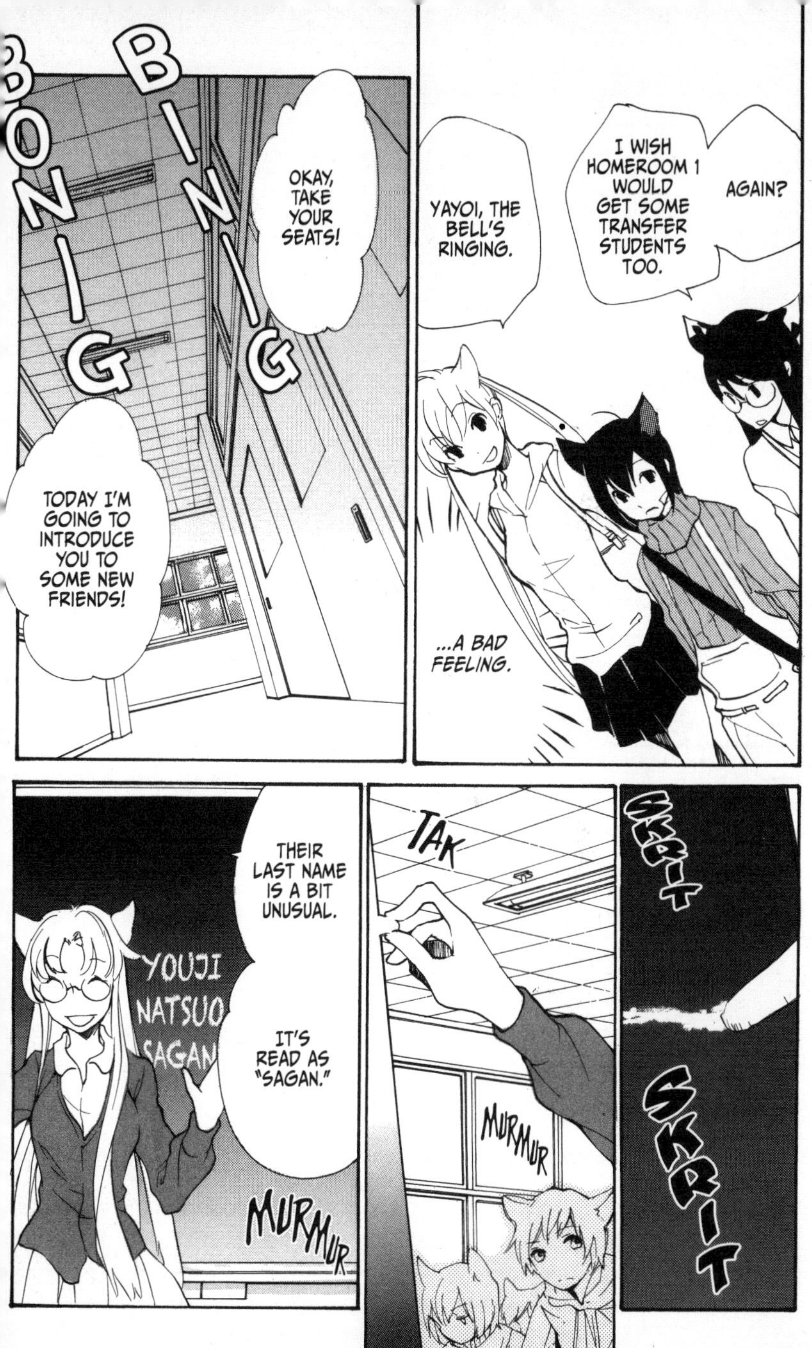
AGAIN?
I WISH HOMEROOM 1 WOULD GET SOME TRANSFER STUDENTS TOO.
YAYOI, THE BELL'S RINGING.
...A BAD FEELING.
BING
BONG
OKAY, TAKE YOUR SEATS!
TODAY I'M GOING TO INTRODUCE YOU TO SOME NEW FRIENDS!
SKRIT
SKRIT
TAK
MURMUR
THEIR LAST NAME IS A BIT UNUSUAL.
IT'S READ AS "SAGAN."
YOUJI
NATSUO
SAGAN
MURMUR

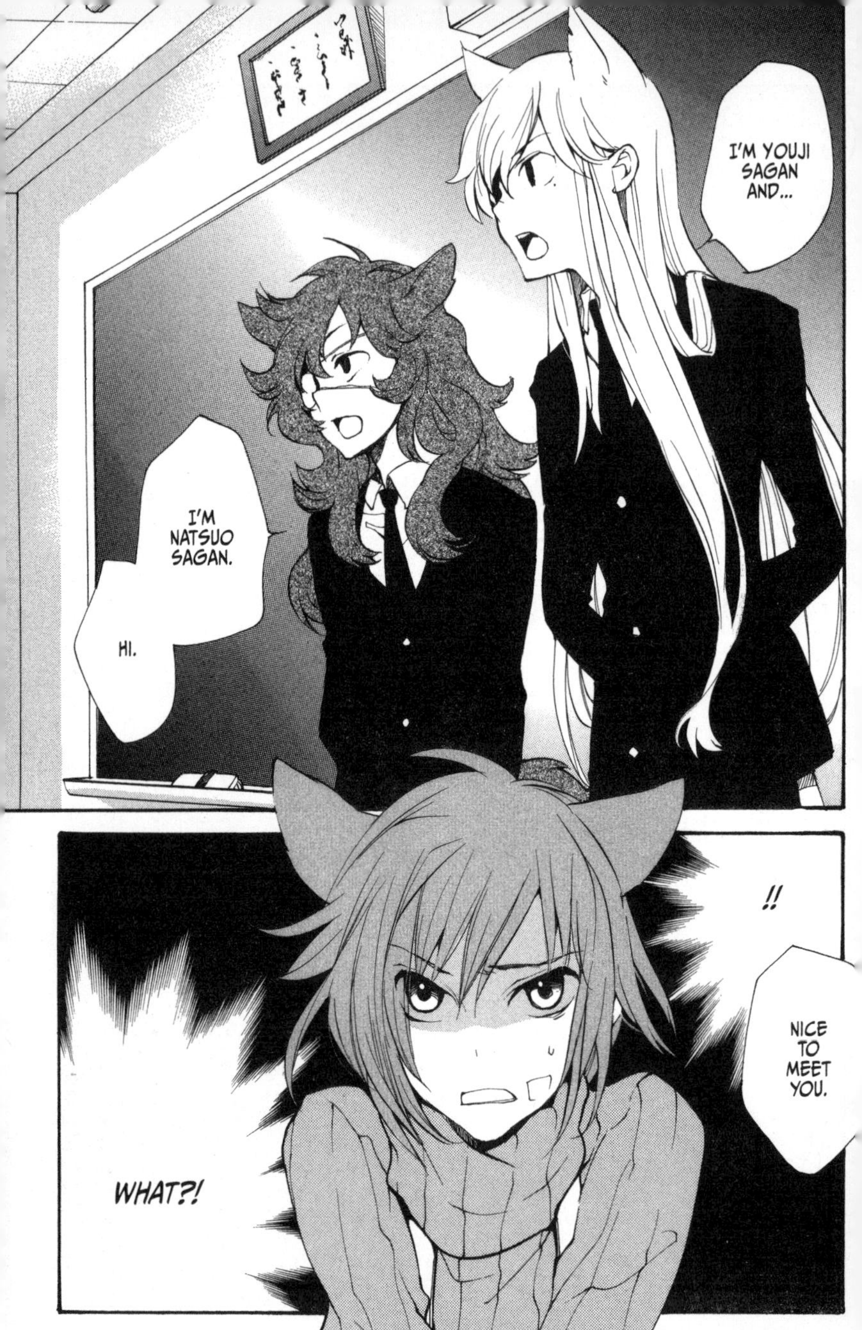
I'M YOUJI SAGAN AND...
I'M NATSUO SAGAN.
HI.
!!
NICE TO MEET YOU.
WHAT?!

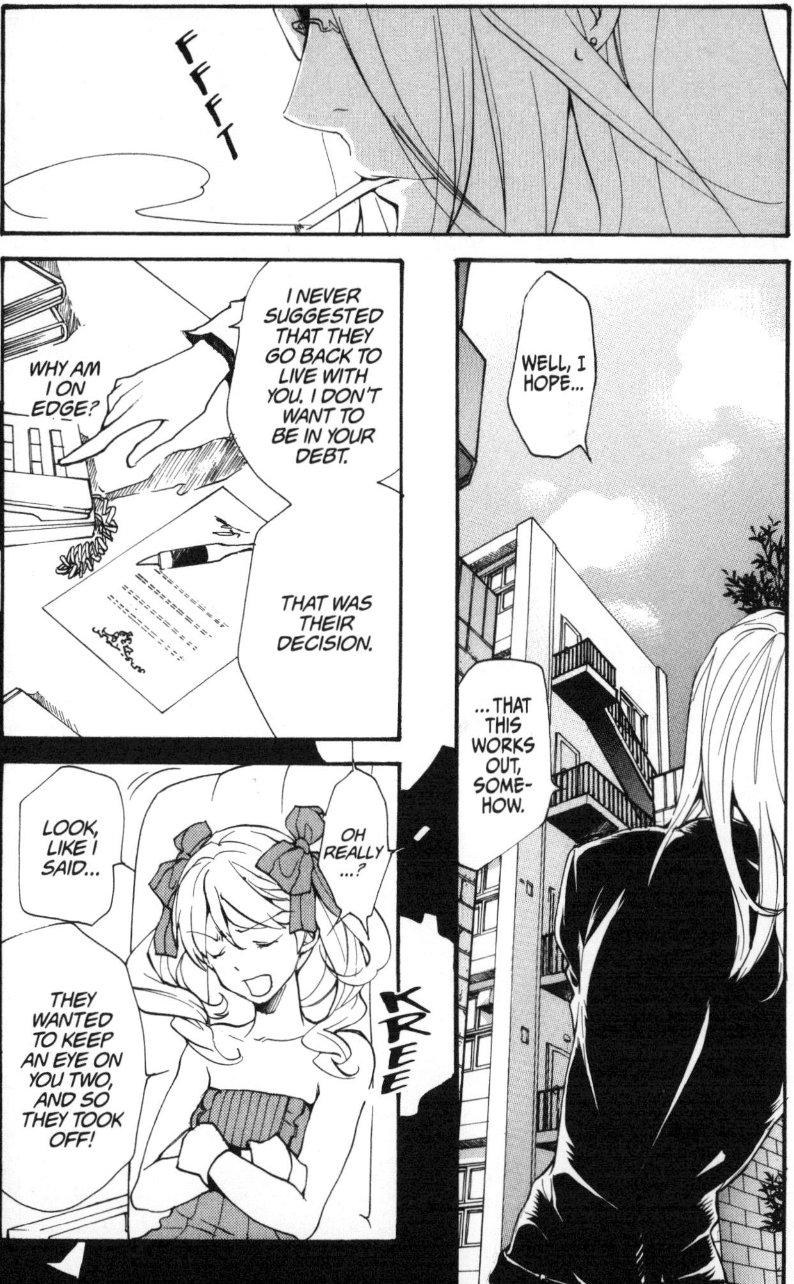
FFFT
WELL, I HOPE...
...THAT THIS WORKS OUT, SOME-HOW.
I NEVER SUGGESTED THAT THEY GO BACK TO LIVE WITH YOU. I DON'T WANT TO BE IN YOUR DEBT.
WHY AM I ON EDGE?
THAT WAS THEIR DECISION.
OH REALLY ...?
LOOK, LIKE I SAID...
KREE
THEY WANTED TO KEEP AN EYE ON YOU TWO, AND SO THEY TOOK OFF!

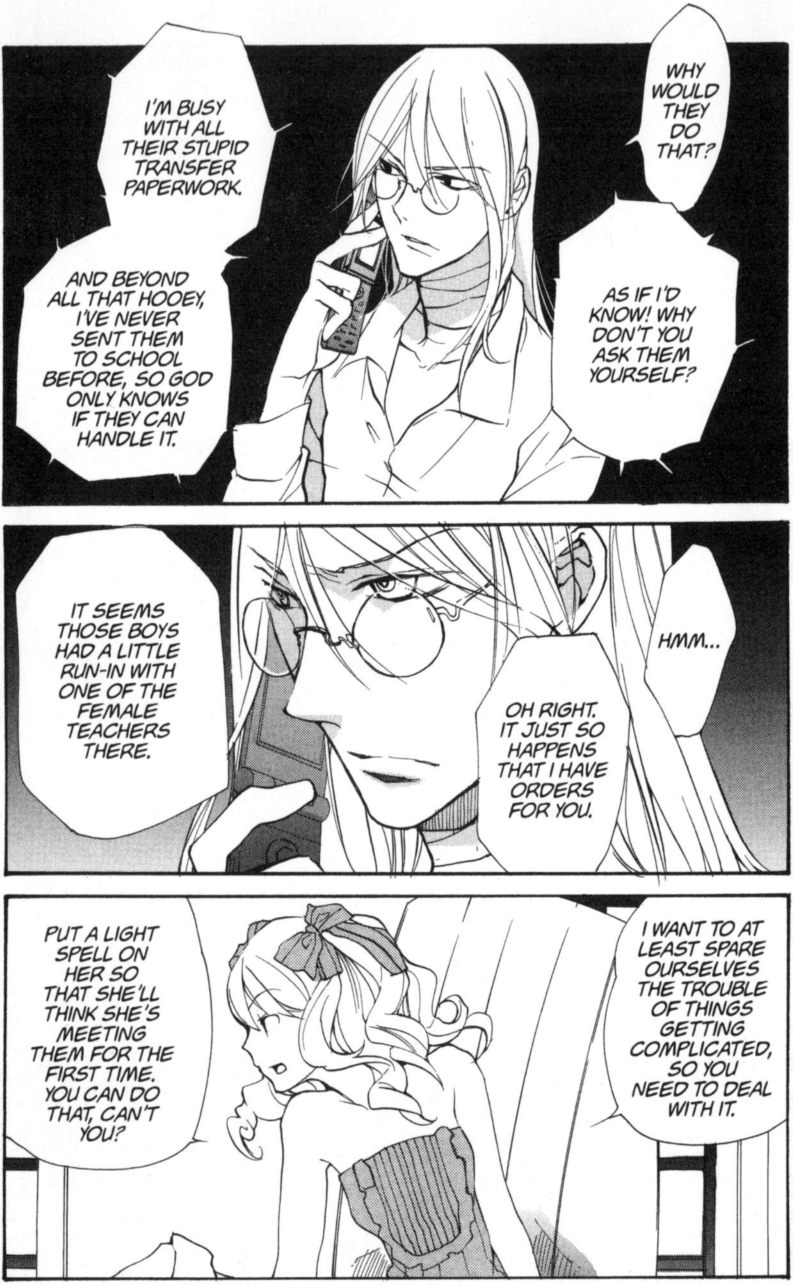
WHY WOULD THEY DO THAT?
AS IF I'D KNOW! WHY DON'T YOU ASK THEM YOURSELF?
I'M BUSY WITH ALL THEIR STUPID TRANSFER PAPERWORK.
AND BEYOND ALL THAT HOOEY, I'VE NEVER SENT THEM TO SCHOOL BEFORE, SO GOD ONLY KNOWS IF THEY CAN HANDLE IT.
HMM...
OH RIGHT. IT JUST SO HAPPENS THAT I HAVE ORDERS FOR YOU.
IT SEEMS THOSE BOYS HAD A LITTLE RUN-IN WITH ONE OF THE FEMALE TEACHERS THERE.
I WANT TO AT LEAST SPARE OURSELVES THE TROUBLE OF THINGS GETTING COMPLICATED, SO YOU NEED TO DEAL WITH IT.
PUT A LIGHT SPELL ON HER SO THAT SHE'LL THINK SHE'S MEETING THEM FOR THE FIRST TIME. YOU CAN DO THAT, CAN'T YOU?

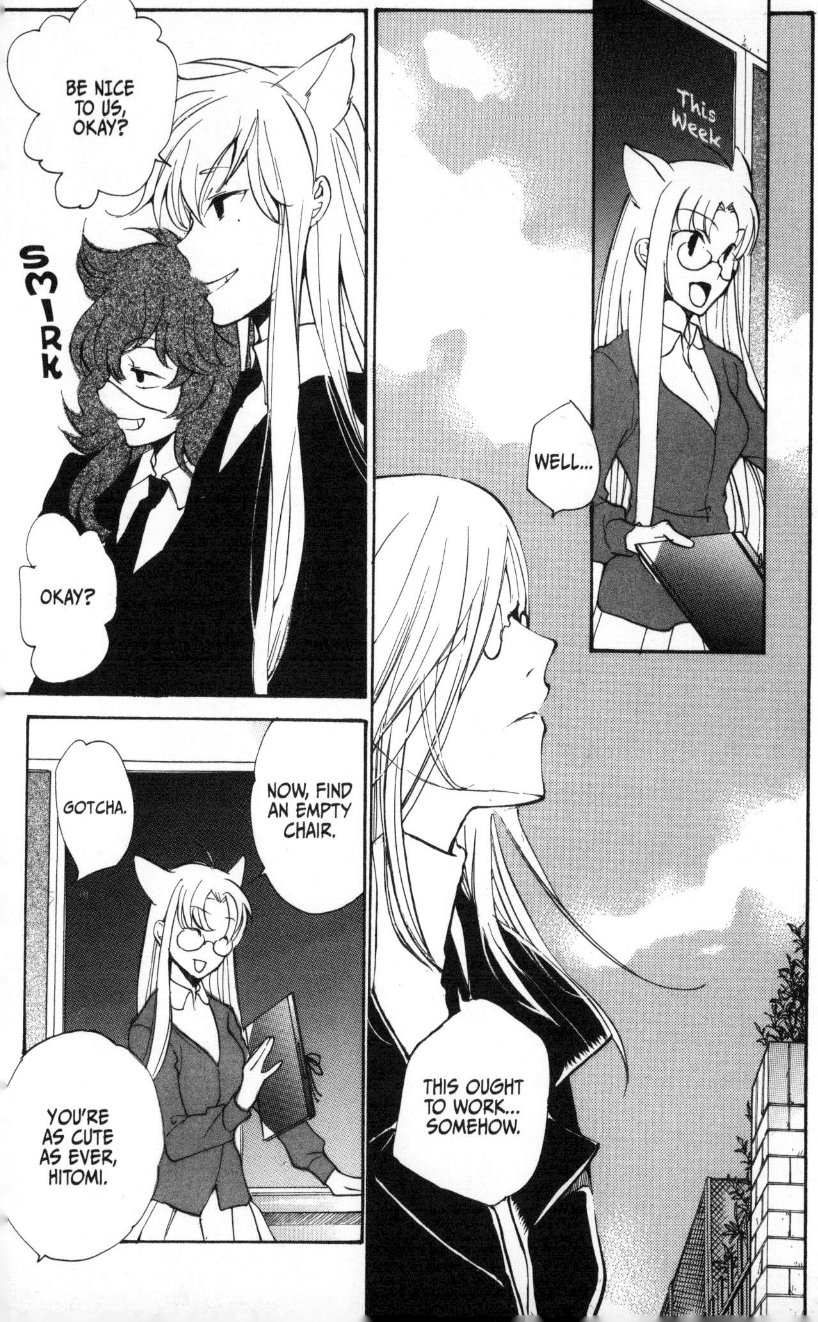
This Week
WELL...
THIS OUGHT TO WORK... SOMEHOW.
BE NICE TO US, OKAY?
SMIRK
OKAY?
NOW, FIND AN EMPTY CHAIR.
GOTCHA.
YOU'RE AS CUTE AS EVER, HITOMI.

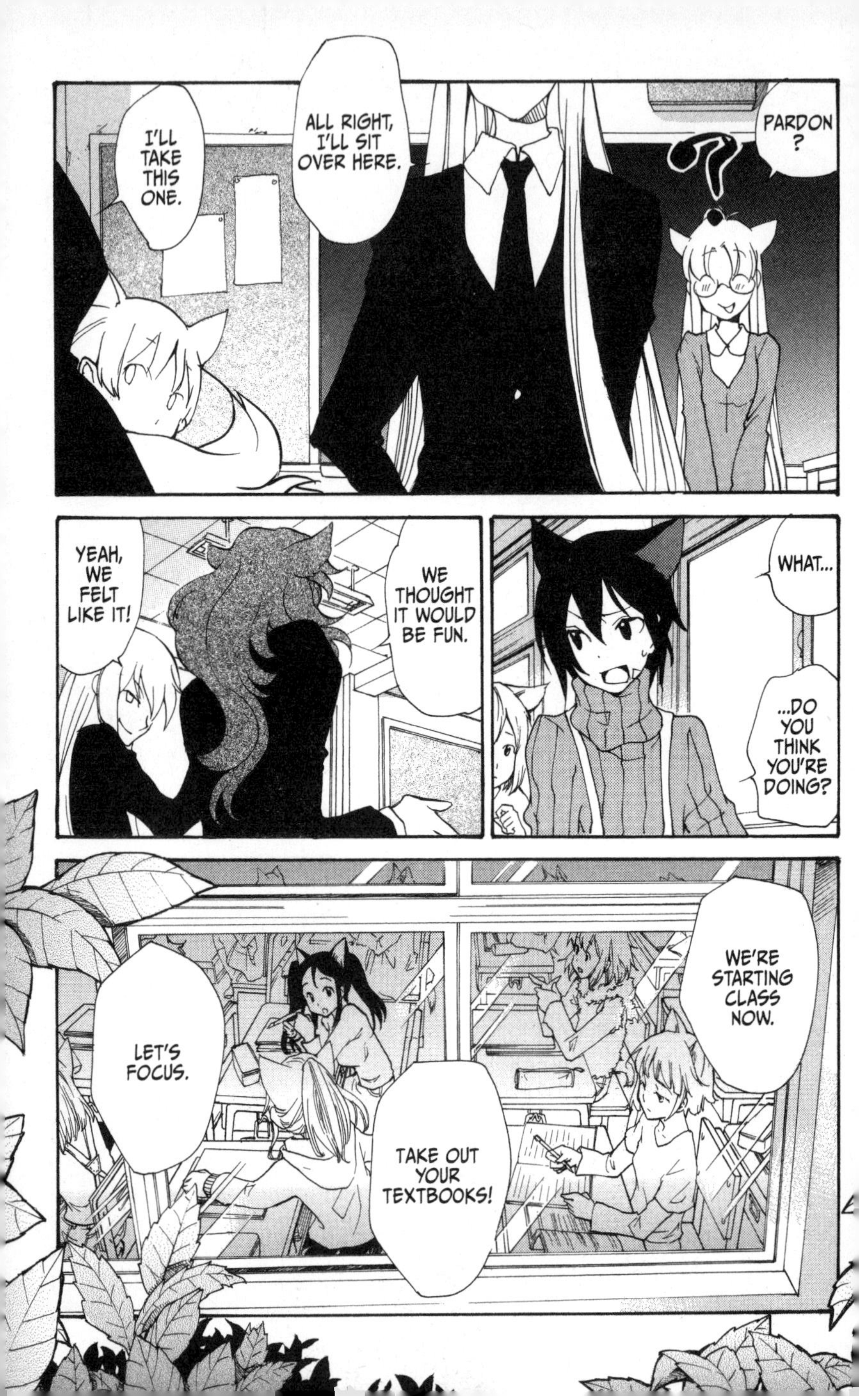
PARDON ?
ALL RIGHT, I'LL SIT OVER HERE.
I'LL TAKE THIS ONE.
WHAT...
...DO YOU THINK YOU'RE DOING?
WE THOUGHT IT WOULD BE FUN.
YEAH, WE FELT LIKE IT!
WE'RE STARTING CLASS NOW.
LET'S FOCUS.
TAKE OUT YOUR TEXTBOOKS!

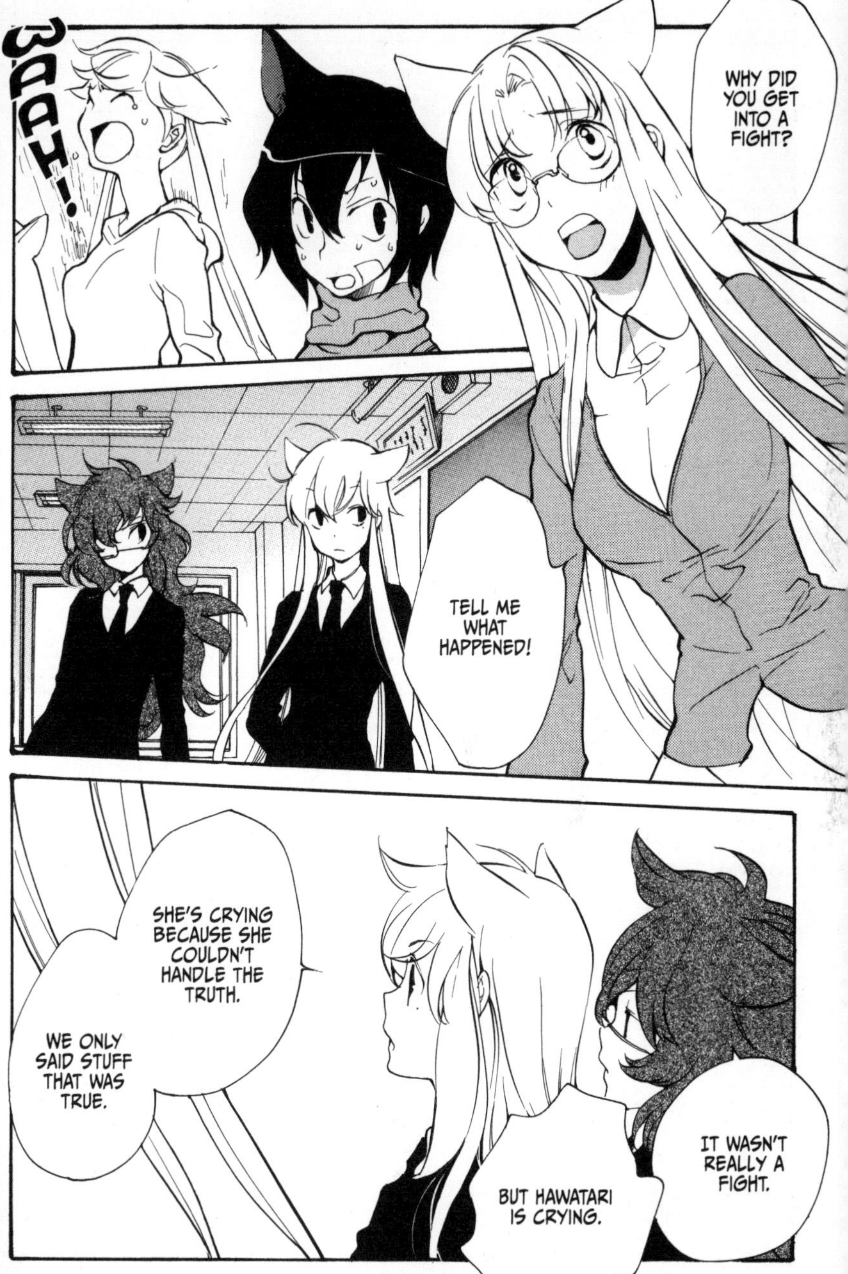
WHY DID YOU GET INTO A FIGHT?
TELL ME WHAT HAPPENED!
WAAH!
IT WASN'T REALLY A FIGHT.
BUT HAWATARI IS CRYING.
SHE'S CRYING BECAUSE SHE COULDN'T HANDLE THE TRUTH.
WE ONLY SAID STUFF THAT WAS TRUE.

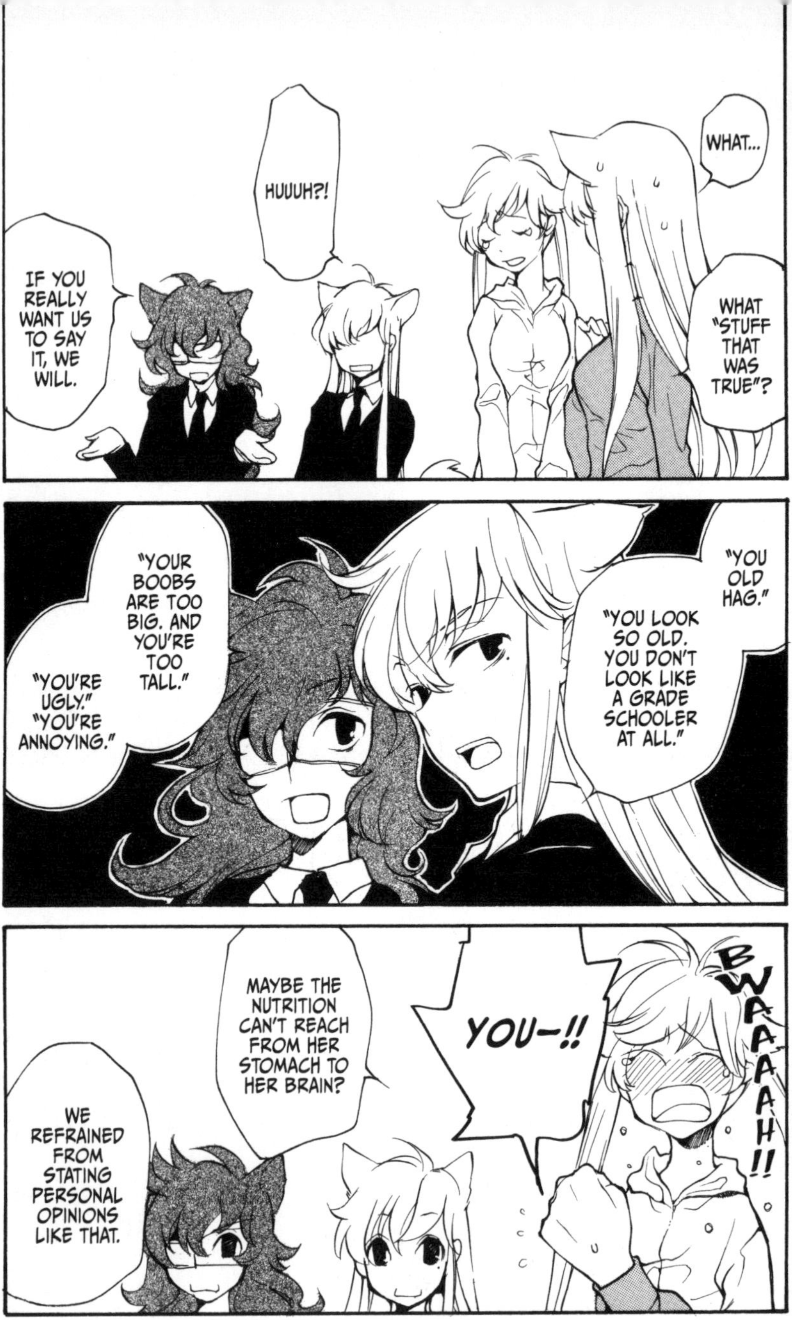
WHAT...
WHAT "STUFF THAT WAS TRUE"?
HUUUH?!
IF YOU REALLY WANT US TO SAY IT, WE WILL.
"YOU OLD HAG."
"YOU LOOK SO OLD. YOU DON'T LOOK LIKE A GRADE SCHOOLER AT ALL."
"YOUR BOOBS ARE TOO BIG. AND YOU'RE TOO TALL."
"YOU'RE UGLY." "YOU'RE ANNOYING."
BWAAAAAH!!
YOU-!!
MAYBE THE NUTRITION CAN'T REACH FROM HER STOMACH TO HER BRAIN?
WE REFRAINED FROM STATING PERSONAL OPINIONS LIKE THAT.

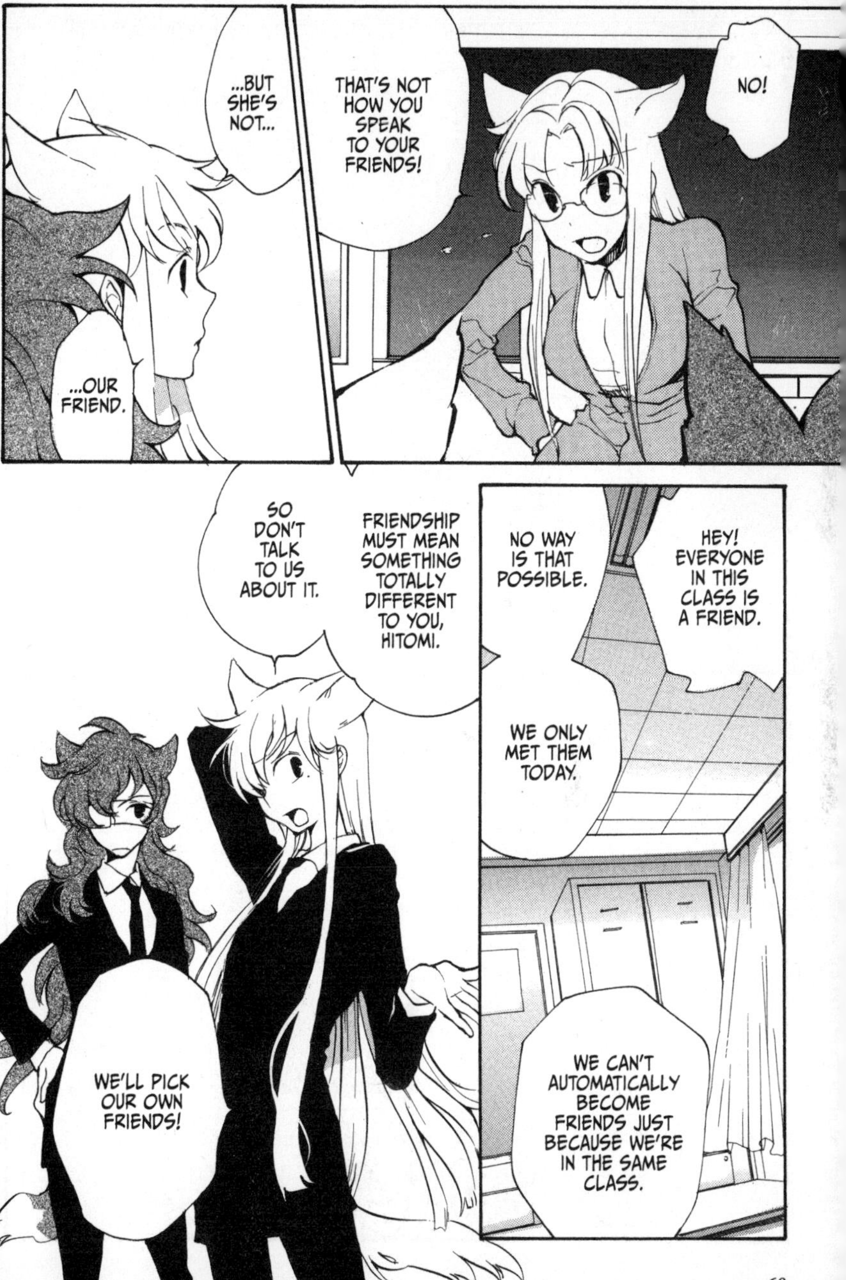
NO!
THAT'S NOT HOW YOU SPEAK TO YOUR FRIENDS!
...BUT SHE'S NOT...
...OUR FRIEND.
HEY! EVERYONE IN THIS CLASS IS A FRIEND.
NO WAY IS THAT POSSIBLE.
WE ONLY MET THEM TODAY.
WE CAN'T AUTOMATICALLY BECOME FRIENDS JUST BECAUSE WE'RE IN THE SAME CLASS.
FRIENDSHIP MUST MEAN SOMETHING TOTALLY DIFFERENT TO YOU, HITOMI.
SO DON'T TALK TO US ABOUT IT.
WE'LL PICK OUR OWN FRIENDS!

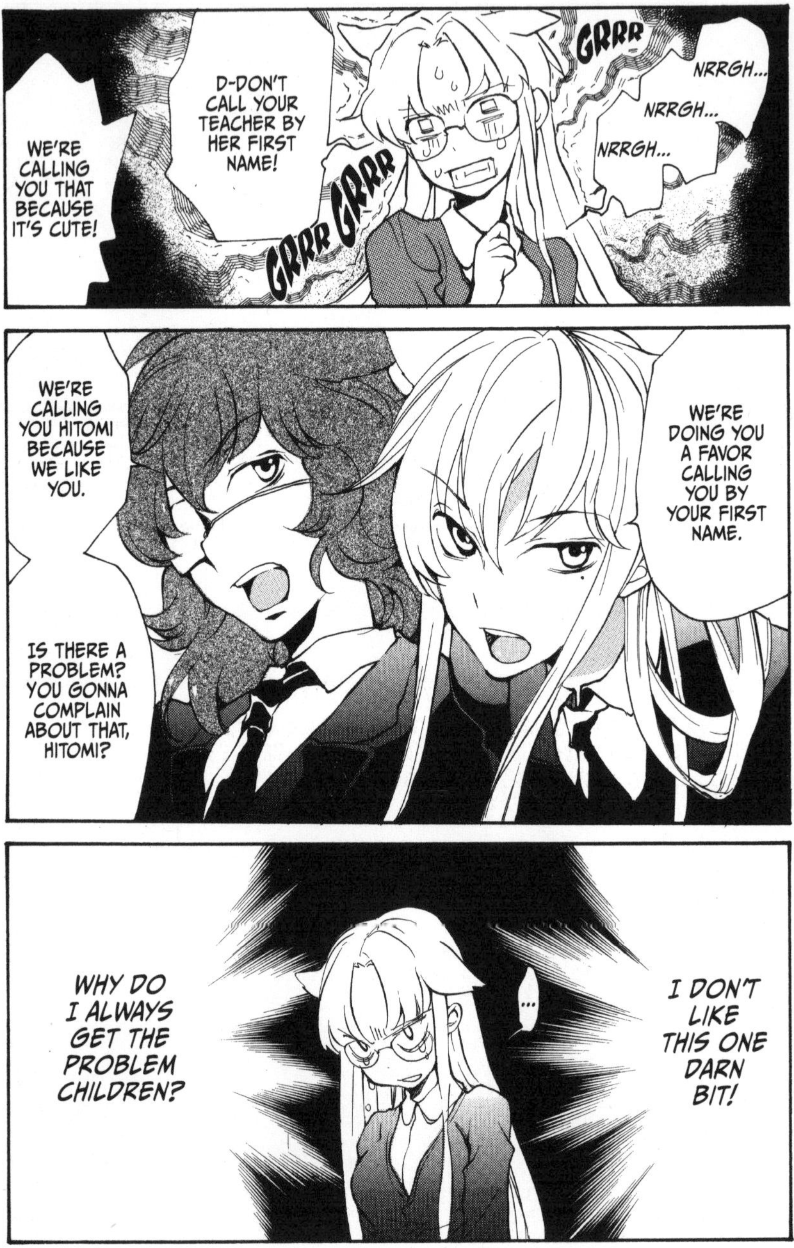
NRRGH... NRRGH... NRRGH...
GRRR
D-DON'T CALL YOUR TEACHER BY HER FIRST NAME!
GRRR GRRR
WE'RE CALLING YOU THAT BECAUSE IT'S CUTE!
WE'RE DOING YOU A FAVOR CALLING YOU BY YOUR FIRST NAME.
WE'RE CALLING YOU HITOMI BECAUSE WE LIKE YOU.
IS THERE A PROBLEM? YOU GONNA COMPLAIN ABOUT THAT, HITOMI?
I DON'T LIKE THIS ONE DARN BIT!
...
WHY DO I ALWAYS GET THE PROBLEM CHILDREN?

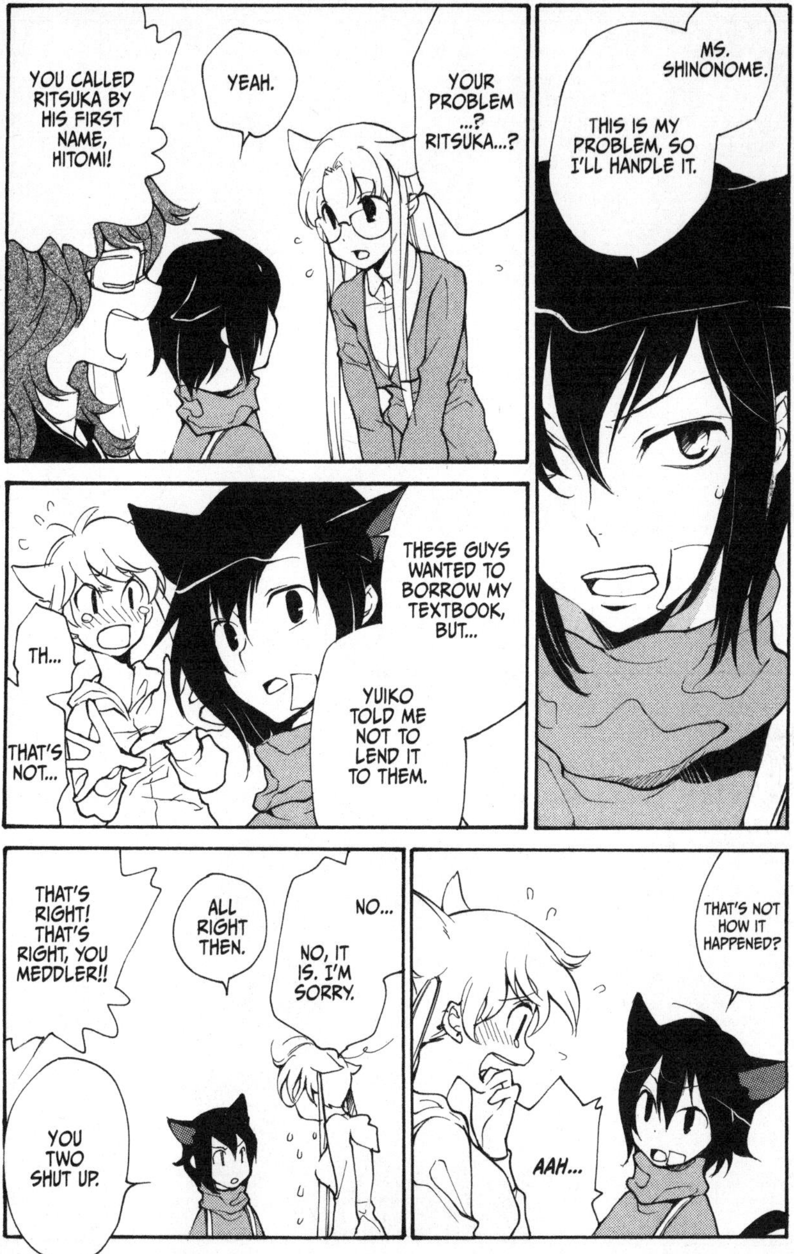
MS. SHINONOME.
THIS IS MY PROBLEM, SO I'LL HANDLE IT.
YOUR PROBLEM ...? RITSUKA...?
YEAH.
YOU CALLED RITSUKA BY HIS FIRST NAME, HITOMI!
THESE GUYS WANTED TO BORROW MY TEXTBOOK, BUT...
YUIKO TOLD ME NOT TO LEND IT TO THEM.
TH...
THAT'S NOT...
THAT'S NOT HOW IT HAPPENED?
AAH...
NO...
NO, IT IS. I'M SORRY.
ALL RIGHT THEN.
THAT'S RIGHT! THAT'S RIGHT, YOU MEDDLER!!
YOU TWO SHUT UP.

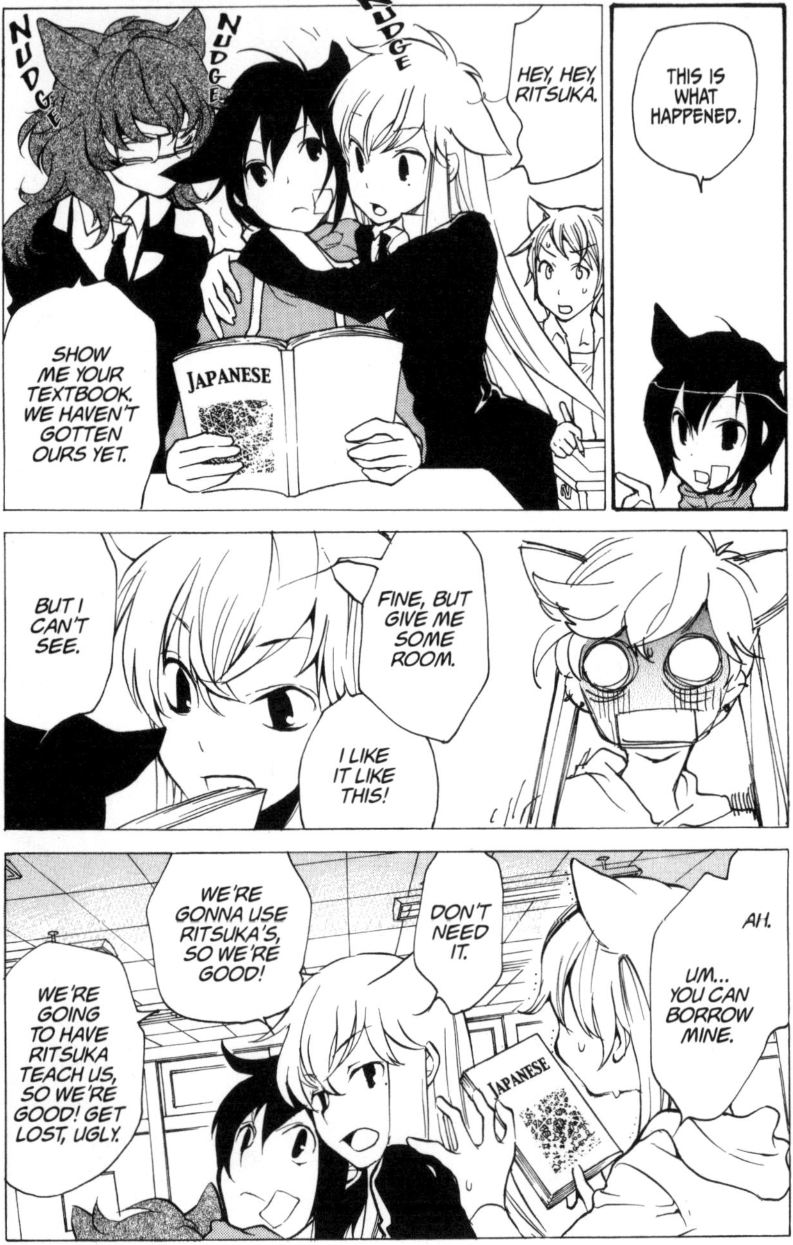

THIS IS WHAT HAPPENED.
HEY, HEY, RITSUKA.
NUDGE
NUDGE
NUDGE
SHOW ME YOUR TEXTBOOK. WE HAVEN'T GOTTEN OURS YET.
JAPANESE
FINE, BUT GIVE ME SOME ROOM.
BUT I CAN'T SEE.
I LIKE IT LIKE THIS!
AH.
UM... YOU CAN BORROW MINE.
DON'T NEED IT.
WE'RE GONNA USE RITSUKA'S, SO WE'RE GOOD!
WE'RE GOING TO HAVE RITSUKA TEACH US, SO WE'RE GOOD! GET LOST, UGLY.
JAPANESE

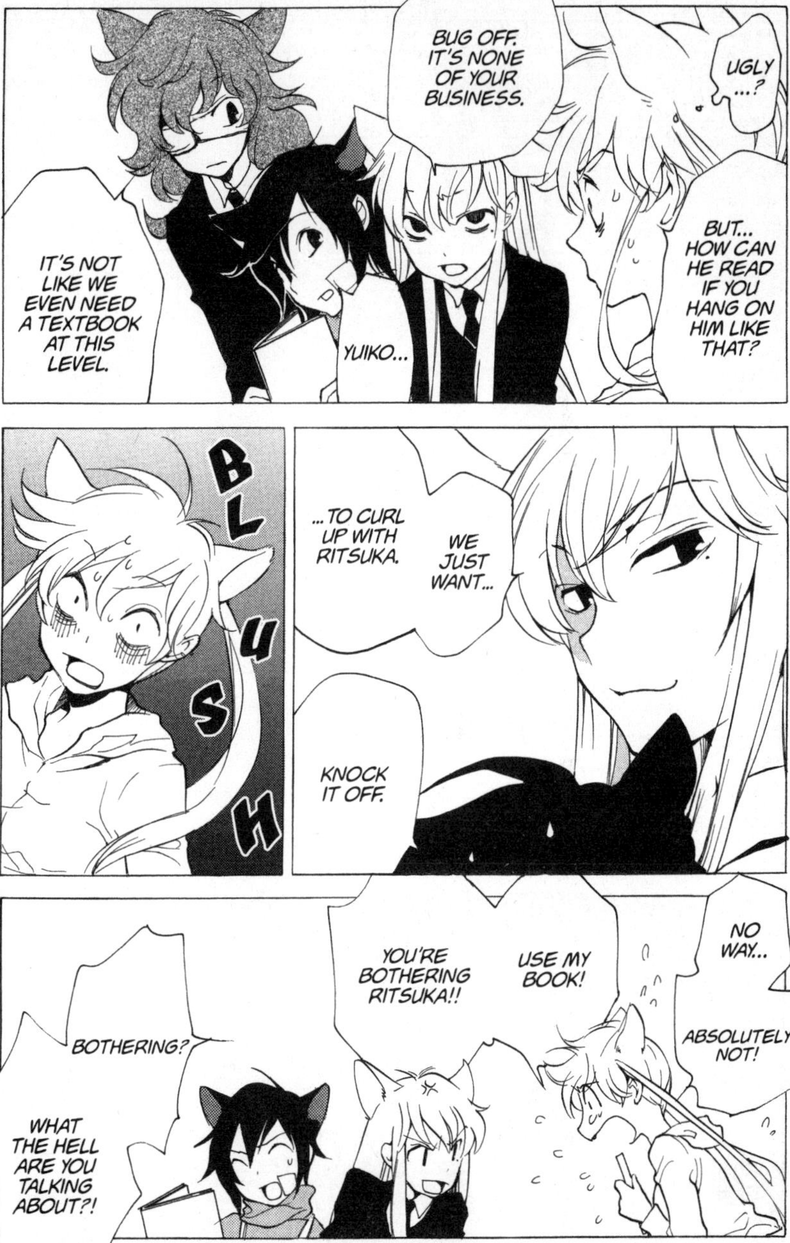
UGLY ...?
BUG OFF. IT'S NONE OF YOUR BUSINESS.
BUT... HOW CAN HE READ IF YOU HANG ON HIM LIKE THAT?
YUIKO...
IT'S NOT LIKE WE EVEN NEED A TEXTBOOK AT THIS LEVEL.
WE JUST WANT...
...TO CURL UP WITH RITSUKA.
KNOCK IT OFF.
BLUSH
NO WAY...
ABSOLUTELY NOT!
USE MY BOOK!
YOU'RE BOTHERING RITSUKA!!
BOTHERING?
WHAT THE HELL ARE YOU TALKING ABOUT?!

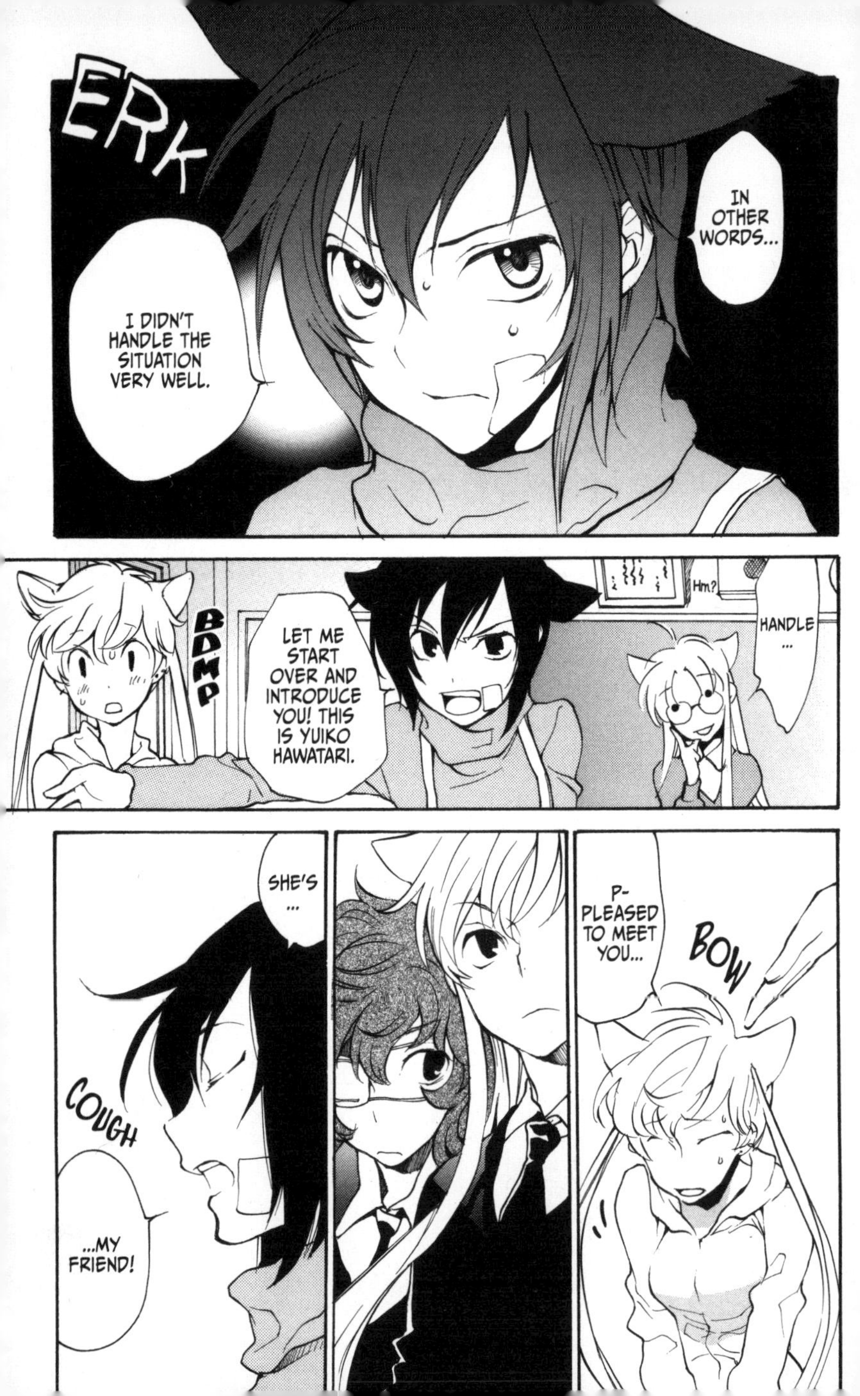
IN OTHER WORDS...
ERK
I DIDN'T HANDLE THE SITUATION VERY WELL.
HANDLE ...
Hm?
LET ME START OVER AND INTRODUCE YOU! THIS IS YUIKO HAWATARI.
BDMP
P-PLEASED TO MEET YOU...
BOW
SHE'S ...
COUGH
...MY FRIEND!

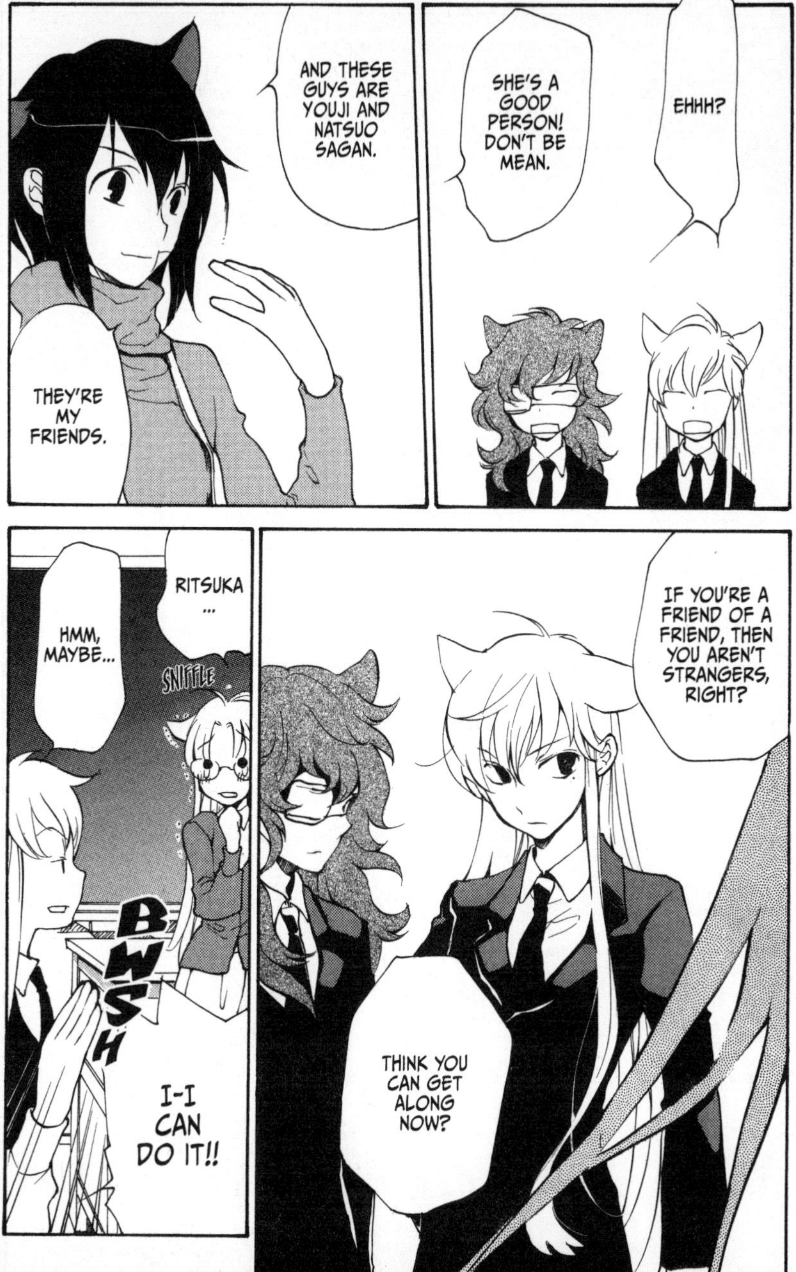
EHHH?
SHE'S A GOOD PERSON! DON'T BE MEAN.
AND THESE GUYS ARE YOUJI AND NATSUO SAGAN.
THEY'RE MY FRIENDS.
IF YOU'RE A FRIEND OF A FRIEND, THEN YOU AREN'T STRANGERS, RIGHT?
THINK YOU CAN GET ALONG NOW?
RITSUKA ...
HMM, MAYBE...
SNIFFLE
BWSH
I-I CAN DO IT!!

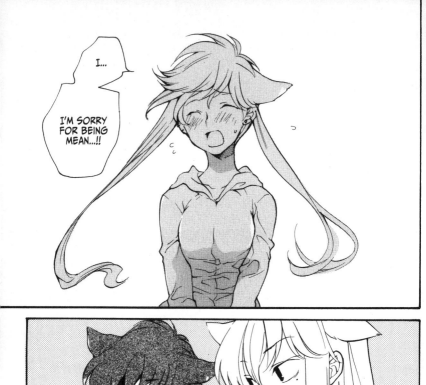

I...

I'M SORRY FOR BEING MEAN...!!

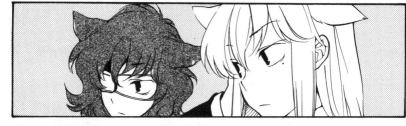

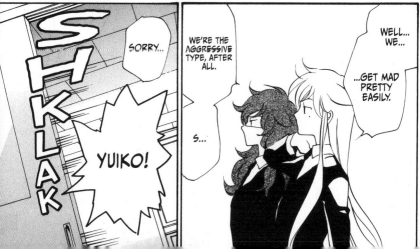

SHKLAK

SORRY...

YUIKO!

WE'RE THE AGGRESSIVE TYPE, AFTER ALL.

S...

WELL... WE...

...GET MAD PRETTY EASILY.

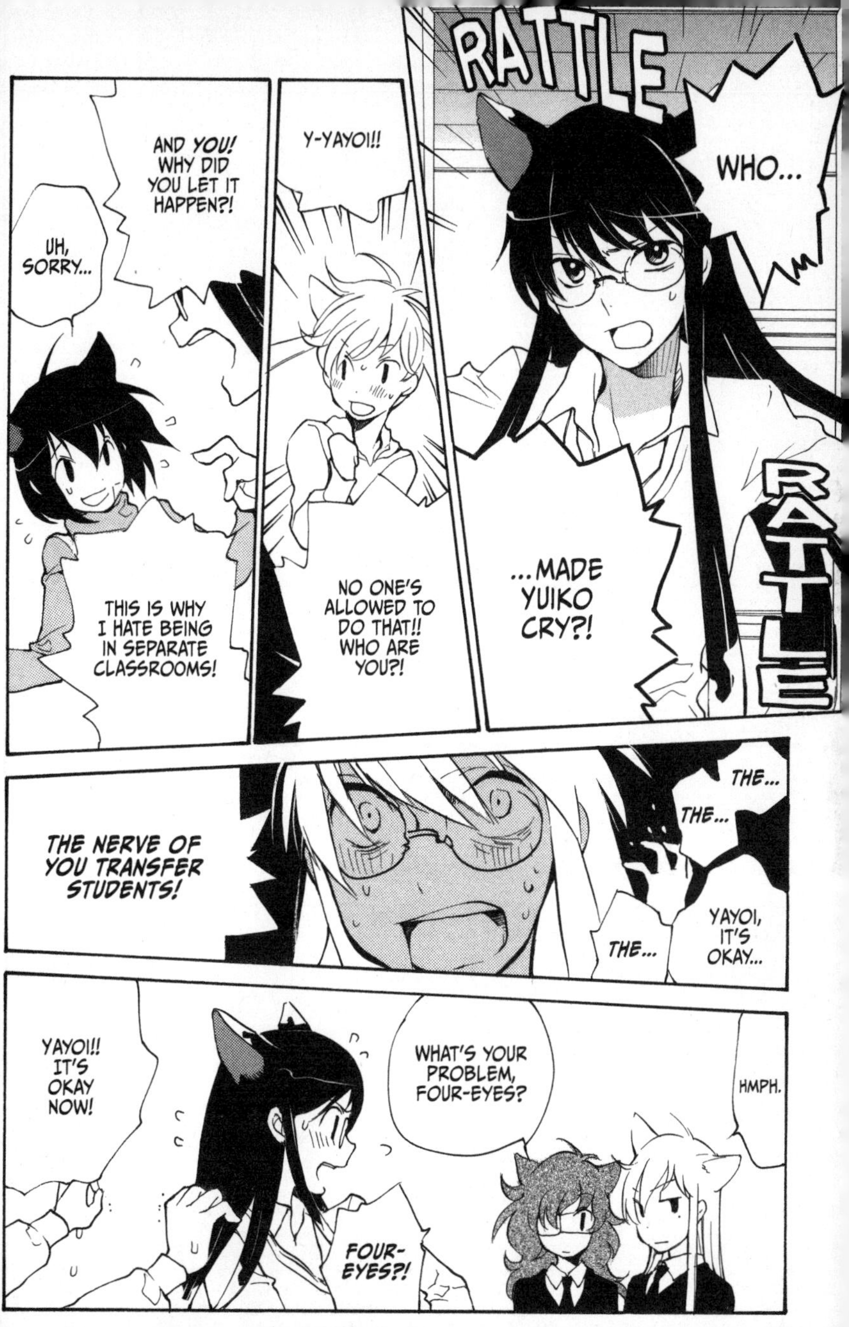
RATTLE
WHO...
...MADE YUIKO CRY?!
RATTLE
Y-YAYOI!!
NO ONE'S ALLOWED TO DO THAT!! WHO ARE YOU?!
AND YOU! WHY DID YOU LET IT HAPPEN?!
UH, SORRY...
THIS IS WHY I HATE BEING IN SEPARATE CLASSROOMS!
THE...
THE...
YAYOI, IT'S OKAY...
THE...
THE NERVE OF YOU TRANSFER STUDENTS!
HMPH.
WHAT'S YOUR PROBLEM, FOUR-EYES?
FOUR-EYES?!
YAYOI!! IT'S OKAY NOW!

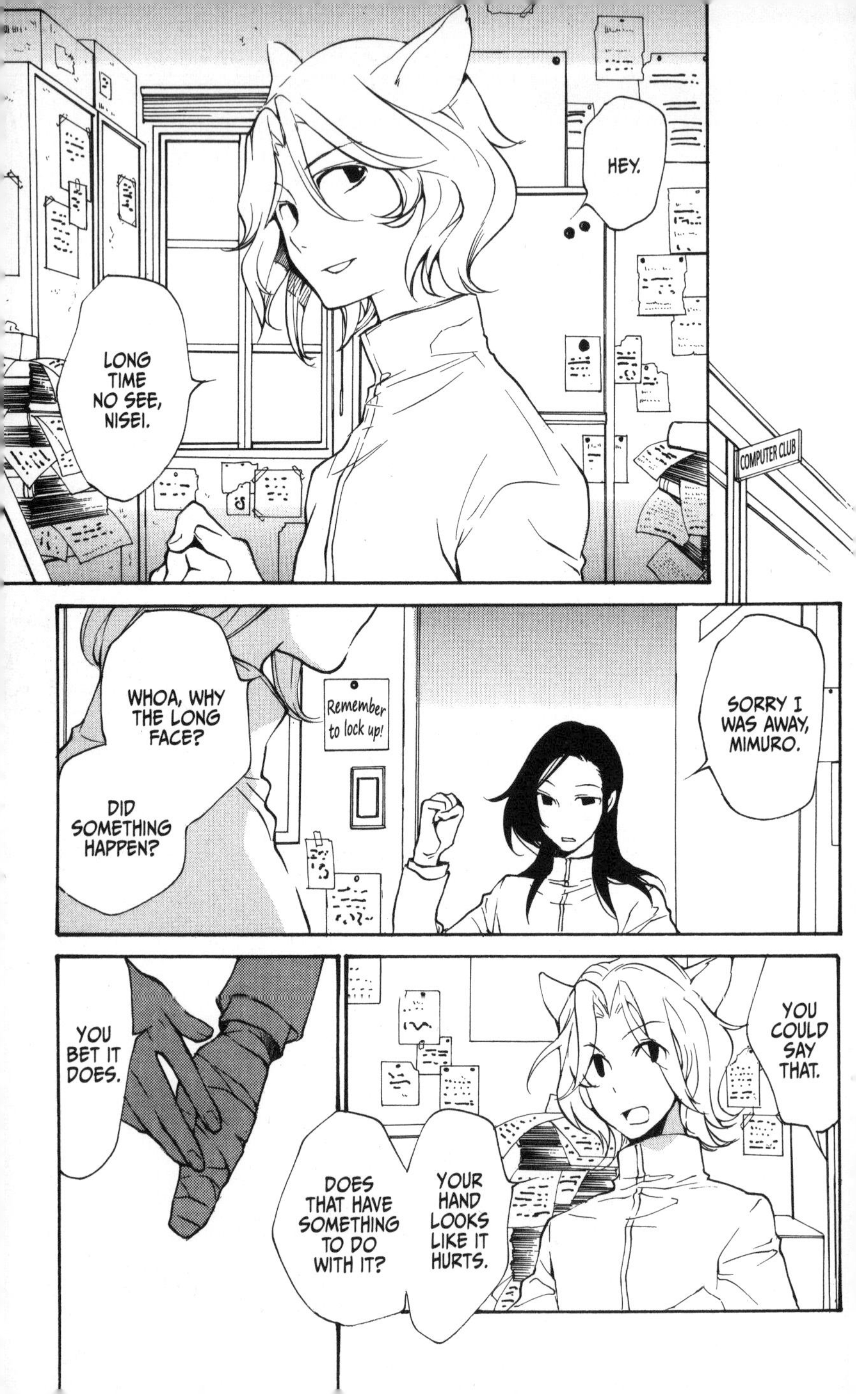
HEY.
LONG TIME NO SEE, NISEI.
COMPUTER CLUB
SORRY I WAS AWAY, MIMURO.
Remember to lock up!
WHOA, WHY THE LONG FACE?
DID SOMETHING HAPPEN?
YOU COULD SAY THAT.
YOUR HAND LOOKS LIKE IT HURTS.
DOES THAT HAVE SOMETHING TO DO WITH IT?
YOU BET IT DOES.

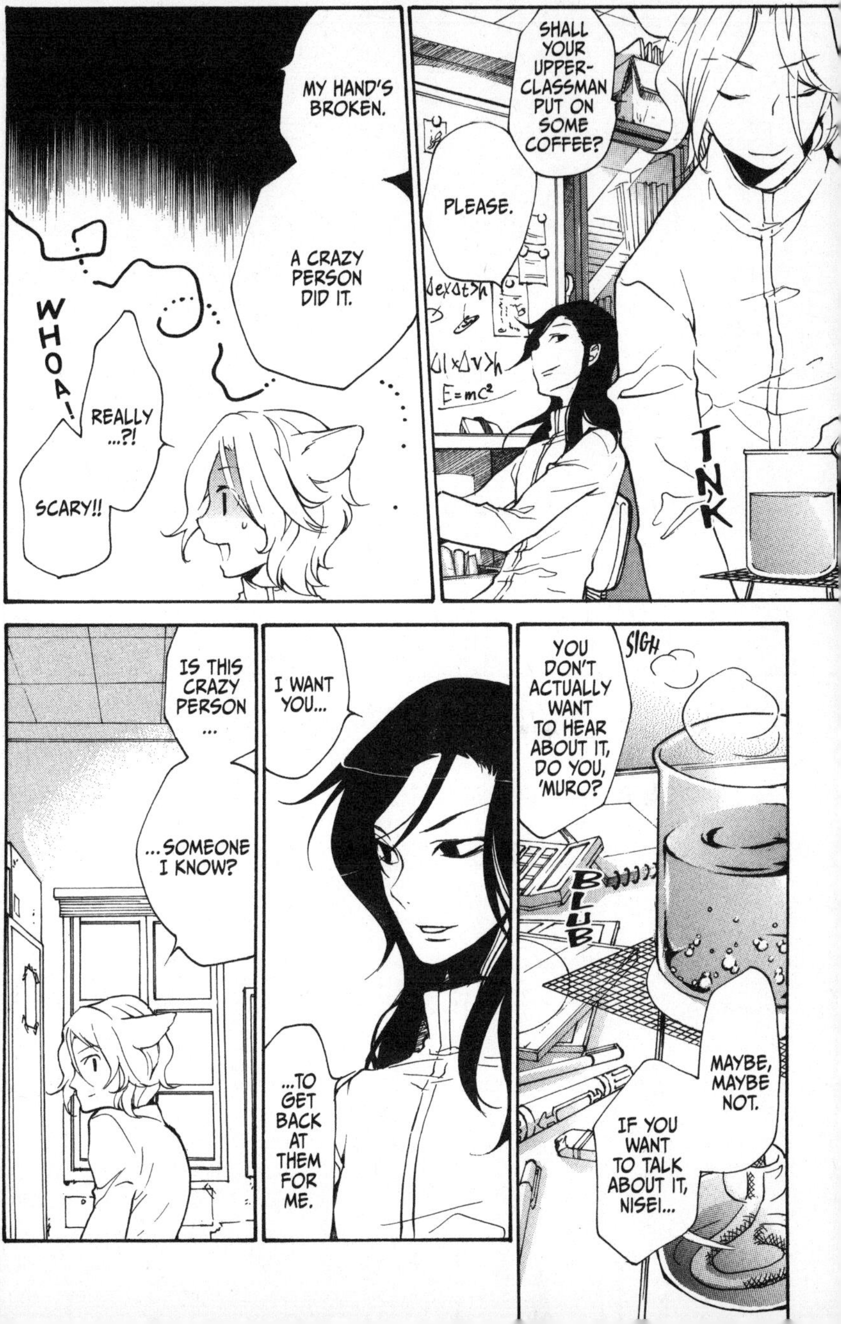
SHALL YOUR UPPER-CLASSMAN PUT ON SOME COFFEE?
PLEASE.
TNK
MY HAND'S BROKEN.
A CRAZY PERSON DID IT.
WHOA!
REALLY ...?!
SCARY!!
SIGH
YOU DON'T ACTUALLY WANT TO HEAR ABOUT IT, DO YOU, 'MURO?
BLUB
MAYBE, MAYBE NOT.
IF YOU WANT TO TALK ABOUT IT, NISEI...
I WANT YOU...
...TO GET BACK AT THEM FOR ME.
IS THIS CRAZY PERSON ...
...SOMEONE I KNOW?

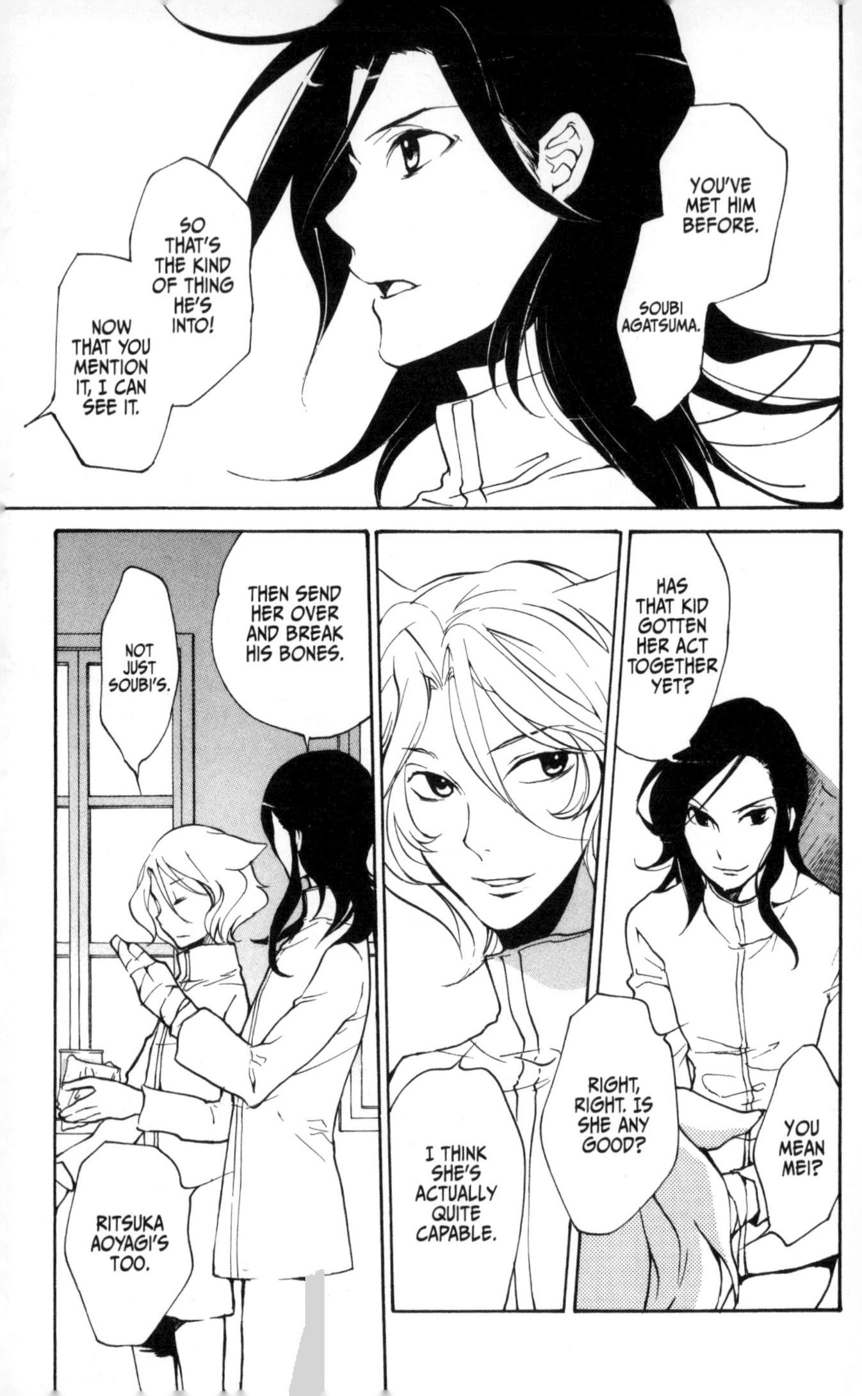
YOU'VE MET HIM BEFORE.
SOUBI AGATSUMA.
SO THAT'S THE KIND OF THING HE'S INTO!
NOW THAT YOU MENTION IT, I CAN SEE IT.
HAS THAT KID GOTTEN HER ACT TOGETHER YET?
YOU MEAN MEI?
RIGHT, RIGHT. IS SHE ANY GOOD?
I THINK SHE'S ACTUALLY QUITE CAPABLE.
THEN SEND HER OVER AND BREAK HIS BONES.
NOT JUST SOUBI'S.
RITSUKA AOYAGI'S TOO.

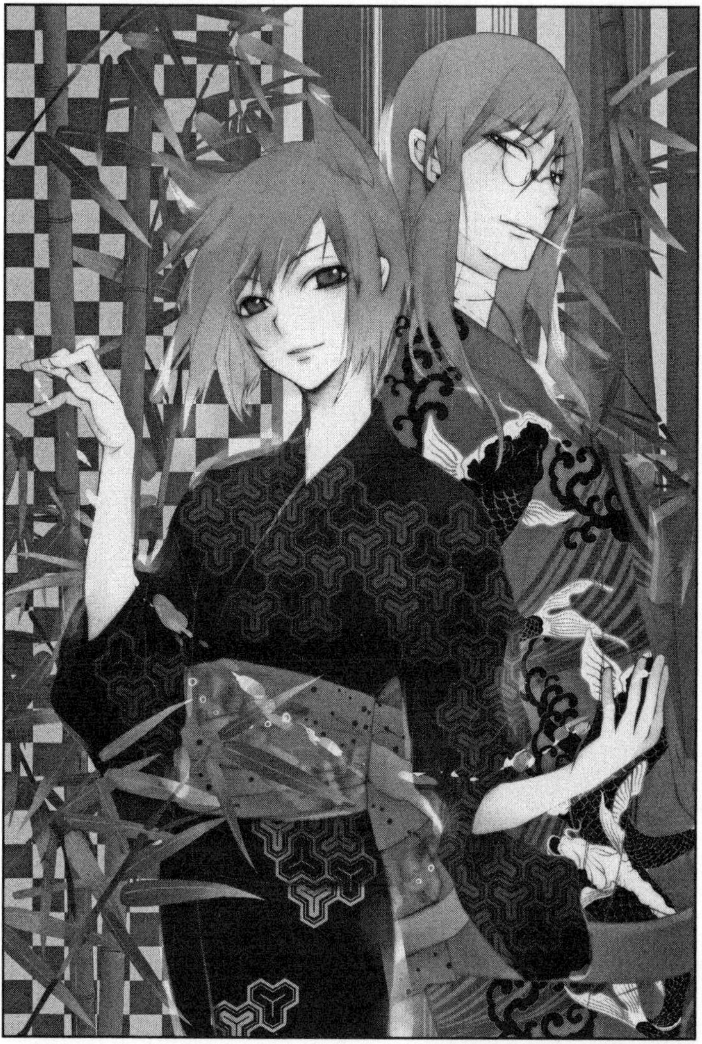

LOVELESS

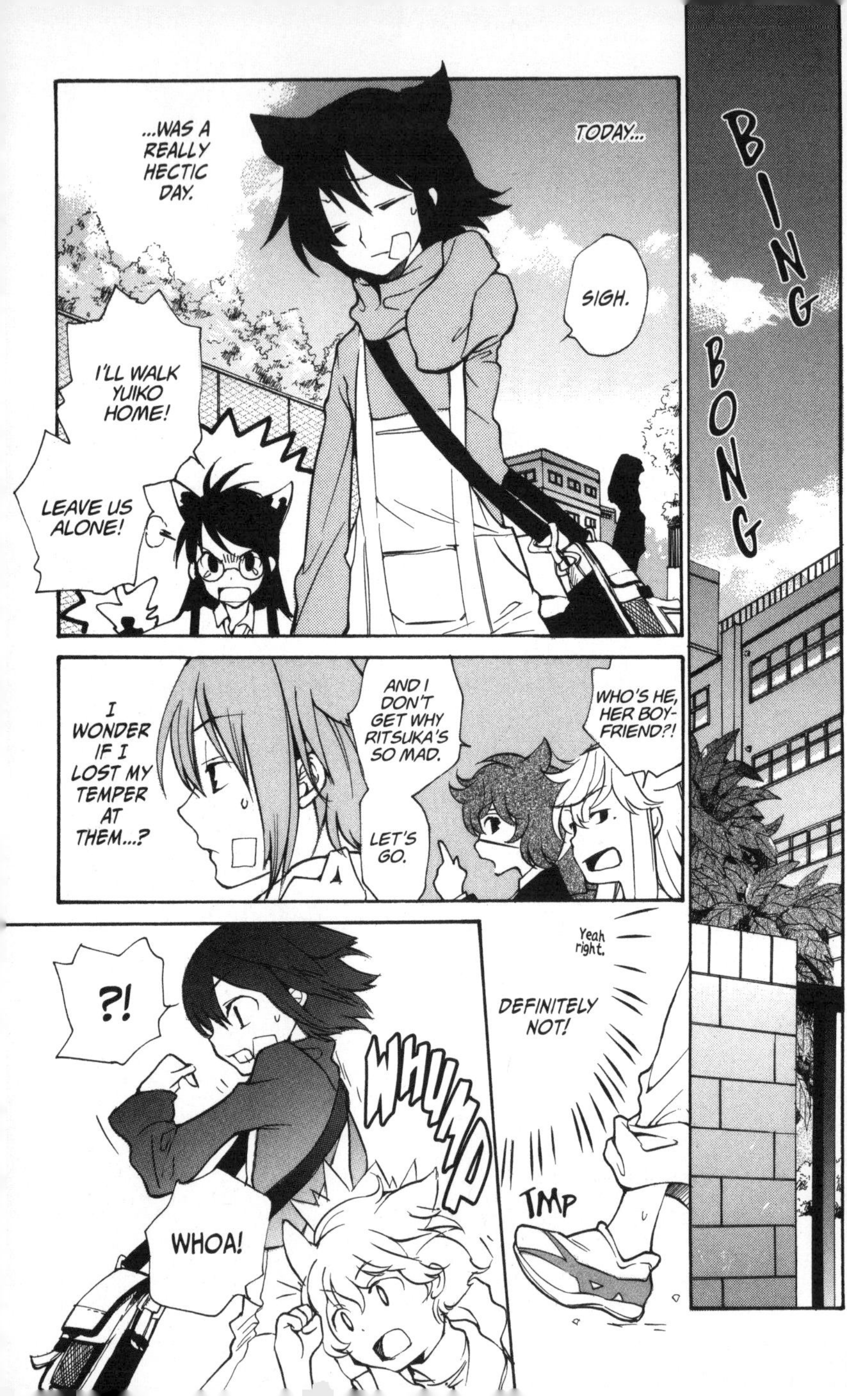
BING BONG
TODAY...
SIGH.
...WAS A REALLY HECTIC DAY.
I'LL WALK YUIKO HOME!
LEAVE US ALONE!
WHO'S HE, HER BOY-FRIEND?!
AND I DON'T GET WHY RITSUKA'S SO MAD.
LET'S GO.
I WONDER IF I LOST MY TEMPER AT THEM...?
Yeah right.
DEFINITELY NOT!
TMP
WHUMP
?!
WHOA!

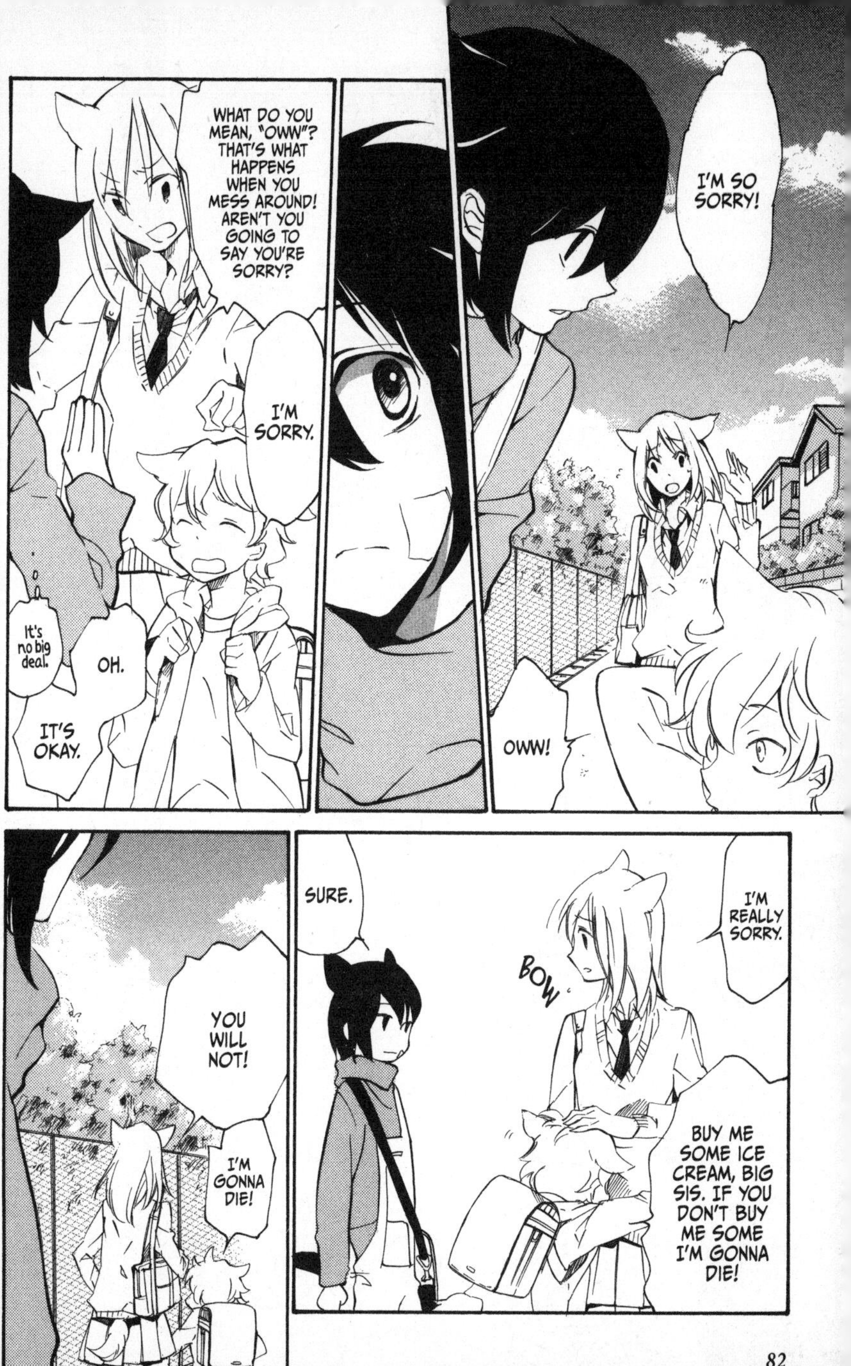
I'M SO SORRY!
OWW!
WHAT DO YOU MEAN, "OWW"? THAT'S WHAT HAPPENS WHEN YOU MESS AROUND! AREN'T YOU GOING TO SAY YOU'RE SORRY?
I'M SORRY.
OH.
It's no big deal.
IT'S OKAY.
I'M REALLY SORRY.
SURE.
BOW
BUY ME SOME ICE CREAM, BIG SIS. IF YOU DON'T BUY ME SOME I'M GONNA DIE!
YOU WILL NOT!
I'M GONNA DIE!

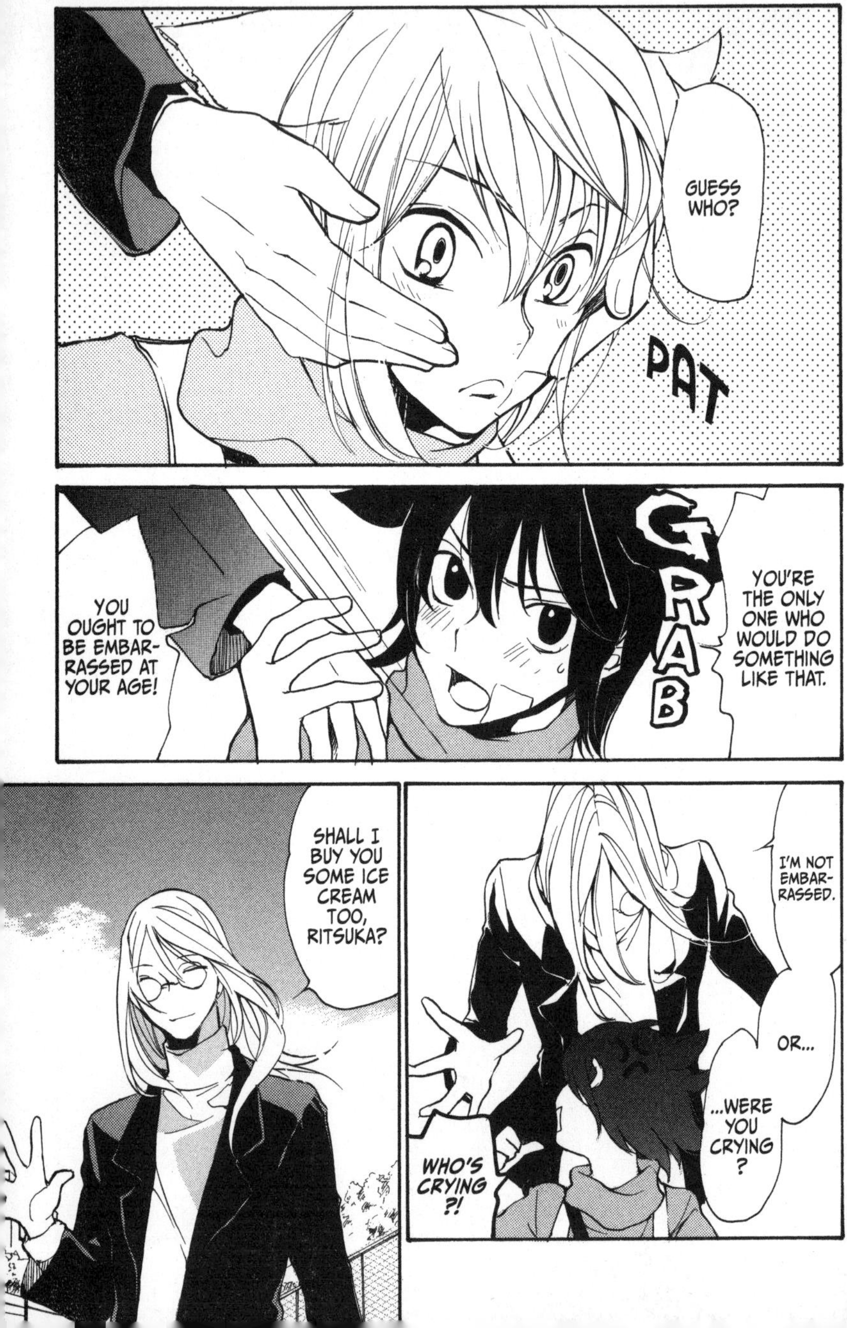
GUESS WHO?
PAT
YOU'RE THE ONLY ONE WHO WOULD DO SOMETHING LIKE THAT.
GRAB
YOU OUGHT TO BE EMBAR-RASSED AT YOUR AGE!
I'M NOT EMBAR-RASSED.
OR...
...WERE YOU CRYING?
WHO'S CRYING?!
SHALL I BUY YOU SOME ICE CREAM TOO, RITSUKA?

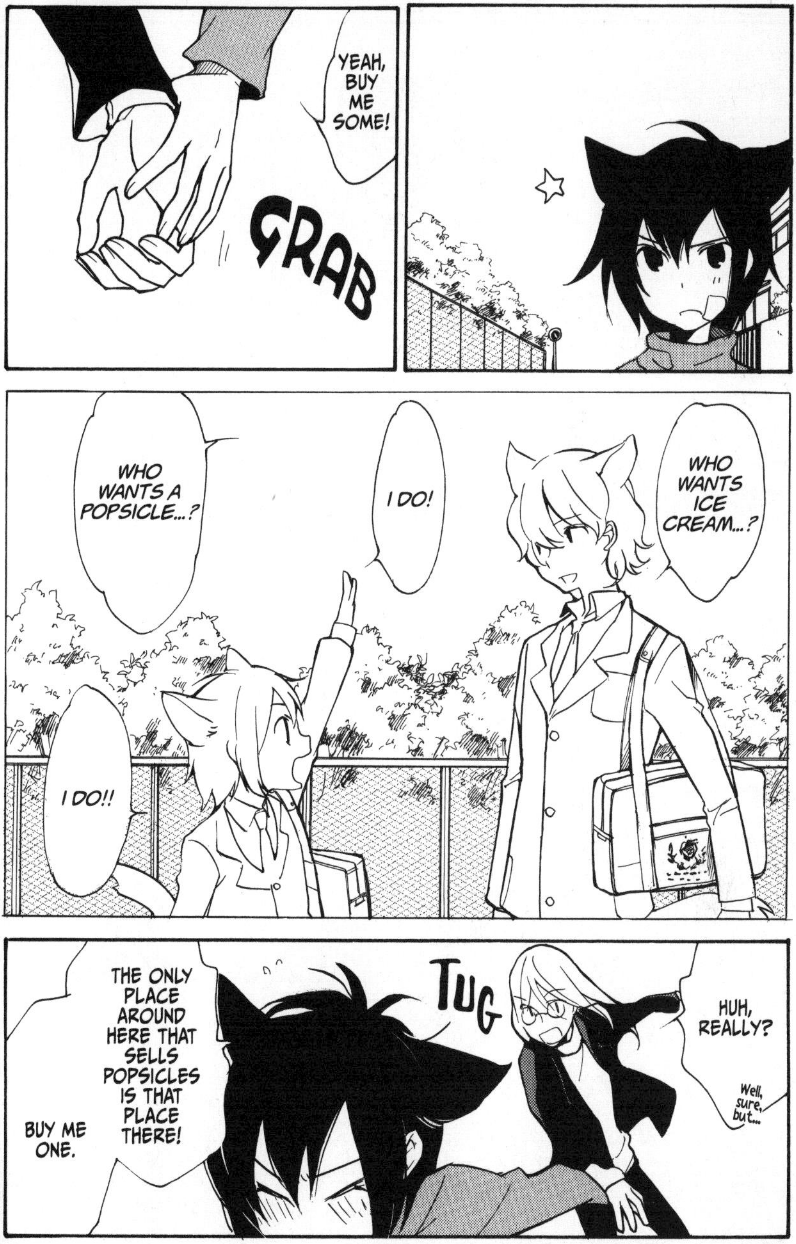
YEAH, BUY ME SOME!
GRAB
WHO WANTS ICE CREAM...?
I DO!
WHO WANTS A POPSICLE...?
I DO!!
HUH, REALLY?
Well, sure, but...
TUG
THE ONLY PLACE AROUND HERE THAT SELLS POPSICLES IS THAT PLACE THERE!
BUY ME ONE.

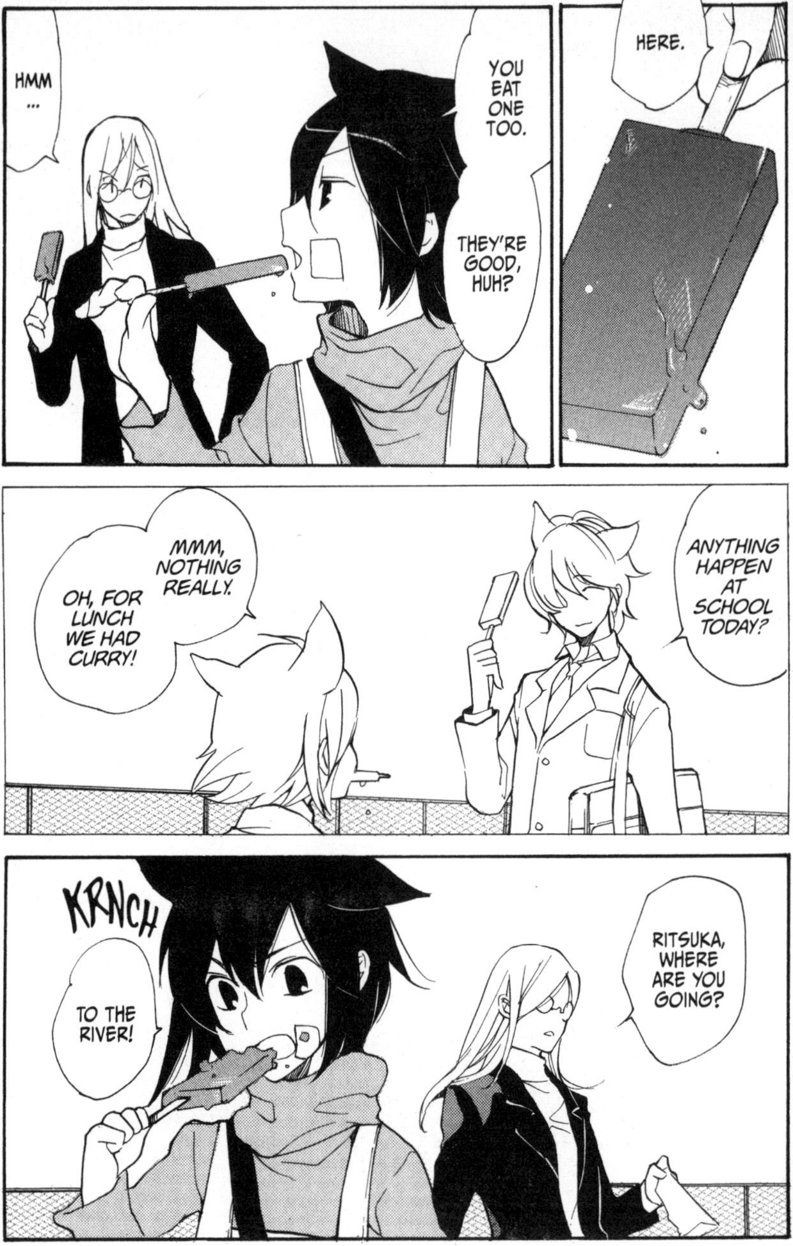
HERE.
YOU EAT ONE TOO.
THEY'RE GOOD, HUH?
HMM ...
ANYTHING HAPPEN AT SCHOOL TODAY?
MMM, NOTHING REALLY.
OH, FOR LUNCH WE HAD CURRY!
RITSUKA, WHERE ARE YOU GOING?
KRNCH
TO THE RIVER!

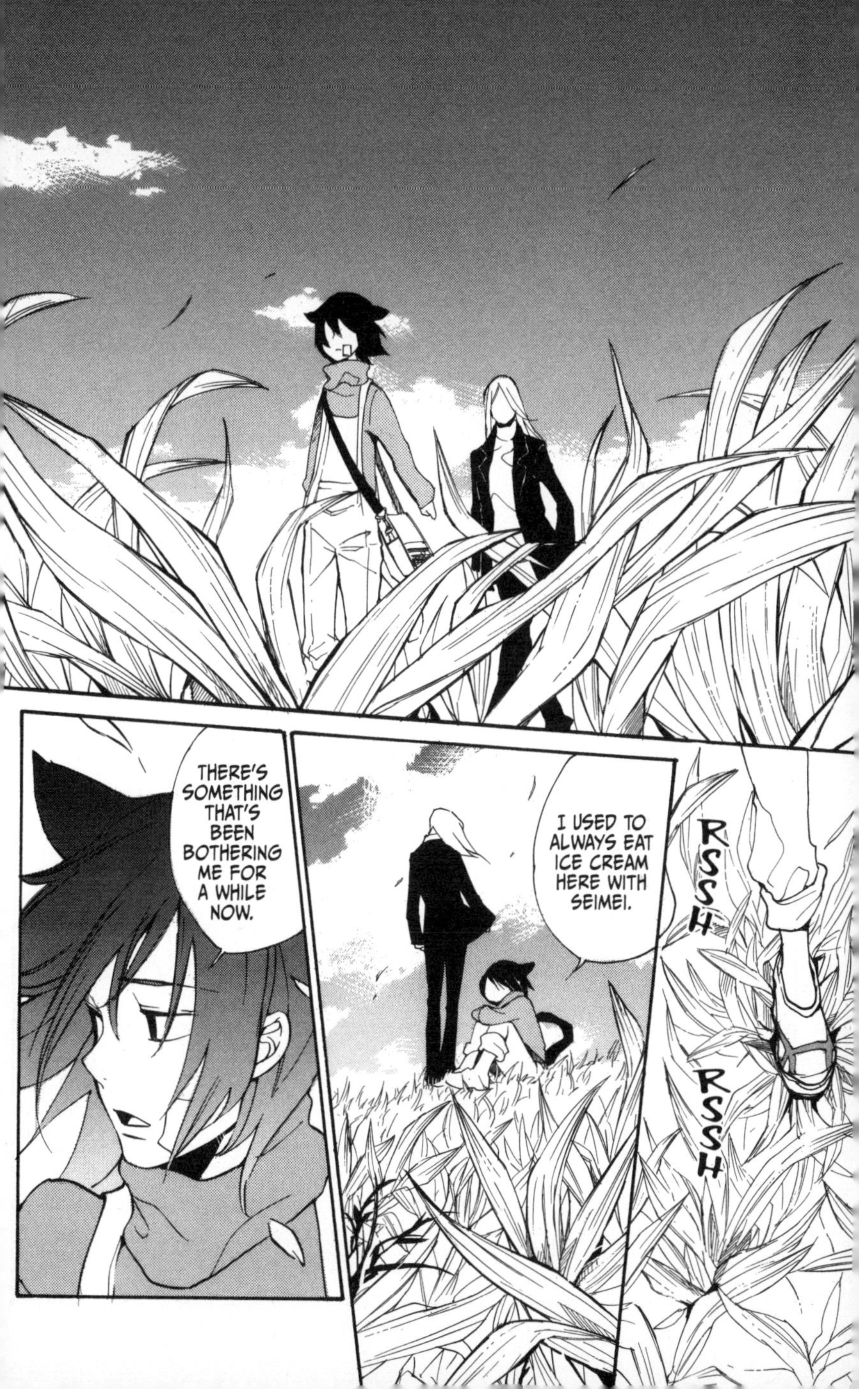
RSSH
RSSH
I USED TO ALWAYS EAT ICE CREAM HERE WITH SEIMEI.
THERE'S SOMETHING THAT'S BEEN BOTHERING ME FOR A WHILE NOW.

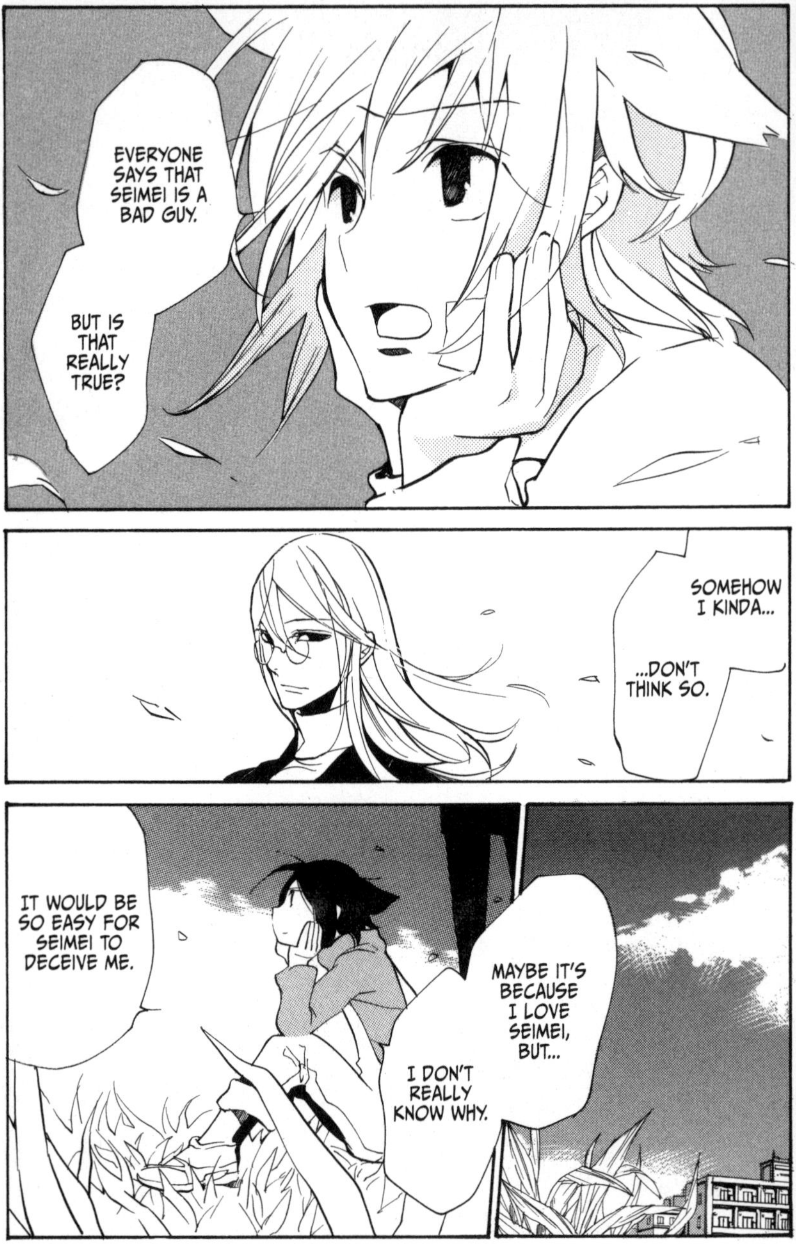
EVERYONE SAYS THAT SEIMEI IS A BAD GUY.
BUT IS THAT REALLY TRUE?
SOMEHOW I KINDA...
...DON'T THINK SO.
MAYBE IT'S BECAUSE I LOVE SEIMEI, BUT...
I DON'T REALLY KNOW WHY.
IT WOULD BE SO EASY FOR SEIMEI TO DECEIVE ME.

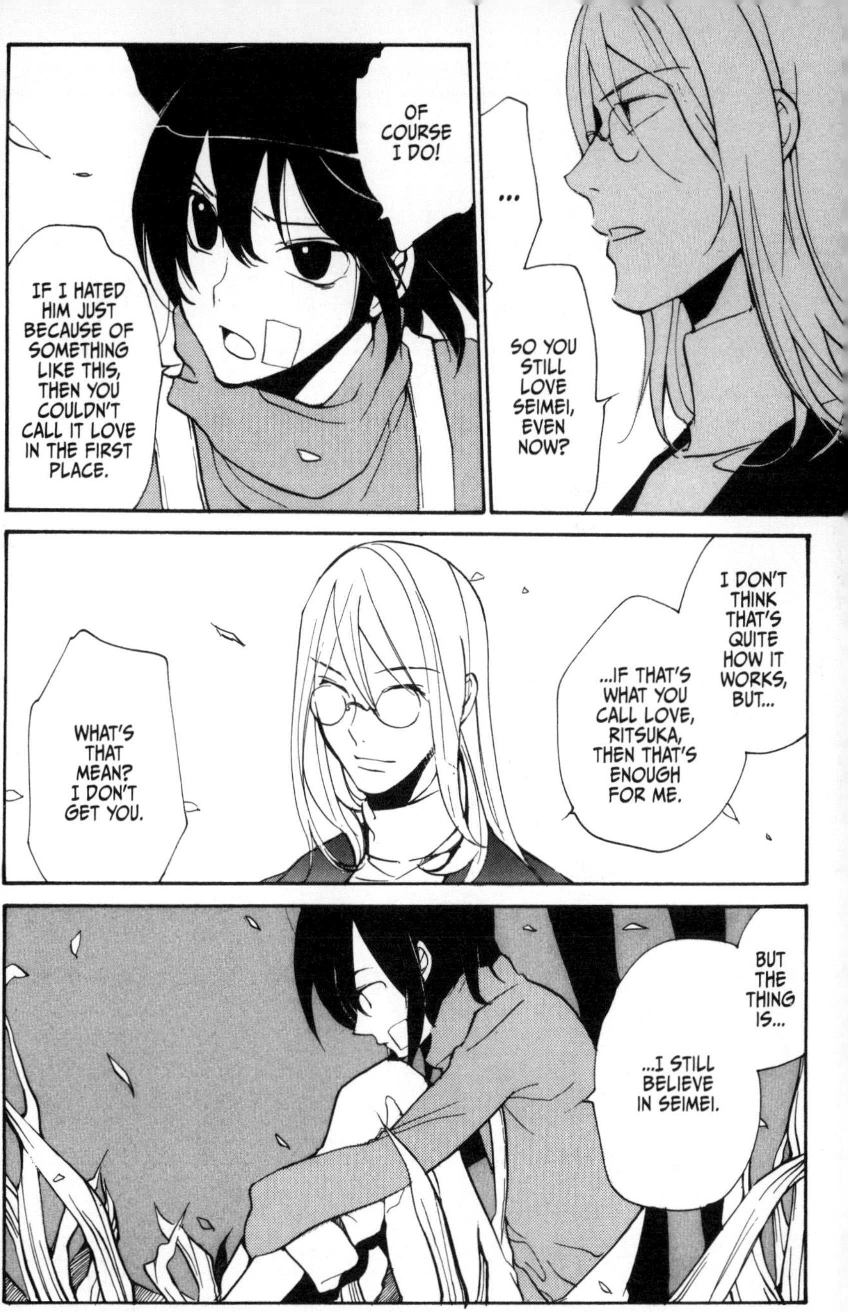
...
SO YOU STILL LOVE SEIMEI, EVEN NOW?
OF COURSE I DO!
IF I HATED HIM JUST BECAUSE OF SOMETHING LIKE THIS, THEN YOU COULDN'T CALL IT LOVE IN THE FIRST PLACE.
I DON'T THINK THAT'S QUITE HOW IT WORKS, BUT...
...IF THAT'S WHAT YOU CALL LOVE, RITSUKA, THEN THAT'S ENOUGH FOR ME.
WHAT'S THAT MEAN? I DON'T GET YOU.
BUT THE THING IS...
...I STILL BELIEVE IN SEIMEI.

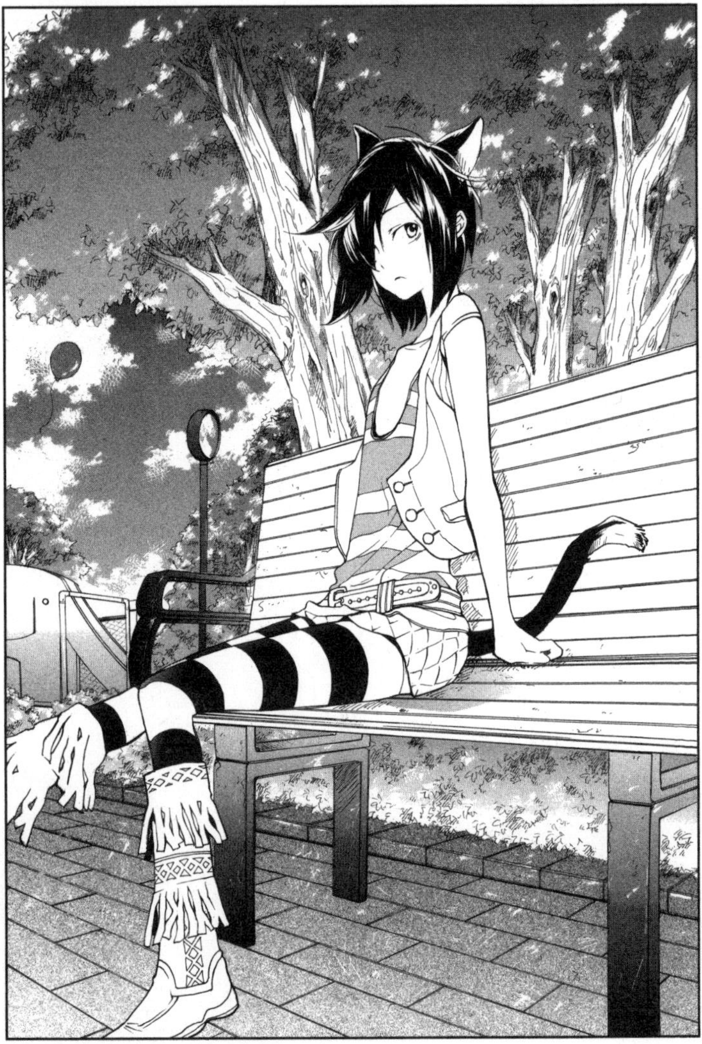

LOVELESS

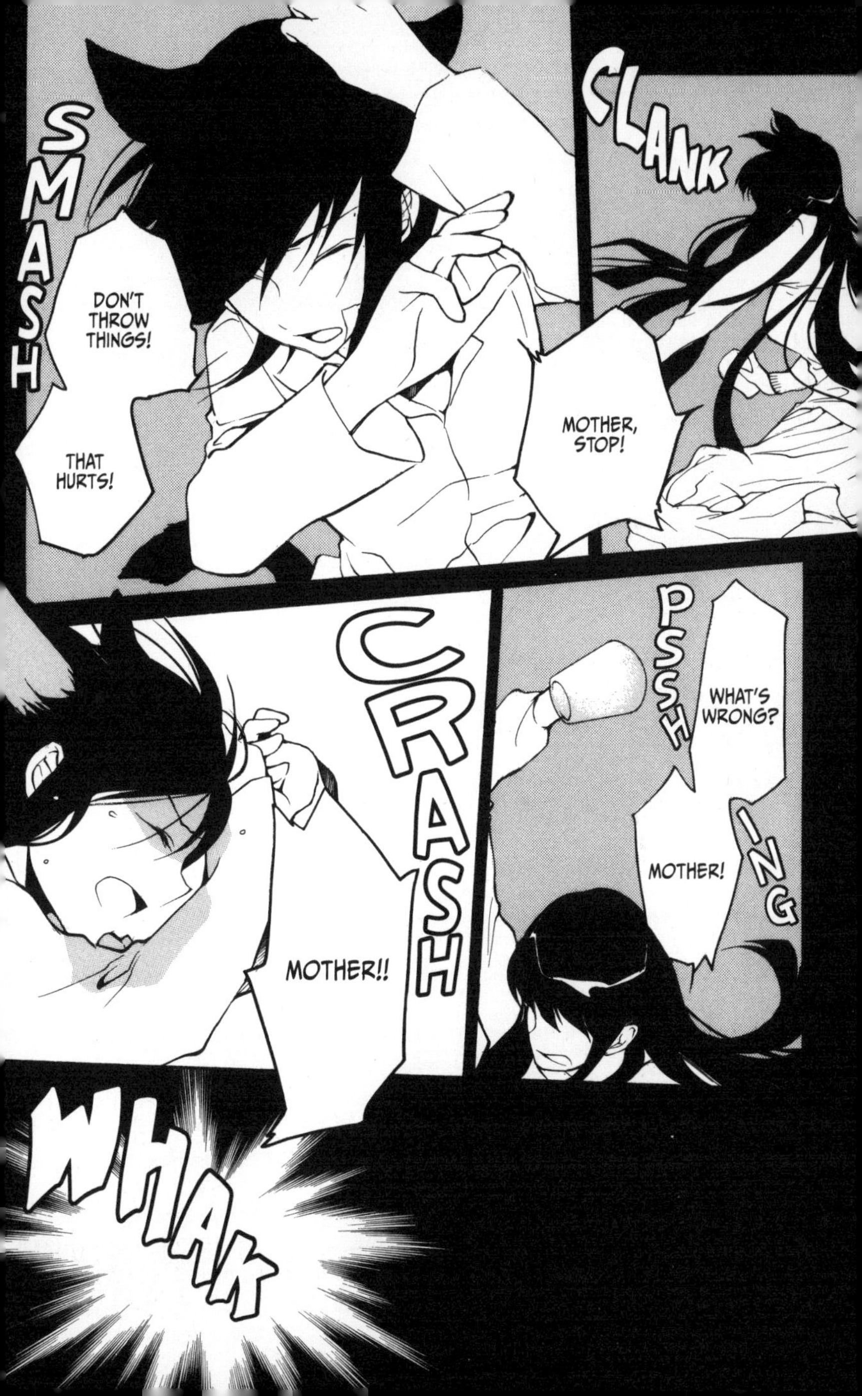
CLANK
MOTHER, STOP!
SMASH
DON'T THROW THINGS!
THAT HURTS!
PSSH
WHAT'S WRONG?
ING
MOTHER!
CRASH
MOTHER!!
WHAK

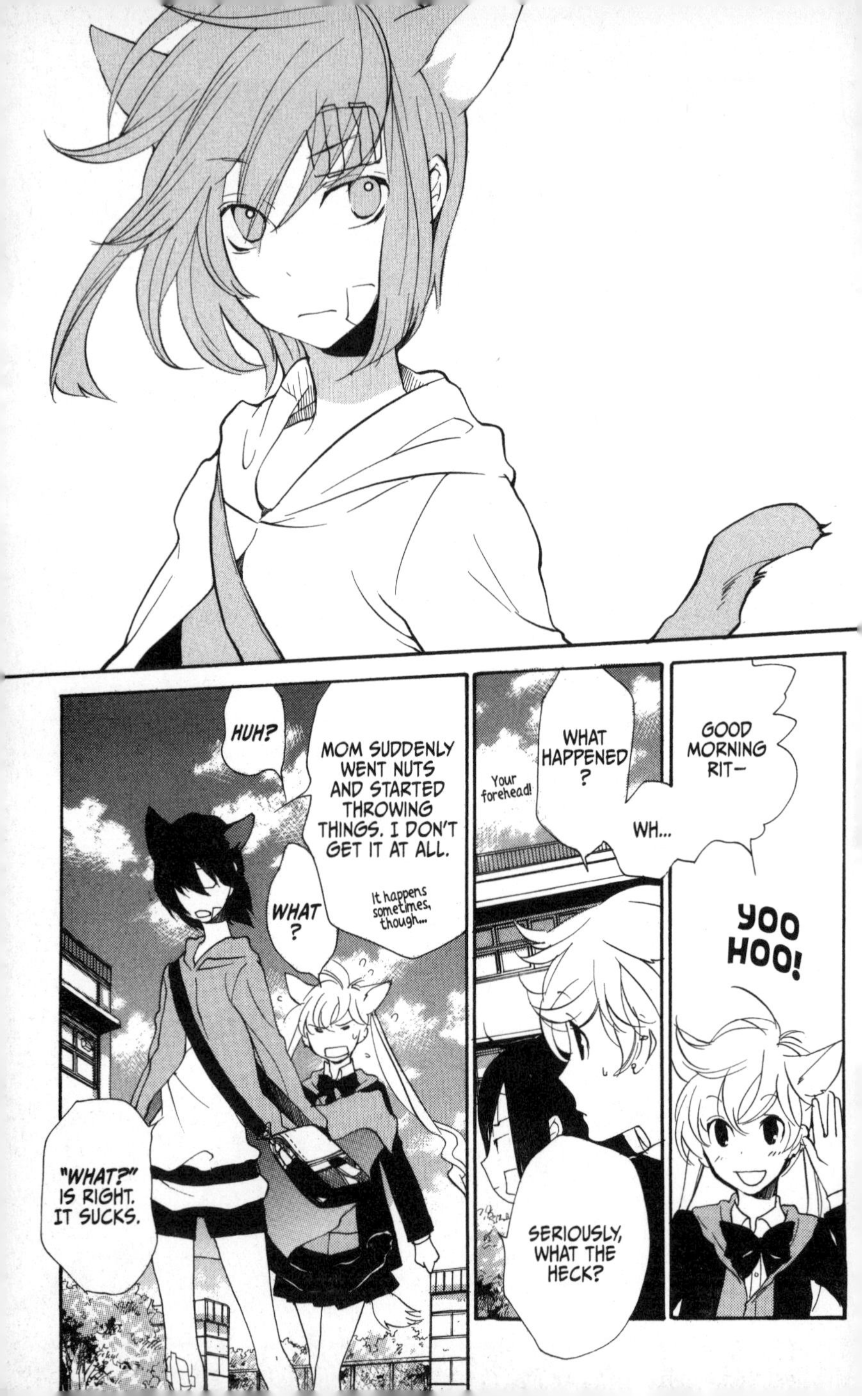

GOOD MORNING RIT—
YOO HOO!
WH...
WHAT HAPPENED?
Your forehead!
SERIOUSLY, WHAT THE HECK?
HUH?
MOM SUDDENLY WENT NUTS AND STARTED THROWING THINGS. I DON'T GET IT AT ALL.
It happens sometimes, though...
WHAT?
"WHAT?" IS RIGHT. IT SUCKS.

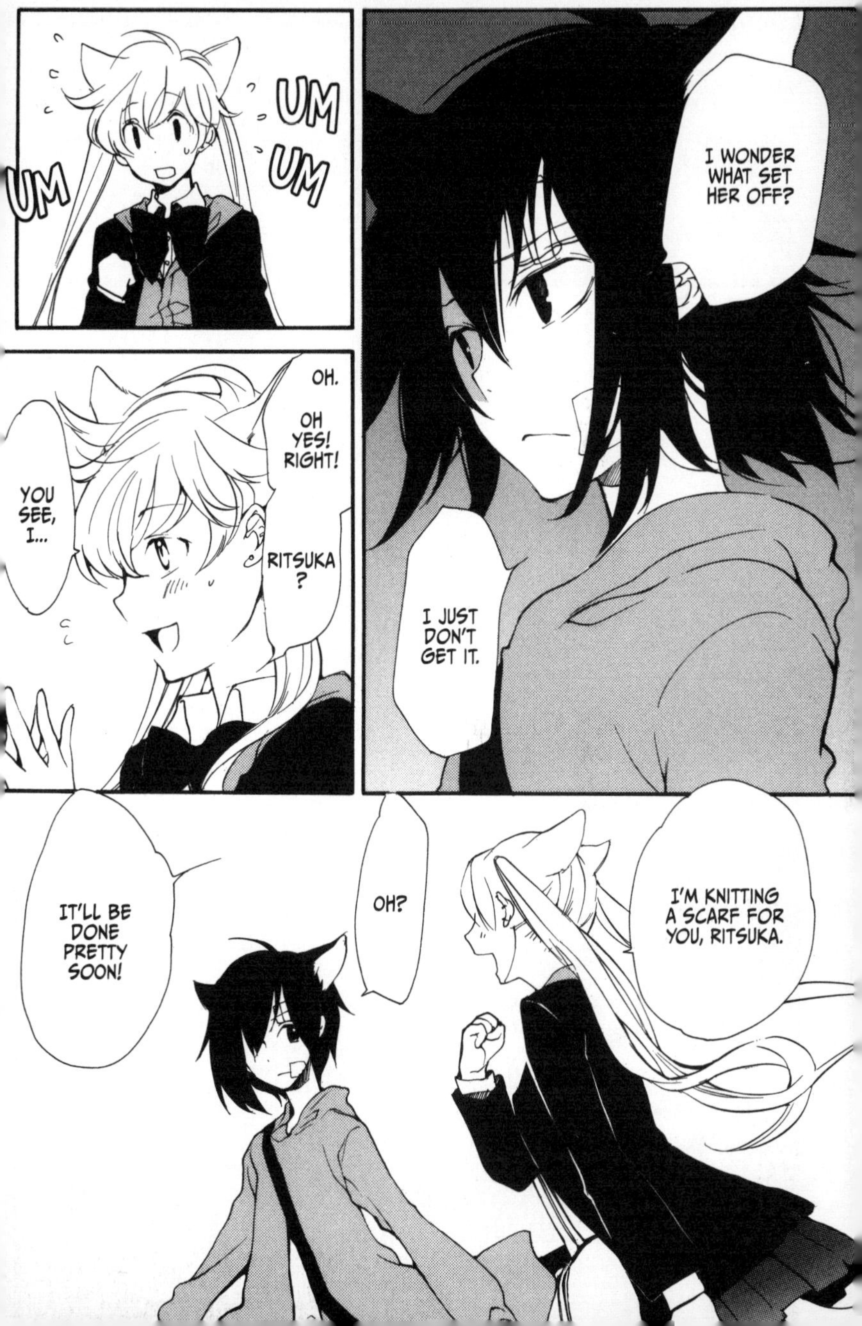
I WONDER WHAT SET HER OFF?
I JUST DON'T GET IT.
UM
UM
UM
OH.
OH YES! RIGHT!
RITSUKA?
YOU SEE, I...
I'M KNITTING A SCARF FOR YOU, RITSUKA.
OH?
IT'LL BE DONE PRETTY SOON!

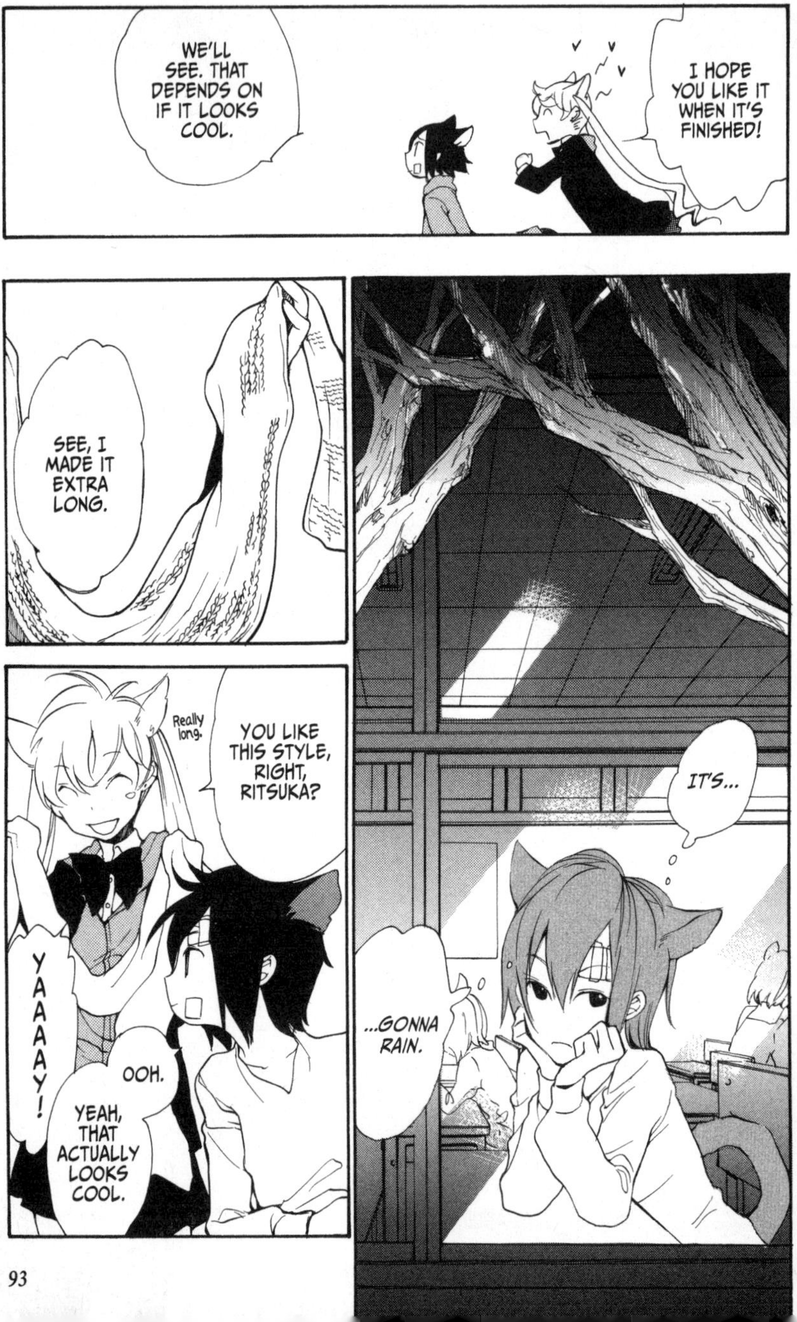
I HOPE YOU LIKE IT WHEN IT'S FINISHED!
WE'LL SEE. THAT DEPENDS ON IF IT LOOKS COOL.
IT'S...
...GONNA RAIN.
SEE, I MADE IT EXTRA LONG.
YOU LIKE THIS STYLE, RITSUKA?
Really long.
YAAAAAY!
OOH.
YEAH, THAT ACTUALLY LOOKS COOL.

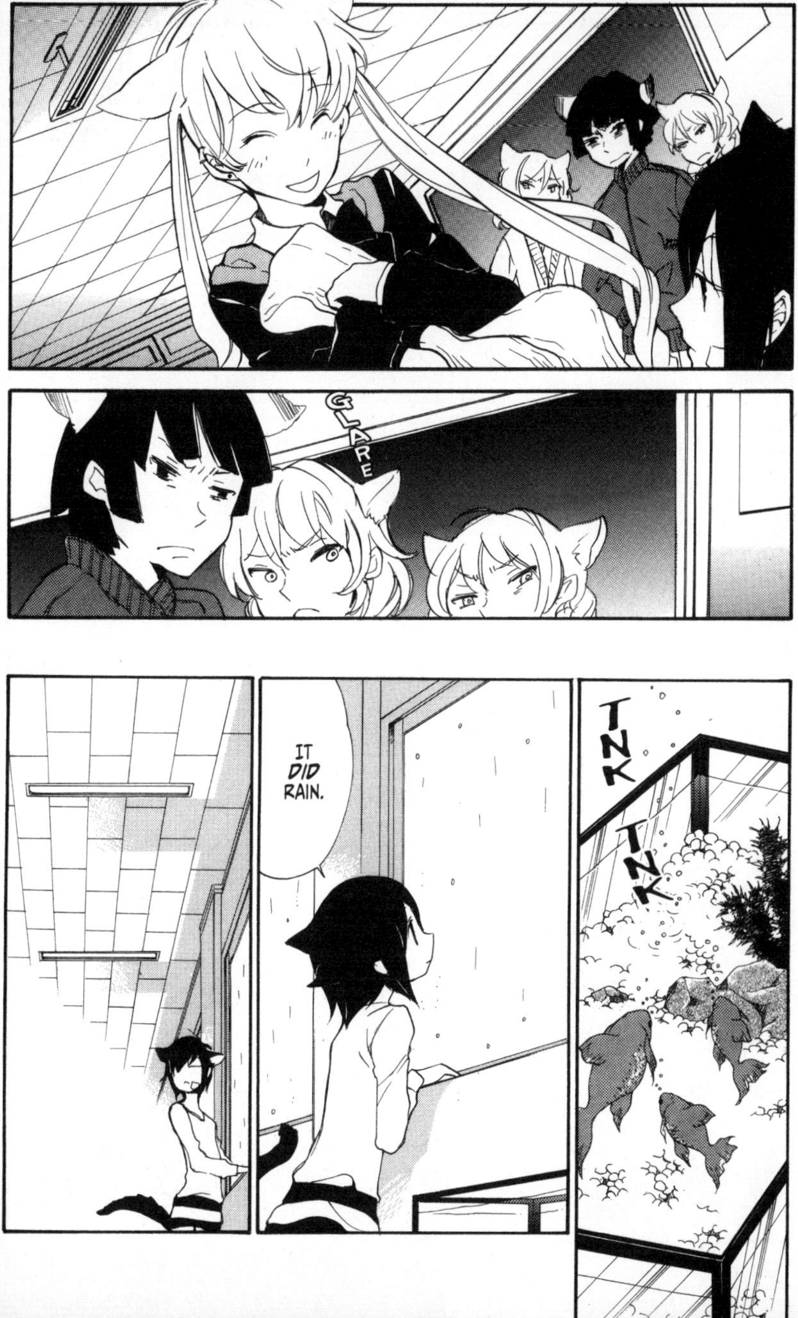
GLARE
TNK
TNK
IT DID RAIN.

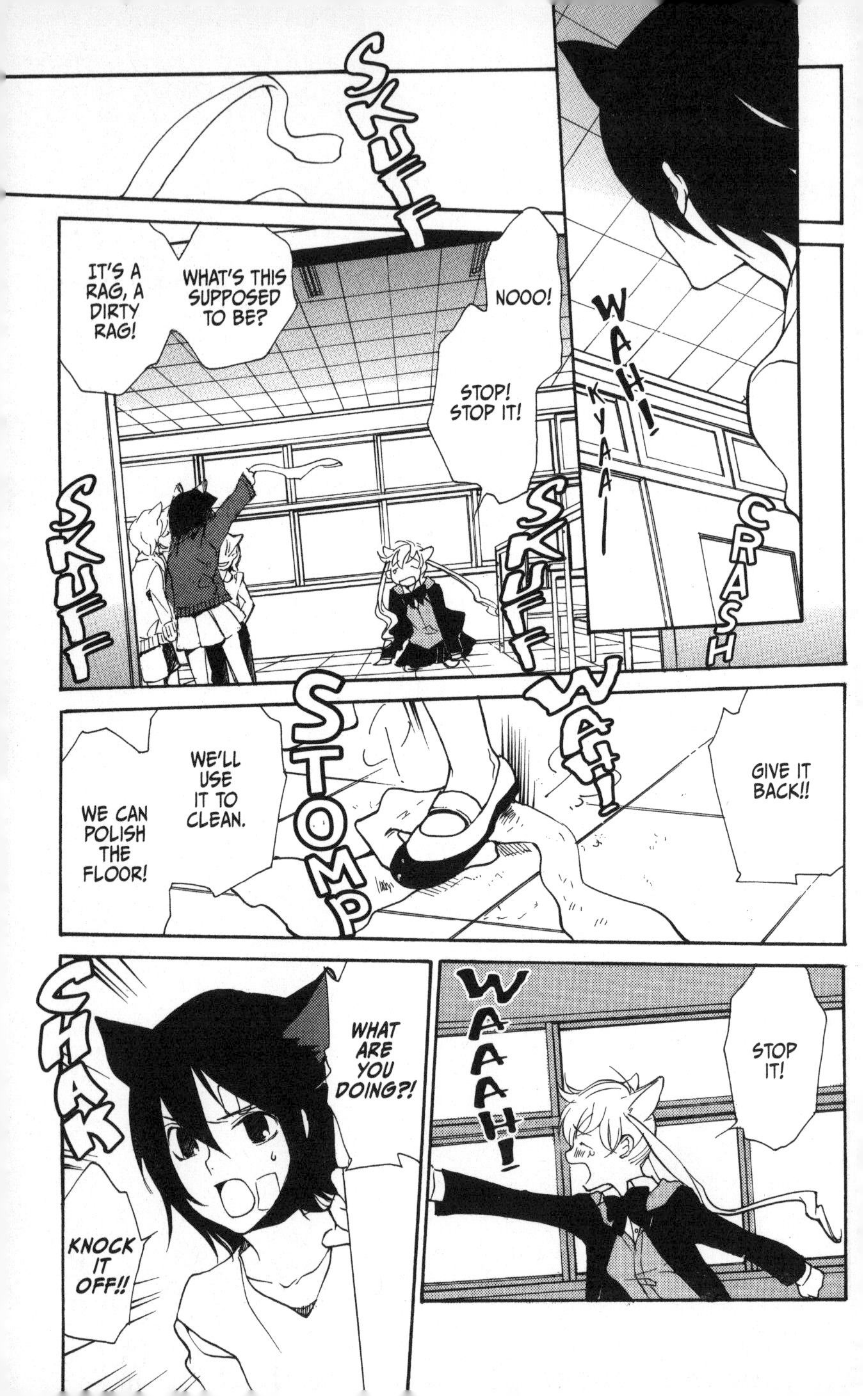
WAH!
KYAAA!
CRASH
SKUFF
NOOO!
STOP! STOP IT!
WHAT'S THIS SUPPOSED TO BE?
IT'S A RAG, A DIRTY RAG!
SKUFF
SKUFF
GIVE IT BACK!!
WAH!
STOMP
WE'LL USE IT TO CLEAN.
WE CAN POLISH THE FLOOR!
STOP IT!
WAAAH!
WHAT ARE YOU DOING?!
KNOCK IT OFF!!
CHAK

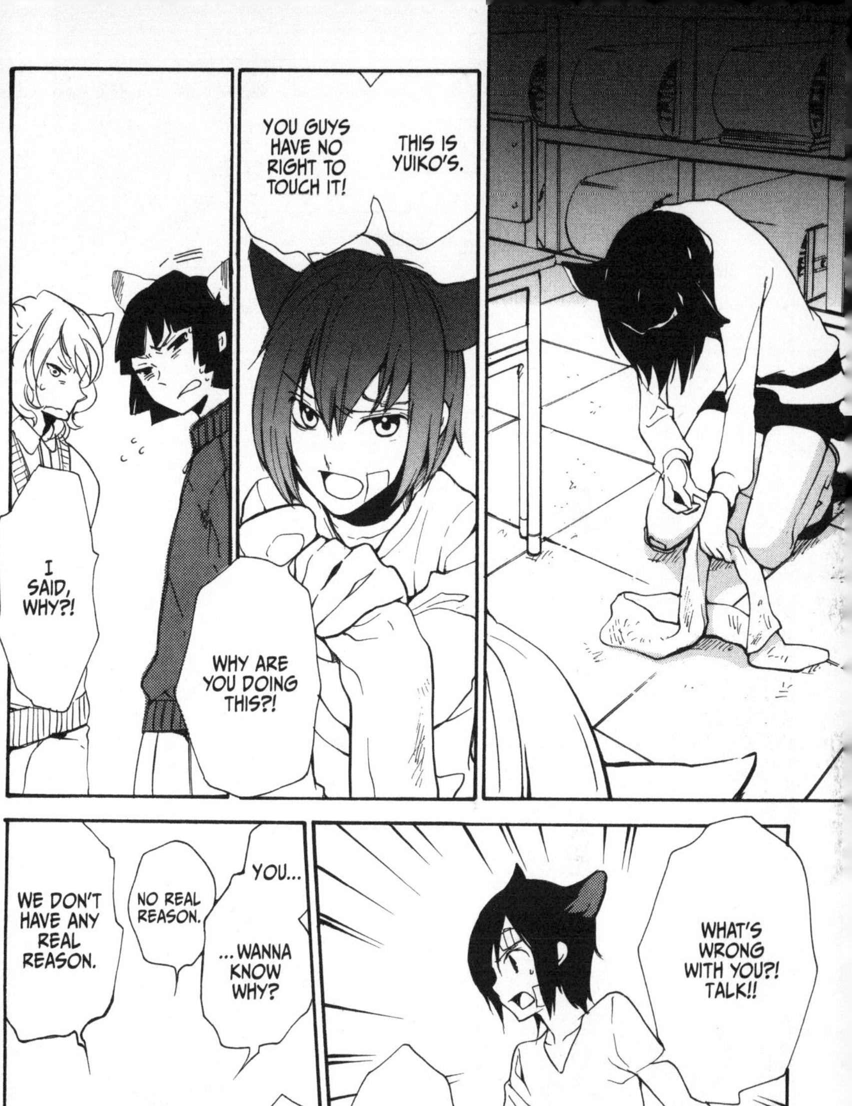
THIS IS YUIKO'S.
YOU GUYS HAVE NO RIGHT TO TOUCH IT!
WHY ARE YOU DOING THIS?!
I SAID, WHY?!
WHAT'S WRONG WITH YOU?! TALK!!
DON'T CLAM UP!
SAY SOMETHING!
YOU...
...WANNA KNOW WHY?
NO REAL REASON.
WE DON'T HAVE ANY REAL REASON.

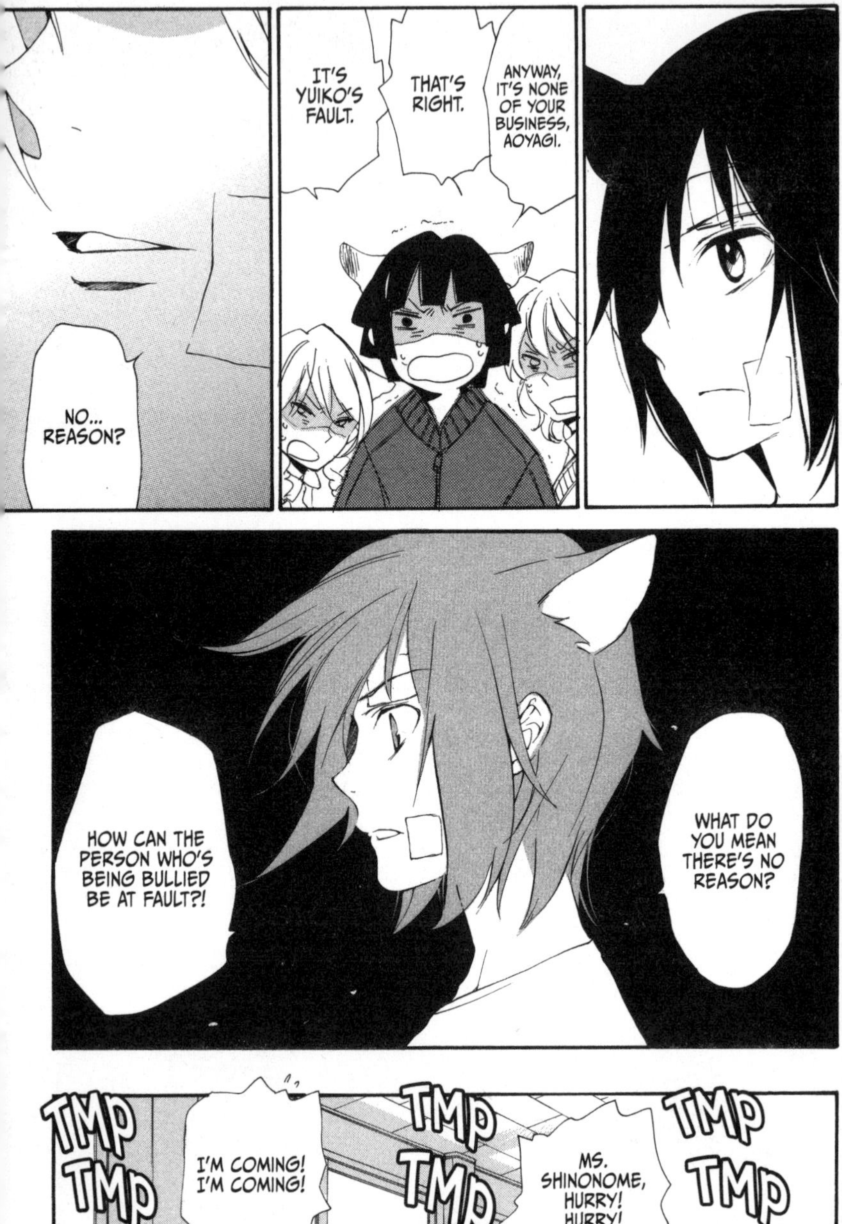
ANYWAY, IT'S NONE OF YOUR BUSINESS, AOYAGI.
THAT'S RIGHT.
IT'S YUIKO'S FAULT.
NO... REASON?
WHAT DO YOU MEAN THERE'S NO REASON?
HOW CAN THE PERSON WHO'S BEING BULLIED BE AT FAULT?!
TMP TMP
MS. SHINONOME, HURRY! HURRY!
TMP TMP
I'M COMING! I'M COMING!
TMP TMP

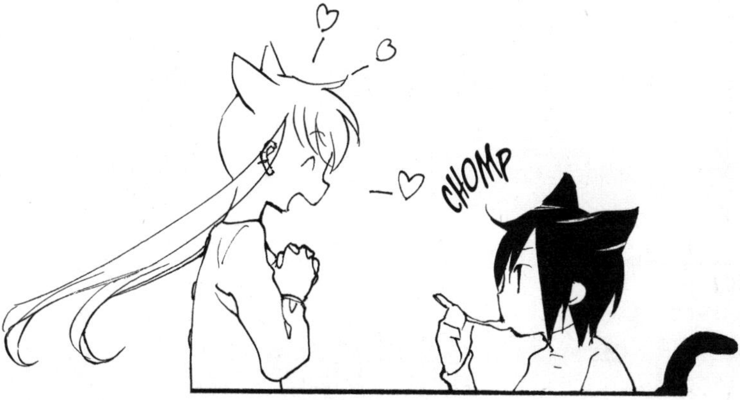
CHOMP

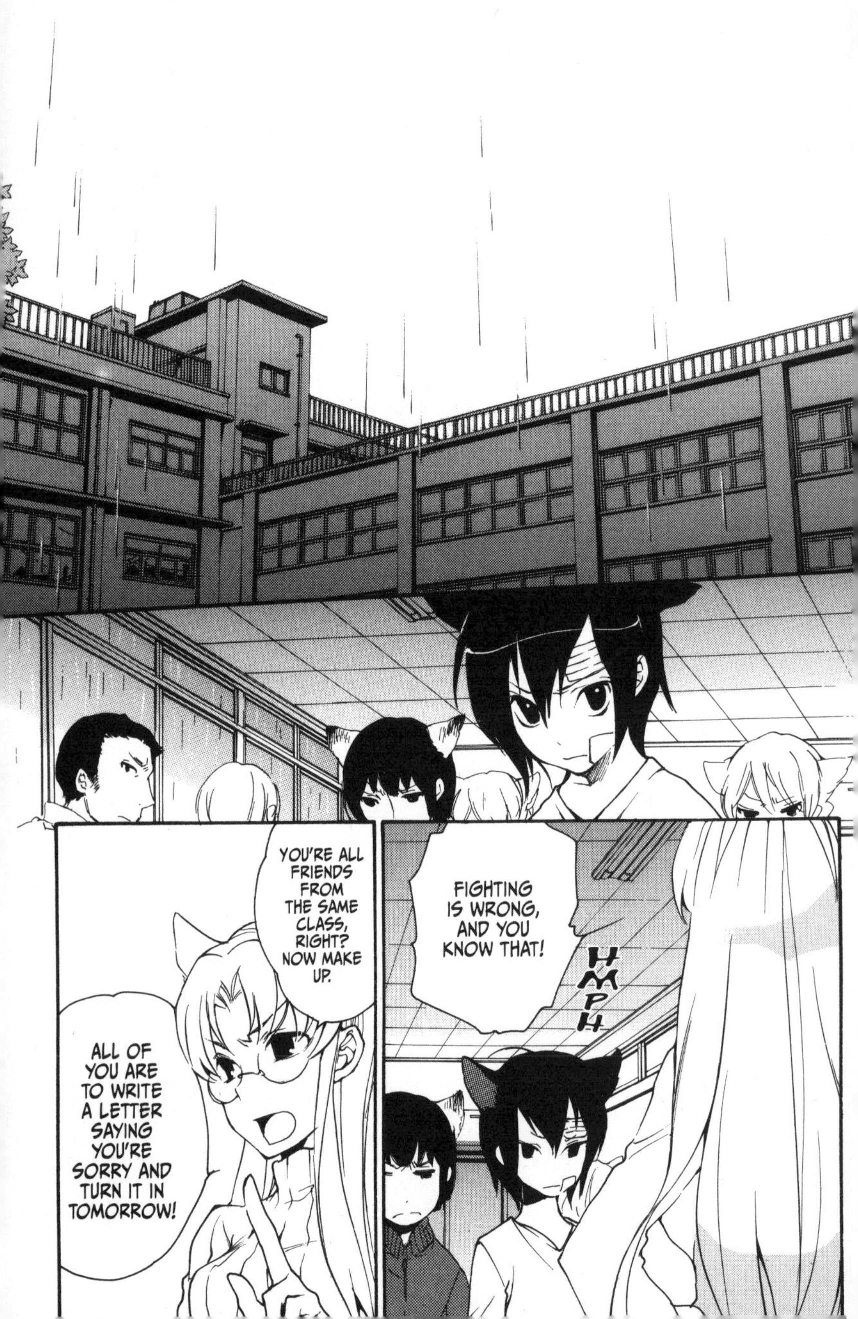
FIGHTING IS WRONG, AND YOU KNOW THAT!
HMPH
YOU'RE ALL FRIENDS FROM THE SAME CLASS, RIGHT? NOW MAKE UP.
ALL OF YOU ARE TO WRITE A LETTER SAYING YOU'RE SORRY AND TURN IT IN TOMORROW!

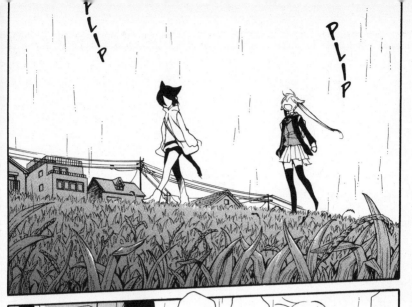

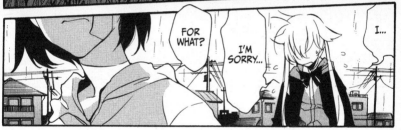

FOR WHAT?

I'M SORRY...

I...

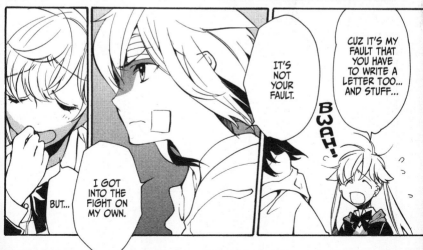

IT'S NOT YOUR FAULT.

CUZ IT'S MY FAULT THAT YOU HAVE TO WRITE A LETTER TOO... AND STUFF...

BWAH!

BUT...

I GOT INTO THE FIGHT ON MY OWN.

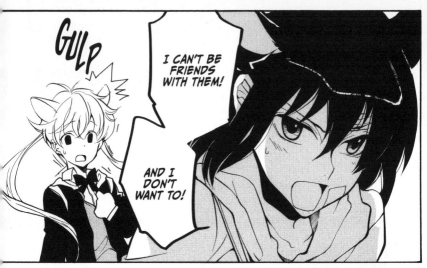

GULP

I CAN'T BE FRIENDS WITH THEM!

AND I DON'T WANT TO!

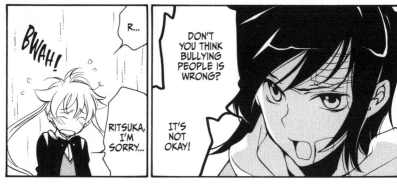

BWAH!

R...

RITSUKA, I'M SORRY...

DON'T YOU THINK BULLYING PEOPLE IS WRONG?

IT'S NOT OKAY!

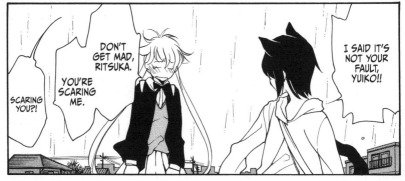

SCARING YOU?!

YOU'RE SCARING ME.

DON'T GET MAD, RITSUKA.

I SAID IT'S NOT YOUR FAULT, YUIKO!!

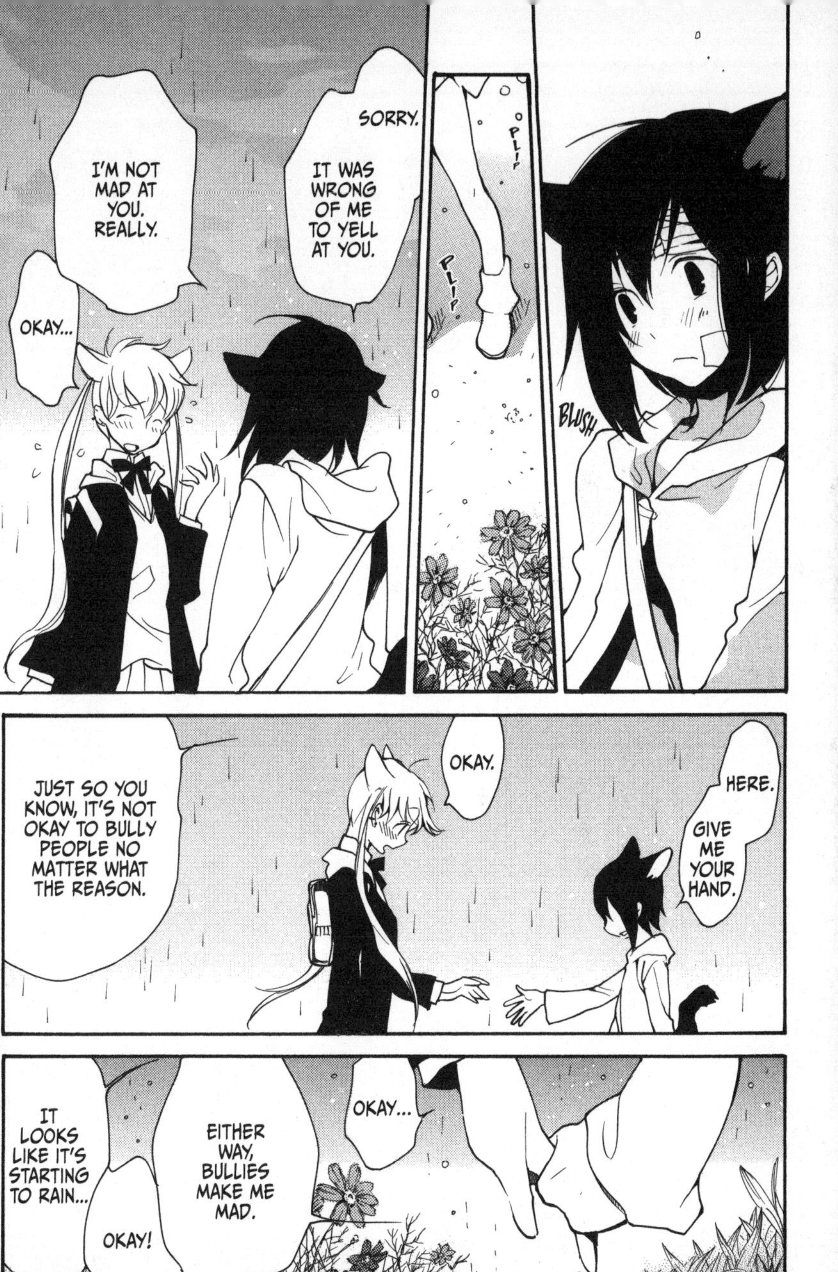
BLUSH
PLIP
PLIP
SORRY.
IT WAS WRONG OF ME TO YELL AT YOU.
I'M NOT MAD AT YOU. REALLY.
OKAY...
HERE.
GIVE ME YOUR HAND.
OKAY.
JUST SO YOU KNOW, IT'S NOT OKAY TO BULLY PEOPLE NO MATTER WHAT THE REASON.
OKAY...
EITHER WAY, BULLIES MAKE ME MAD.
IT LOOKS LIKE IT'S STARTING TO RAIN...
OKAY!

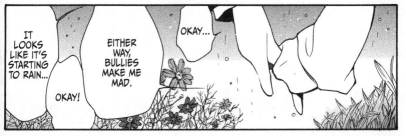

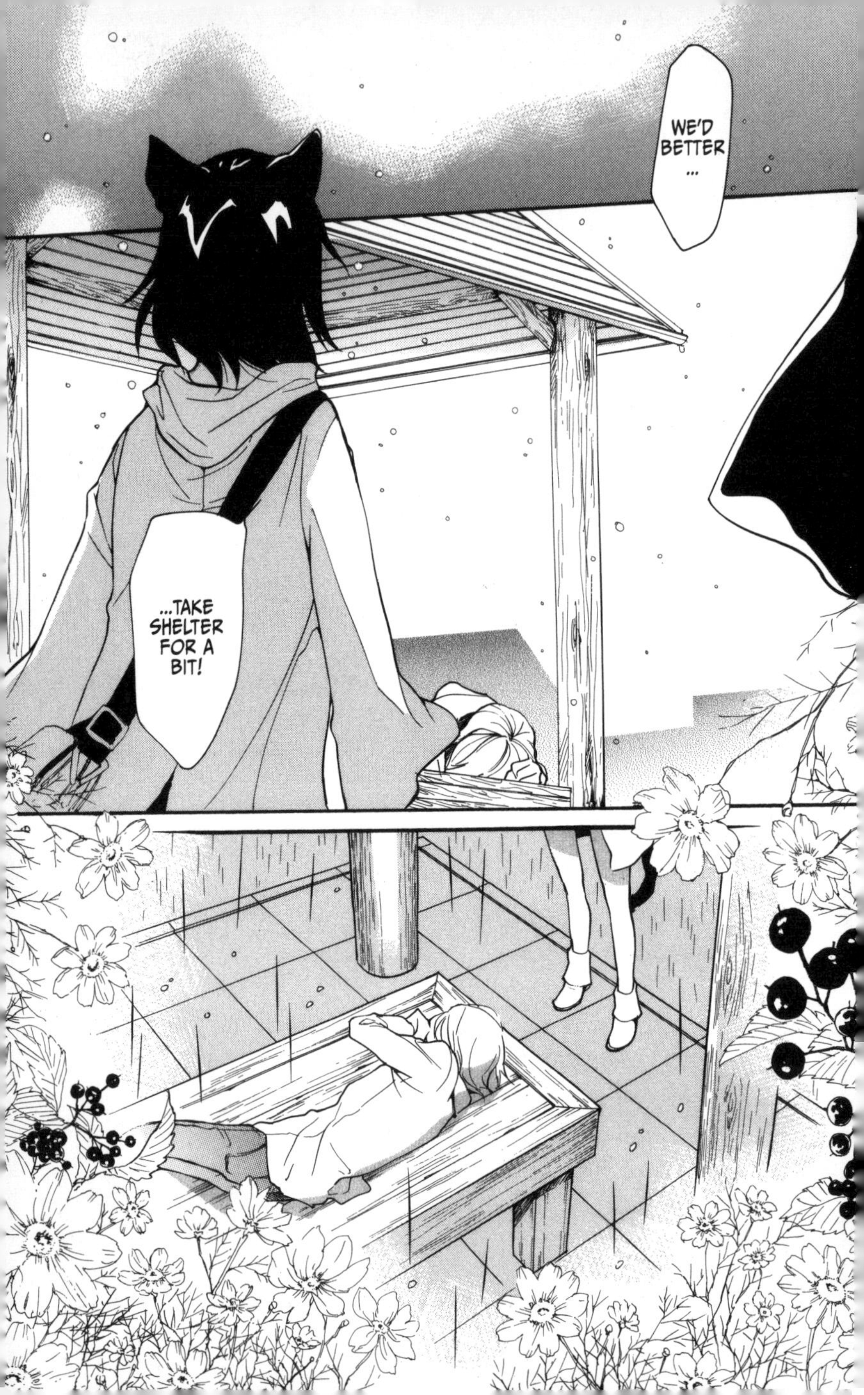
WE'D BETTER ...
...TAKE SHELTER FOR A BIT!

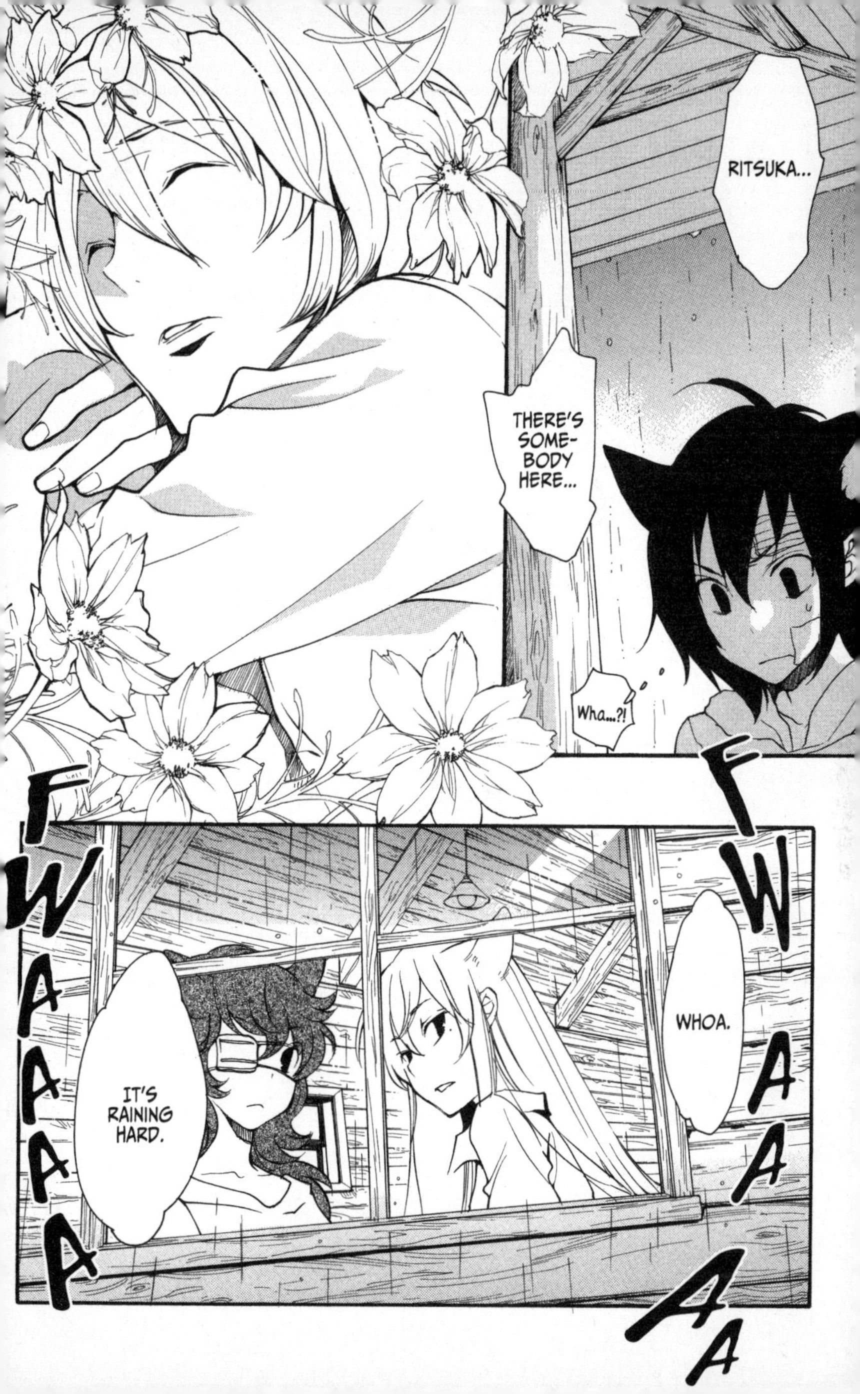
RITSUKA...
THERE'S SOME-BODY HERE...
Wha...?!
FWAAAAA
WHOA.
IT'S RAINING HARD.
FWAAAAA

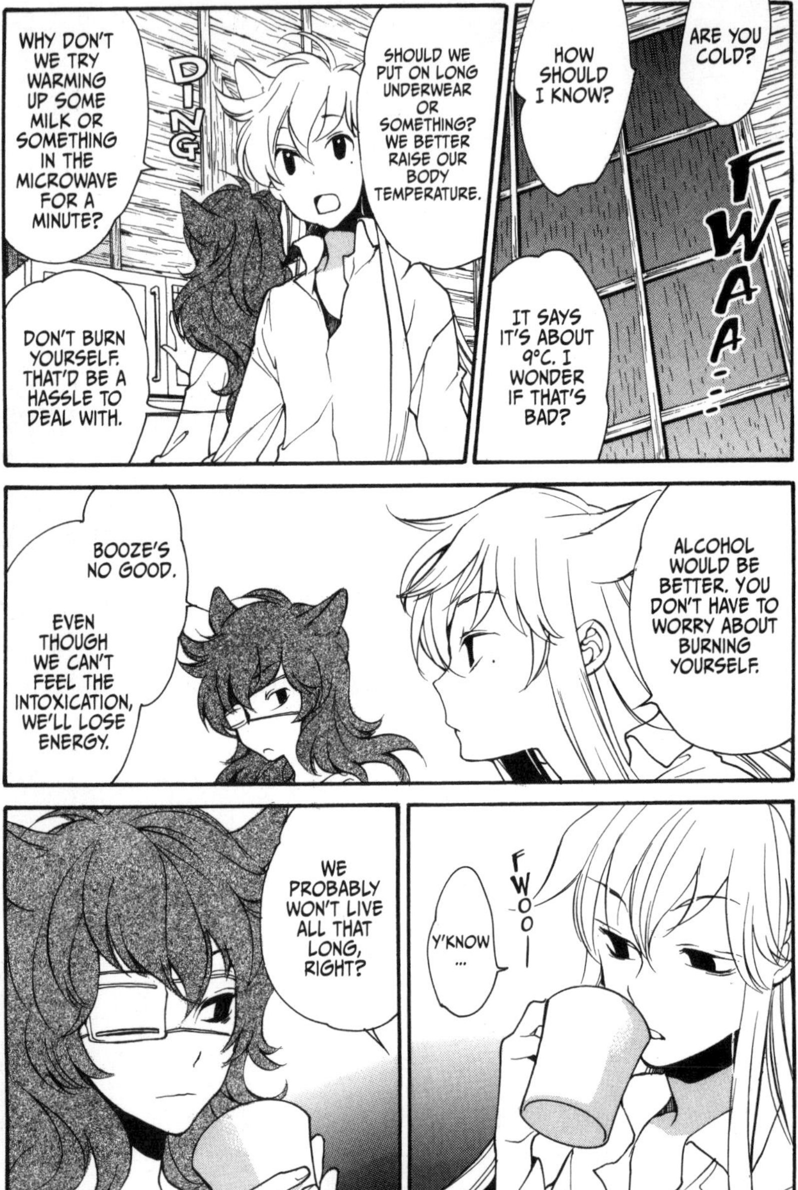
ARE YOU COLD?
HOW SHOULD I KNOW?
FWAA...
IT SAYS IT'S ABOUT 9°C. I WONDER IF THAT'S BAD?
SHOULD WE PUT ON LONG UNDERWEAR OR SOMETHING? WE BETTER RAISE OUR BODY TEMPERATURE.
DING
WHY DON'T WE TRY WARMING UP SOME MILK OR SOMETHING IN THE MICROWAVE FOR A MINUTE?
DON'T BURN YOURSELF. THAT'D BE A HASSLE TO DEAL WITH.
ALCOHOL WOULD BE BETTER. YOU DON'T HAVE TO WORRY ABOUT BURNING YOURSELF.
BOOZE'S NO GOOD.
EVEN THOUGH WE CAN'T FEEL THE INTOXICATION, WE'LL LOSE ENERGY.
FWOO
Y'KNOW ...
WE PROBABLY WON'T LIVE ALL THAT LONG, RIGHT?

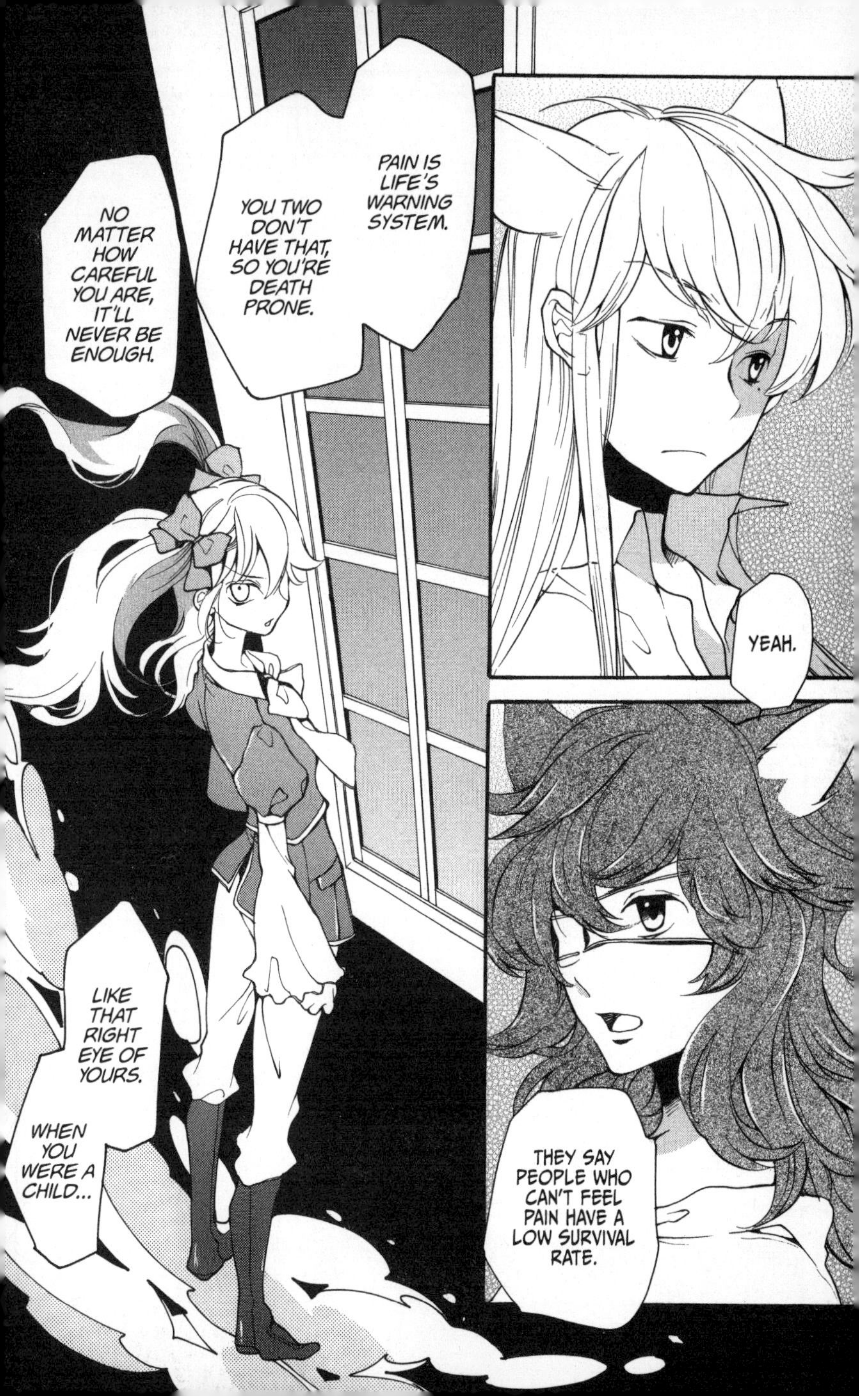
YEAH.
THEY SAY PEOPLE WHO CAN'T FEEL PAIN HAVE A LOW SURVIVAL RATE.
PAIN IS LIFE'S WARNING SYSTEM.
YOU TWO DON'T HAVE THAT, SO YOU'RE DEATH PRONE.
NO MATTER HOW CAREFUL YOU ARE, IT'LL NEVER BE ENOUGH.
LIKE THAT RIGHT EYE OF YOURS.
WHEN YOU WERE A CHILD...

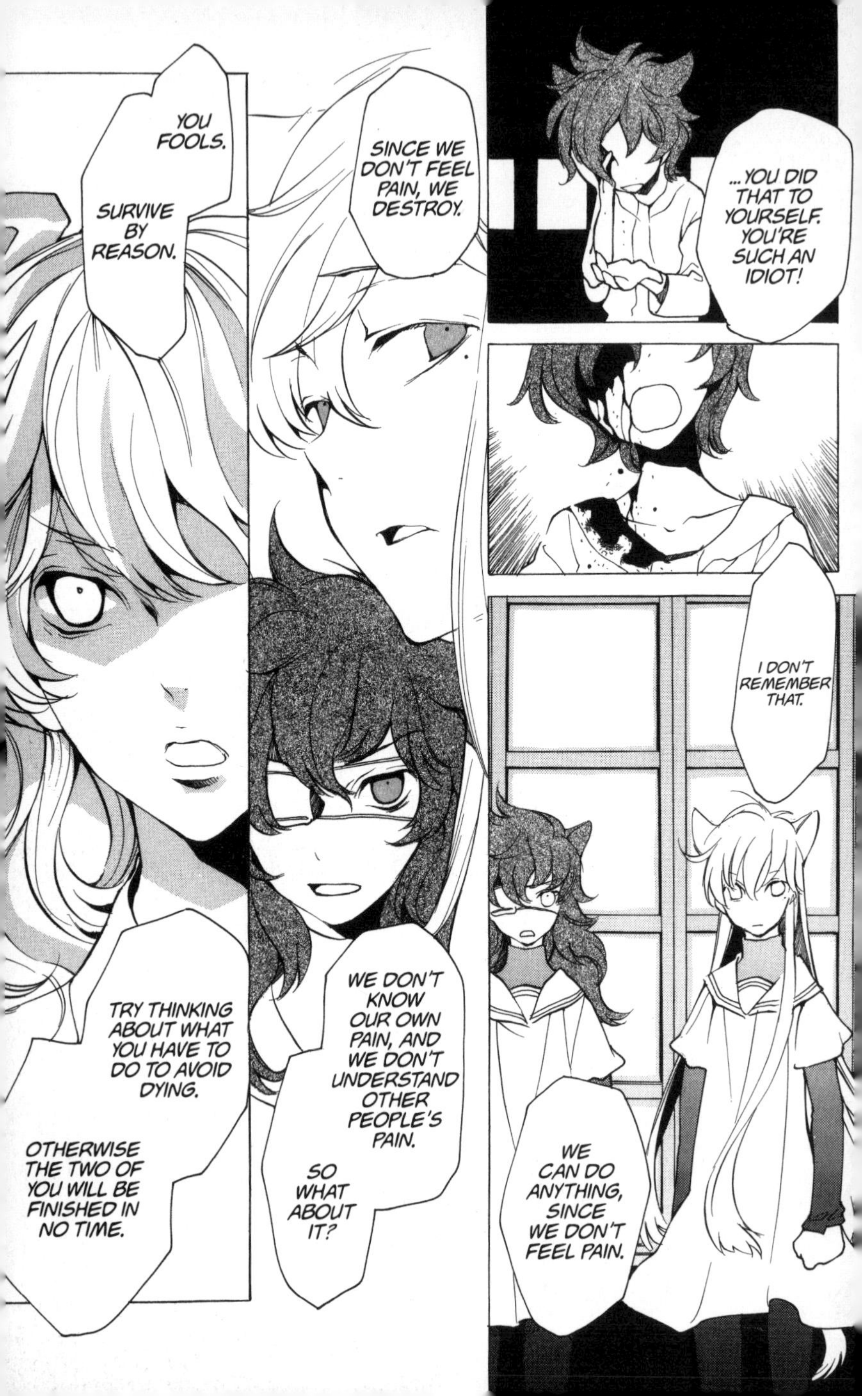
...YOU DID THAT TO YOURSELF. YOU'RE SUCH AN IDIOT!
I DON'T REMEMBER THAT.
WE CAN DO ANYTHING, SINCE WE DON'T FEEL PAIN.
SINCE WE DON'T FEEL PAIN, WE DESTROY.
WE DON'T KNOW OUR OWN PAIN, AND WE DON'T UNDERSTAND OTHER PEOPLE'S PAIN.
SO WHAT ABOUT IT?
YOU FOOLS.
SURVIVE BY REASON.
TRY THINKING ABOUT WHAT YOU HAVE TO DO TO AVOID DYING.
OTHERWISE THE TWO OF YOU WILL BE FINISHED IN NO TIME.

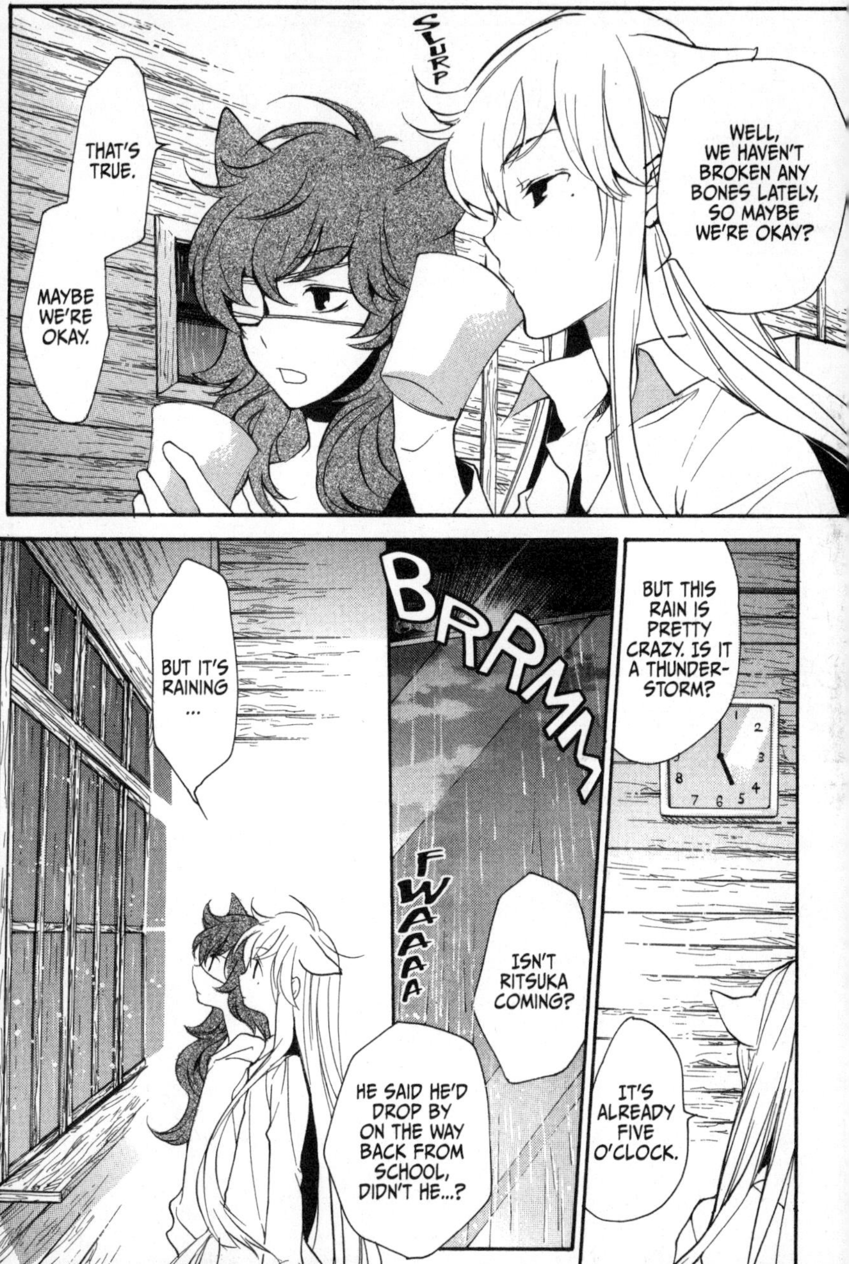
WELL, WE HAVEN'T BROKEN ANY BONES LATELY, SO MAYBE WE'RE OKAY?
SLURP
THAT'S TRUE.
MAYBE WE'RE OKAY.
BUT THIS RAIN IS PRETTY CRAZY. IS IT A THUNDER-STORM?
IT'S ALREADY FIVE O'CLOCK.
BRRMM
BUT IT'S RAINING...
FWAAAAA
ISN'T RITSUKA COMING?
HE SAID HE'D DROP BY ON THE WAY BACK FROM SCHOOL, DIDN'T HE...?

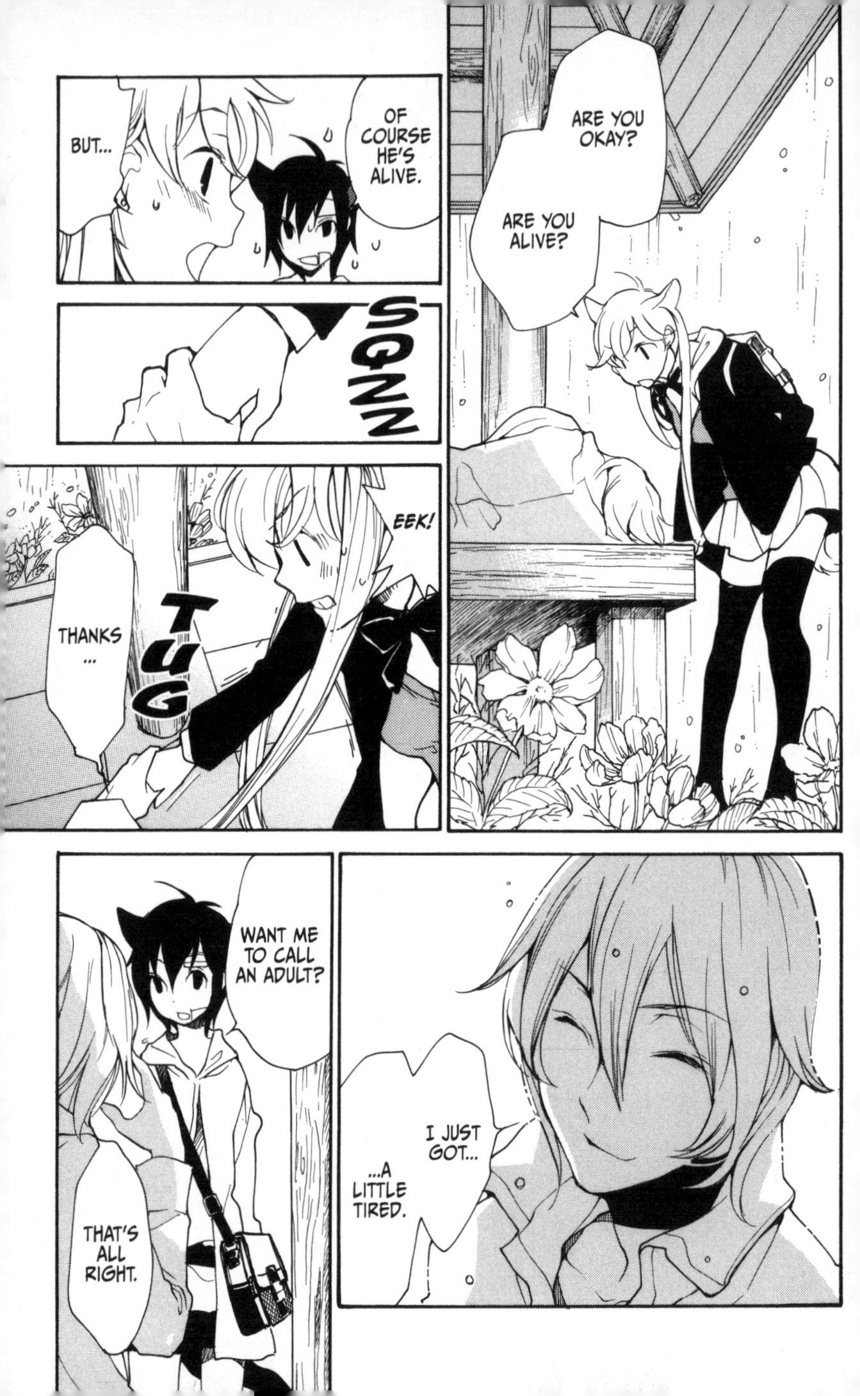
ARE YOU OKAY?
ARE YOU ALIVE?
OF COURSE HE'S ALIVE.
BUT...
SQNN
EEK!
TUG
THANKS...
I JUST GOT...
...A LITTLE TIRED.
WANT ME TO CALL AN ADULT?
THAT'S ALL RIGHT.

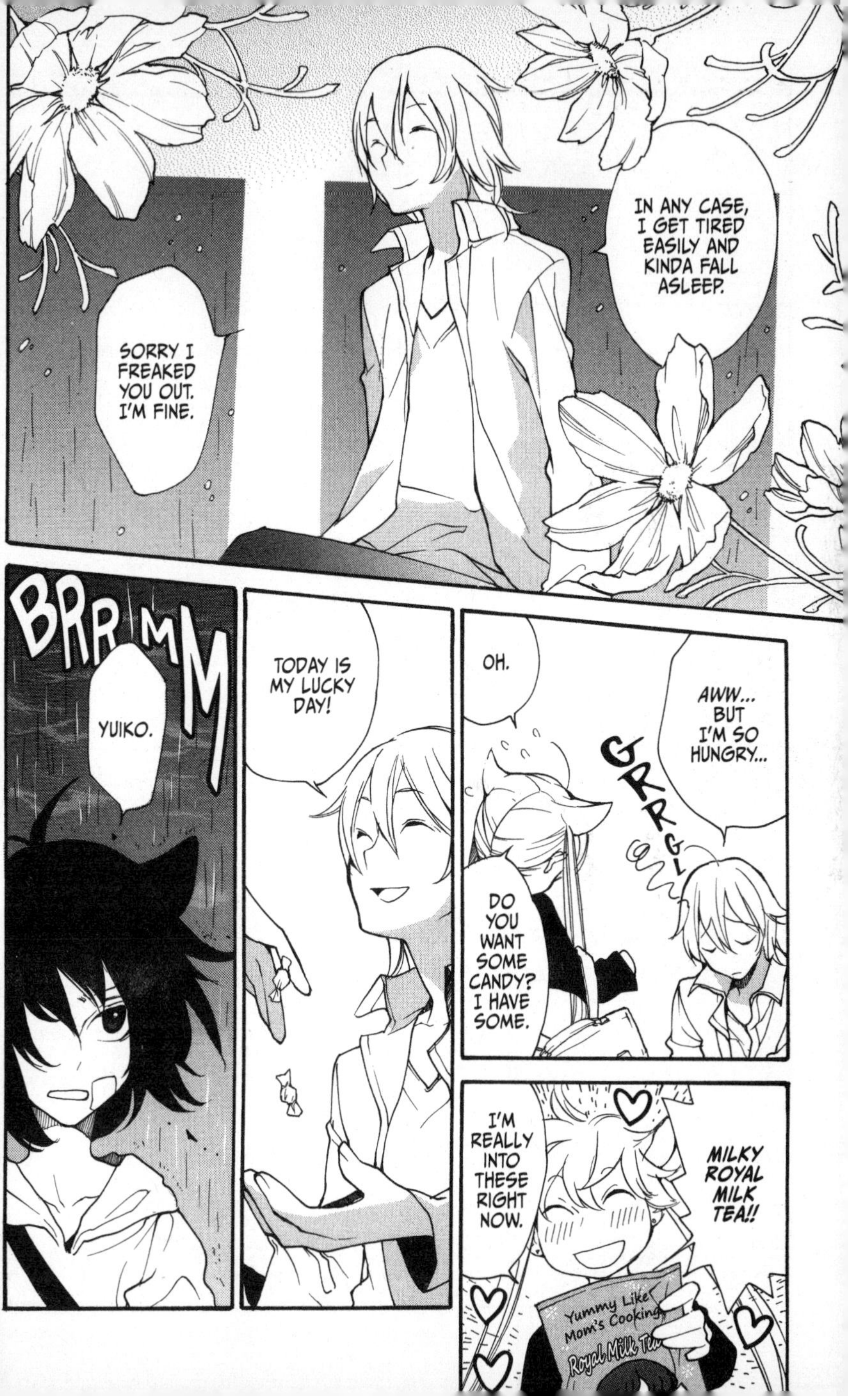
IN ANY CASE, I GET TIRED EASILY AND KINDA FALL ASLEEP.
SORRY I FREAKED YOU OUT. I'M FINE.
AWW... BUT I'M SO HUNGRY...
GRRRGL
OH.
DO YOU WANT SOME CANDY? I HAVE SOME.
MILKY ROYAL MILK TEA!!
I'M REALLY INTO THESE RIGHT NOW.
Yummy Like Mom's Cooking
Royal Milk Tea
TODAY IS MY LUCKY DAY!
BRRMMM
YUIKO.

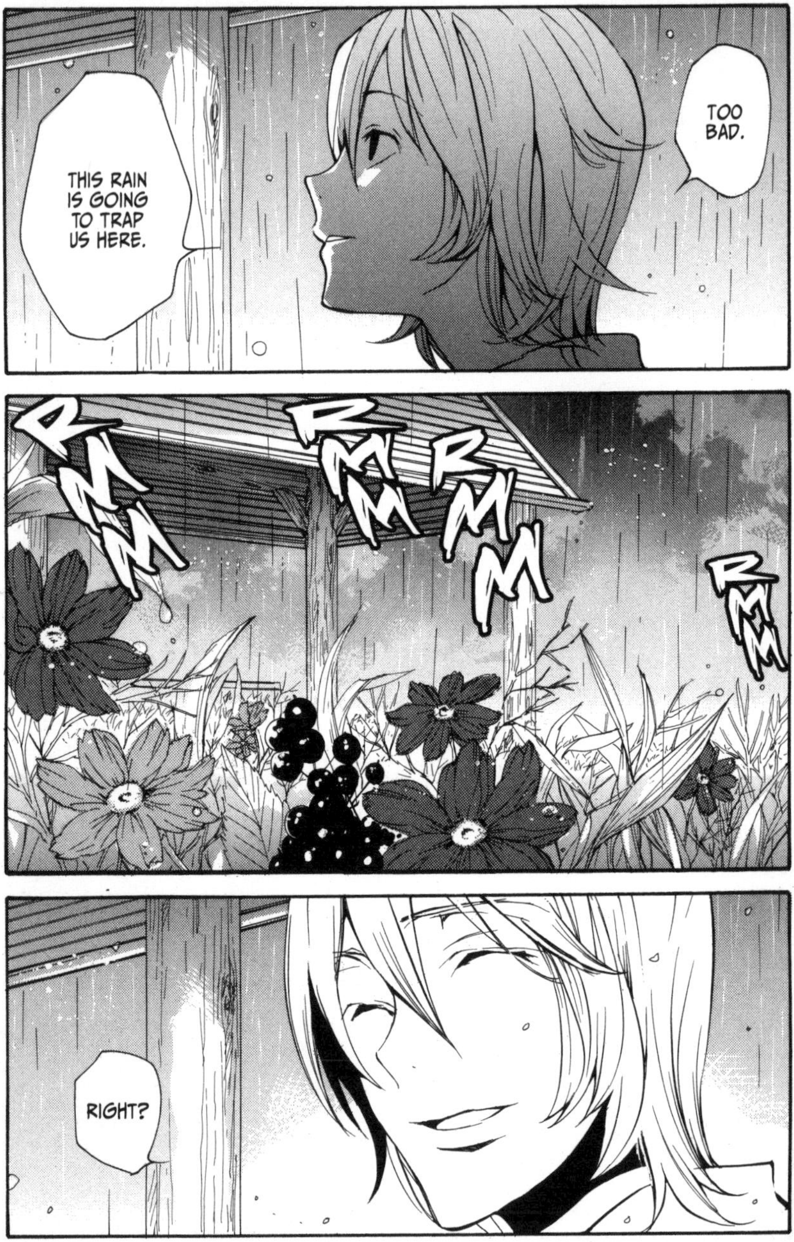
TOO BAD.
THIS RAIN IS GOING TO TRAP US HERE.
RMM
RMMM
RMM
RMMM
RIGHT?

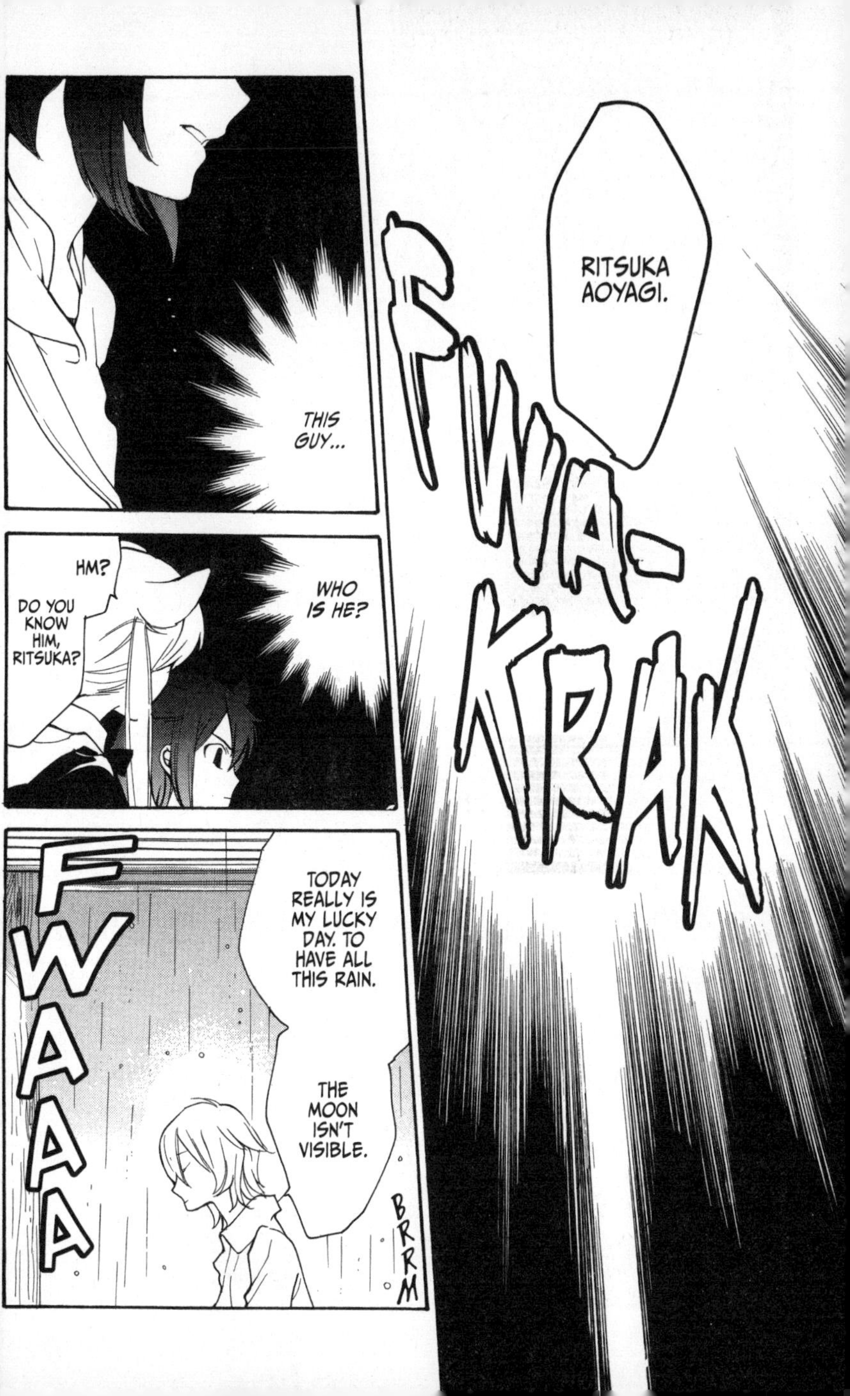
RITSUKA AOYAGI.
FWA-KRAK
THIS GUY...
WHO IS HE?
HM?
DO YOU KNOW HIM, RITSUKA?
TODAY REALLY IS MY LUCKY DAY. TO HAVE ALL THIS RAIN.
THE MOON ISN'T VISIBLE.
BRRM
FWAAAA

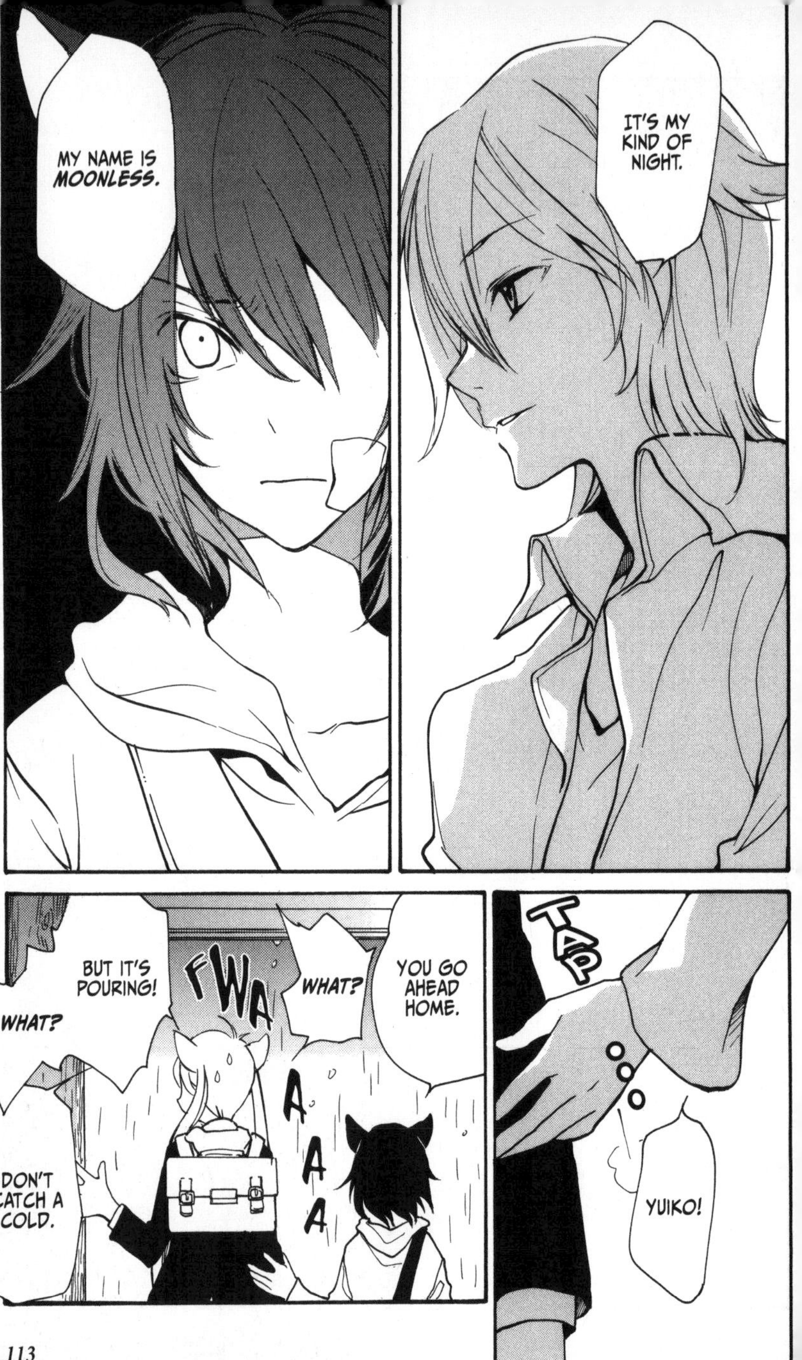
IT'S MY KIND OF NIGHT.
MY NAME IS *MOONLESS.*
TAP
YUIKO!
YOU GO AHEAD HOME.
WHAT?
FWAAAA
BUT IT'S POURING!
WHAT?
DON'T CATCH A COLD.

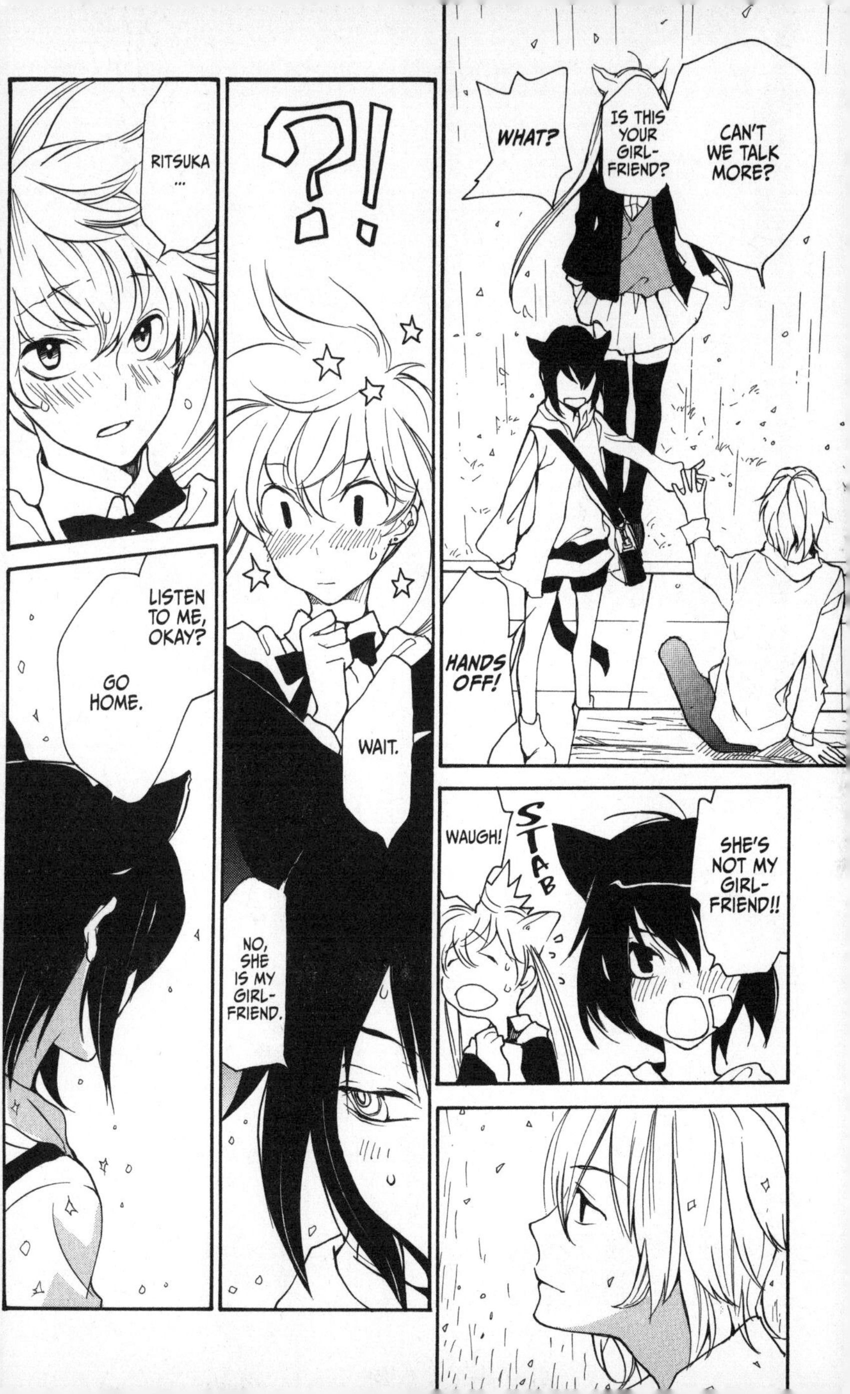
CAN'T WE TALK MORE?
IS THIS YOUR GIRL-FRIEND?
WHAT?
HANDS OFF!
SHE'S NOT MY GIRL-FRIEND!!
STAB
WAUGH!
?!
WAIT.
NO, SHE IS MY GIRL-FRIEND.
RITSUKA ...
LISTEN TO ME, OKAY?
GO HOME.

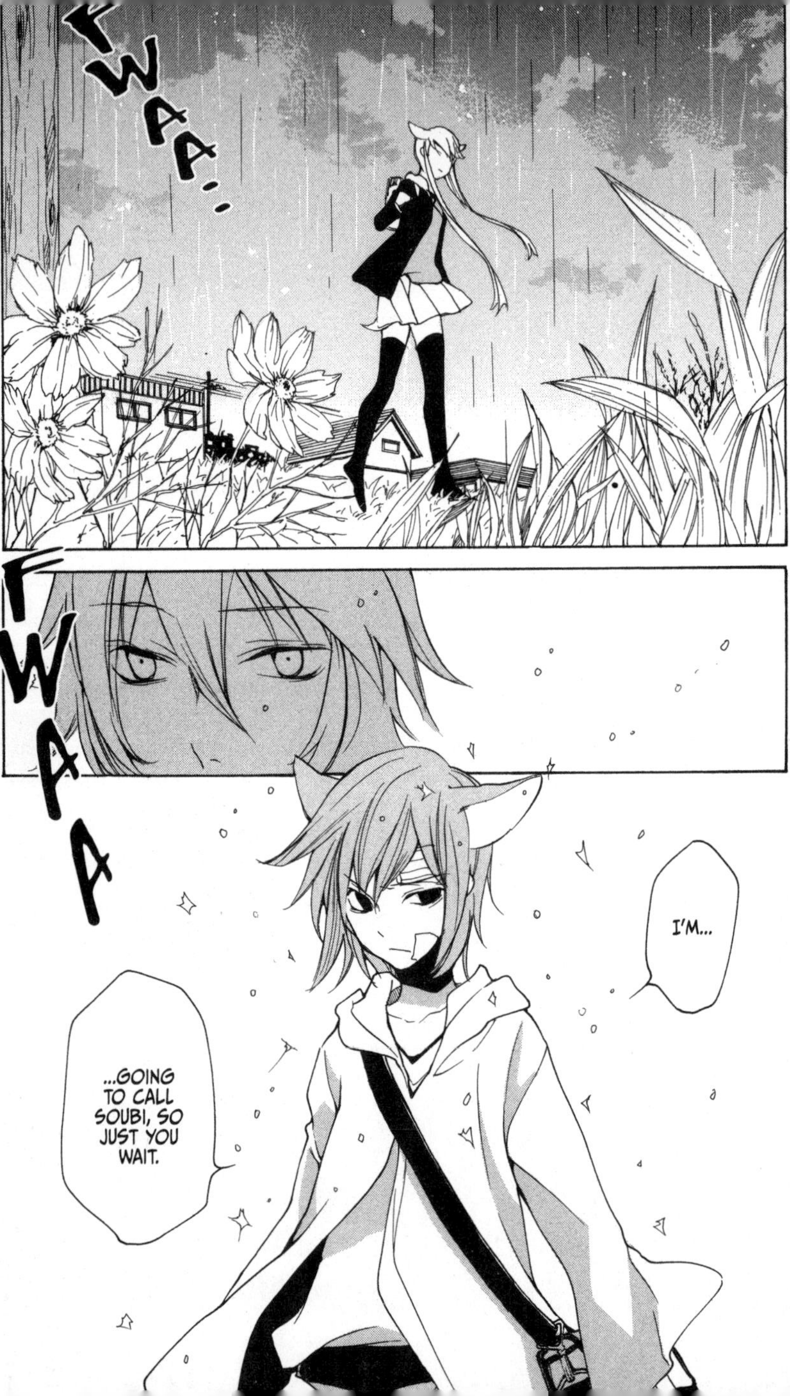
FWAA...
FWAA
I'M...
...GOING TO CALL SOUBI, SO JUST YOU WAIT.

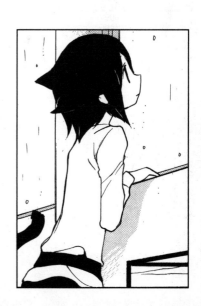

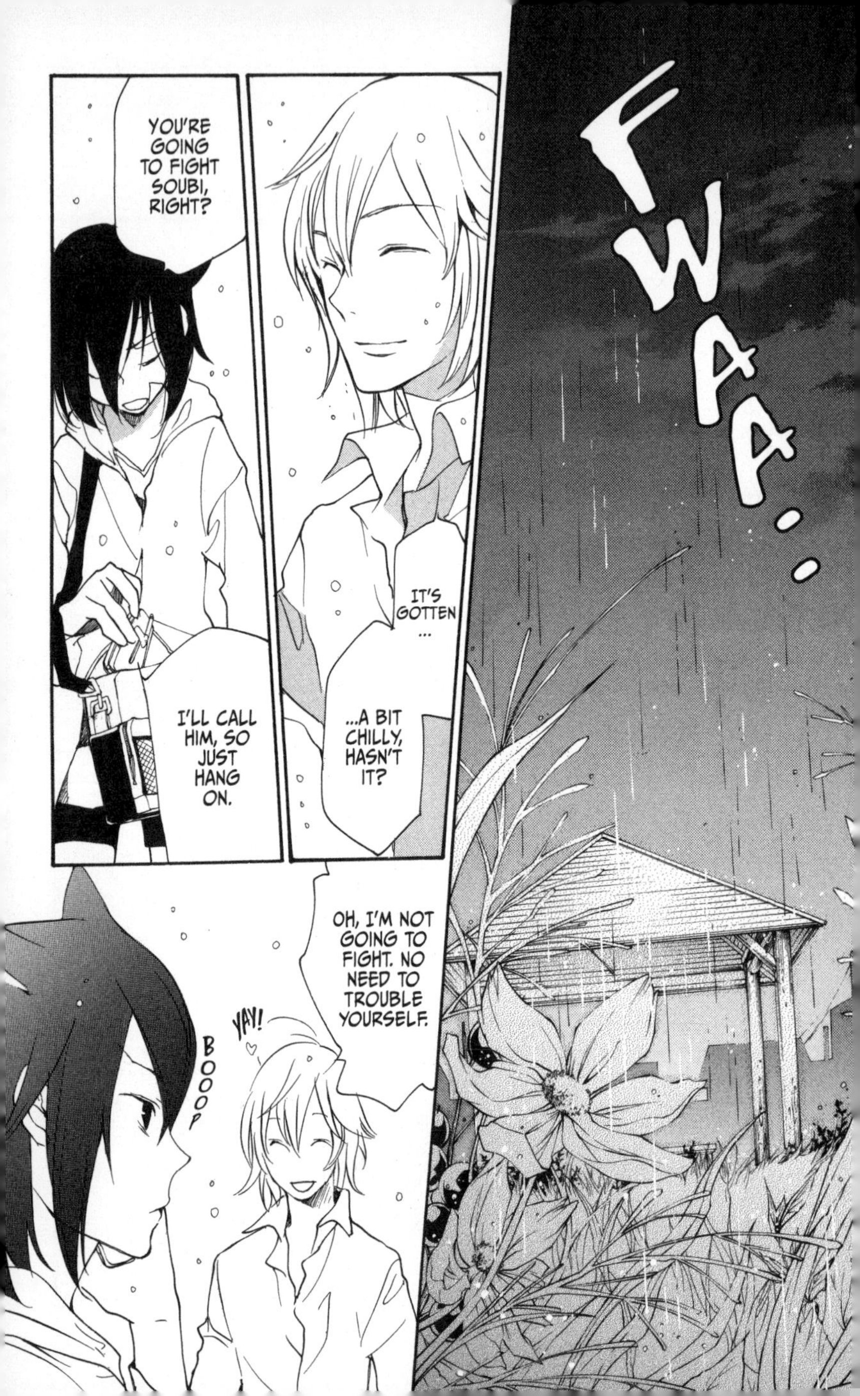
FWAA...
IT'S GOTTEN...
...A BIT CHILLY, HASN'T IT?
YOU'RE GOING TO FIGHT SOUBI, RIGHT?
I'LL CALL HIM, SO JUST HANG ON.
OH, I'M NOT GOING TO FIGHT. NO NEED TO TROUBLE YOURSELF.
YAY!
BOOOP

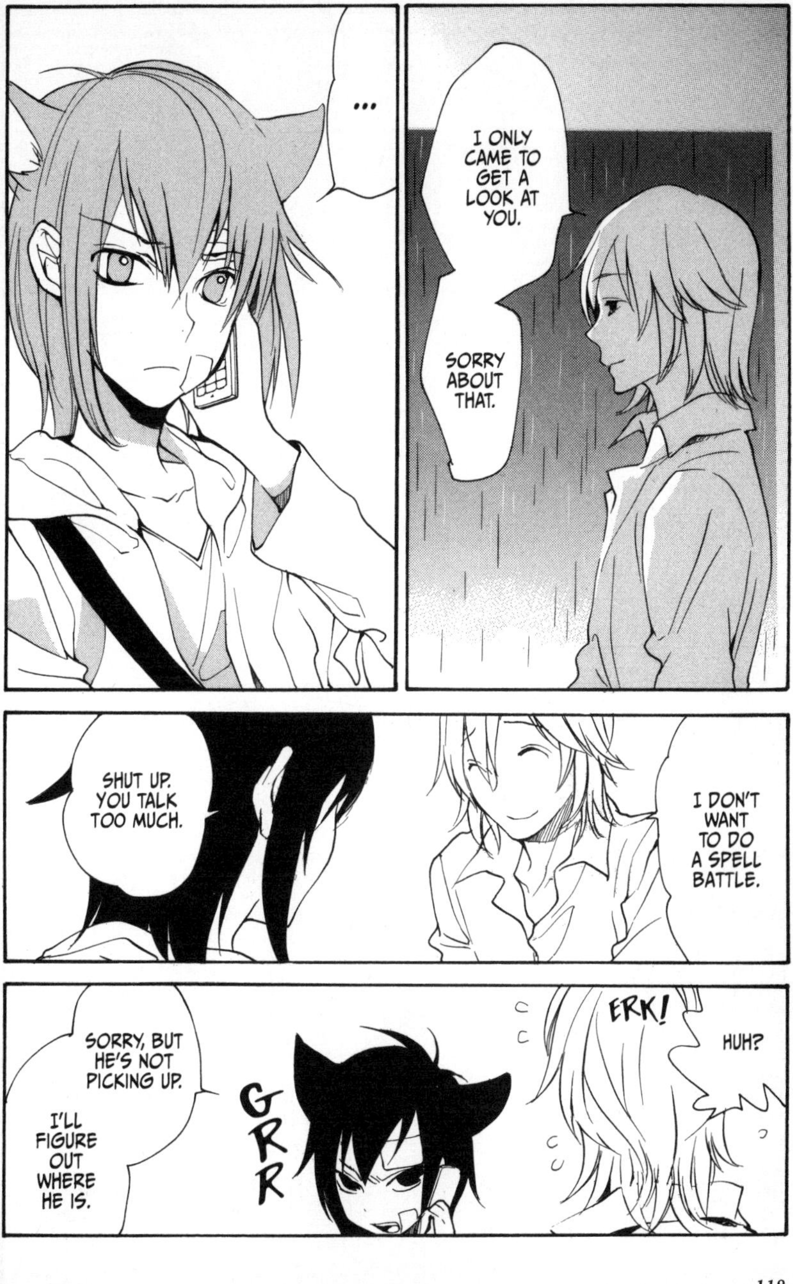
I ONLY CAME TO GET A LOOK AT YOU.
SORRY ABOUT THAT.
...
I DON'T WANT TO DO A SPELL BATTLE.
SHUT UP. YOU TALK TOO MUCH.
HUH?
ERK!
GRR
SORRY, BUT HE'S NOT PICKING UP.
I'LL FIGURE OUT WHERE HE IS.

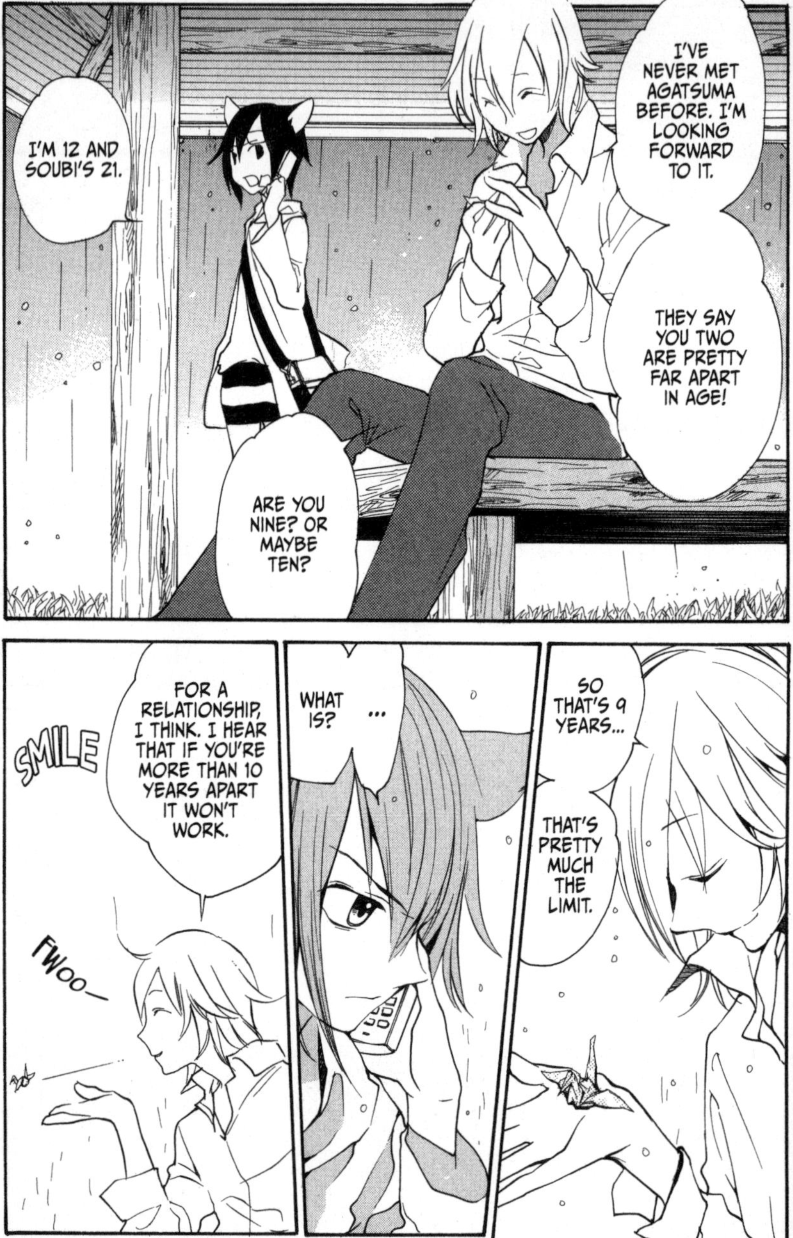
I'VE NEVER MET AGATSUMA BEFORE. I'M LOOKING FORWARD TO IT.
THEY SAY YOU TWO ARE PRETTY FAR APART IN AGE!
ARE YOU NINE? OR MAYBE TEN?
I'M 12 AND SOUBI'S 21.
SO THAT'S 9 YEARS...
THAT'S PRETTY MUCH THE LIMIT.
...
WHAT IS?
FOR A RELATIONSHIP, I THINK. I HEAR THAT IF YOU'RE MORE THAN 10 YEARS APART IT WON'T WORK.
SMILE
FWOO-

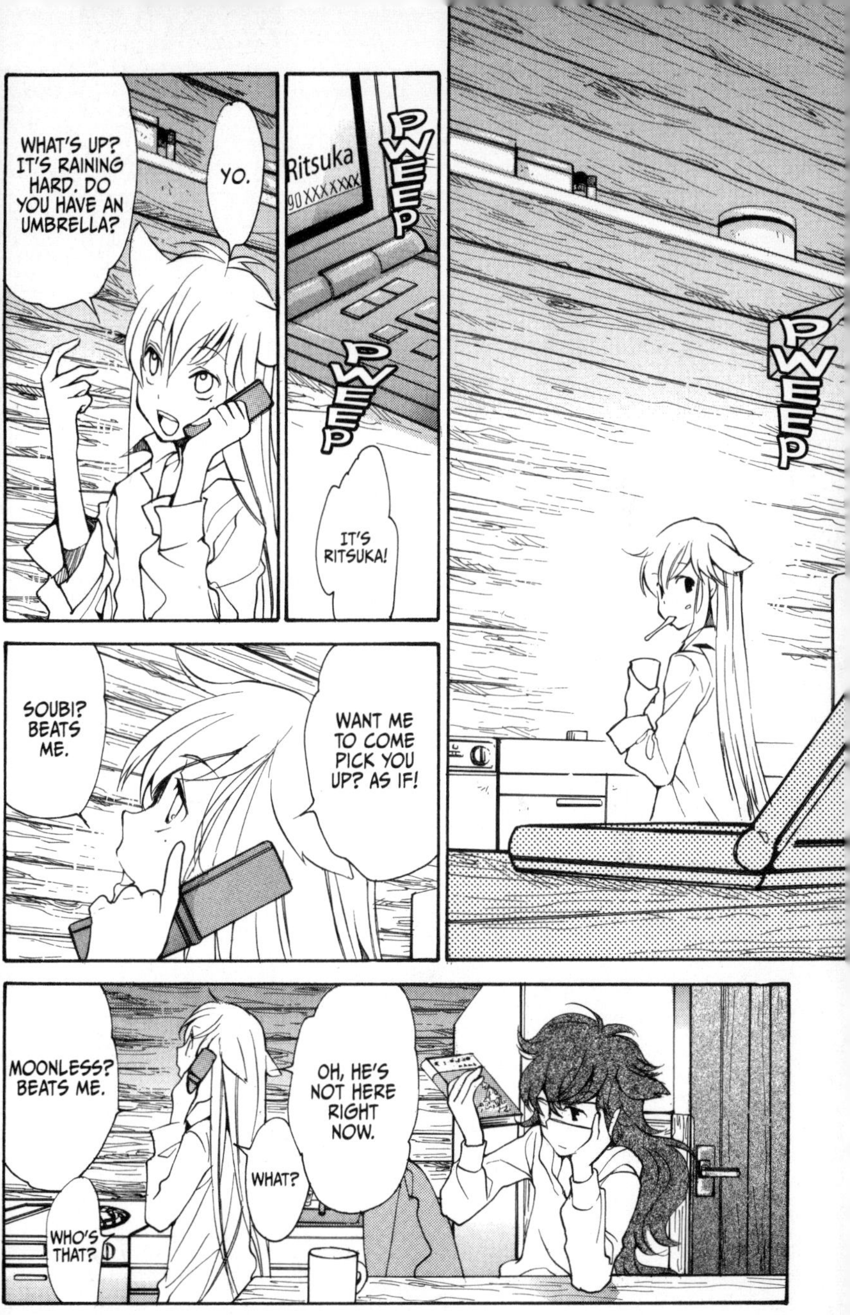
PWEEP
Ritsuka
90XXXXXXX
PWEEP
PWEEP
IT'S RITSUKA!
YO.
WHAT'S UP? IT'S RAINING HARD. DO YOU HAVE AN UMBRELLA?
WANT ME TO COME PICK YOU UP? AS IF!
SOUBI? BEATS ME.
OH, HE'S NOT HERE RIGHT NOW.
MOONLESS? BEATS ME.
WHAT?
WHO'S THAT?

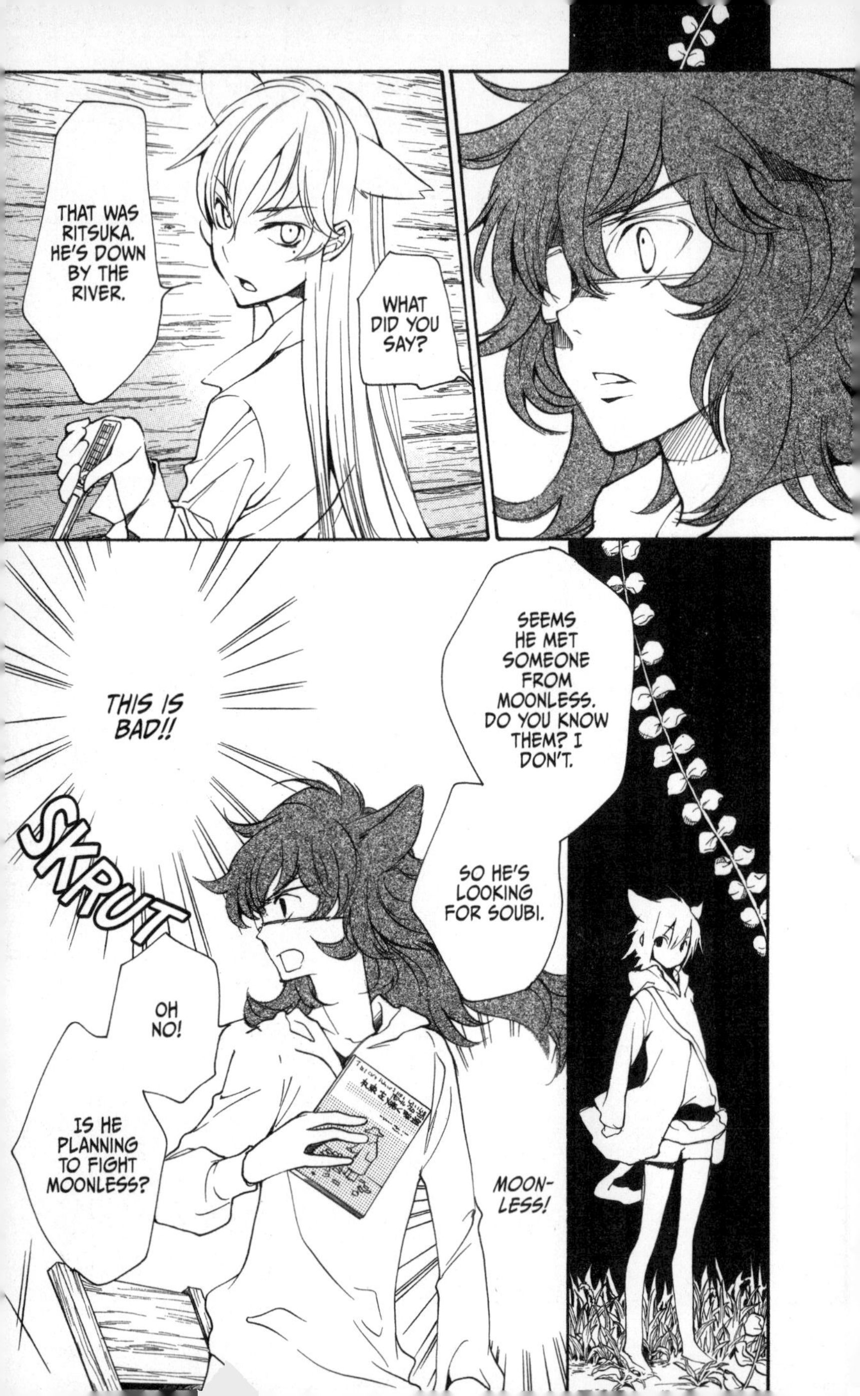
THAT WAS RITSUKA. HE'S DOWN BY THE RIVER.
WHAT DID YOU SAY?
SEEMS HE MET SOMEONE FROM MOONLESS. DO YOU KNOW THEM? I DON'T.
SO HE'S LOOKING FOR SOUBI.
THIS IS BAD!!
SKRUT
OH NO!
IS HE PLANNING TO FIGHT MOONLESS?
MOON-LESS!

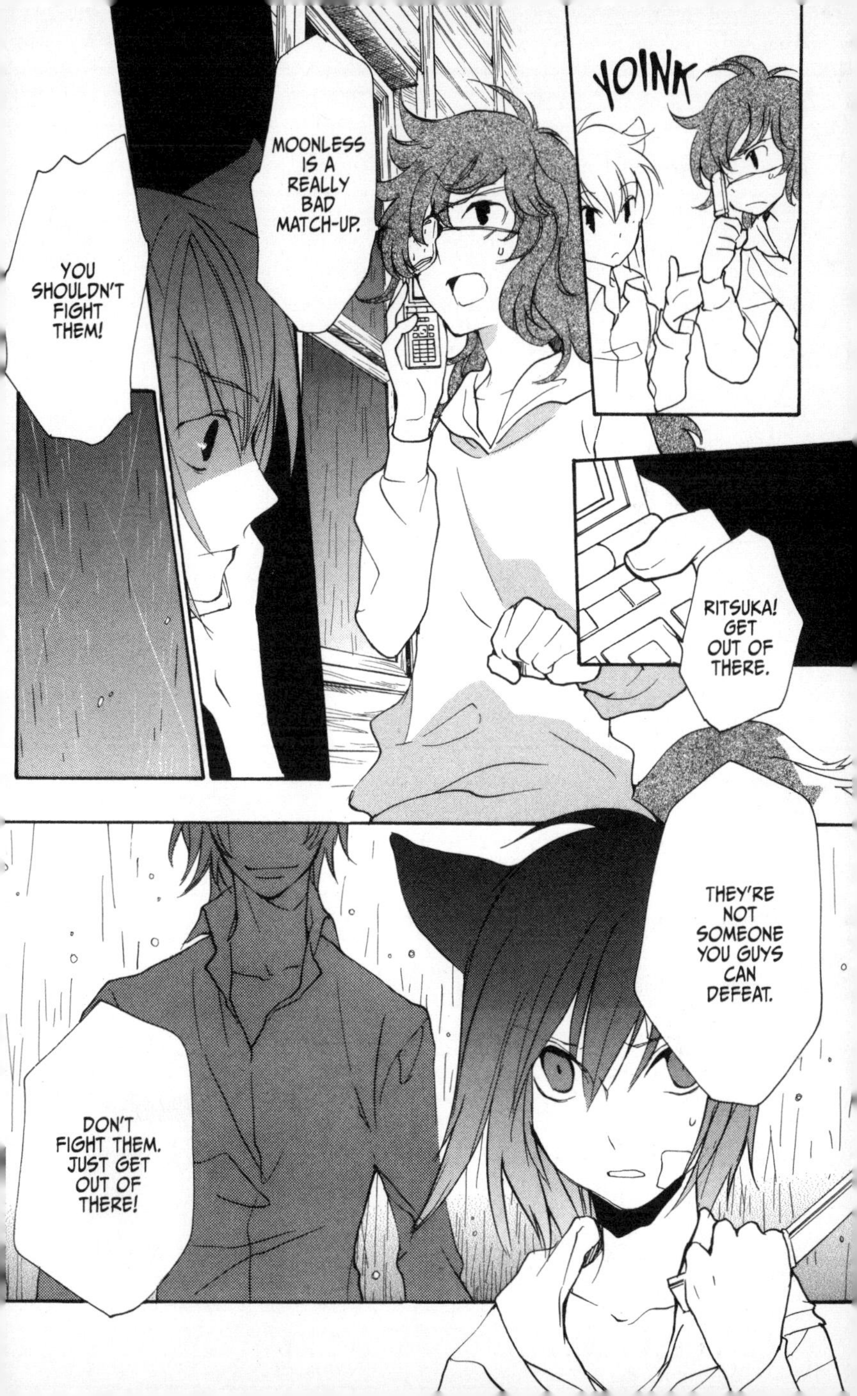
MOONLESS IS A REALLY BAD MATCH-UP.
YOINK
RITSUKA! GET OUT OF THERE.
YOU SHOULDN'T FIGHT THEM!
THEY'RE NOT SOMEONE YOU GUYS CAN DEFEAT.
DON'T FIGHT THEM. JUST GET OUT OF THERE!

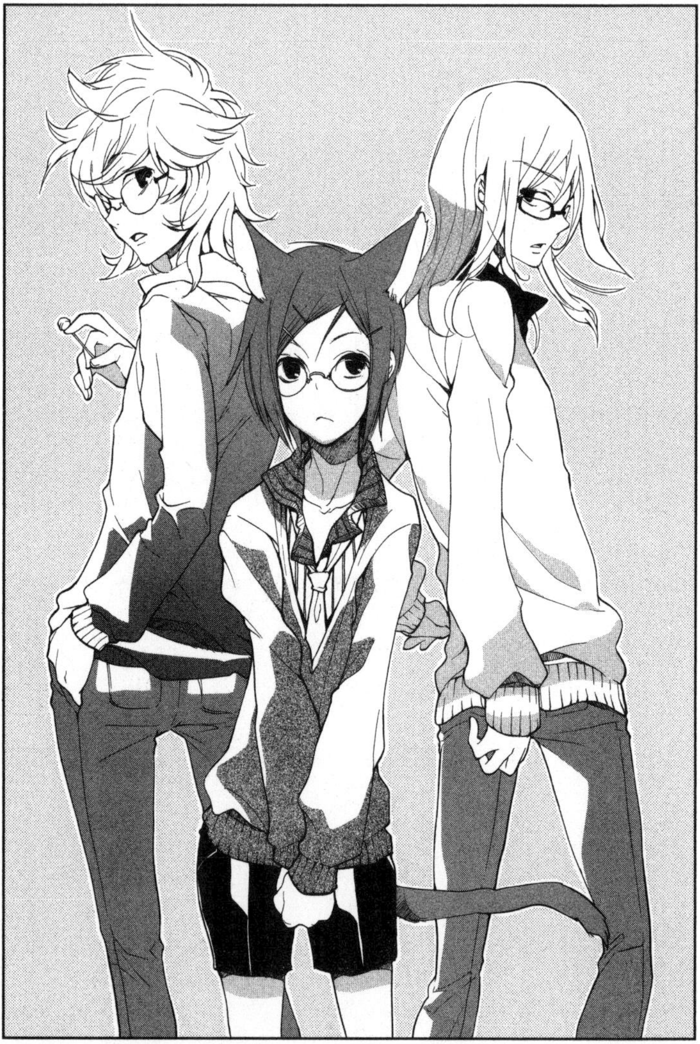

LOVELESS

LOVELESS

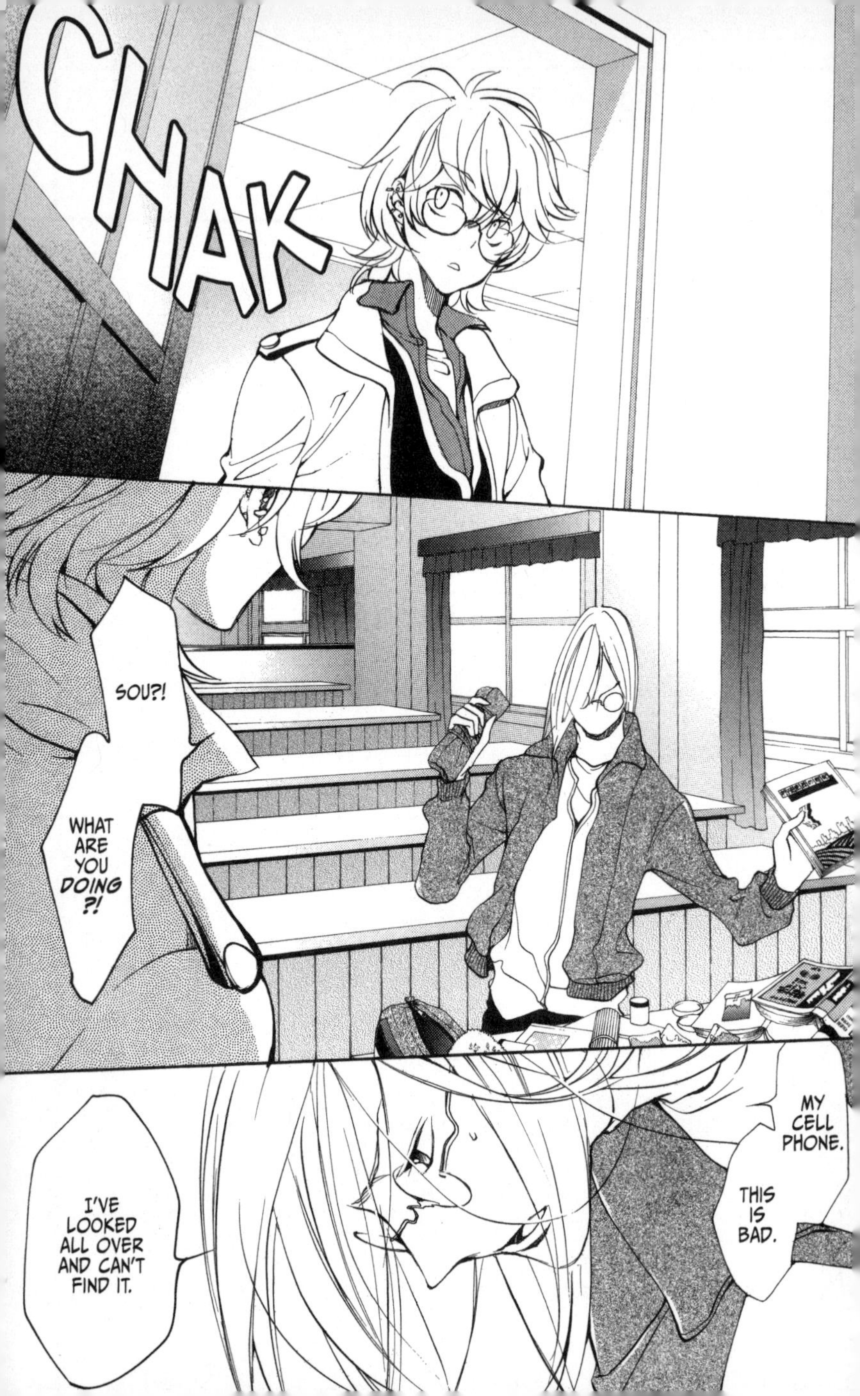
CHAK
SOU?!
WHAT ARE YOU DOING?!
MY CELL PHONE.
THIS IS BAD.
I'VE LOOKED ALL OVER AND CAN'T FIND IT.

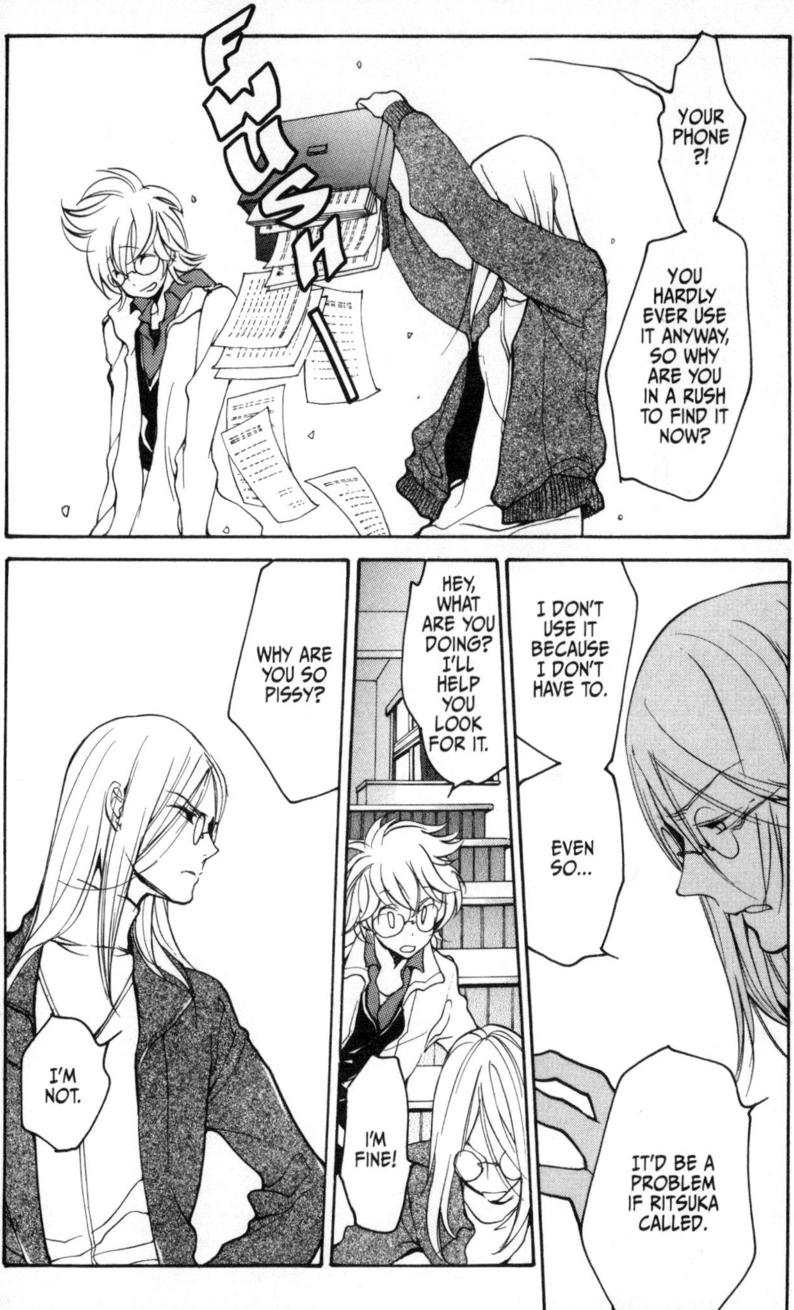
YOUR PHONE?!
YOU HARDLY EVER USE IT ANYWAY, SO WHY ARE YOU IN A RUSH TO FIND IT NOW?
FWUSH
I DON'T USE IT BECAUSE I DON'T HAVE TO.
EVEN SO...
IT'D BE A PROBLEM IF RITSUKA CALLED.
HEY, WHAT ARE YOU DOING? I'LL HELP YOU LOOK FOR IT.
I'M FINE!
WHY ARE YOU SO PISSY?
I'M NOT.

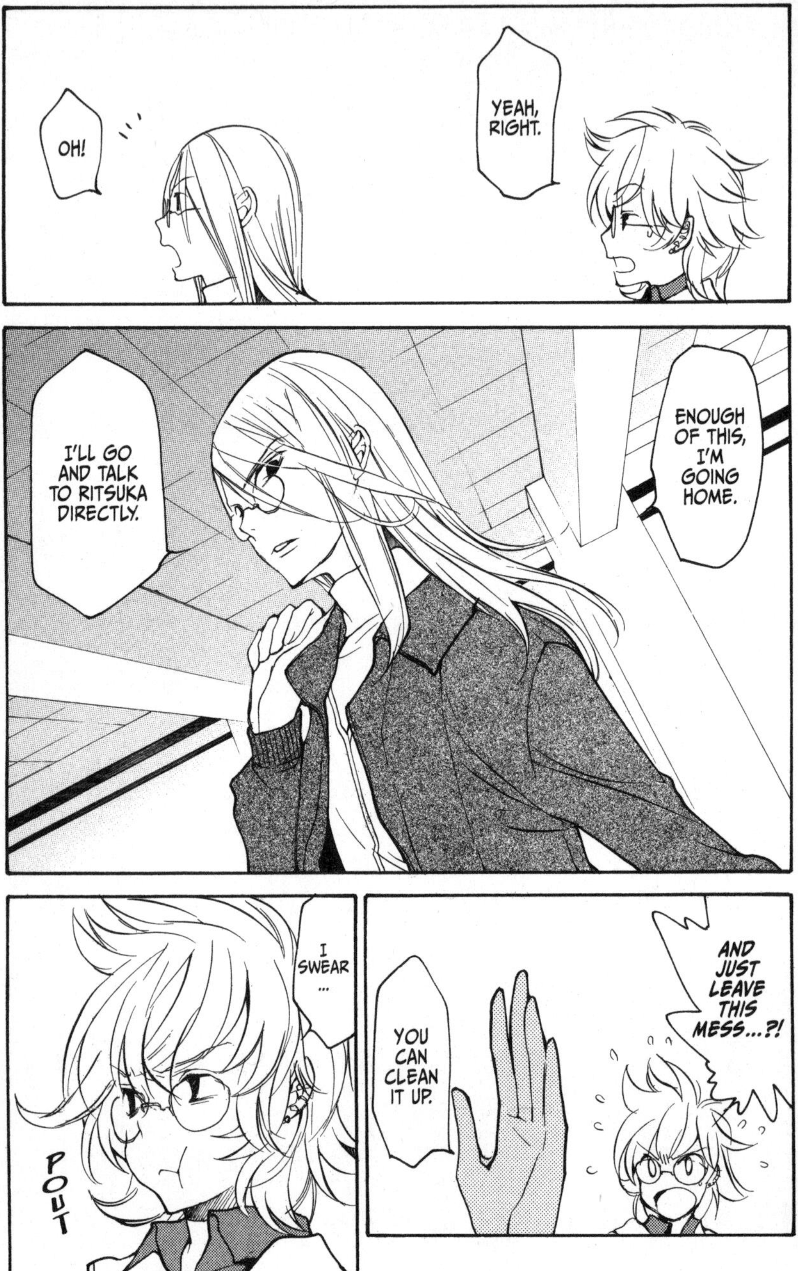
YEAH, RIGHT.
OH!
ENOUGH OF THIS, I'M GOING HOME.
I'LL GO AND TALK TO RITSUKA DIRECTLY.
AND JUST LEAVE THIS MESS...?!
YOU CAN CLEAN IT UP.
I SWEAR ...
POUT

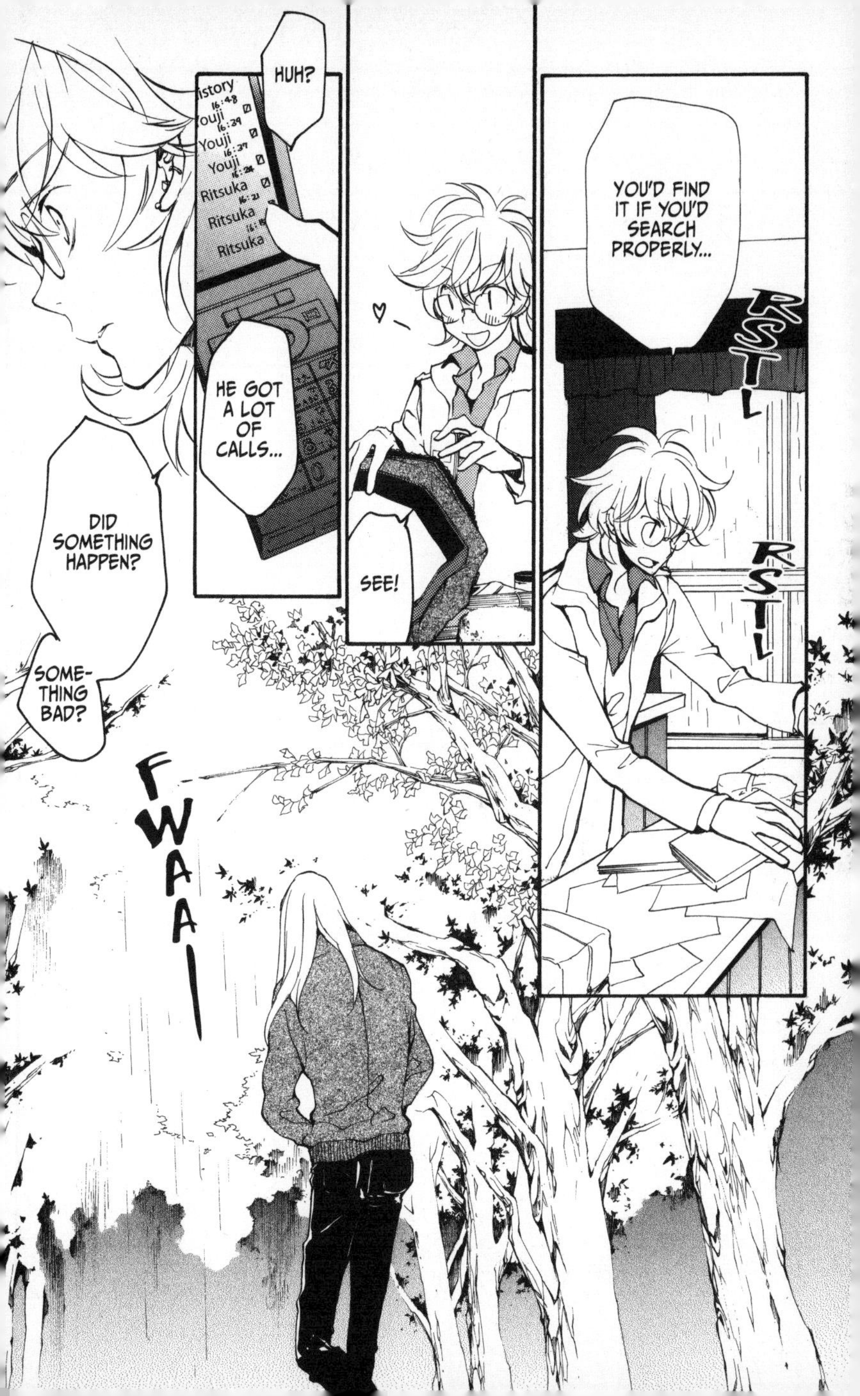
YOU'D FIND IT IF YOU'D SEARCH PROPERLY...
RSTL
RSTL
SEE!
HUH?
istory
Youji
Youji
Youji
Ritsuka
Ritsuka
Ritsuka
HE GOT A LOT OF CALLS...
DID SOMETHING HAPPEN?
SOME-THING BAD?
FWAAI

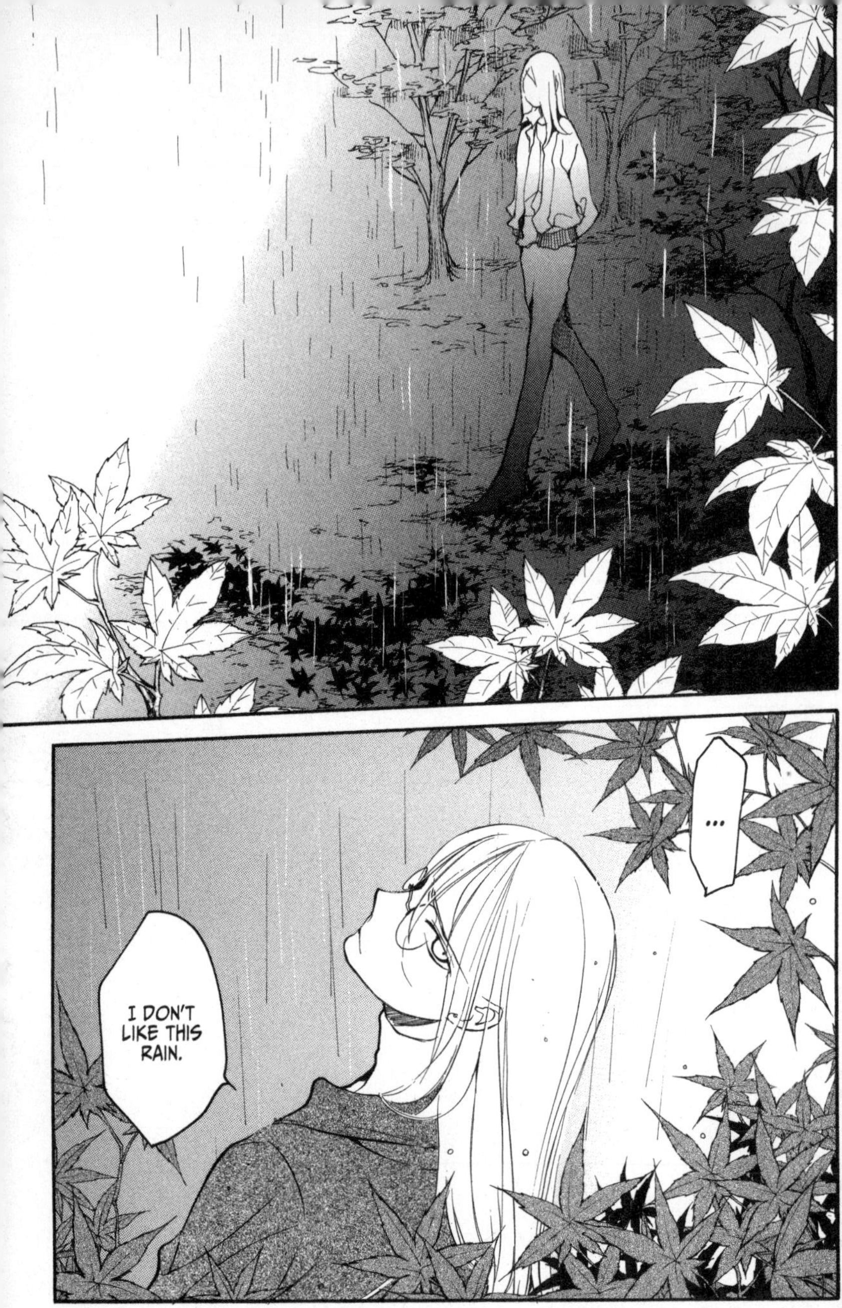
...
I DON'T LIKE THIS RAIN.

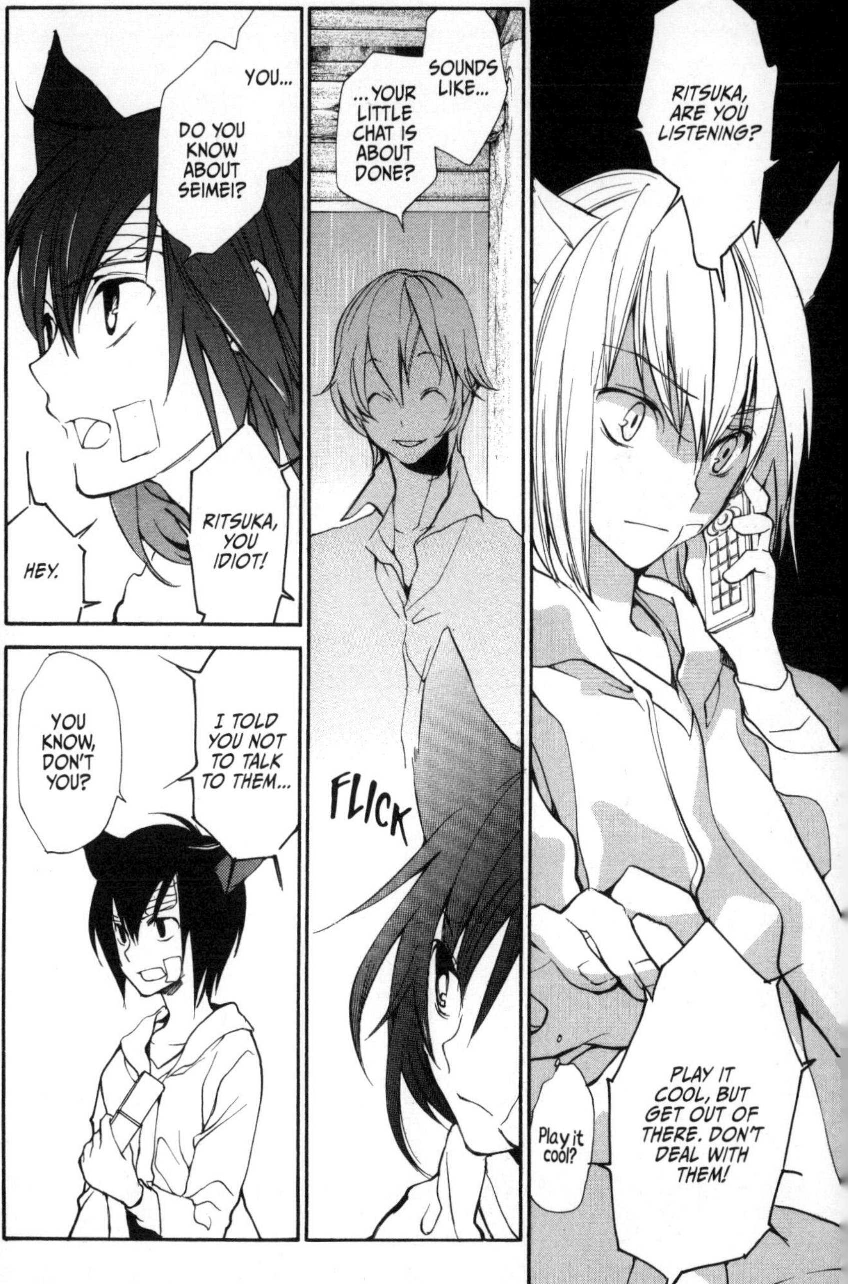
RITSUKA, ARE YOU LISTENING?
PLAY IT COOL, BUT GET OUT OF THERE. DON'T DEAL WITH THEM!
Play it cool?
SOUNDS LIKE...
...YOUR LITTLE CHAT IS ABOUT DONE?
FLICK
YOU...
DO YOU KNOW ABOUT SEIMEI?
RITSUKA, YOU IDIOT!
HEY.
I TOLD YOU NOT TO TALK TO THEM...
YOU KNOW, DON'T YOU?

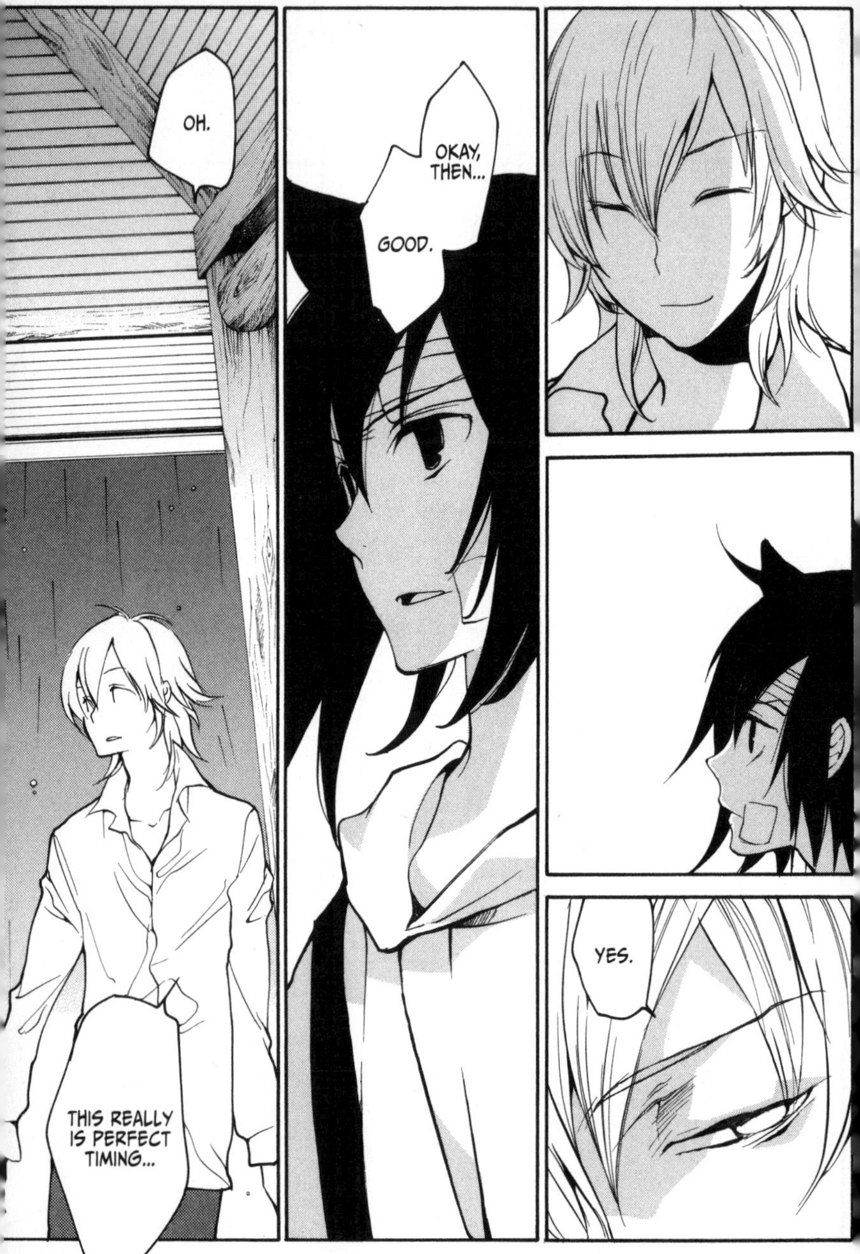
YES.
OKAY, THEN...
GOOD.
OH.
THIS REALLY IS PERFECT TIMING...

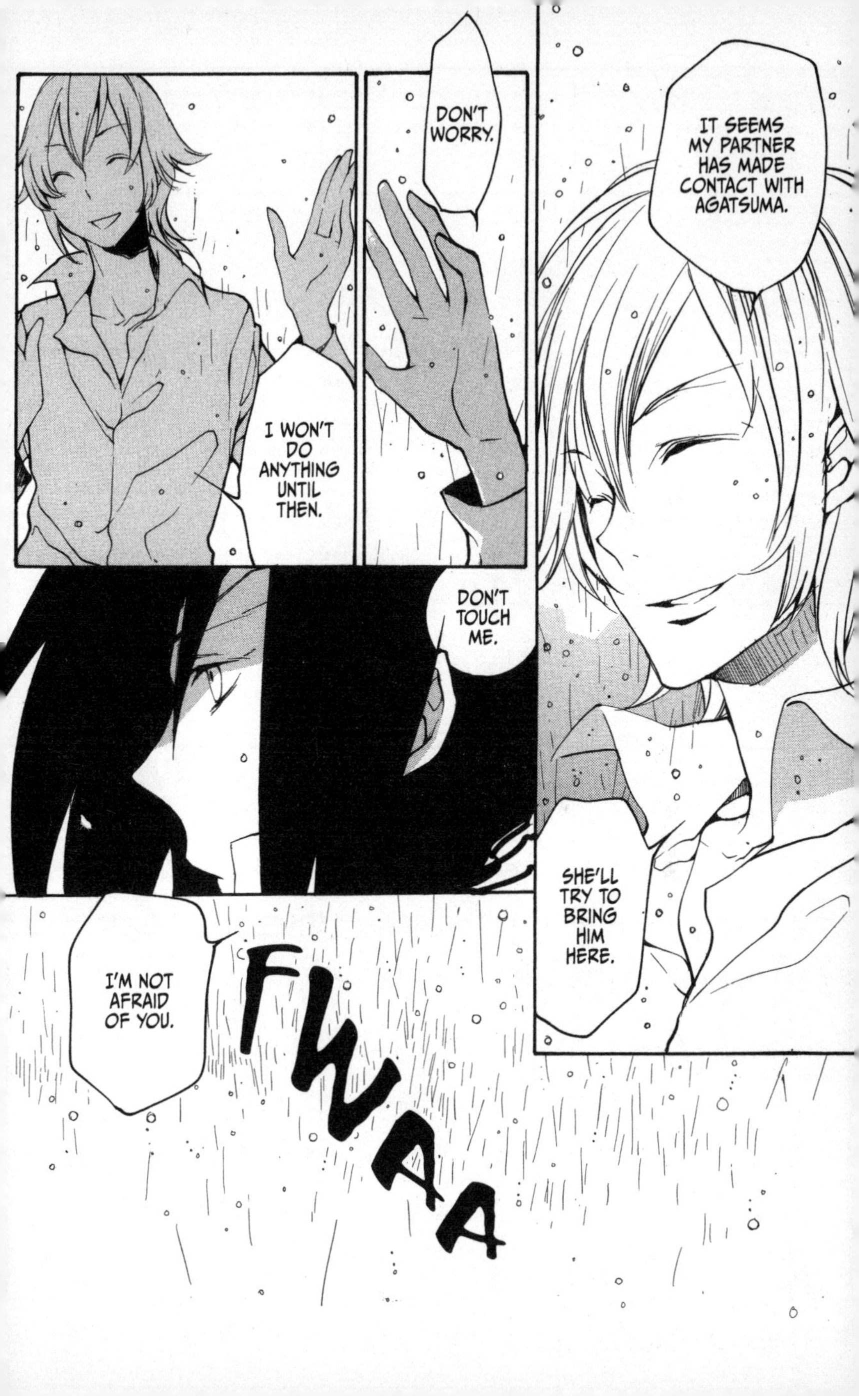
IT SEEMS MY PARTNER HAS MADE CONTACT WITH AGATSUMA.
SHE'LL TRY TO BRING HIM HERE.
DON'T WORRY.
I WON'T DO ANYTHING UNTIL THEN.
DON'T TOUCH ME.
I'M NOT AFRAID OF YOU.
FWAA

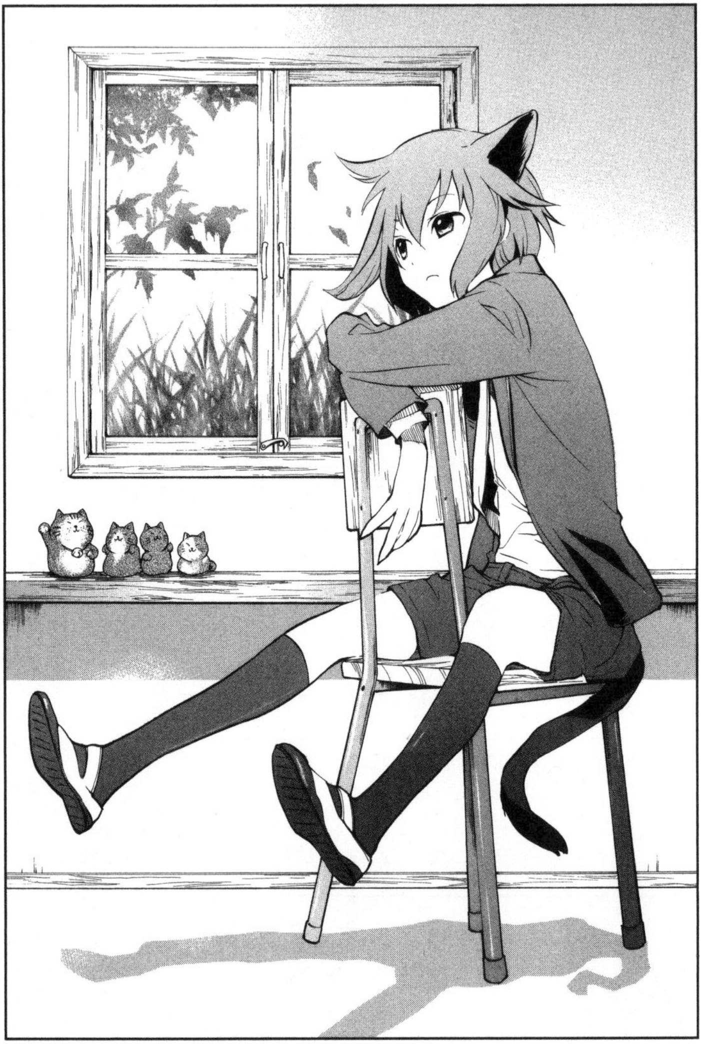

LOVELESS

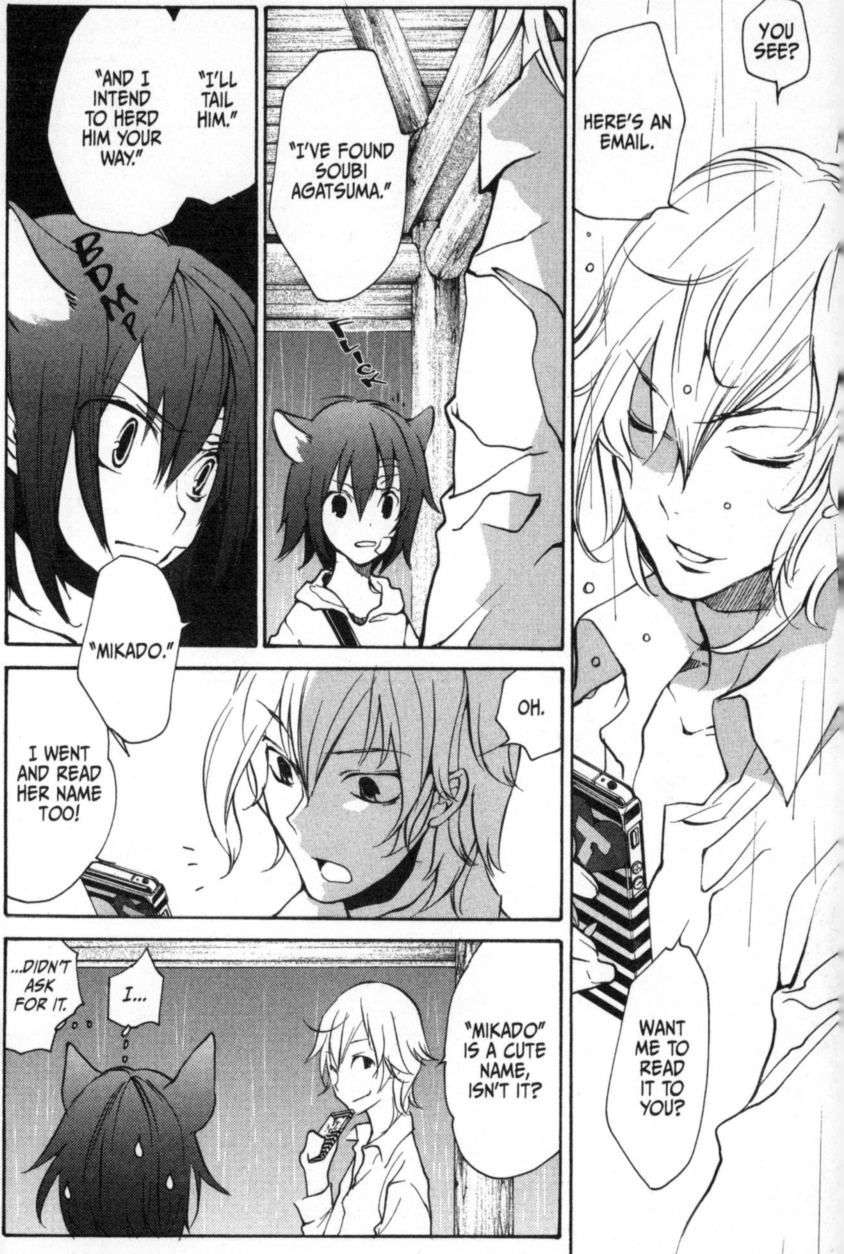
YOU SEE?
HERE'S AN EMAIL.
WANT ME TO READ IT TO YOU?
"I'VE FOUND SOUBI AGATSUMA."
FLICK
"I'LL TAIL HIM."
"AND I INTEND TO HERD HIM YOUR WAY."
BDMP
"MIKADO."
OH.
I WENT AND READ HER NAME TOO!
"MIKADO" IS A CUTE NAME, ISN'T IT?
I...
...DIDN'T ASK FOR IT.

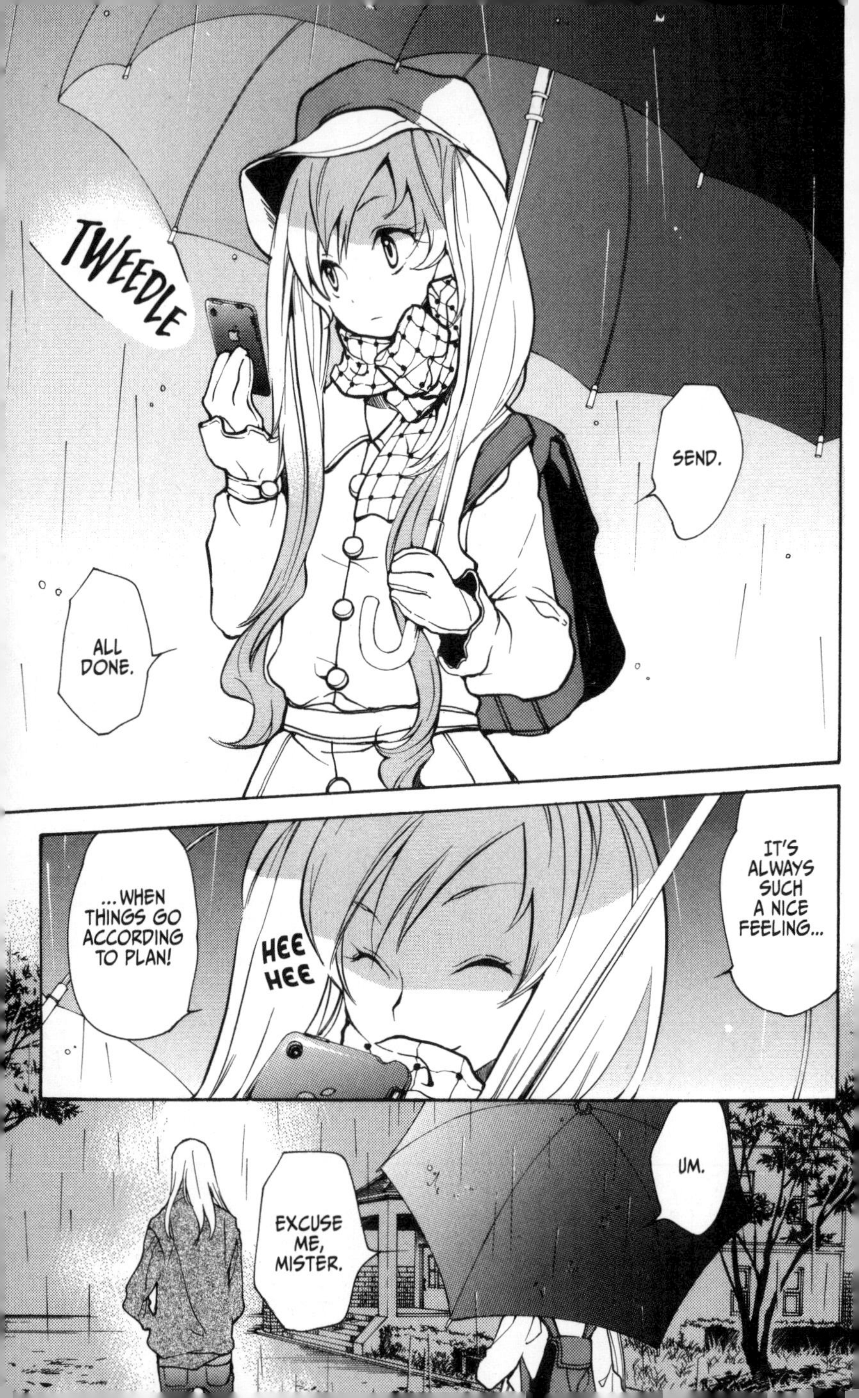
SEND.
TWEEDLE
ALL DONE.
IT'S ALWAYS SUCH A NICE FEELING...
HEE HEE
...WHEN THINGS GO ACCORDING TO PLAN!
UM.
EXCUSE ME, MISTER.

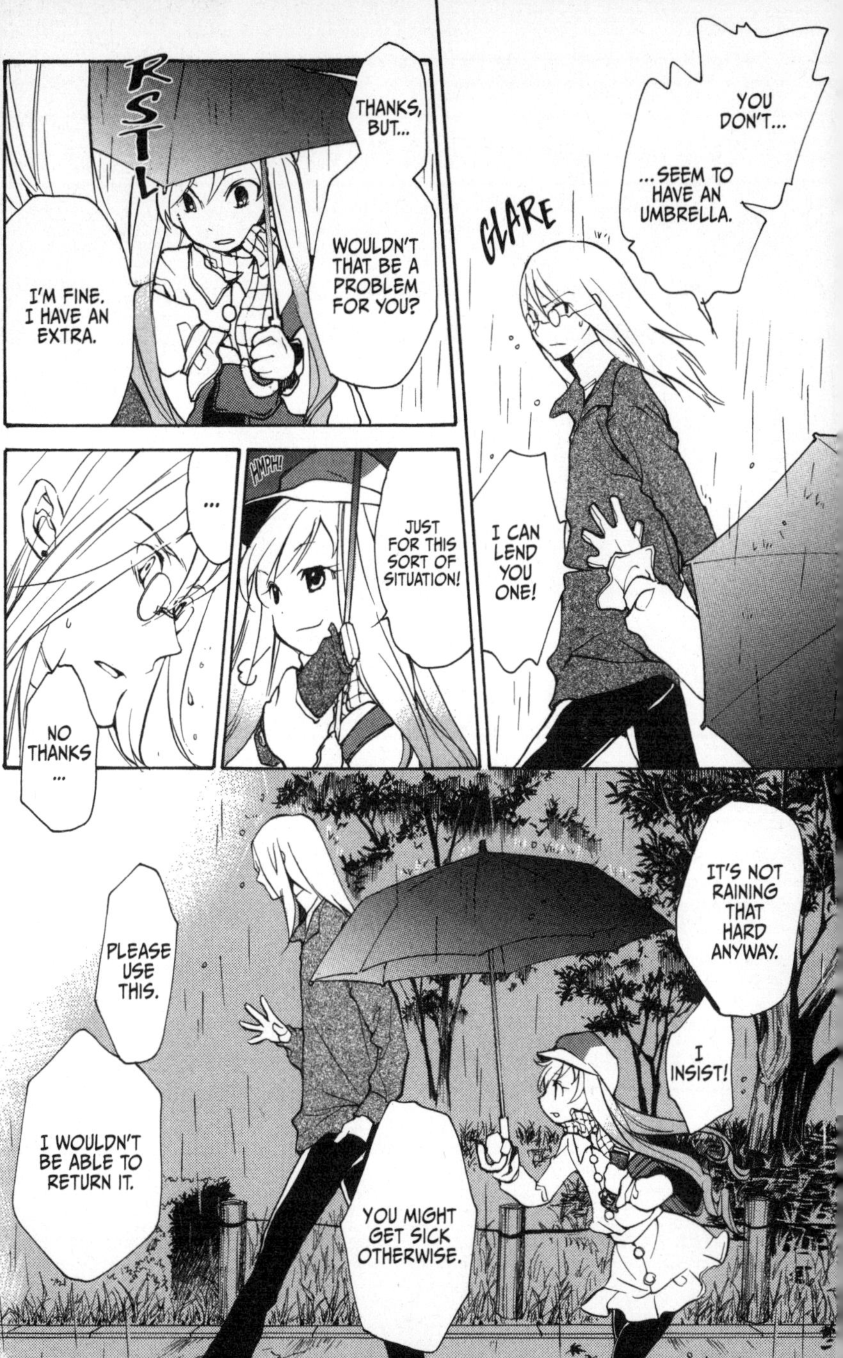
YOU DON'T...
...SEEM TO HAVE AN UMBRELLA.
GLARE
I CAN LEND YOU ONE!
RSTL
THANKS, BUT...
WOULDN'T THAT BE A PROBLEM FOR YOU?
I'M FINE. I HAVE AN EXTRA.
HMPH!
JUST FOR THIS SORT OF SITUATION!
...
NO THANKS ...
IT'S NOT RAINING THAT HARD ANYWAY.
I INSIST!
PLEASE USE THIS.
YOU MIGHT GET SICK OTHERWISE.
I WOULDN'T BE ABLE TO RETURN IT.

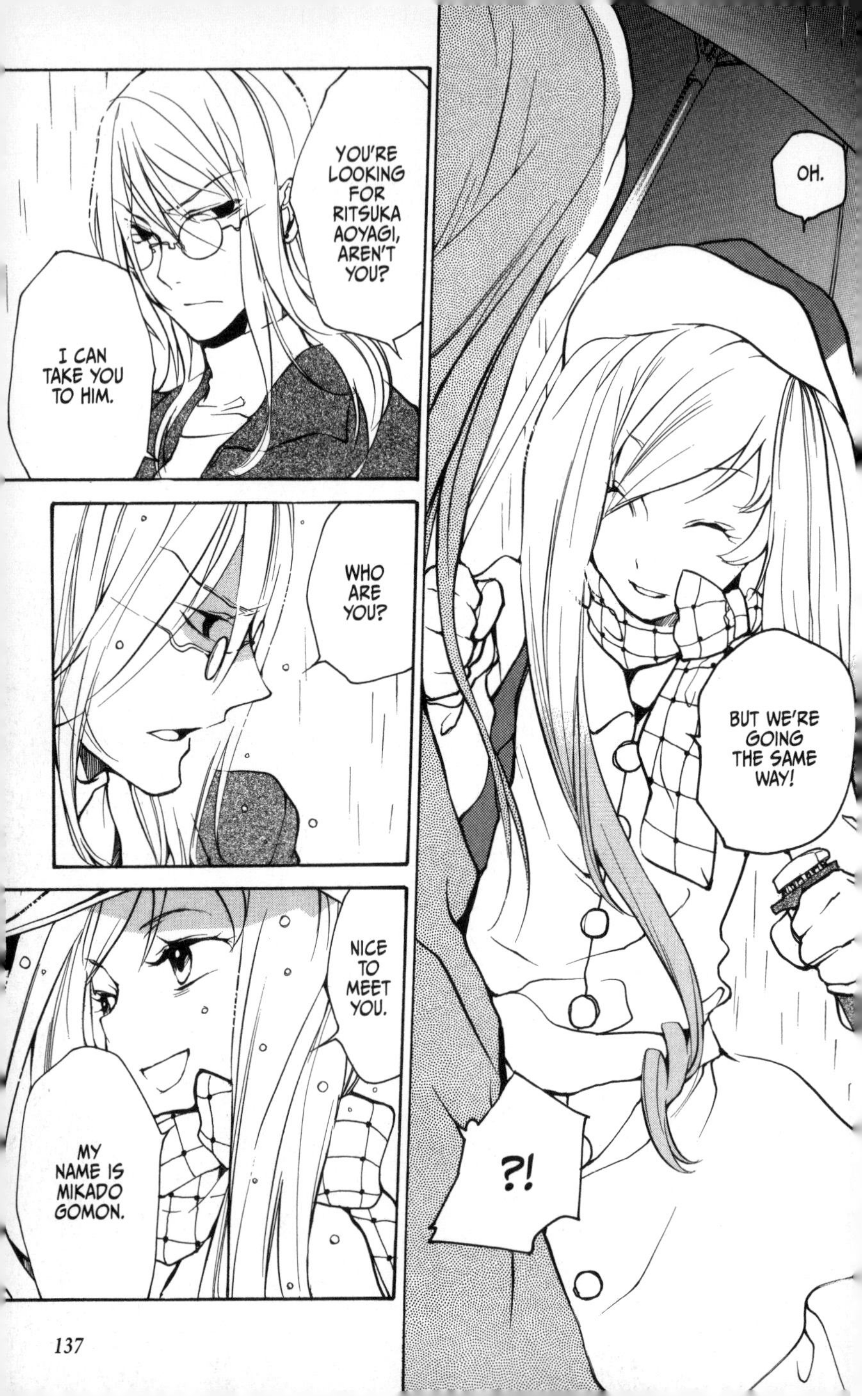
OH.
BUT WE'RE GOING THE SAME WAY!
?!
YOU'RE LOOKING FOR RITSUKA AOYAGI, AREN'T YOU?
I CAN TAKE YOU TO HIM.
WHO ARE YOU?
NICE TO MEET YOU.
MY NAME IS MIKADO GOMON.

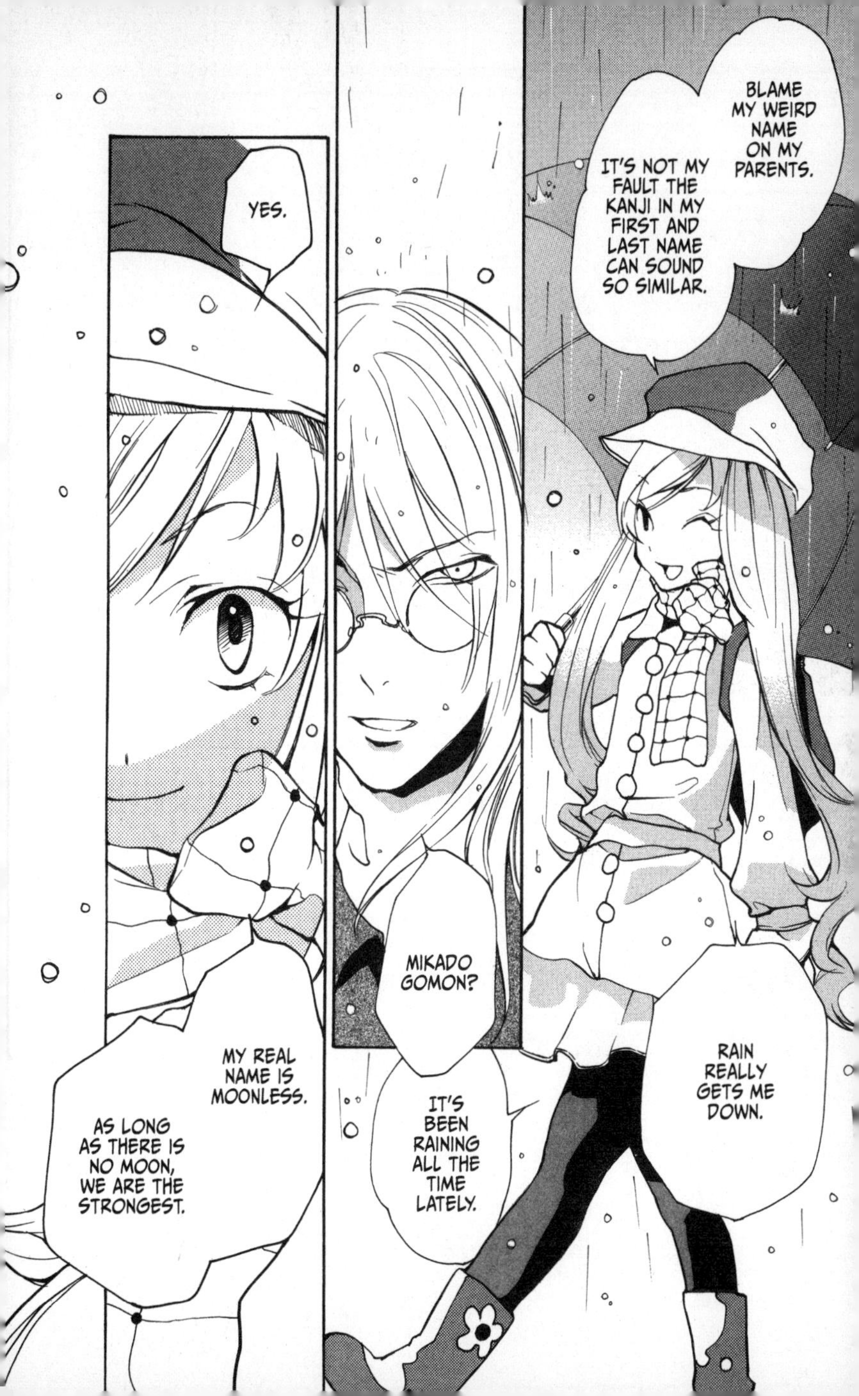
BLAME MY WEIRD NAME ON MY PARENTS.
IT'S NOT MY FAULT THE KANJI IN MY FIRST AND LAST NAME CAN SOUND SO SIMILAR.
RAIN REALLY GETS ME DOWN.
MIKADO GOMON?
IT'S BEEN RAINING ALL THE TIME LATELY.
YES.
MY REAL NAME IS MOONLESS.
AS LONG AS THERE IS NO MOON, WE ARE THE STRONGEST.

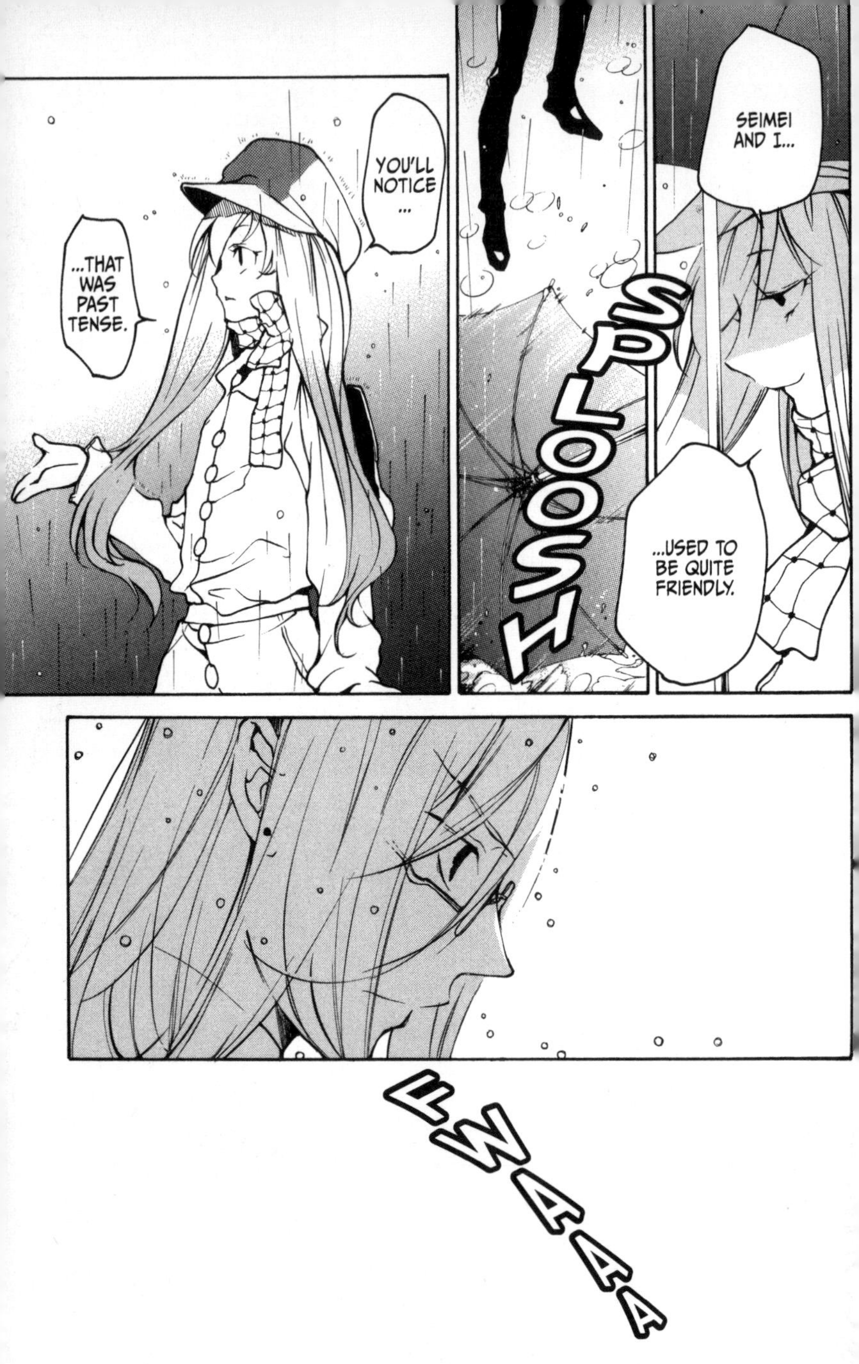
SEIMEI AND I...
...USED TO BE QUITE FRIENDLY.
SPLOOSH
YOU'LL NOTICE ...
...THAT WAS PAST TENSE.
EWAAA

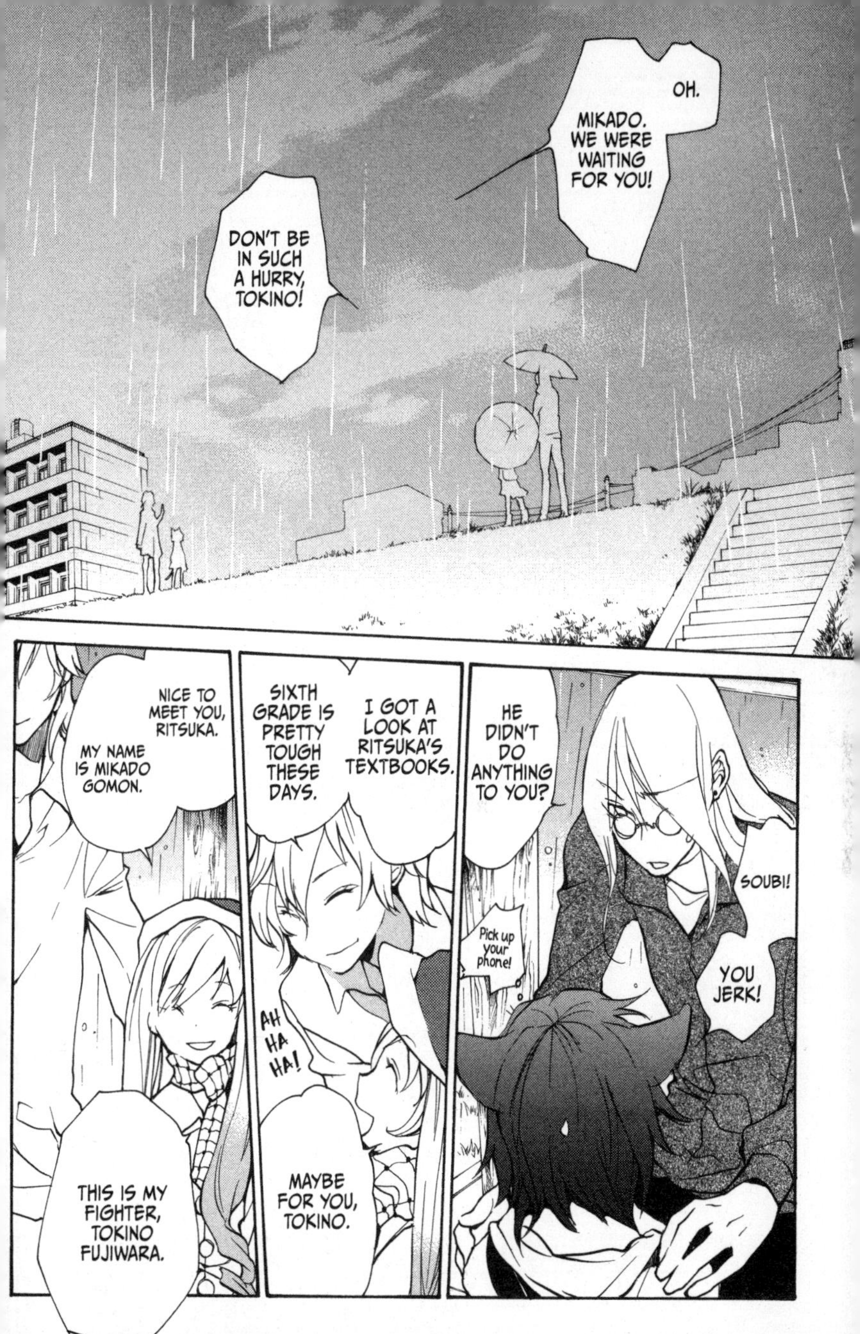
OH.
MIKADO. WE WERE WAITING FOR YOU!
DON'T BE IN SUCH A HURRY, TOKINO!
HE DIDN'T DO ANYTHING TO YOU?
SOUBI!
YOU JERK!
Pick up your phone!
I GOT A LOOK AT RITSUKA'S TEXTBOOKS.
SIXTH GRADE IS PRETTY TOUGH THESE DAYS.
AH HA HA!
MAYBE FOR YOU, TOKINO.
NICE TO MEET YOU, RITSUKA.
MY NAME IS MIKADO GOMON.
THIS IS MY FIGHTER, TOKINO FUJIWARA.

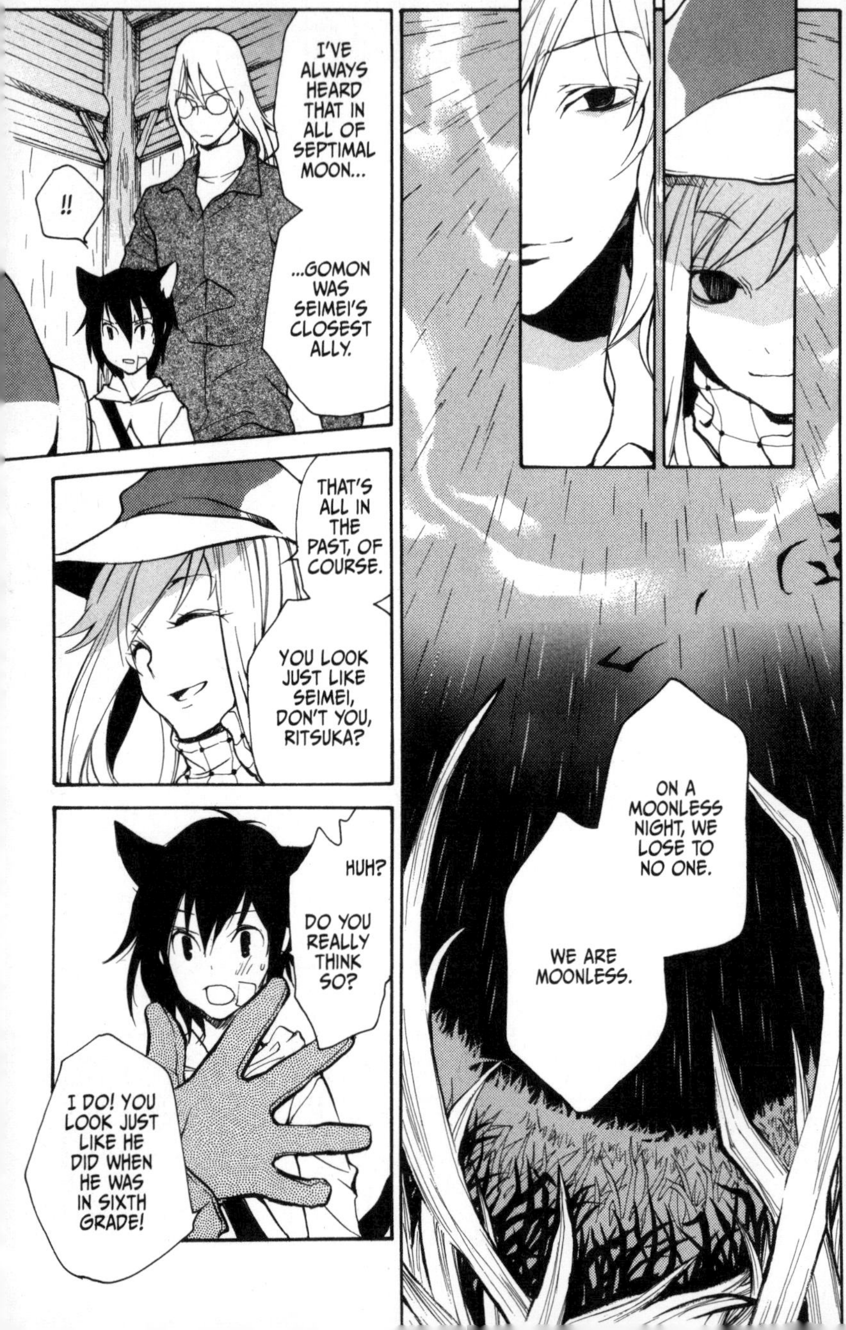
ON A MOONLESS NIGHT, WE LOSE TO NO ONE.
WE ARE MOONLESS.
I'VE ALWAYS HEARD THAT IN ALL OF SEPTIMAL MOON...
...GOMON WAS SEIMEI'S CLOSEST ALLY.
!!
THAT'S ALL IN THE PAST, OF COURSE.
YOU LOOK JUST LIKE SEIMEI, DON'T YOU, RITSUKA?
HUH?
DO YOU REALLY THINK SO?
I DO! YOU LOOK JUST LIKE HE DID WHEN HE WAS IN SIXTH GRADE!

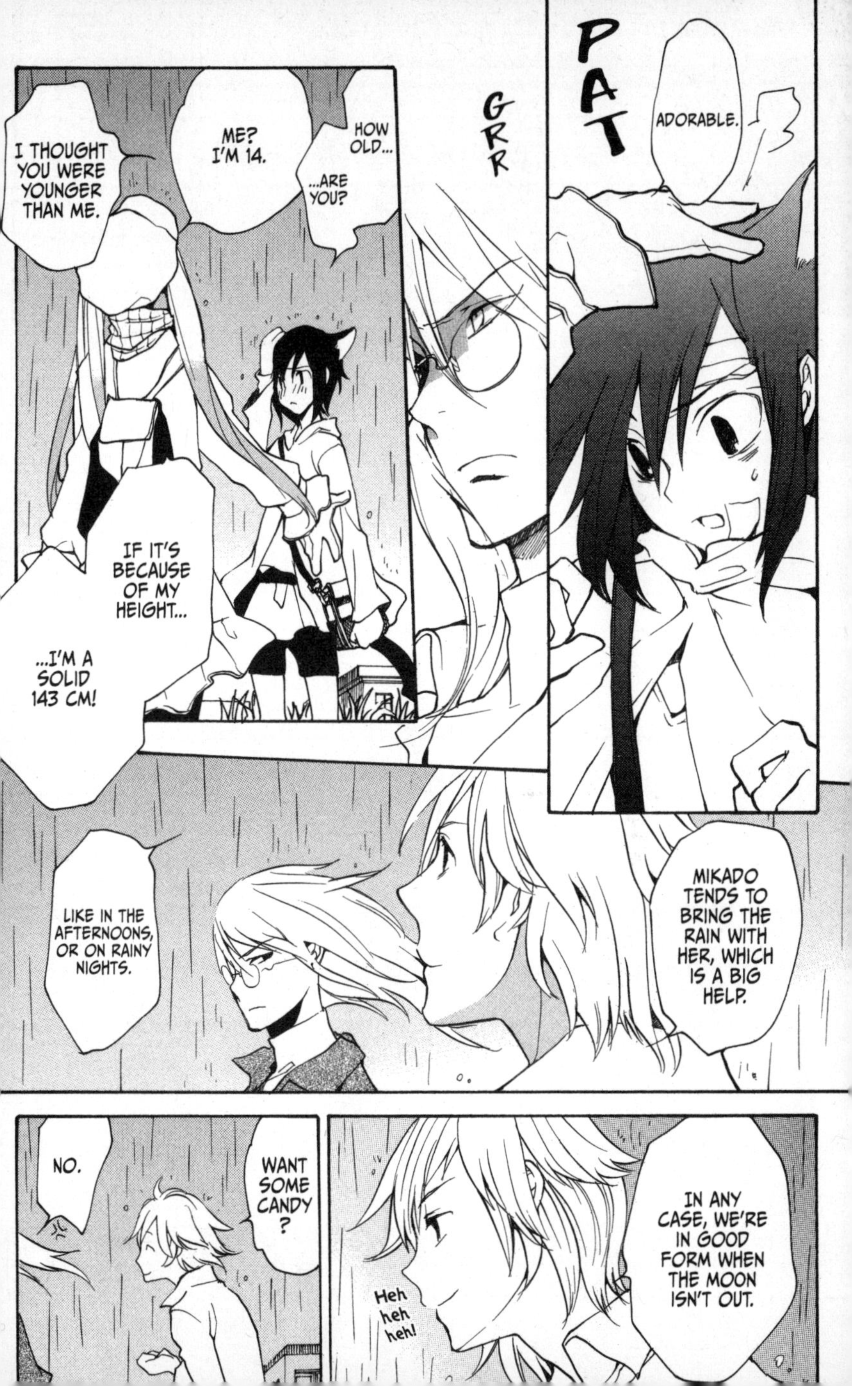
PAT
ADORABLE.
GRR
HOW OLD...
...ARE YOU?
ME? I'M 14.
I THOUGHT YOU WERE YOUNGER THAN ME.
IF IT'S BECAUSE OF MY HEIGHT...
...I'M A SOLID 143 CM!
MIKADO TENDS TO BRING THE RAIN WITH HER, WHICH IS A BIG HELP.
LIKE IN THE AFTERNOONS, OR ON RAINY NIGHTS.
IN ANY CASE, WE'RE IN GOOD FORM WHEN THE MOON ISN'T OUT.
Heh heh heh!
WANT SOME CANDY?
NO.

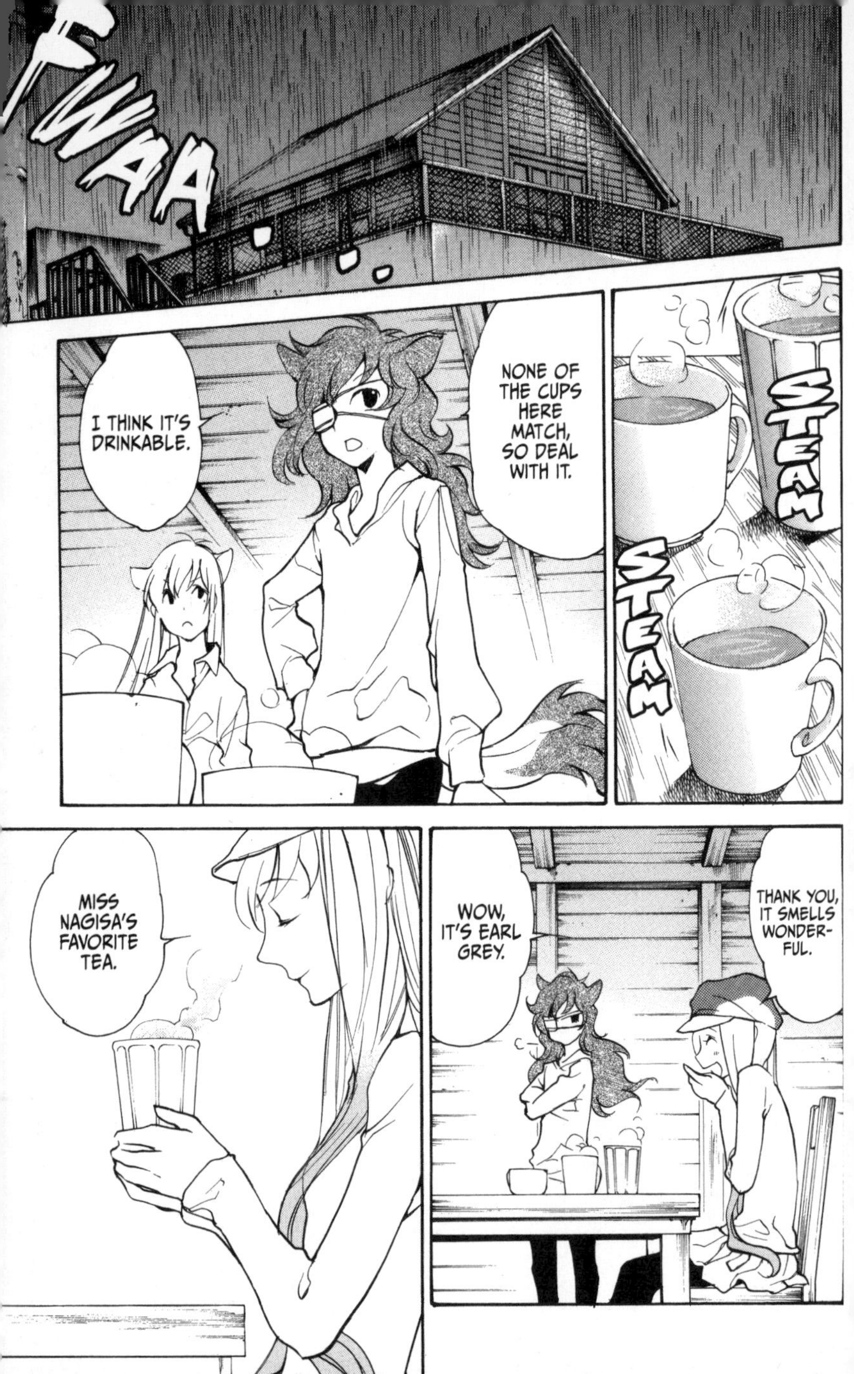
FWAA
STEAM
STEAM
NONE OF THE CUPS HERE MATCH, SO DEAL WITH IT.
I THINK IT'S DRINKABLE.
THANK YOU, IT SMELLS WONDER-FUL.
WOW, IT'S EARL GREY.
MISS NAGISA'S FAVORITE TEA.

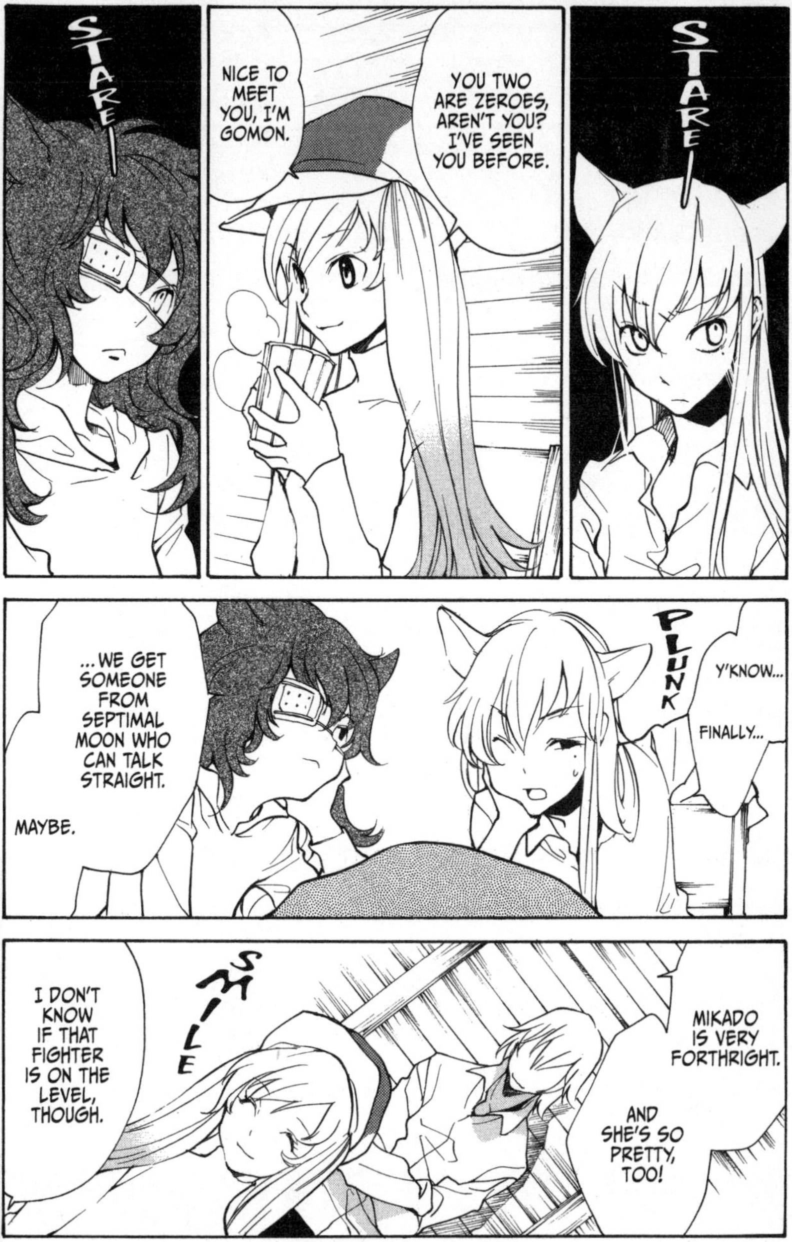
STARE
YOU TWO ARE ZEROES, AREN'T YOU? I'VE SEEN YOU BEFORE.
NICE TO MEET YOU, I'M GOMON.
STARE
Y'KNOW...
FINALLY...
PLUNK
...WE GET SOMEONE FROM SEPTIMAL MOON WHO CAN TALK STRAIGHT.
MAYBE.
MIKADO IS VERY FORTHRIGHT.
AND SHE'S SO PRETTY, TOO!
SMILE
I DON'T KNOW IF THAT FIGHTER IS ON THE LEVEL, THOUGH.

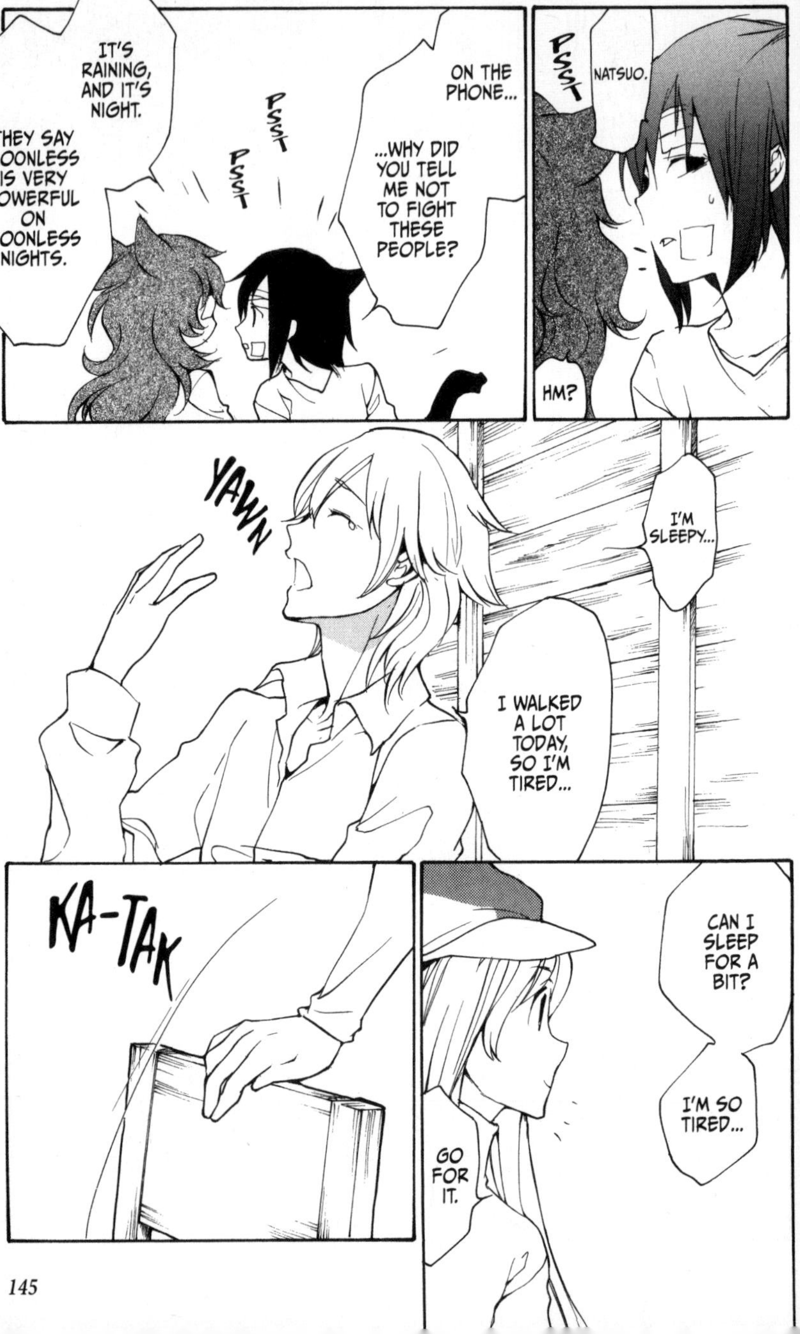
PSST
NATSUO.
HM?
ON THE PHONE...
...WHY DID YOU TELL ME NOT TO FIGHT THESE PEOPLE?
PSST
PSST
IT'S RAINING, AND IT'S NIGHT.
THEY SAY MOONLESS IS VERY POWERFUL ON MOONLESS NIGHTS.
I'M SLEEPY...
YAWN
I WALKED A LOT TODAY, SO I'M TIRED...
CAN I SLEEP FOR A BIT?
I'M SO TIRED...
GO FOR IT.
KA-TAK

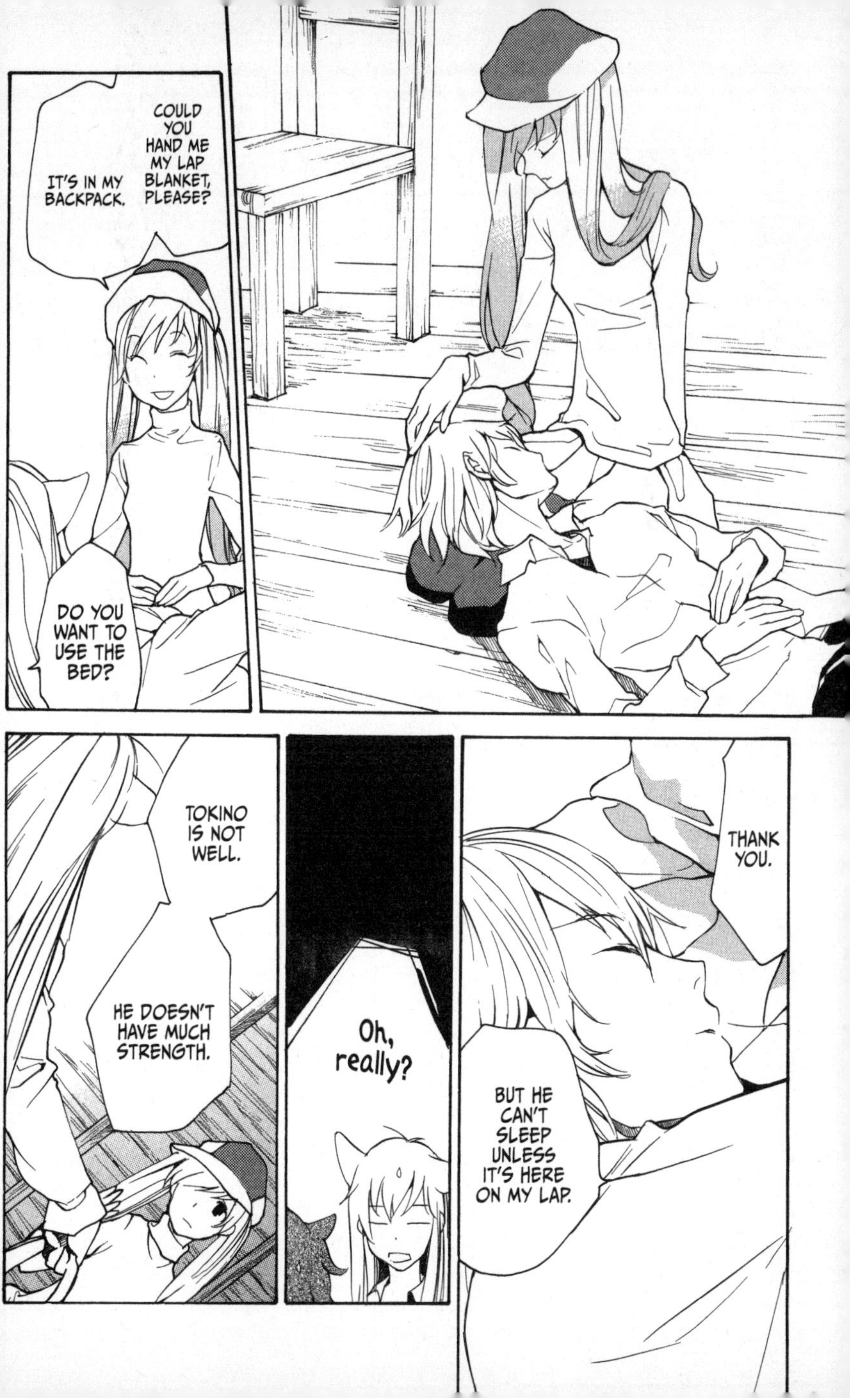
COULD YOU HAND ME MY LAP BLANKET, PLEASE?
IT'S IN MY BACKPACK.
DO YOU WANT TO USE THE BED?
THANK YOU.
BUT HE CAN'T SLEEP UNLESS IT'S HERE ON MY LAP.
Oh, really?
TOKINO IS NOT WELL.
HE DOESN'T HAVE MUCH STRENGTH.

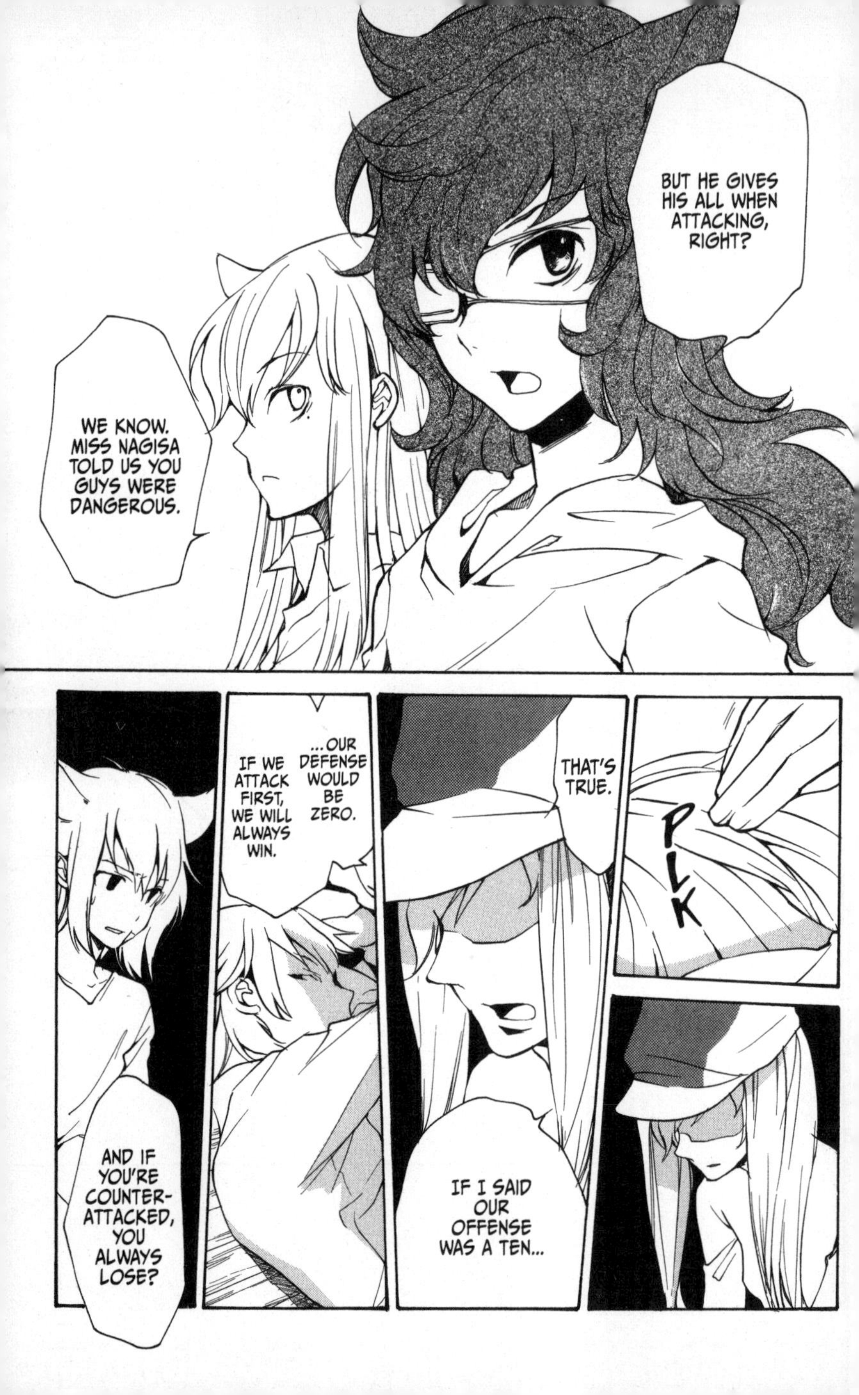
BUT HE GIVES HIS ALL WHEN ATTACKING, RIGHT?
WE KNOW. MISS NAGISA TOLD US YOU GUYS WERE DANGEROUS.
PLK
THAT'S TRUE.
IF I SAID OUR OFFENSE WAS A TEN...
...OUR DEFENSE WOULD BE ZERO.
IF WE ATTACK FIRST, WE WILL ALWAYS WIN.
AND IF YOU'RE COUNTER-ATTACKED, YOU ALWAYS LOSE?

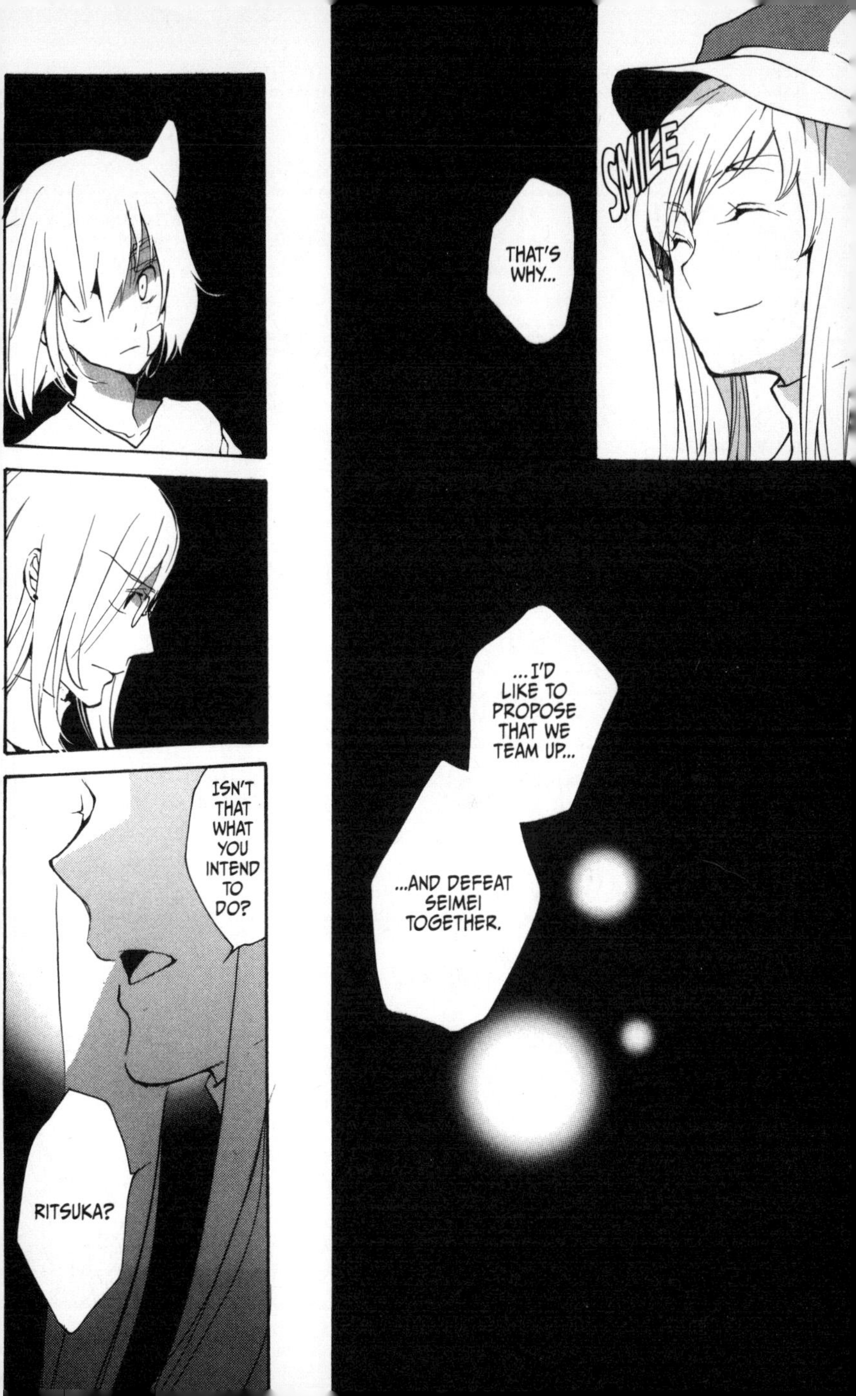
SMILE
THAT'S WHY...
...I'D LIKE TO PROPOSE THAT WE TEAM UP...
...AND DEFEAT SEIMEI TOGETHER.
ISN'T THAT WHAT YOU INTEND TO DO?
RITSUKA?

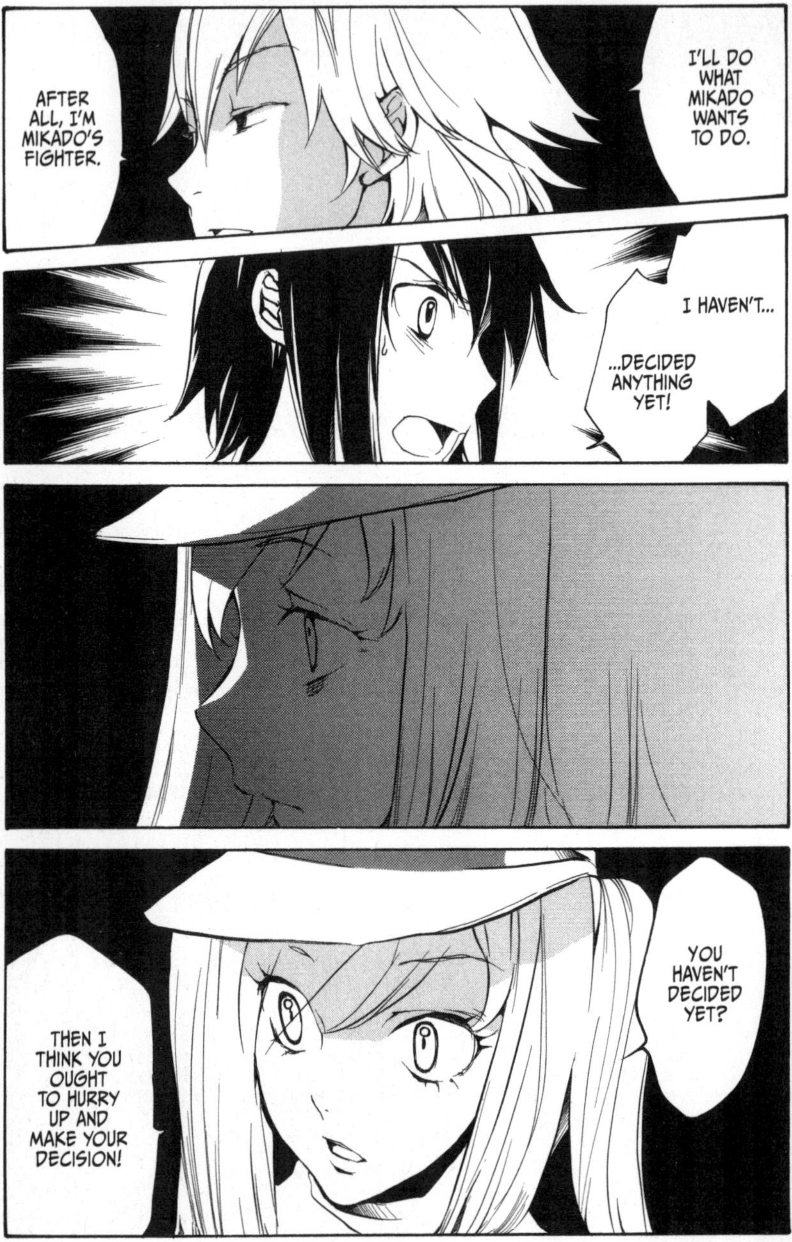
I'LL DO WHAT MIKADO WANTS TO DO.
AFTER ALL, I'M MIKADO'S FIGHTER.
I HAVEN'T...
...DECIDED ANYTHING YET!
YOU HAVEN'T DECIDED YET?
THEN I THINK YOU OUGHT TO HURRY UP AND MAKE YOUR DECISION!

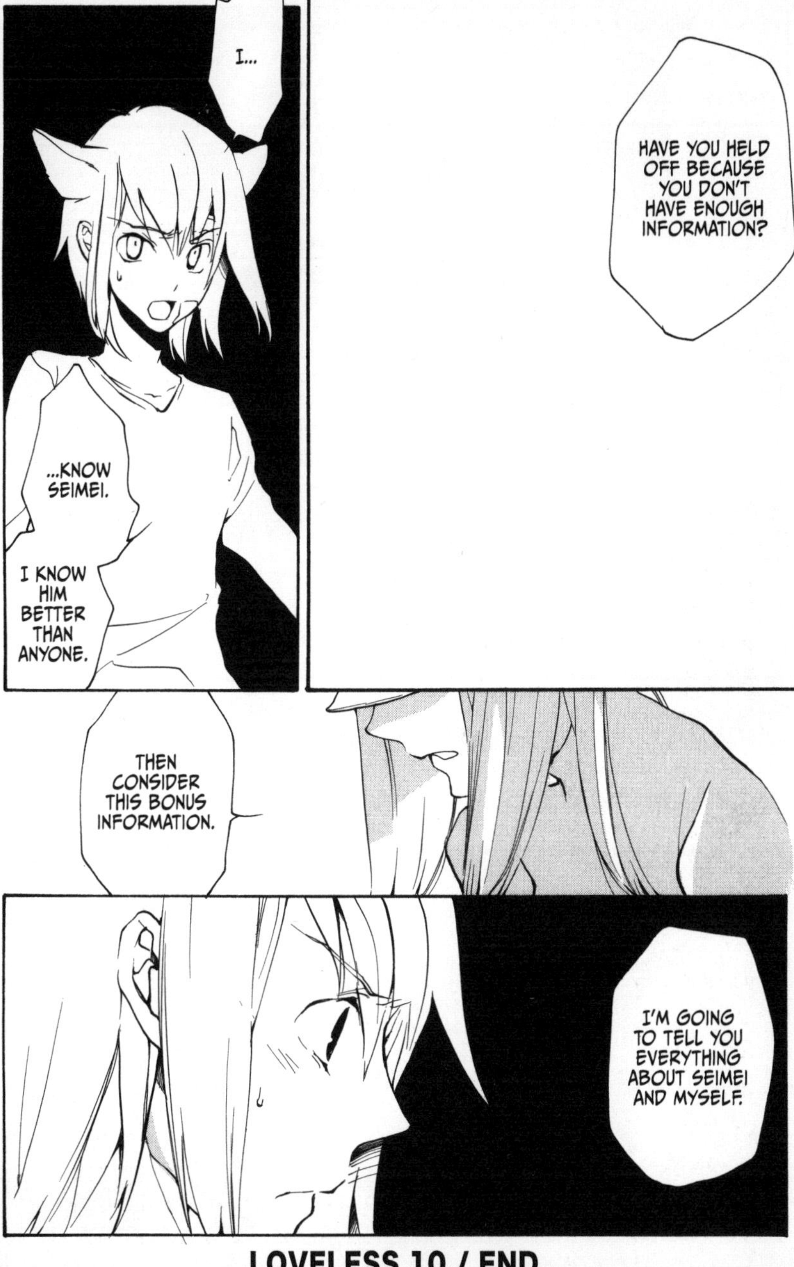
HAVE YOU HELD OFF BECAUSE YOU DON'T HAVE ENOUGH INFORMATION?
I...
...KNOW SEIMEI.
I KNOW HIM BETTER THAN ANYONE.
THEN CONSIDER THIS BONUS INFORMATION.
I'M GOING TO TELL YOU EVERYTHING ABOUT SEIMEI AND MYSELF.

LOVELESS 10 / END

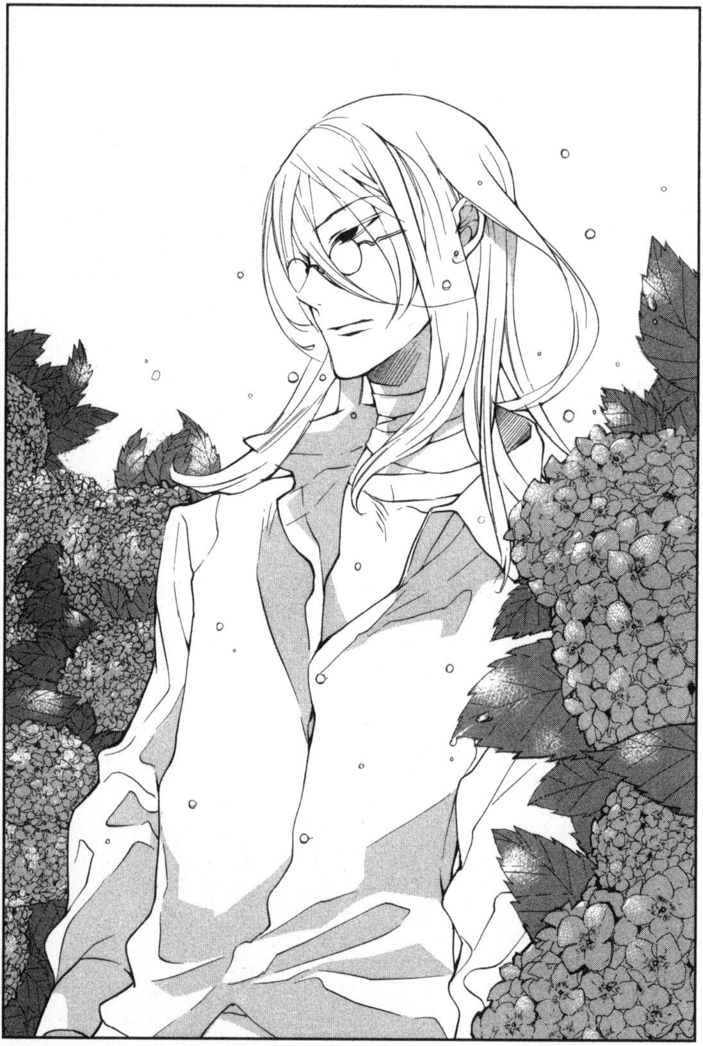

LOVELESS

LOVELESS

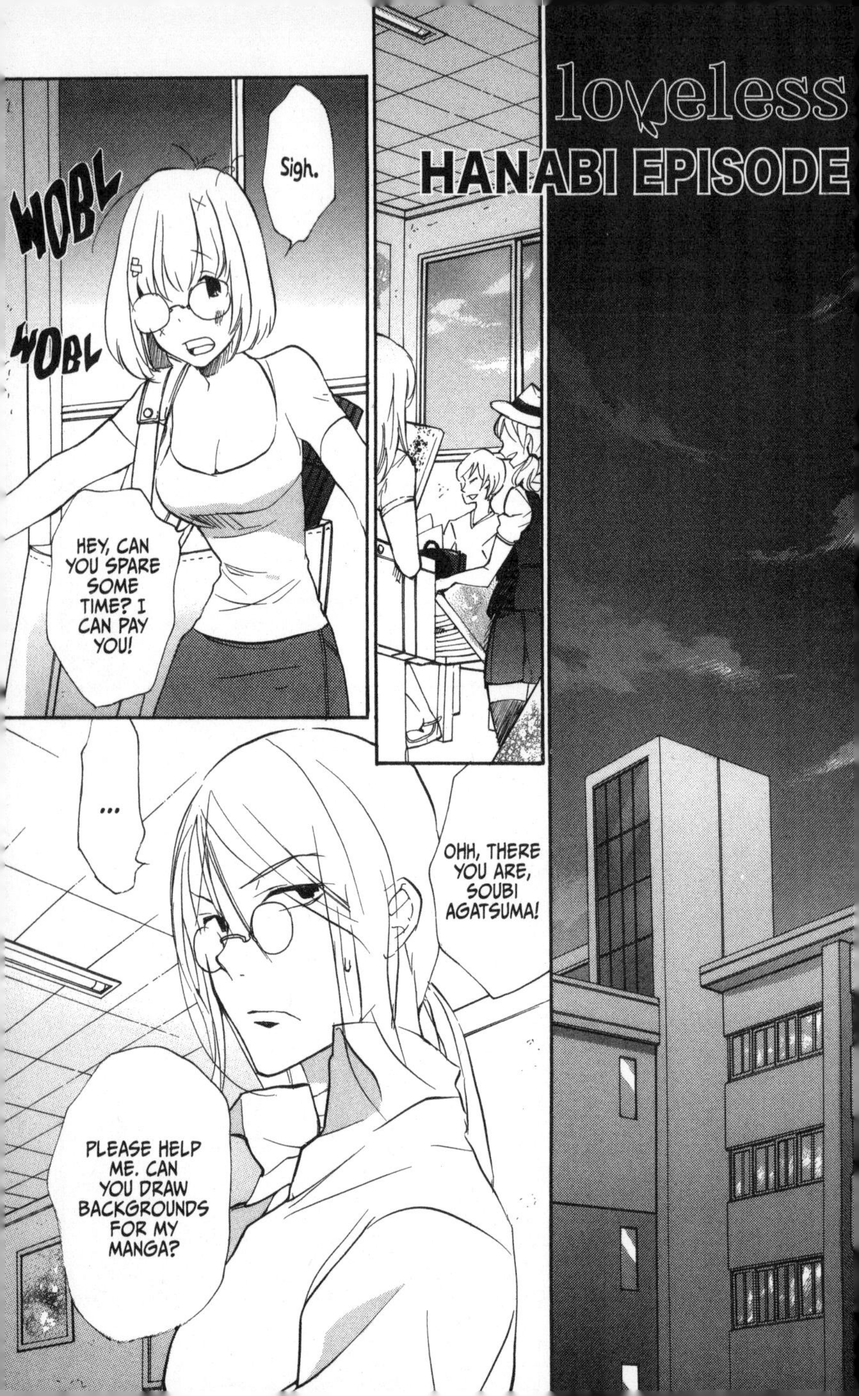
loveless
HANABI EPISODE
Sigh.
WOBL
WOBL
HEY, CAN YOU SPARE SOME TIME? I CAN PAY YOU!
OHH, THERE YOU ARE, SOUBI AGATSUMA!
...
PLEASE HELP ME. CAN YOU DRAW BACKGROUNDS FOR MY MANGA?

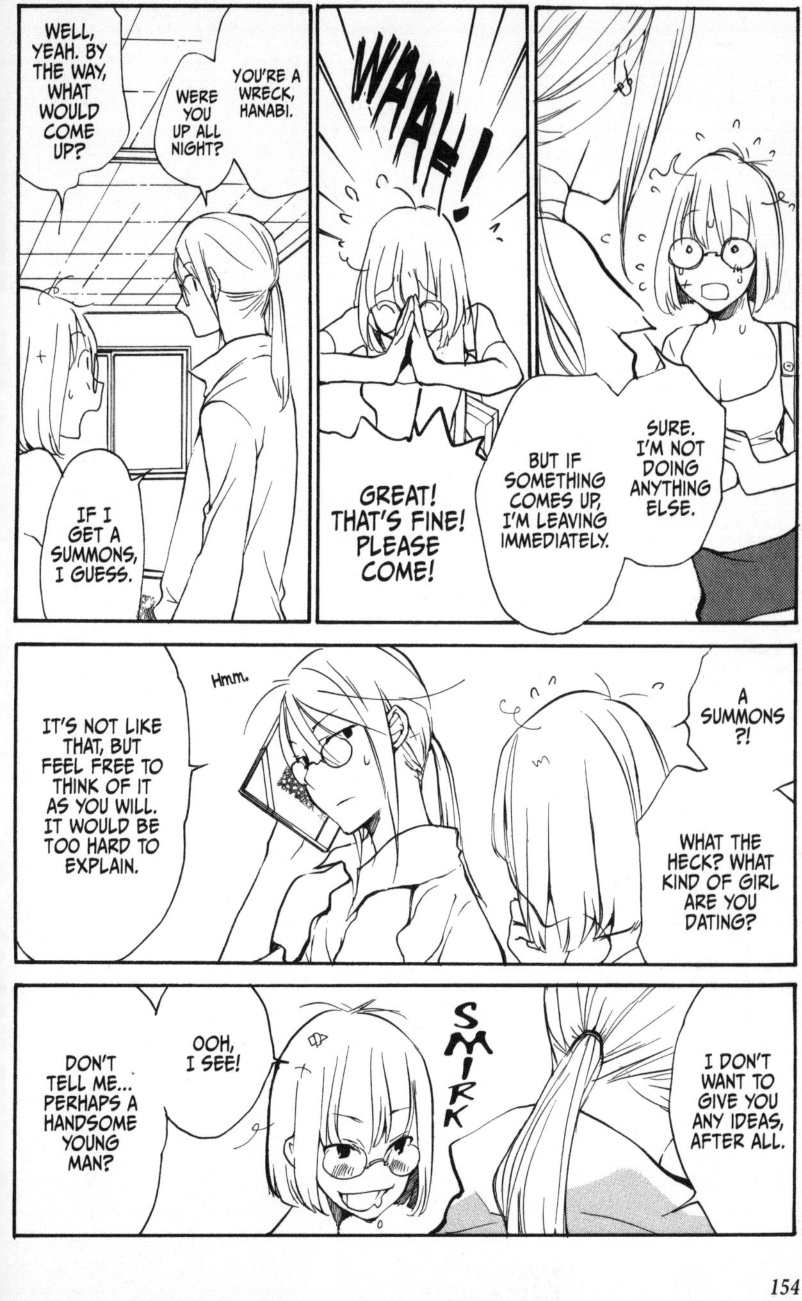
SURE. I'M NOT DOING ANYTHING ELSE.
BUT IF SOMETHING COMES UP, I'M LEAVING IMMEDIATELY.
WAAH!
GREAT! THAT'S FINE! PLEASE COME!
YOU'RE A WRECK, HANABI.
WERE YOU UP ALL NIGHT?
WELL, YEAH. BY THE WAY, WHAT WOULD COME UP?
IF I GET A SUMMONS, I GUESS.
A SUMMONS?!
WHAT THE HECK? WHAT KIND OF GIRL ARE YOU DATING?
Hmm.
IT'S NOT LIKE THAT, BUT FEEL FREE TO THINK OF IT AS YOU WILL. IT WOULD BE TOO HARD TO EXPLAIN.
I DON'T WANT TO GIVE YOU ANY IDEAS, AFTER ALL.
SMIRK
OOH, I SEE!
DON'T TELL ME... PERHAPS A HANDSOME YOUNG MAN?

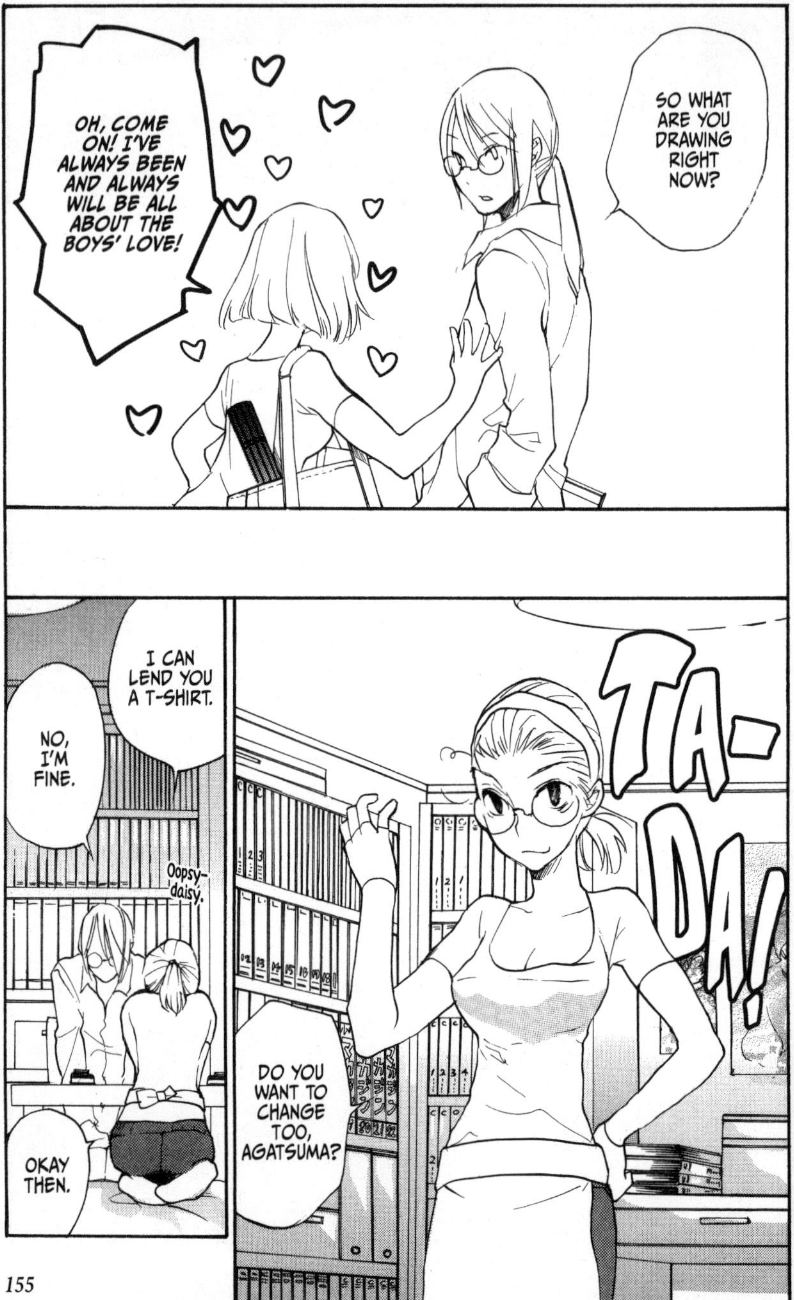
SO WHAT ARE YOU DRAWING RIGHT NOW?
OH, COME ON! I'VE ALWAYS BEEN AND ALWAYS WILL BE ALL ABOUT THE BOYS' LOVE!
TA-DA!
DO YOU WANT TO CHANGE TOO, AGATSUMA?
I CAN LEND YOU A T-SHIRT.
NO, I'M FINE.
Oopsy-daisy.
OKAY THEN.

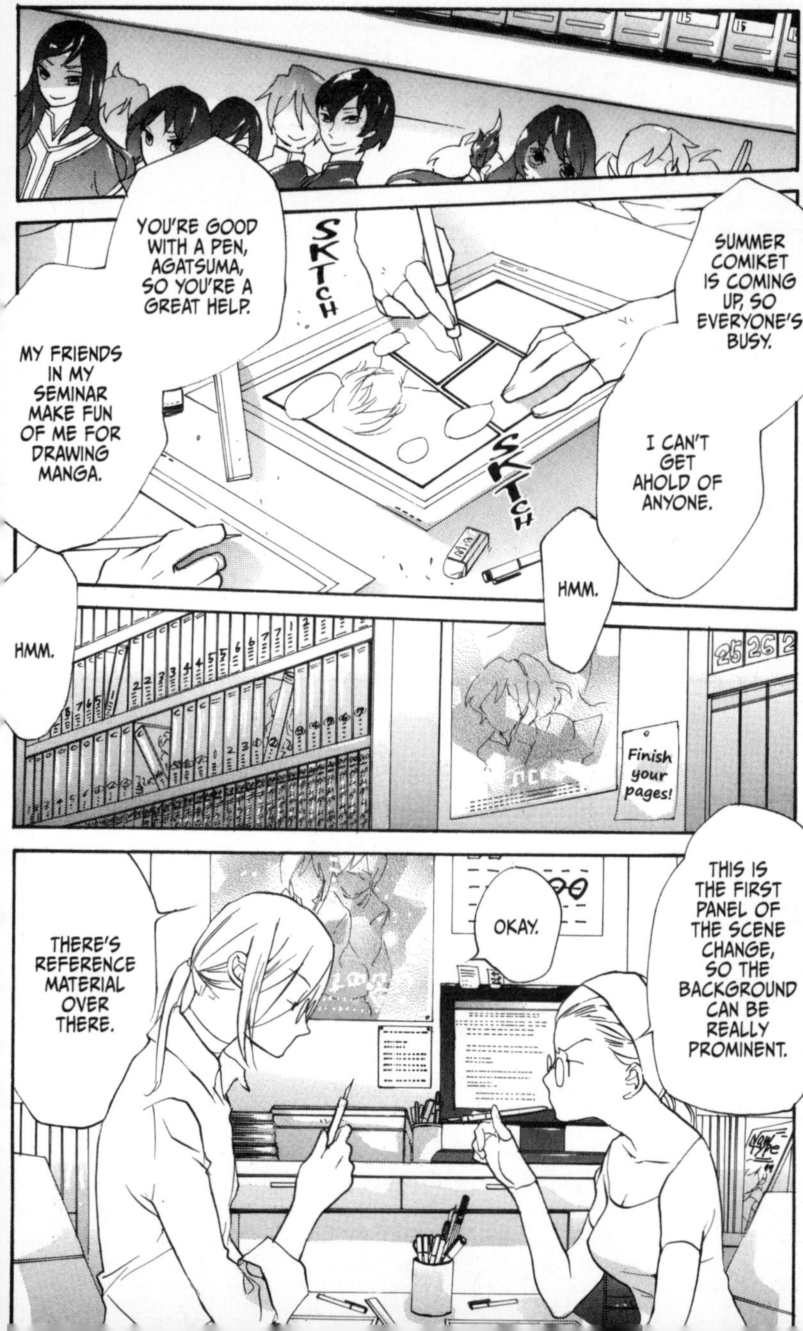
SUMMER COMIKET IS COMING UP, SO EVERYONE'S BUSY.
SKTCH
YOU'RE GOOD WITH A PEN, AGATSUMA, SO YOU'RE A GREAT HELP.
I CAN'T GET AHOLD OF ANYONE.
SKTCH
MY FRIENDS IN MY SEMINAR MAKE FUN OF ME FOR DRAWING MANGA.
HMM.
HMM.
Finish your pages!
THIS IS THE FIRST PANEL OF THE SCENE CHANGE, SO THE BACKGROUND CAN BE REALLY PROMINENT.
OKAY.
THERE'S REFERENCE MATERIAL OVER THERE.

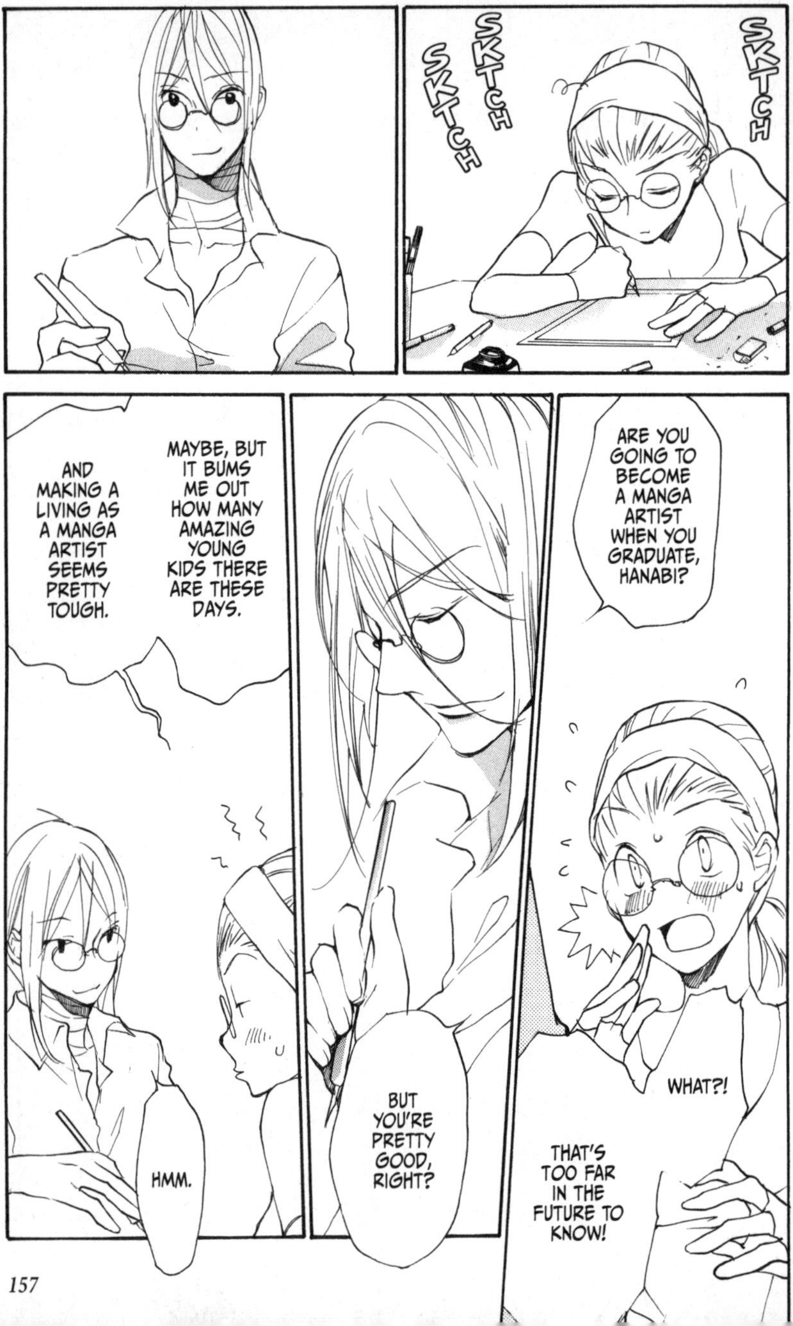
SKTCH
SKTCH
SKTCH
ARE YOU GOING TO BECOME A MANGA ARTIST WHEN YOU GRADUATE, HANABI?
WHAT?!
THAT'S TOO FAR IN THE FUTURE TO KNOW!
BUT YOU'RE PRETTY GOOD, RIGHT?
MAYBE, BUT IT BUMS ME OUT HOW MANY AMAZING YOUNG KIDS THERE ARE THESE DAYS.
AND MAKING A LIVING AS A MANGA ARTIST SEEMS PRETTY TOUGH.
HMM.

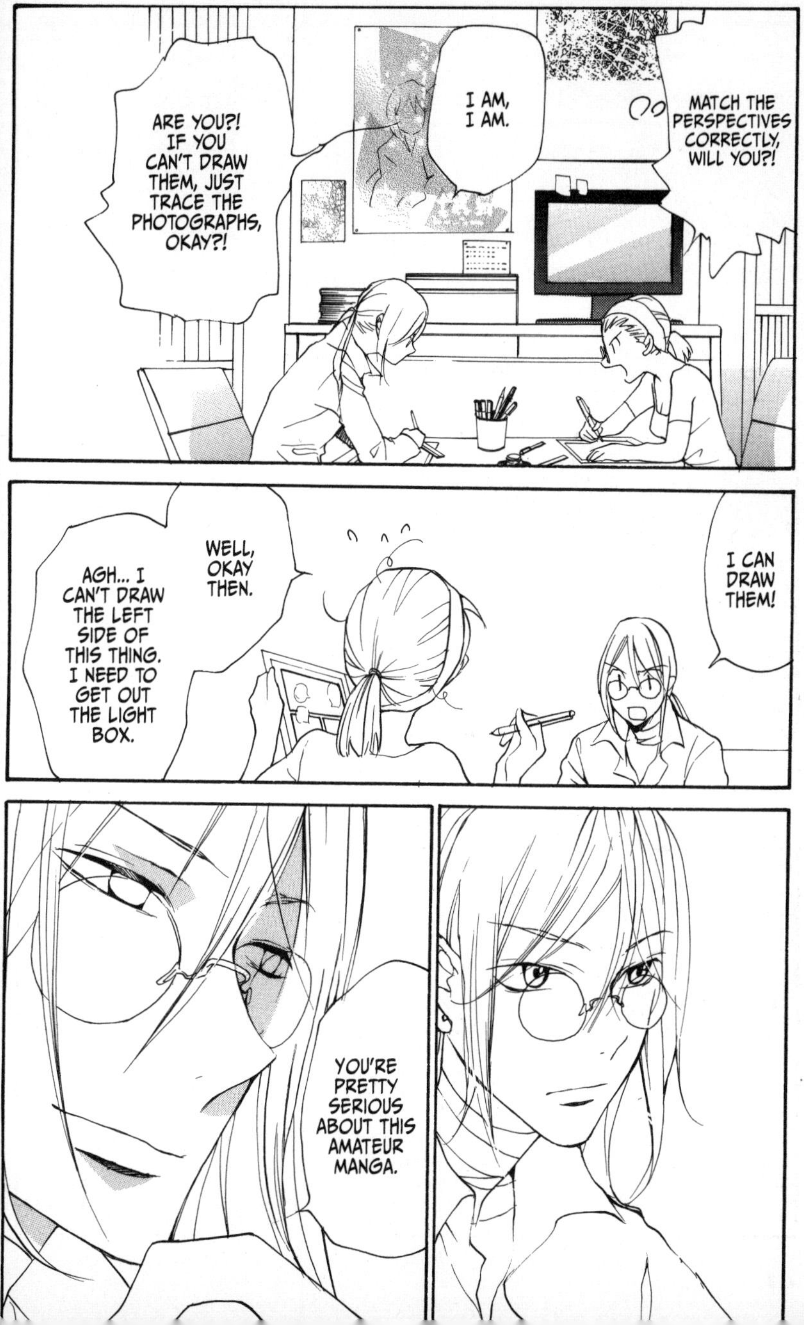
MATCH THE PERSPECTIVES CORRECTLY, WILL YOU?!
I AM, I AM.
ARE YOU?! IF YOU CAN'T DRAW THEM, JUST TRACE THE PHOTOGRAPHS, OKAY?!
I CAN DRAW THEM!
WELL, OKAY THEN.
AGH... I CAN'T DRAW THE LEFT SIDE OF THIS THING. I NEED TO GET OUT THE LIGHT BOX.
YOU'RE PRETTY SERIOUS ABOUT THIS AMATEUR MANGA.

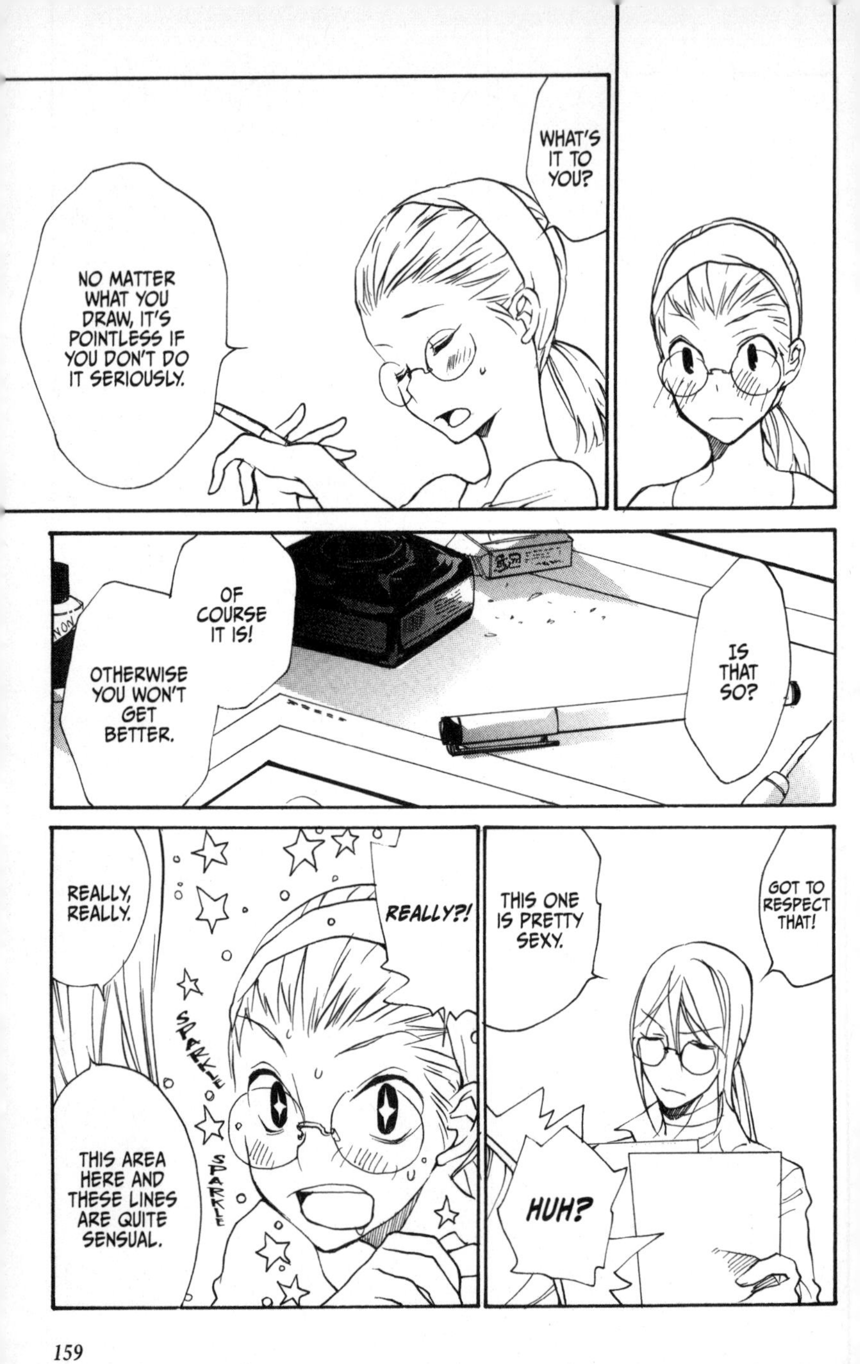
WHAT'S IT TO YOU?
NO MATTER WHAT YOU DRAW, IT'S POINTLESS IF YOU DON'T DO IT SERIOUSLY.
IS THAT SO?
OF COURSE IT IS!
OTHERWISE YOU WON'T GET BETTER.
GOT TO RESPECT THAT!
THIS ONE IS PRETTY SEXY.
HUH?
REALLY?!
REALLY, REALLY.
SPARKLE
SPARKLE
THIS AREA HERE AND THESE LINES ARE QUITE SENSUAL.

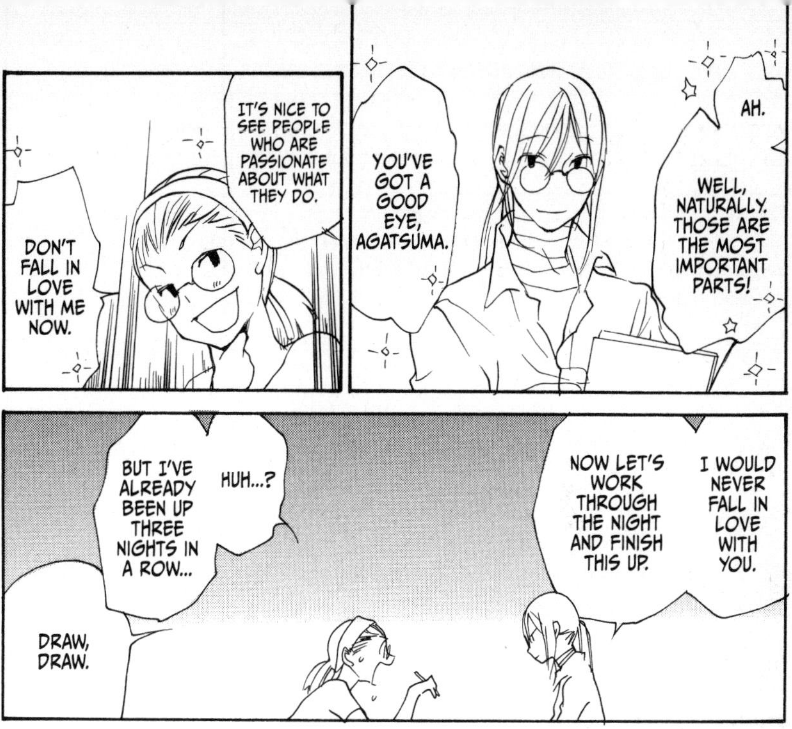
AH.
WELL, NATURALLY. THOSE ARE THE MOST IMPORTANT PARTS!
YOU'VE GOT A GOOD EYE, AGATSUMA.
IT'S NICE TO SEE PEOPLE WHO ARE PASSIONATE ABOUT WHAT THEY DO.
DON'T FALL IN LOVE WITH ME NOW.
I WOULD NEVER FALL IN LOVE WITH YOU.
NOW LET'S WORK THROUGH THE NIGHT AND FINISH THIS UP.
HUH...?
BUT I'VE ALREADY BEEN UP THREE NIGHTS IN A ROW...
DRAW, DRAW.

The midnight snack

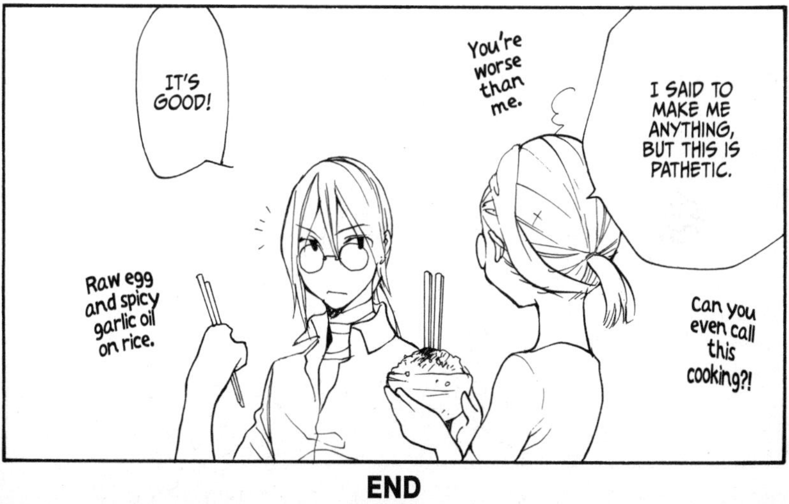
I SAID TO MAKE ME ANYTHING, BUT THIS IS PATHETIC.
You're worse than me.
IT'S GOOD!
Can you even call this cooking?!
Raw egg and spicy garlic oil on rice.

END

MOBILE SUIT GUNDAM 00 MOVIE RELEASE/ LOVELESS CROSSOVER

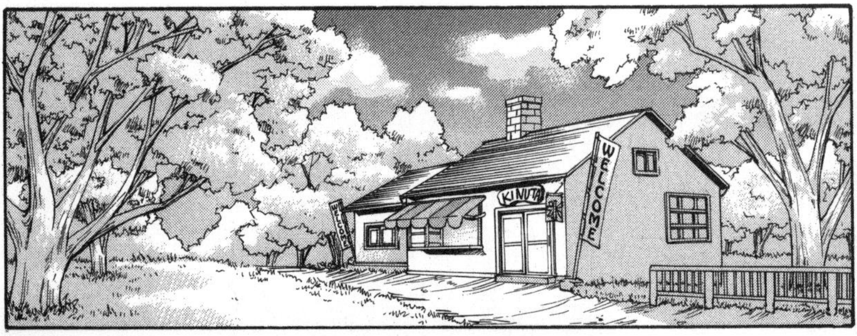
WELCOME
KINUTA
WELCOME

SOMETIME, SOMEPLACE ON A STREET CORNER

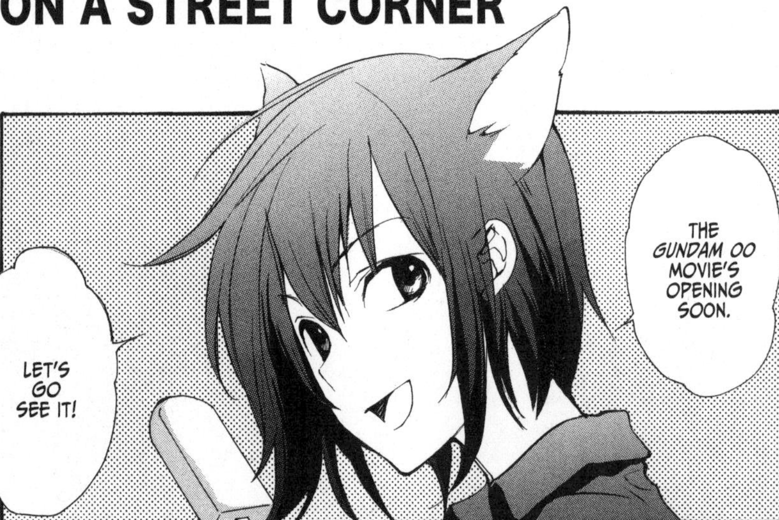
THE GUNDAM 00 MOVIE'S OPENING SOON.
LET'S GO SEE IT!

Mobile Suit Gundam 00 –A Wakening of the Trailblazer– national roadshow!

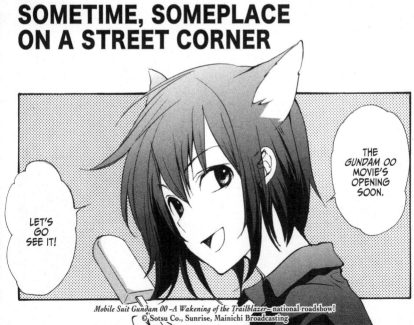

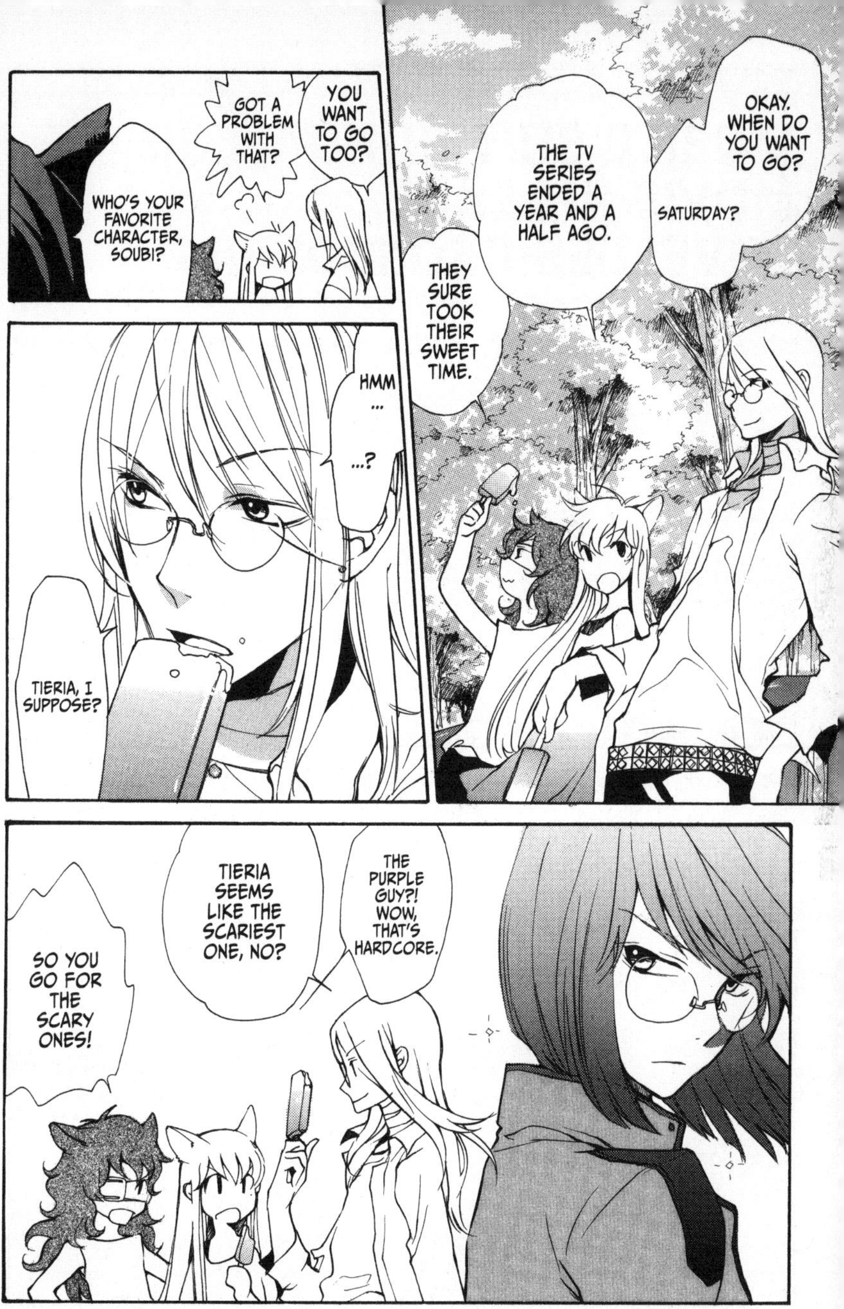
OKAY. WHEN DO YOU WANT TO GO?
SATURDAY?
THE TV SERIES ENDED A YEAR AND A HALF AGO.
THEY SURE TOOK THEIR SWEET TIME.
YOU WANT TO GO TOO?
GOT A PROBLEM WITH THAT?
WHO'S YOUR FAVORITE CHARACTER, SOUBI?
HMM ...
...?
TIERIA, I SUPPOSE?
THE PURPLE GUY?! WOW, THAT'S HARDCORE.
TIERIA SEEMS LIKE THE SCARIEST ONE, NO?
SO YOU GO FOR THE SCARY ONES!

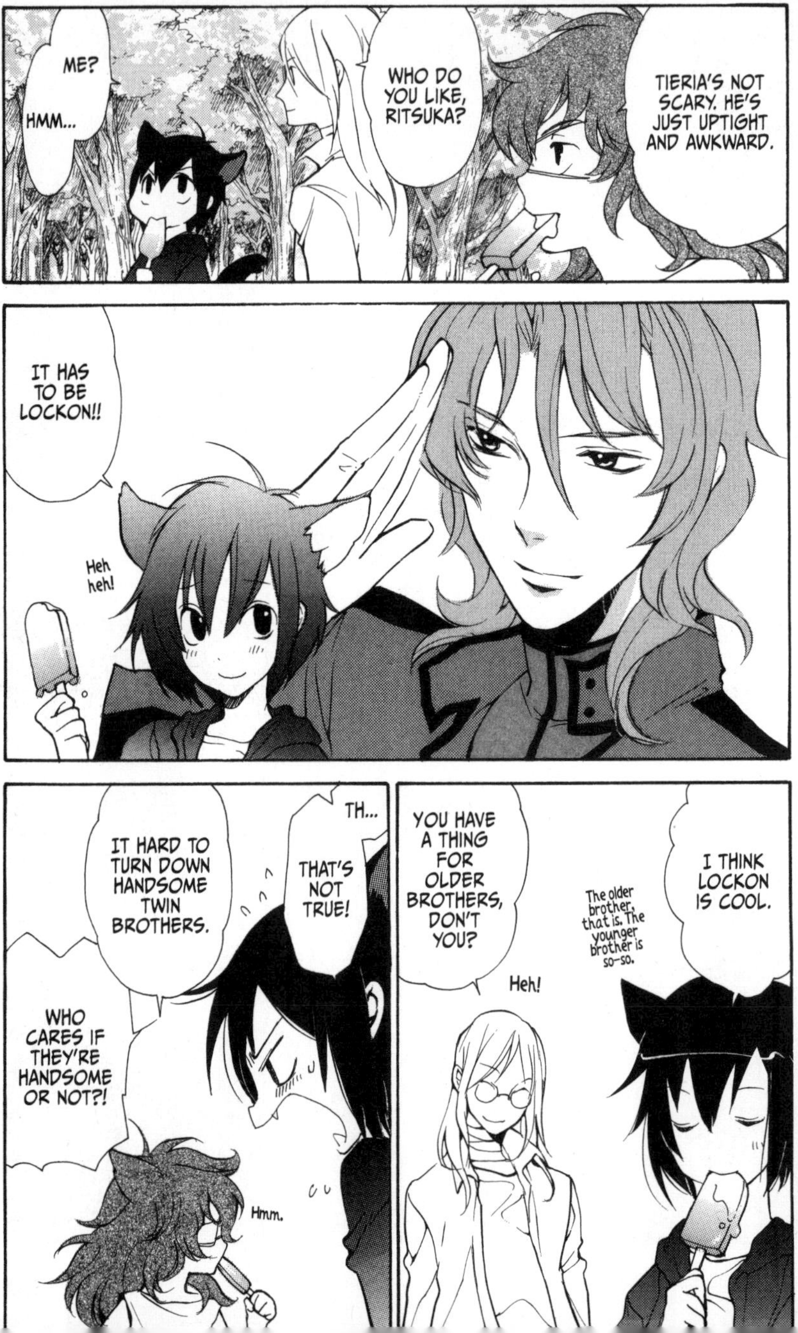

TIERIA'S NOT SCARY. HE'S JUST UPTIGHT AND AWKWARD.
WHO DO YOU LIKE, RITSUKA?
ME?
HMM...
IT HAS TO BE LOCKON!!
Heh heh!
I THINK LOCKON IS COOL.
The older brother, that is. The younger brother is so-so.
YOU HAVE A THING FOR OLDER BROTHERS, DON'T YOU?
Heh!
TH...
THAT'S NOT TRUE!
IT HARD TO TURN DOWN HANDSOME TWIN BROTHERS.
WHO CARES IF THEY'RE HANDSOME OR NOT?!
Hmm.

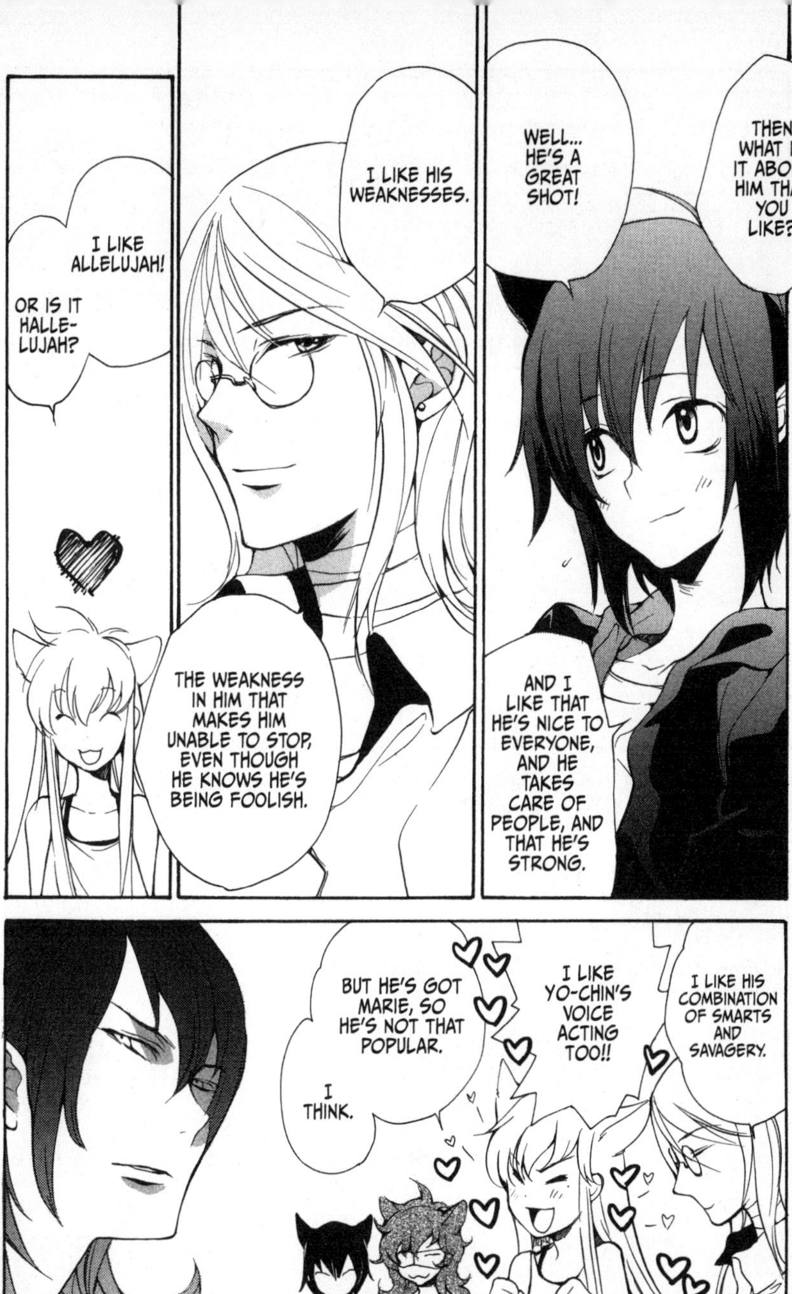
THEN WHAT IS IT ABOUT HIM THAT YOU LIKE?
WELL... HE'S A GREAT SHOT!
AND I LIKE THAT HE'S NICE TO EVERYONE, AND HE TAKES CARE OF PEOPLE, AND THAT HE'S STRONG.
I LIKE HIS WEAKNESSES.
THE WEAKNESS IN HIM THAT MAKES HIM UNABLE TO STOP, EVEN THOUGH HE KNOWS HE'S BEING FOOLISH.
I LIKE ALLELUJAH!
OR IS IT HALLE-LUJAH?
I LIKE HIS COMBINATION OF SMARTS AND SAVAGERY.
I LIKE YO-CHIN'S VOICE ACTING TOO!!
BUT HE'S GOT MARIE, SO HE'S NOT THAT POPULAR.
I THINK.

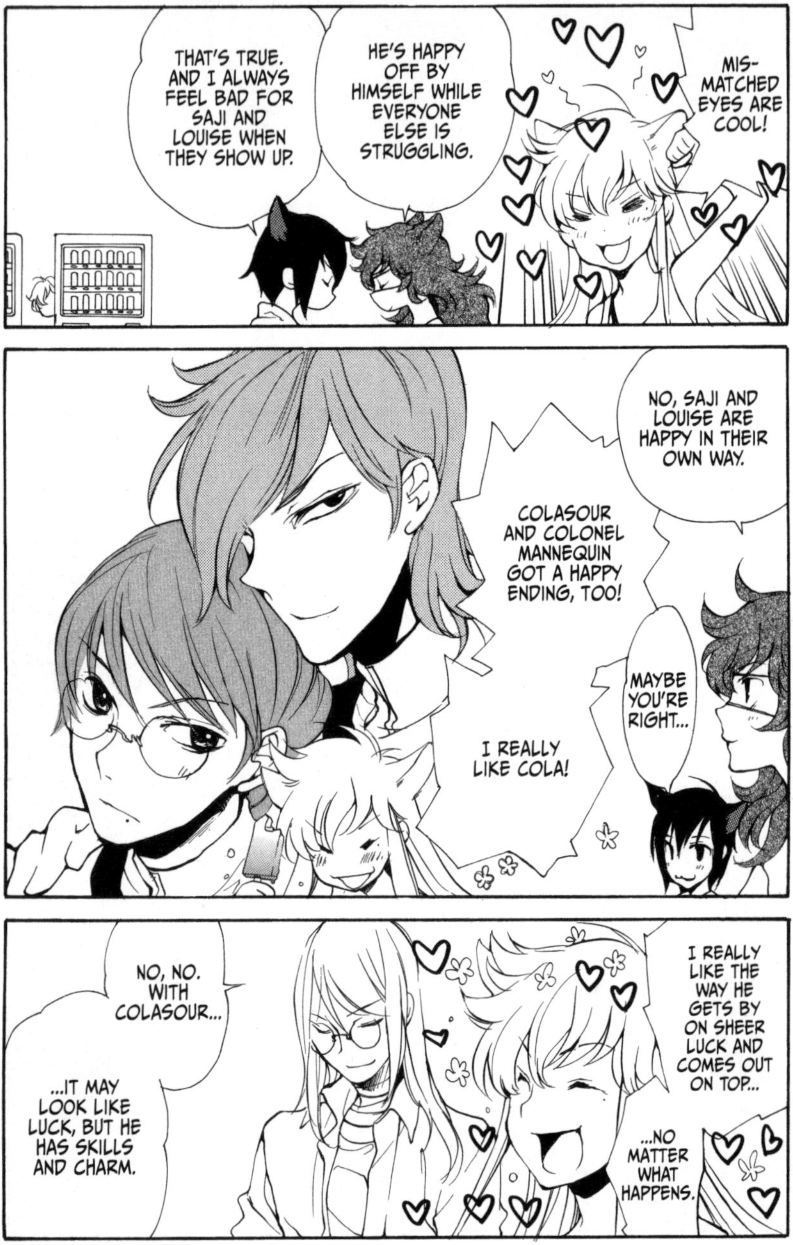
MIS-MATCHED EYES ARE COOL!
HE'S HAPPY OFF BY HIMSELF WHILE EVERYONE ELSE IS STRUGGLING.
THAT'S TRUE. AND I ALWAYS FEEL BAD FOR SAJI AND LOUISE WHEN THEY SHOW UP.
NO, SAJI AND LOUISE ARE HAPPY IN THEIR OWN WAY.
COLASOUR AND COLONEL MANNEQUIN GOT A HAPPY ENDING, TOO!
MAYBE YOU'RE RIGHT...
I REALLY LIKE COLA!
I REALLY LIKE THE WAY HE GETS BY ON SHEER LUCK AND COMES OUT ON TOP...
...NO MATTER WHAT HAPPENS.
NO, NO. WITH COLASOUR...
...IT MAY LOOK LIKE LUCK, BUT HE HAS SKILLS AND CHARM.

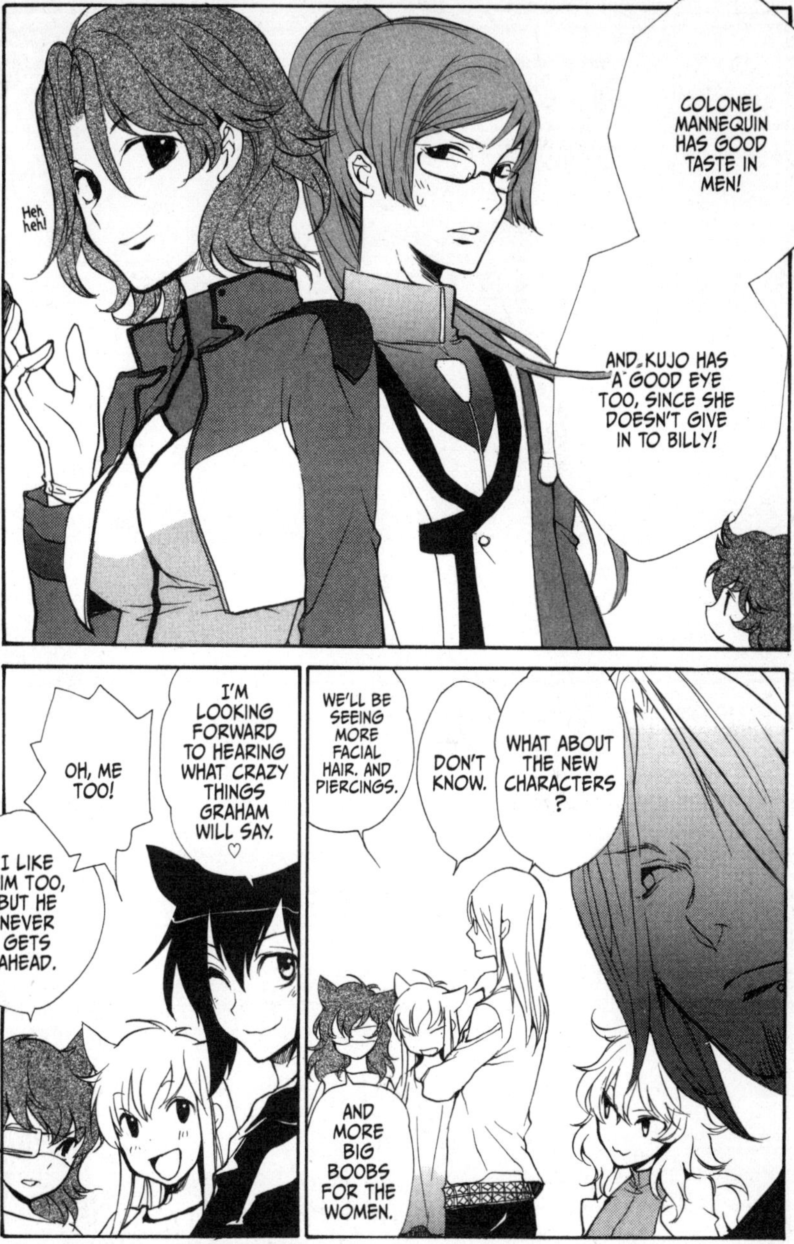
COLONEL MANNEQUIN HAS GOOD TASTE IN MEN!
AND KUJO HAS A GOOD EYE TOO, SINCE SHE DOESN'T GIVE IN TO BILLY!
Heh heh!
WHAT ABOUT THE NEW CHARACTERS?
DON'T KNOW.
WE'LL BE SEEING MORE FACIAL HAIR. AND PIERCINGS.
AND MORE BIG BOOBS FOR THE WOMEN.
I'M LOOKING FORWARD TO HEARING WHAT CRAZY THINGS GRAHAM WILL SAY. ♡
OH, ME TOO!
I LIKE HIM TOO, BUT HE NEVER GETS AHEAD.

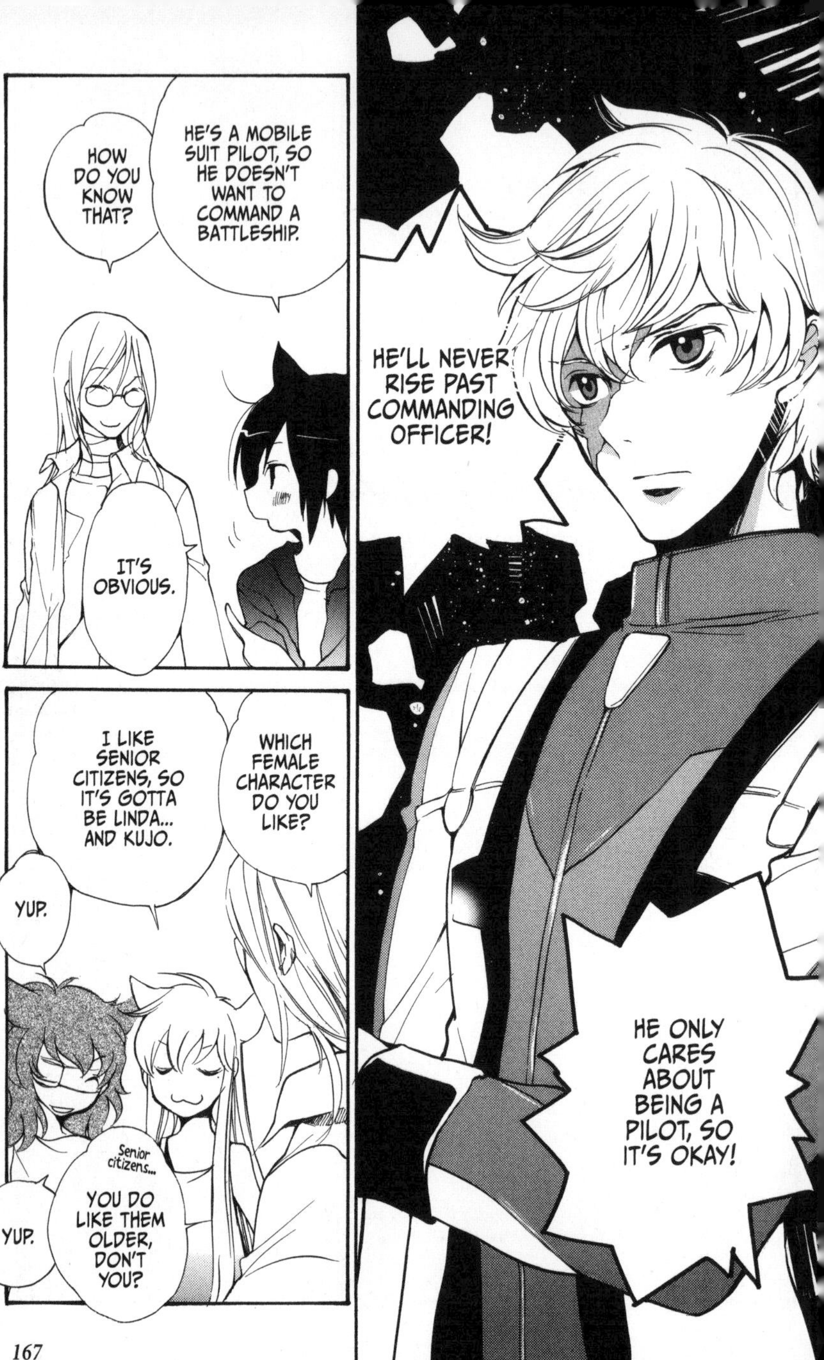
HE'LL NEVER RISE PAST COMMANDING OFFICER!
HE ONLY CARES ABOUT BEING A PILOT, SO IT'S OKAY!
HE'S A MOBILE SUIT PILOT, SO HE DOESN'T WANT TO COMMAND A BATTLESHIP.
HOW DO YOU KNOW THAT?
IT'S OBVIOUS.
WHICH FEMALE CHARACTER DO YOU LIKE?
I LIKE SENIOR CITIZENS, SO IT'S GOTTA BE LINDA... AND KUJO.
YUP.
Senior citizens...
YOU DO LIKE THEM OLDER, DON'T YOU?
YUP.

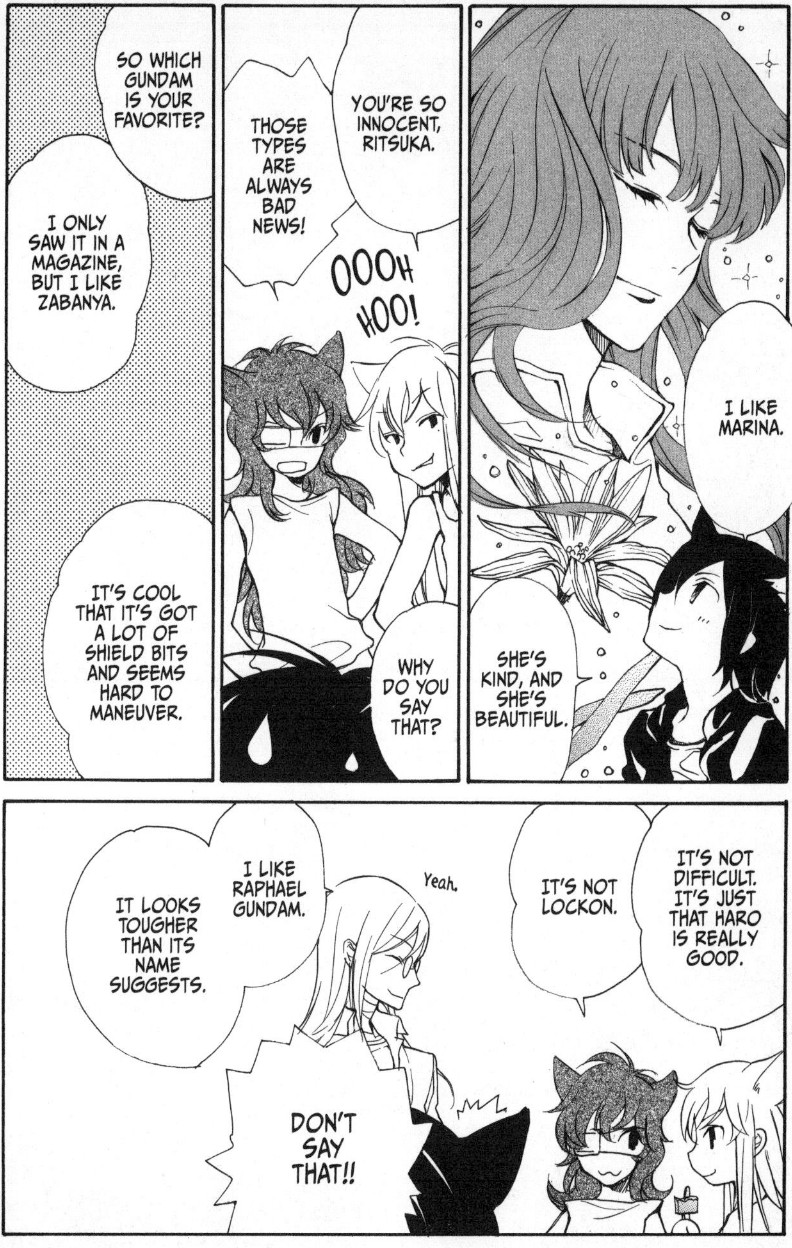
I LIKE MARINA.
SHE'S KIND, AND SHE'S BEAUTIFUL.
YOU'RE SO INNOCENT, RITSUKA.
THOSE TYPES ARE ALWAYS BAD NEWS!
OOOH HOO!
WHY DO YOU SAY THAT?
SO WHICH GUNDAM IS YOUR FAVORITE?
I ONLY SAW IT IN A MAGAZINE, BUT I LIKE ZABANYA.
IT'S COOL THAT IT'S GOT A LOT OF SHIELD BITS AND SEEMS HARD TO MANEUVER.
IT'S NOT DIFFICULT. IT'S JUST THAT HARO IS REALLY GOOD.
IT'S NOT LOCKON.
Yeah.
I LIKE RAPHAEL GUNDAM.
IT LOOKS TOUGHER THAN ITS NAME SUGGESTS.
DON'T SAY THAT!!

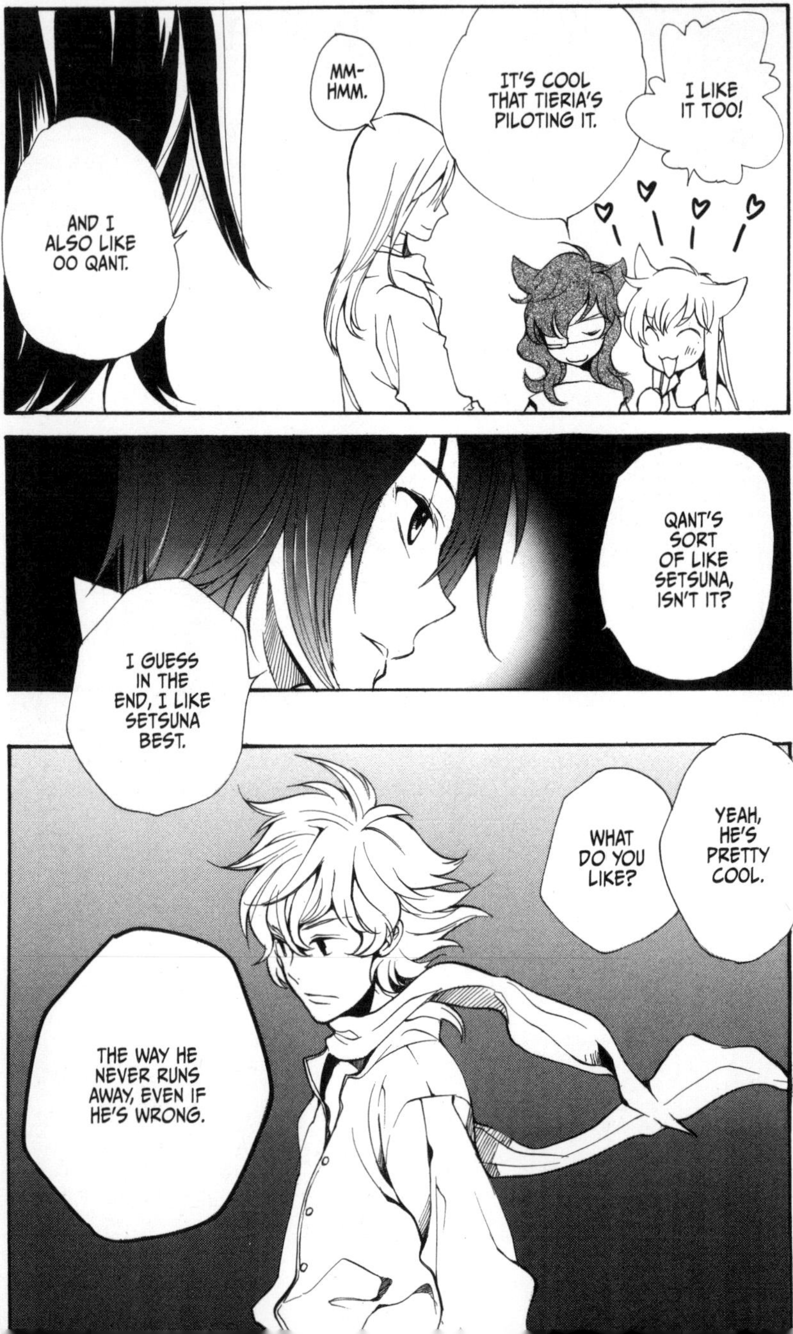
I LIKE IT TOO!
IT'S COOL THAT TIERIA'S PILOTING IT.
MM-HMM.
AND I ALSO LIKE OO QANT.
QANT'S SORT OF LIKE SETSUNA, ISN'T IT?
I GUESS IN THE END, I LIKE SETSUNA BEST.
YEAH, HE'S PRETTY COOL.
WHAT DO YOU LIKE?
THE WAY HE NEVER RUNS AWAY, EVEN IF HE'S WRONG.

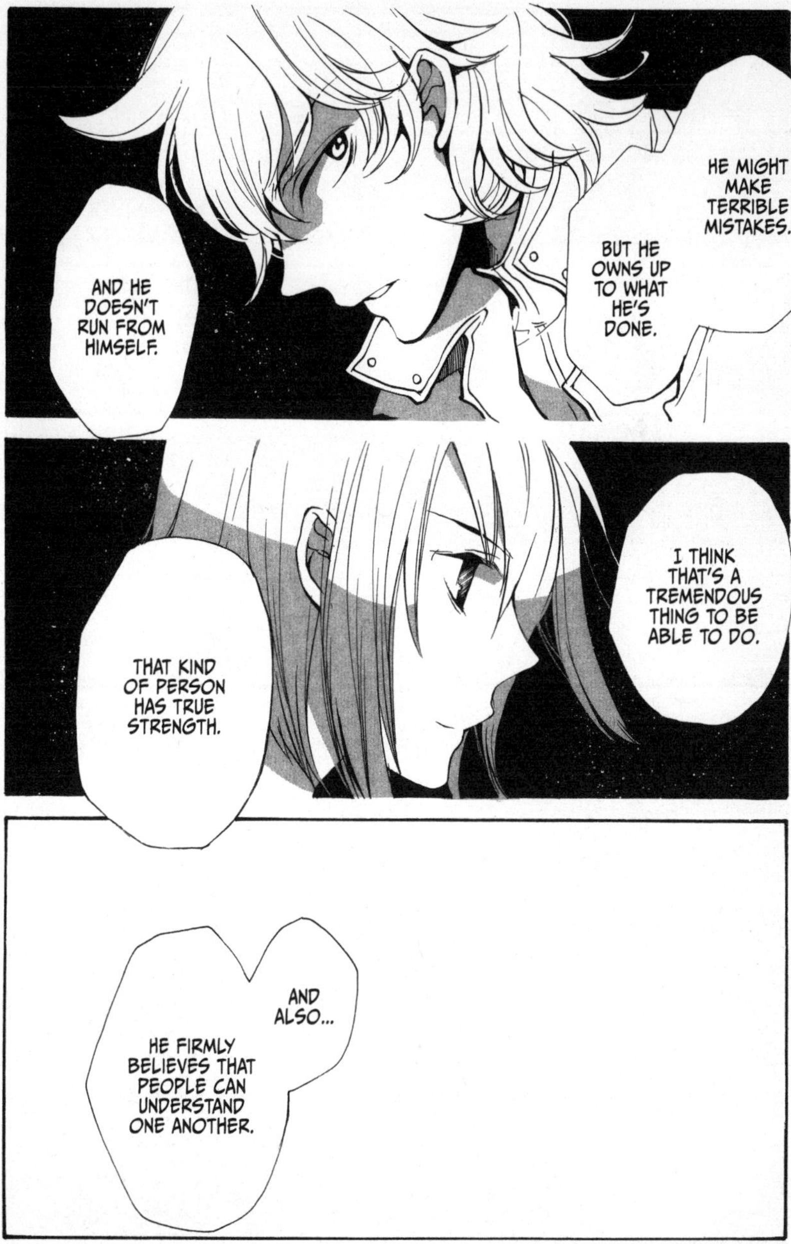
HE MIGHT MAKE TERRIBLE MISTAKES.
BUT HE OWNS UP TO WHAT HE'S DONE.
AND HE DOESN'T RUN FROM HIMSELF.
I THINK THAT'S A TREMENDOUS THING TO BE ABLE TO DO.
THAT KIND OF PERSON HAS TRUE STRENGTH.
AND ALSO...
HE FIRMLY BELIEVES THAT PEOPLE CAN UNDERSTAND ONE ANOTHER.

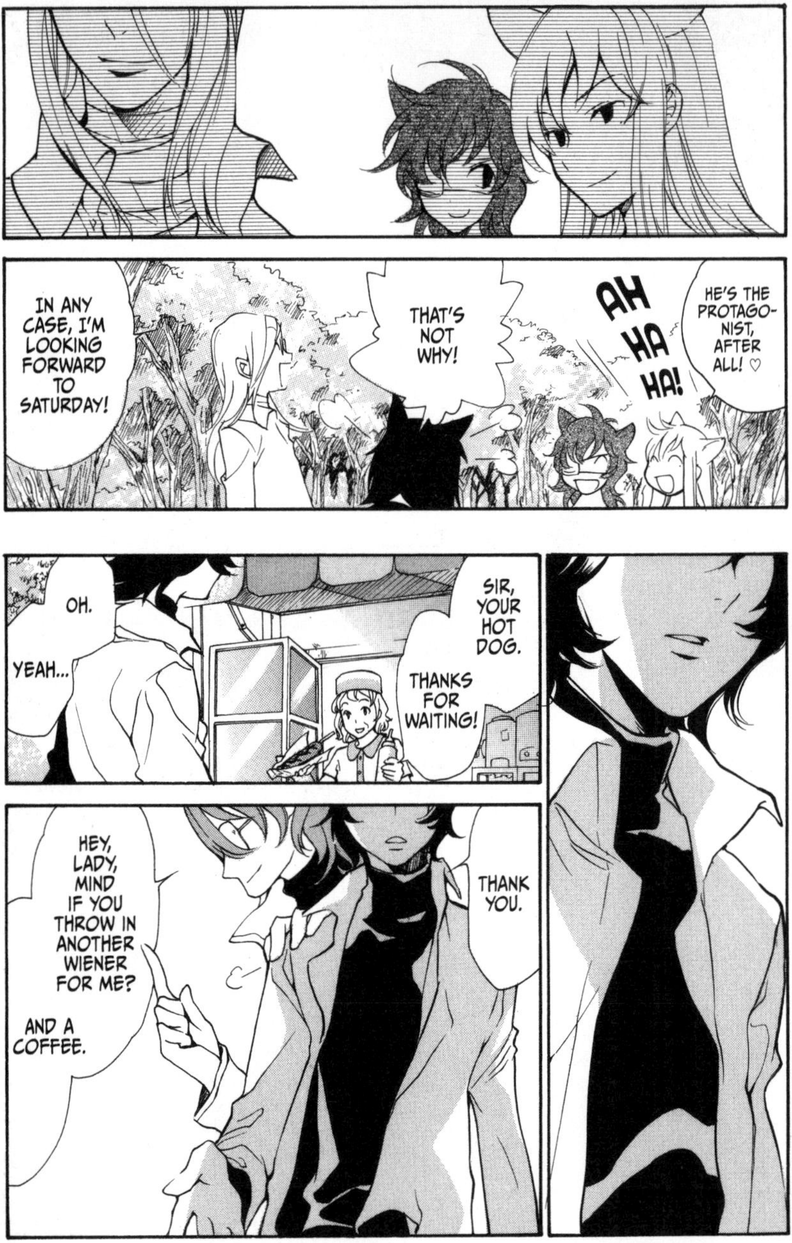
HE'S THE PROTAGO-NIST, AFTER ALL! ♡
AH HA HA!
THAT'S NOT WHY!
IN ANY CASE, I'M LOOKING FORWARD TO SATURDAY!
SIR, YOUR HOT DOG.
THANKS FOR WAITING!
OH.
YEAH...
THANK YOU.
HEY, LADY, MIND IF YOU THROW IN ANOTHER WIENER FOR ME?
AND A COFFEE.

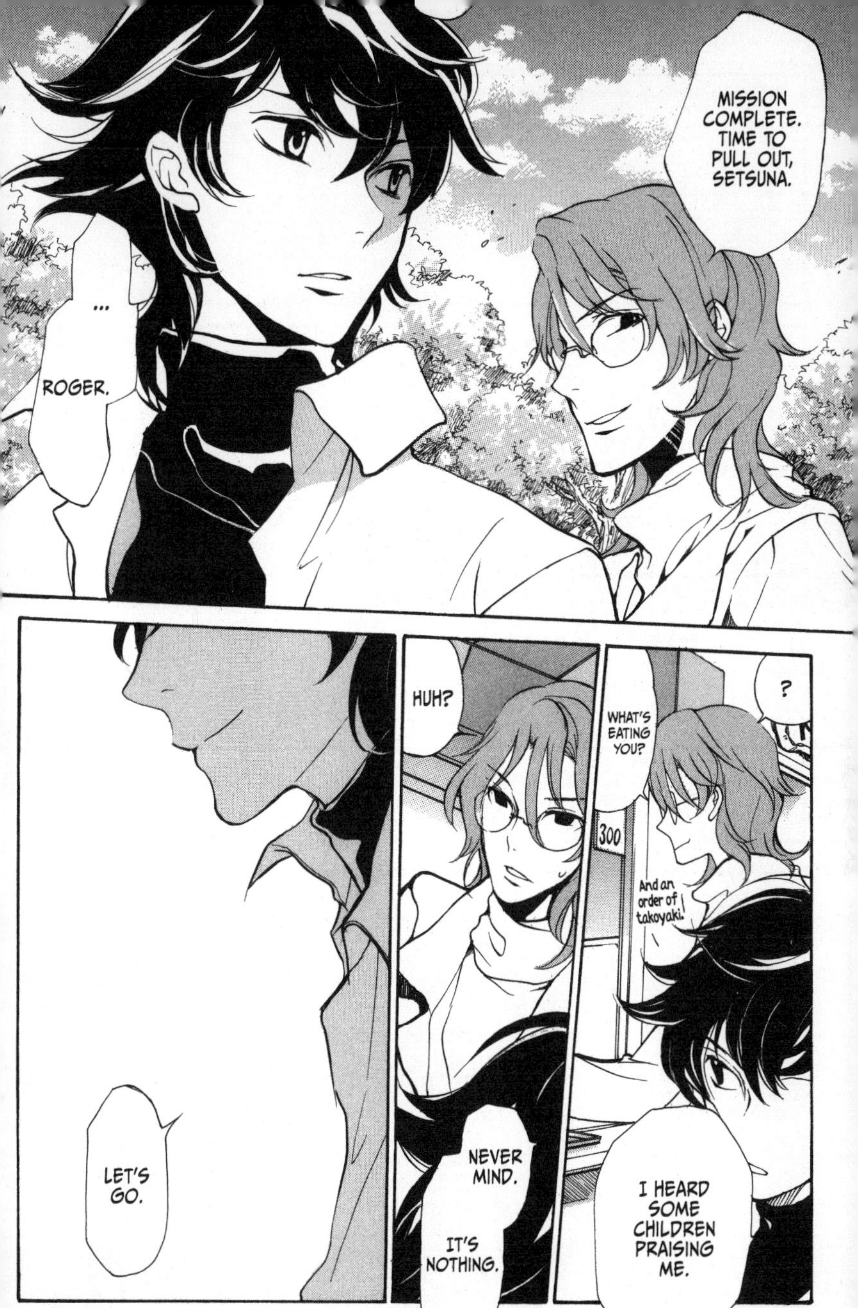
MISSION COMPLETE. TIME TO PULL OUT, SETSUNA.
...
ROGER.
?
WHAT'S EATING YOU?
300
And an order of takoyaki!
I HEARD SOME CHILDREN PRAISING ME.
HUH?
NEVER MIND.
IT'S NOTHING.
LET'S GO.

END

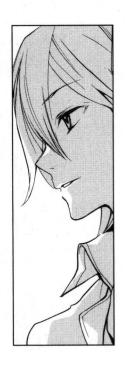

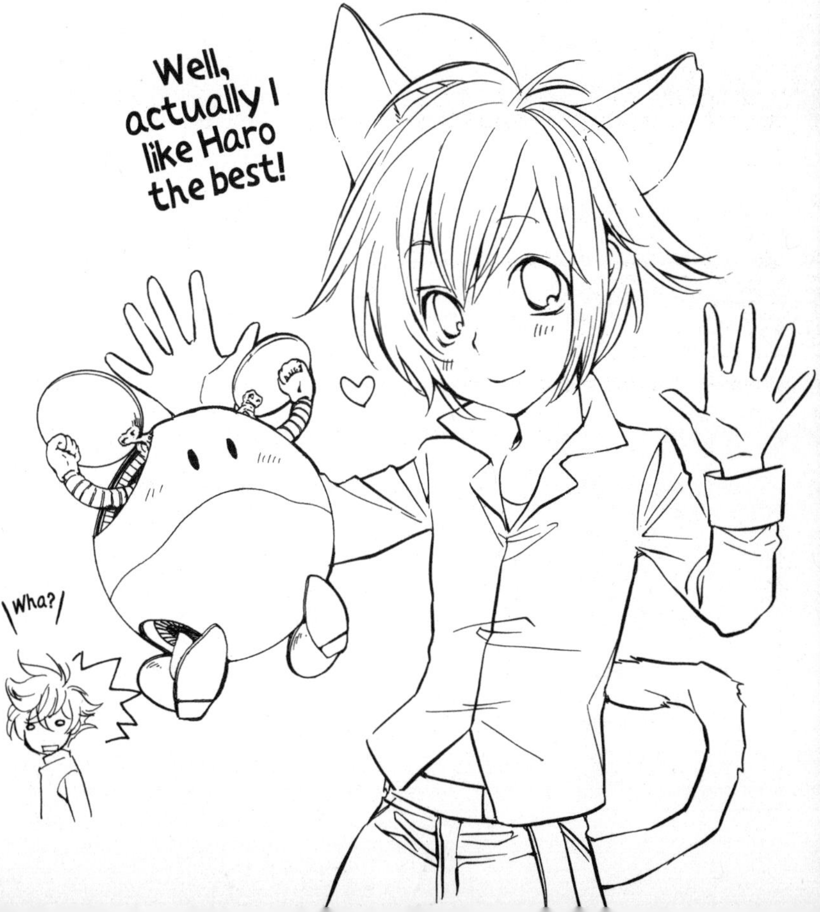
Well, actually I like Haro the best!
Wha?

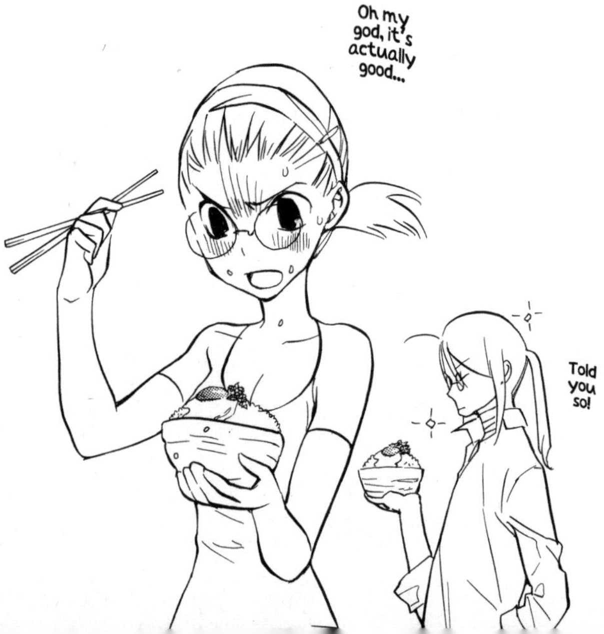
Told you so!
Oh my god, it's actually good...

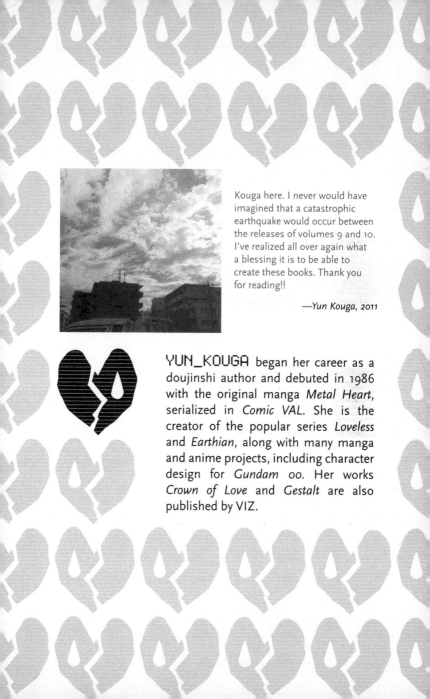

Kouga here. I never would have imagined that a catastrophic earthquake would occur between the releases of volumes 9 and 10. I've realized all over again what a blessing it is to be able to create these books. Thank you for reading!!

—*Yun Kouga, 2011*

YUN_KOUGA began her career as a doujinshi author and debuted in 1986 with the original manga *Metal Heart*, serialized in *Comic VAL*. She is the creator of the popular series *Loveless* and *Earthian*, along with many manga and anime projects, including character design for *Gundam 00*. Her works *Crown of Love* and *Gestalt* are also published by VIZ.

Loveless

Volume 10
VIZ Media Edition

Story and Art by YUN KOUGA

Translation // RAY YOSHIMOTO
English Adaptation // LILLIAN DIAZ-PRZYBYL
Touch-Up Art + Lettering // ERIC ERBES
Design // FAWN LAU
Editor // HOPE DONOVAN

Loveless © 2011 by Yun Kouga
All rights reserved.
Original Japanese edition published by ICHIJINSHA, INC., Tokyo.
English translation rights arranged with ICHIJINSHA, INC.

Printed in the U.S.A.

Published by VIZ Media, LLC
P.O. Box 77010
San Francisco, CA 94107

10 9 8 7 6 5 4 3 2 1
First printing, January 2013

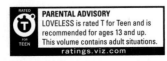

www.viz.com

THIS IS THE END OF THE BOOK.

Loveless is printed from right to left in the original Japanese format in order to present Yun Kouga's art as it was meant to be seen.